School Administrator's Guide to COMPUTERS IN EDUCATION

D1518043

DANIEL S. CHEEVER, JR.
PETER COBURN
FRANK DIGIAMMARINO
PETER KELMAN
BETH T. LOWD
ADELINE NAIMAN
GUS A. SAYER
KENNETH TEMKIN
ISA KAFTAL ZIMMERMAN

▲▼ ADDISON-WESLEY
PUBLISHING COMPANY, INC.

Reading, Massachusetts · Menlo Park, California
Don Mills, Ontario · Wokingham, England · Amsterdam
Sydney · Singapore · Tokyo · Mexico City · Bogota
Santiago · San Juan

Intentional Educations, Series Developer
Peter Kelman, Series Editor
Richard Hannus, Cover Designer

This book is in the
Addison-Wesley Series on Computers in Education

Illustration credits:
Pages x, 92, 102, photos: Sharon Bazarian. Page 105, photo: Courtesy of International Business Machines Corporation. Page 132, photos courtesy of Arrakis Technologies. Page 134, photo reprinted by permission from COMPress. © 1983,84 by COMPress. From *The Molecular Animator*. Page 135, photo courtesy DLM. Page 158, photo: Sharon Bazarian. Page 192, photo courtesy Intel Corporation. Page 199, photo courtesy Texas Instruments Incorporated. Page 204, photo: Sharon Bazarian. Page 206, photo courtesy of Honeywell Inc. Page 207, photo: Sharon Bazarian. Page 209, photo courtesy of Cromemco, Inc. Page 210, photo courtesy of Morrow Designs, Inc. Page 212, photo courtesy Micro Control Systems, Vernon, CT. Page 213 (top), photo courtesy Microsoft Corporation. Page 213 (bottom) photo courtesy Hewlett-Packard Company. Page 214, photo courtesy of Koala Technologies Corp. Page 215, photo courtesy Visual Technology Incorporated—1985. Page 216 (top) photo use courtesy of Nixdorf Computer Corporation. Page 216 (bottom) photo courtesy of Tandy Corporation/Radio Shack. Page 217, photo courtesy of Amdek Corp., Elk Grove Village, Illinois 60007, 1985. Page 218, photo courtesy Wang Laboratories, Inc. Page 219, printout copyright © 1983 Epson America, Inc. Pages 220, 221, photo and print sample courtesy Qume Corporation, a subsidiary of ITT. Pages 222, 224, photos courtesy of Amdek Corp., Elk Grove Village, Illinois 60007, 1985. Page 232, photo courtesy of Apple Computer, Inc. Page 244, photo courtesy of Casio, Inc. Page 246, photo courtesy of CardCo, Inc. Page 249 (top), photo courtesy of Tandy Corporation/Radio Shack. Pages 252, 260, photos: Sharon Bazarian.

Library of Congress Cataloging-in-Publication Data

Main entry under title:

School administrator's guide to computers in education.

    Bibliography: p.
    Includes index.
    1. Education—Data processing.   I. Cheever, Daniel S.
LB1028.43.S35   1985   370'.285   85-19969
ISBN 0-201-10564-0

ISBN 0-201-10564-0
ABCDEFGHIJ-AL-898765

Foreword

The computer is a rich and complex tool that is increasingly within the financial means of schools to acquire. Like any educational tool, it comes with inherent advantages and disadvantages, is more appropriate for some uses than others, is more suited to some teaching styles than others, and is neither the answer to all our educational ills nor the end of all that is great and good in our educational system. Like any tool, it can be used well or poorly, it can be overemphasized or ignored, and it depends on the human qualities of the wielder for its effectiveness.

The purpose of the Addison-Wesley Series on *Computers in Education* is to persuade you, as educators, that the future of computers in education is in your hands. Your interest and involvement in educational computer applications will determine whether computers will be the textbook, the TV, or the chalkboard of education for the next generation.

For years, textbooks have dominated school curricula with little input from classroom teachers or local communities. Recently, television has become the most influential and ubiquitous educator in society, yet it has not been widely or particularly successfully used by teachers in schools. On the other hand, for over one hundred years the chalkboard has been the most individualized, interactive, and creatively used technology in schools.

Already, textbook-like computerized curricula are being churned out with little teacher or local community input. Already, computers are available for home use at prices comparable to that of a good color television set and with programs at the educational level of the soaps. If teachers are to gain control over computers in education and make them be their chalkboards, the time to act is now.

Each book in the *Computers in Education* series is intended to provide teachers, school administrators, and parents with information and ideas that will help them begin to meet the educational challenge computers present. Taken as a whole, the series has been designed to help the reader:

- Appreciate the potential and the limits of computers in education.
- Develop a functional understanding of the computer.

- Overcome apprehension about and fear of the computer.
- Participate in efforts to introduce and integrate computers into a school.
- Use the computer creatively and effectively in teaching and administration.
- Apply a discerning and critical attitude toward the myriad computer-related products offered in increasing volume to the education market.
- Consider seriously the ethical, political, and philosophical ramifications of computer use in education.

Practical Guide to Computers in Education is the basic primer for the series. *School Administrator's Guide to Computers in Education* is one of several books in the second tier of the series, each dealing with computer applications in particular educational contexts. Other books in the second tier already published are: *Computers and Reading Instruction, Computers in Teaching Mathematics,* and *Computers, Education, and Special Needs.* Also under preparation are volumes dealing with computers in teaching science and social studies. Each book in this second tier of the series picks up where *Practical Guide to Computers in Education* leaves off. Each is more focused and provides far more practical detail to educators seriously considering computer use in their schools and curricula.

It is my hope, as series editor, that *School Administrator's Guide to Computers in Education* will provide the same kind of solid foundation for school leaders that *Practical Guide to Computers in Education* has for teachers, parents, and interested citizens. It is intended to help administrators and other school leaders in planning and implementing computer use in their districts; for ultimately it is they who will determine whether educational computing succeeds or becomes yet another failed fad in education.

Peter Kelman
Series Editor

Preface

"The computers are coming, The computers are coming!" This book carries a message of vital importance for school leaders. Something significant is happening. It is a time for alertness, for preparation. Careful planning is in order. Major changes loom large on the horizon and are approaching rapidly. A warning issued by Machiavelli in 1518 in *The Prince* somehow seems appropriate:

> It must be remembered that there is nothing more difficult to plan, more doubtful
> of success, nor more dangerous to manage than the creation of a new system.

Computers are being brought into schools. They can prove to be an immense benefit to administrators and to teachers, contributing greatly to the quality of management and instruction. They can, on the other hand, prove to be the most significant boondoggle, the most expensive mistake ever made in schools. The actual outcome lies in the hands of school leaders who must guide the appropriate assimilation of computers into the managerial and instructional operations of schools.

You may be a leader at the district level (the superintendent, assistant superintendent, or director), who presides over the planning, organizing, coordinating, and controlling functions of the district. If so, you need to recognize the implications of computers for district operations such as the budget, the instructional program, support services, business and personnel actions, and communications. You must then initiate an appropriate preparation and planning effort for computer implementation.

If you work at the school level (the principal, assistant principal, department head, or program coordinator), you are one of the leaders who is or will be directing the planning and the implementation of computer use within a school. Your efforts to apply the computer to administrative and instructional processes must mesh with the efforts of those in other schools and at the district level.

In either case, as a leader in a district either considering computer use or in the process of using computers in your schools, you will have many questions to be answered and a great deal to learn. Especially if you are new to computers, you will have to develop an appropriate base of knowledge about their characteristics, capabilities, and possible applications. It is not necessary that you become a systems analyst, a computer expert, a programmer, or a computer operator. But you must know enough to be wary of those who would offer advice or "just the right" computer for your needs.

Moreover, if you are at the stage of contemplating computer use in the schools, you should, for the time being, deflect the promotional presentations of sales representatives, the advice of consultants or computer users in your school or community, and the recommendations of computer-using friends or colleagues in other school systems. Decisions about computer acquisition and implementation should be made only after you have completed a thorough system-wide planning effort.

One of the problems with such sensible-sounding advice is that computers have already begun to infiltrate most school systems. Already, a number of teachers are using microcomputers in their classrooms and agitating for more. Already, principals are buying word processors and are trying to sell their districts on a particular brand's superiority. Already, PTAs are asking which kind of micros they should buy for the elementary schools, and parents are beginning to ask administrators about their plans.

So, you may be behind, playing catch-up, instead of out in front, leading. What can you do to start taking the lead in this new area, which has grown without systematic planning, research, or officially arranged resources?

We have organized this book to help you get a handle quickly on what you need to know and how to make it happen.

If you are new to computers and need some background knowledge before you plunge into the practical "how-to" portions of the book, turn first to Chapters 7 through 10.

- *Chapter 7*, "Instructional Applications of Computers," presents a comprehensive overview of the uses of computers in instruction and a balanced view of those related issues that should be in the forefront of your mind as an instructional leader in your district or school.
- *Chapter 8*, "Computer Applications in Educational Administration," gives you a vision of how computers can help you administratively, and provides many practical examples of the types of information-handling tasks for which software has been developed.
- *Chapter 9*, "Bits and Bytes," introduces you to computer terminology, components, and functions so you can participate knowledgeably in discussions of hardware and software capabilities. If you're a total novice to computers, read this chapter first.
- *Chapter 10*, "Choosing Your Computer System," you may wish to save until last, but don't ignore it! It is full of detailed information and practical concerns that you'll want to review as you choose your hardware and software systems.

The core of this book and the result of our collective experiences in computer implementation, is to be found in Chapters 1 through 6. Here is what we'd tell you if you called for advice or visited our schools. Here, too, are the detailed examples from real life that we hope will help you during each step of the process of planning and implementation.

- *Chapter 1*, "Computers in Schools: Promises and Pitfalls," provides an overview of advantages and potential hazards in implementing a computer system in your district.
- *Chapter 2*, "Planning Computer Implementation," is the key to the book, carefully walking you through the planning process and its pitfalls.
- *Chapter 3*, "Politics and Funding," gives sound advice on establishing political support for your plan and finding funds to make it begin to happen.
- *Chapter 4*, "Implementing and Supporting a One-Year Plan," follows the cycle of creating and implementing a one-year plan, complete with sample goals and step-by-step advice.
- *Chapter 5*, "Staff Development," discusses staff development and the issues, methods, and goals for such efforts during various stages of computer activity.
- *Chapter 6*, "Management and Operational Control," catalogs the nitty-gritty concerns and tasks that you will run into during implementation, and offers some thoughtful ideas on dealing with these.

The book concludes on a more philosophical note with Chapter 11, "Transforming the Schools." This chapter describes the tremendous potential computers offer educators for bringing about significant changes in our schools, and it urges administrators to take up this challenge.

This book has been a long time in the making and many people have contributed ideas and suggestions to it. Some of us began work on the book in August 1981, just as the educational computing "revolution" was moving into high gear. But events moved so quickly that ideas we committed to paper became out of date almost before our editors returned our drafts to us. Ultimately, we decided to focus on issues that we felt would be relevant for some years to come, and leave the fast-changing details of computer technology to the magazines and newspapers.

Among those who have been particularly helpful are David Dennen and Zeke Finch, members of the original authorship team; Carl Clauset whose thoughtful critique of an earlier version of the book caused us to redefine our task; Alan Ellis whose vision and intensity helped us to develop a clearer focus for our work; and Don McIsaac and Dave Kenniston whose suggestions led us to a last set of changes; Rudy Satlak and Michael Ananis whose comments helped us polish our final draft.

We also wish to thank the patient folks at Addison-Wesley who bore with us during the many changes and delays, especially Peter Gordon, Gail Goodell, Cheryl Wurzbacher, and Ellen Chaffin.

Finally, we wish to thank Elydia Siegel and her colleagues at Superscript Associates for taking our torn and tattered, cut-and-pasted manuscript and turning it into a book in half the time it should have taken.

Contents

Computers in Schools: *1* Promises and Pitfalls

Once again our schools are under fire. From every corner of society we hear criticisms of the ways in which schools are run and the results they attain. Articles in the press, various commission studies, special interest groups, and the periodic best-selling exposés all attack the schools. However, there is little agreement among these critics as to what should be changed or how to do it. Some are concerned with poor student performance in basic skills and gaps in traditional knowledge areas. Most often this group calls for a return to traditional methods to teach these basics. Others believe the major problem with schools to be one of poor management, resulting in waste and low levels of personnel performance. This group usually demands greater accountability at all personnel levels. Still others believe the school environment to be dull, oppressive, uncreative, and dangerous to the mental and physical health of children. Many people in this group have given up trying to change the public schools and either are sending their children to private schools or, in growing numbers, are educating them at home. Periodically, poor teaching becomes the focus of critics, who call for increased incentives for bright and talented people to enter the profession and for improvements in teacher training.

A list of current criticisms of the schools and suggested solutions would be practically endless. Everyone seems to have their own bone to pick with the schools and their own pet solution. There appears to be only one point of agreement: the schools must change. And change they will, although not necessarily due to the pressures of critics, but rather because of the technological breakthroughs radically altering all social institutions today.

Indeed, we appear to be in the early stages of a genuine technological revolution, one that promises to produce major changes in the ways we lead our lives. Fueling this technological whirlwind is the computer, which through incredibly rapid development and application is today playing a major role in the operations of government, business and industry, the armed forces, universities, hospitals, and homes. In these varied sectors of society, computers are used to control and exploit the ongoing explosion of information, to coordinate complex tasks, to facilitate communication and understanding, to provide entertainment, and to support individual and organizational work in myriad ways.

As one of the major institutions in our society, it is inevitable that schools become involved in this computer revolution, if only to prepare workers and citizens for it. However, the impact of computers on schooling is likely to be both more profound and more extensive than this. Computers are already affecting the schools through their influence on children who encounter them in their everyday lives. "Television Age" students are fast becoming "Computer Age" students with attitudes and values that are strange to many educators and with a new set of skills and "disabilities" for us to cope with. And on the proactive side, educators are fast discovering that computers may be applied as tools of instruction and management in numerous ways, many of which can greatly improve the operations and effectiveness of schools, even perhaps addressing many of the criticisms currently being leveled at the schools.

A BRIEF HISTORY OF EDUCATIONAL COMPUTING

This is not to suggest that computers are brand new to society or even to schools. Electronic computers have existed since the late 1930s and have been widely used in government and industry since the fifties. However, those multi-million dollar computers that occupied whole rooms or even buildings bear little resemblance to the affordable desk top computers we know today.

As for use in schools, even as recently as 1978, only a few high schools were using computers in instructional programs in any significant way, though many were doing their scheduling, budgets, and reports on big computers within the district or were buying data processing services. For instructional use, some high schools were connected to large computers (mainframes), often located in a university. Some used terminals wired to the school or town hall business computer, or connected by phone lines to a shared computer. Most of the instructional programs were located in the mathematics or business departments. Nobody considered using computers in elementary school: they were enormously expensive to own, to operate, to maintain, and to house, and there was virtually nothing to teach with them. Certainly no textbook publisher offered software that schools could adopt, and very few teachers knew how to operate computers, let alone write programs for them.

The advent of the personal computer in the late seventies changed all that. All of a sudden, a low-cost, powerful stand-alone computer system was manufactured in quantity. It didn't require space or on-site expensive maintenance. It didn't need telephone wires or charges. Above all, it was easy and fun to use. For many instructional as well as administrative purposes, especially in small school systems or within a school, the microcomputer offered distinct advantages.

What happened is history, and also, incidentally, the source of our present dilemma. Teachers bought their own microcomputers and brought them into schools for themselves, their colleagues, and their students to use. Parents lent their computers to their children's classrooms. Students brought in computers. PTAs began to raise money to buy microcomputers for their schools. School boards began to pressure school administrators to "go computer," especially in regions of the United States where high-technology industries were centered. Software networks and user groups sprang up to exchange courseware developed or modified by teachers, as well as commercial software, which by now was being produced by small independent companies in kitchens and basements and garages in the Sunbelt and Northeast, in Oregon, Minnesota, and Long Island . . . everywhere. A breath of fresh air blew into schools that had been suffocating under declining birthrates and rising taxes in a tight economy.

The 1982–83 school year proved to be a pivotal one, as district after district found the money for hardware and began to look for help in training teachers and choosing software for computer literacy and computer-based instruction in a range of subject areas.

Since then, the trend has intensified. Most surveys estimate that by the end of the 1984–85 school year, computers were being used for instructional purposes in over 75 percent of all schools and that few, if any districts, were without computers altogether. Many of these same surveys point out, however, that the uneven distribution of computer resources across socio-economic groups and the lack of evidence of effectiveness are beginning to cast a cloud of concern over these figures.

CAVEAT EMPTOR

It is becoming increasingly obvious that without proper preparation and planning, those who seek to use the computer to promote improvement in the quality and effectiveness of schools are probably doomed to repeat a well known lesson of history: the more things change, the more they remain the same. We suggest that it is a time for caution; a time that calls for the development of an informed perspective on computers; a time which demands thorough assessment, planning, and tactics for producing change. The siren song of those who promote the computer as the solution to a number of long-standing problems and dilemmas should be resisted. The truth is that the computer could generate as many new problems as solutions to existing ones.

While the computer might offer the means for achieving a quantum leap in the quality of schooling, there are no guarantees. It remains to be seen whether educators can harness computers to facilitate new concepts of learning, new curricula, new instructional and administrative support systems, and new architectural and organizational designs. To do so will require dramatic changes in long-standing traditions, familiar organizational patterns with comfortable role definitions, and entrenched ways of doing business. Otherwise, the computer will likely become the latest disappointment in a series of fads and technological innovations that never achieved their potential in schools.

PROMISES

Despite the warnings offered above, there are strong reasons to be optimistic about the potential uses of computers in educational settings. Computers with appropriate capabilities, used in an intelligent manner, are capable of contributing greatly to the processes of instruction and the procedures of administration. The major areas of school operations in which computers may be most beneficial are:

1. Resource utilization
2. Management
3. Assessment
4. Communication
5. Instruction

Throughout this book, we detail numerous examples of computer use in these five areas. For now we offer a few brief case studies to whet the appetite. These cases are based on real situations, although names and some situational details have been changed for the sake of anonymity and narrative clarity.

More Effective and Efficient Resource Utilization

Dr. Stanley Thomas, Superintendent of the Blytheville School District, typed in a response to the query from the computer terminal located in his outer office. A graph of the distribution of the annual budget among the schools in his district immediately appeared on the screen. He nodded approvingly and directed the computer to provide him with another menu from which to select. He entered his next selection and the percentage allocated to each category of the budget appeared on the screen in the form of figures listed under each of the school names. Another entry brought up a profile of salaries compared to all other expenditures, for each school. Dr. Thomas continued to enter requests as he methodically interrogated a financial database his staff had painstakingly constructed over the past year.

Using the computer in this way as an analytical tool, Dr. Thomas, over the past few months, was able to clearly recognize the way funds were being allocated. With this ability to trace funds, he now found himself able to support the annual district goals with larger resource allocations, to shift funds away from areas deemed less important, and to identify areas where economy was possible. Prior to the installation of the computer system, Dr. Thomas had regularly been frustrated by the difficulty of getting fast, accurate answers to the many questions he had about the way limited resources were being utilized in his district. With the computer, he was now able to monitor budget allocations, analyze the distribution pattern to intelligently question its appropriateness, and plan a new budget with far greater precision.

Improved Management of People, Places, Things, and Time

For years, the high school had used the services of a timeshare computer company to assist with the scheduling of its 1500 students. Paul Riley, the principal, had become increasingly frustrated during the past several years with the quality of the service. Not only had the company dictated all of the time parameters for the project, but it also insisted on a number of constraints which limited Mr. Riley's flexibility and made it next to impossible for him to develop a master schedule that did not freeze many students out of desired courses. He dreaded the predictable calls of outraged parents that followed the summer mailing of schedules. In addition, he was thoroughly irritated by the nuisance of his guidance staff having to hand-schedule all transfer students and to coordinate schedule changes of students with a manual card system.

Finally, last year, Mr. Riley took action. He joined with several other administrators to formulate a district-wide plan for an administrative computer support system. Now that system was in place and he was using it to schedule the high school. Using the computer in a planning mode, Mr. Riley discovered that he now had the ability to weigh different patterns and combinations and to use his years of experience as a principal to try out alternative combinations. The final configuration of selections then became the master schedule—one with the lowest number of conflicts he had ever seen. And to his great satisfaction, the computer continued to coordinate scheduling when the school year began. All new students and all schedule changes were processed quickly and accurately through a computer terminal in the guidance office. Not only had the amount of confusion and unhappiness been drastically reduced, but large amounts of time were saved. With the support of the computer, Mr. Riley now had a system that allowed him to manage scheduling and enabled the guidance department to obtain an accurate profile of one or more student schedules with the press of a key on their terminal. Gone were the long lines in the guidance office, the piles of paper waiting to be posted, and the general sense of confusion which had always marred a smooth opening of school.

Facilitation of Performance Evaluation
and Needs Assessment

Sarah Jenkins, Reading Coordinator for the district, examined the reading scores she had recently received, which summarized the performance of all students in grades one to six on the standardized test given each year. She noticed that scores of approximately one-fourth of the students were below national norms. Using an item analysis profile she had requested, she carefully identified the areas in which students had experienced the greatest difficulty. Getting up from her desk, she walked across the hall to the program planning center established by the assistant superintendent and sat down at the computer terminal. Mrs. Jenkins typed in a request for the computer to display an outline of reading objectives for the district. She then brought up on the screen a scope and sequence chart which identified the delivery points for specific skills. Finally, she instructed the computer to print out hard copies of what she had been examining and she left the room to pick them up at the printer in the next office.

With the newly acquired information in front of her, Mrs. Jenkins prepared a series of questions about the materials being used, the methods of the elementary teachers and reading specialists, and the time currently being allocated for reading. At the next elementary school program council meeting, she intended to introduce a suggestion for modifications which might strengthen the skill areas which were deficient for too many students. As part of her preparation, Mrs. Jenkins arranged to have the data from the reading profile entered into a database program on the computer. She planned later to request class lists in which students' specific reading deficiencies were indicated. With the aid of these computerized records, she hoped to begin an effort to address the skill deficiencies of students through the school reading specialists while at the same time strengthening portions of the regular curriculum.

Greater Clarity and Timeliness of Communication

Ellie Sanchez, guidance coordinator for the Monroe Elementary School, was noticeably pleased. The new student performance reporting system which she had so carefully designed for the elementary schools had been fully operational for a month. Initially, many teachers had questioned the appropriateness of computer printed messages about student performance in class and were leery of sitting at the terminal in the guidance office to select the comments they wished to have appear on the reports being sent to parents. Several teachers complained that they'd been unable to find appropriate comments in the extensive menu of comments. But Ms. Sanchez had shown these teachers how to enter a code which permitted them to type in their own messages and slowly, but surely, teacher resistance melted away.

The system was designed to take advantage of the school computer system to address a long-standing communication problem. Sending out report cards four times a year was proving to be unsatisfactory. It did not provide parents with the kind of detailed information they needed to help their children and, in any case, the information usually arrived too late to be of much use. Some teachers tried to address this problem with mid-term "progress reports" but they had become frustrated with the difficulty of trying to telephone parents and the unreliability of sending notes home with students.

Leaving the regular report card system intact, Ellie created a supplementary system which allowed teachers to prepare mid-term student performance reports consisting of one or more messages selected by teachers from a simple computer menu. With the new system, a precisely written statement describing the performance of a student could be produced with a couple of minutes of effort, resulting in a letter which was mailed to parents by the guidance secretary, with a copy provided for both the teacher and the guidance counselor. Despite initial skepticism, the teachers recognized that the system was easy for them to use, and parents' reaction was very positive, as well.

Expanded Instructional Methods and Improved Instructional Outcomes

The students worked quietly on a set of assigned problems in John D'Urbo's Algebra I class. In a corner of the room, two students sat at desk-top computers which were presenting a review of fractions with bold colored graphics. Mr. D'Urbo had discovered that these two students came into algebra with serious gaps in their mathematics background that were hindering their advancement into algebraic concepts. Rather than transfer them out of his class, Mr. D'Urbo obtained use of two of the school's microcomputers and borrowed some arithmetic review software from the junior high school to use with the students. These two students thus were able to work on individualized review programs during a part of each class, while other students worked on assigned algebra problems, and to return once each week after school for a session. During the rest of the time in class, the two students learned algebra alongside their classmates. A monitoring program built into the arithmetic review series allowed Mr. D'Urbo to examine the progress of the students regularly and to plan for the next unit to be given to them. Using the computer in this way, Mr. D'Urbo found that he was able to both address skill weaknesses in these students and focus his attention on teaching algebra to the whole·class. As a bonus, Mr. D'Urbo discovered that he could use the computer to demonstrate key concepts in algebra as well. He ran demonstration programs on one of the computers which he placed on a tall audio-visual cart at the front of the classroom. These programs allowed his students to experience algebra in highly visual and structured ways. He found that his students' understanding of algebra and their motivation was at an all-time high, that both he and his students felt more confident about what they were doing, and that his relationship with the students had become more relaxed.

PITFALLS

While the promises of computer applications in schools, such as those just described, are great, the road to implementation is fraught with dangers. Following are several case studies which illustrate some of the most common mistakes made when school districts acquire computers. Each case study is followed by a brief discussion of several of these common pitfalls.

Much Ado About Nothing

Daisydale High School has 1350 students and is part of a district which includes two junior high schools and five elementary schools. Upon learning that state occupational education funds could be used to obtain computers, the school principal asked George Jones, a calculus teacher who was the only person in the school with any knowledge of computers, if he would be willing to prepare a proposal for the funds. Mr. Jones regarded the opportunity to submit a proposal as a piece of good fortune because he had been lobbying vigorously for a computer to support mathematics instruction.

As Mr. Jones began his efforts, the principal took a supportive stance but left the preparation of the proposal to Mr. Jones. With high hopes, Mr. Jones attempted to solicit ideas from other teachers, but quickly discovered that his colleagues had almost no knowledge of how to use computers for instruction. Nevertheless, Mr. Jones threw himself into the task, doing all kinds of reading and research into instructional applications of computers. Eventually the proposal was completed. It outlined the school's intention to teach programming, to use the computers as tools in the mathematics curriculum, and to provide business education students with an opportunity to become familiar with the computer.

Much to Mr. Jones' delight the proposal was accepted and a combination of that money and a corporate gift from a local high-tech company enabled the school to obtain a high quality timesharing minicomputer with ten terminals. The value of the equipment alone was estimated to be $75,000.

When the equipment arrived at Daisydale High, the principal directed that the main unit and three terminals be installed in an unused storage room on the first floor. As a result, the connection of the terminals was delayed for several weeks because of a structural steel barrier which blocked planned cable routes and because an air conditioning unit had to be installed in the new "computer room" to protect the equipment. Finally, after many unforeseen delays and expenditures the system became operational.

During the first year, a total of 51 students completed an introductory programming course and approximately a dozen computer buffs logged many hours with practice and experimentation. On many days the system lay idle because there was no one to supervise students and no instruction planned. During this first year, George Jones continued to be the only staff member who seemed to know anything about computers. The mathematics department made little use of the computer, despite having one of the terminals in the math office, because the teachers did not know how to use it and seemed disinclined to learn. The business education students had very little opportunity to become familiar with the computer because the cost of running cable to the second floor where the business education classrooms were located was considered prohibitive. Six of the terminals were located in Mr. Jones' classroom so he could keep an eye on the students learning to program while he taught his regular calculus course.

Nevertheless, the local newspaper published a front page article which extolled the virtues of the new computer system and its potential benefits for students. In reading the article, one formed an image of wonderful educational experiences, of the intelligent use of grant funds, and great enthusiasm for the computer by students and teachers.

During this same year, the school district continued to pay $30,000 a year to a company for scheduling, attendance, and report card services of limited quality. The company was largely unresponsive to requests from the school district for modification of their services.

At the end of the first year, school leaders representing the administration, the mathematics department, the business education department, and the guidance department came together to see what could be done to make better use of this expensive equipment and possibly to expand the system to address some of the administrative tasks now done through the computer services company. However, as they began planning by polling their staffs, they encountered a lot of resistance. Many of the teachers had adopted a point of view which was reflected in statements such as these:

"Why do we need more computer equipment? We don't seem to use what we have now very well."

"Let's get back to basics and stop worrying about all these frills."

"You computer nuts can use that stuff all you want, but don't try to force me to use it. I like things the way they are."

"There are other more important priorities right now; try again next year."

Shortly thereafter, the committee disbanded and asked George Jones to continue his efforts to find uses for the equipment now on hand. The committee gave George a gentle hint that there would be very little money budgeted for support materials or any more unforeseen costs such as the air-conditioner.

Pitfall #1: Failure to plan systematically for computer acquisition.   In this school, the efforts to computerize instruction were piecemeal, unrelated, and limited in scope. The needs of the school, much less those of the district, were not considered. At the same time that a system was being installed for instructional applications, a substantial amount of money was being spent for leased computer support for administrative applications with no apparent thought for plans to eventually transfer the latter tasks to the new in-house computers.

Moreover, the computer system was acquired with no planning with respect to important issues such as:

- Who would operate the computer?
- Where would it be placed?
- What types of uses would be possible given available software?
- How would decisions be made about access and use?
- How would the equipment be protected from vandalism, theft, or misuse?

Pitfall #2: Failure of school leaders to actively coordinate the planning, design, acquisition, and implementation processes.   The principal, the mathematics department head, and the business education head all had remained uninvolved. Rather than leading a comprehensive effort, these administrators sat on the sidelines and "let George do it." They allowed an expensive computer system to arrive without creating any readiness for it, either in terms of physical plant or staff. Any potential which might have existed for instructional use of the computer was squandered by placement of the computers in locations that hindered access and by lack of skills or interest on the part of the staff. In short, computers were obtained by this school because they were available at "no cost" to the school and because one staff member believed that computers could support instruction. Unfortunately, the vision of this teacher had no concrete management support to help bring it to life.

Pitfall #3: Failure to involve a broad base of staff and community participation in the entire process from initial planning to active implementation. The computer at Daisydale High became "George Jones' folly." Instead of campaigning to encourage widespread involvement, Mr. Jones merely made a brief *pro forma* effort to solicit ideas. He abandoned this approach when it did not quickly produce either good ideas or enthusiasm. The article in the newspaper was completely counterproductive, touting an accomplished fact that was imaginary, rather than presenting a description of the potential and calling for some help to realize that potential. Moreover, although the computers were intended to serve the interests of both the mathematics and business education departments, Mr. Jones made practically no effort to involve members of either department in planning their purchase or use. As a result, by the time the administration recognized the need for broader participation to plan an expanded system, it was too late. As often happens, once computers are present in a school and some less than positive experiences have taken place, school staffs do not look favorably upon attempts to expand the system. Nor are taxpayers likely to approve expenditures for equipment that has been utilized poorly in the past.

Trying to Do Too Much with Too Little

Harbrace Union had wanted to obtain computers for several years, but waited patiently for costs to become more reasonable. As a rural regional secondary school containing grades 7–12 with just under 700 students, the budget simply would not accommodate the purchase of a minicomputer system. However, as microcomputers became available at attractive prices, the principal, Dr. Sarah Brown, began to investigate various models. She hoped that one of these microcomputers could manage scheduling, grades, attendance, and, to a limited extent, be available to students for supplementary work in math, business, and science. Promotional materials from the various manufacturers, done in eye-catching colors, suggested that all of these applications were possible. Educational computing magazines carried a variety of articles describing the virtues of microcomputers and created the impression that they were the answer to every school administrator's prayer. For once in the history of Harbrace Union, consensus existed. Dr. Brown wanted a computer; the teachers wanted one; the school committee, believing this request to be most progressive and modern, voted the funds.

Fred Pierson, the sales rep from the computer store in the state's only real city, delivered the computer, installed it, and turned it on. It seemed to run marvelously well, as Fred demonstrated one feature after another. Dr. Brown was delighted. "Let's start with the attendance report for yesterday," she exclaimed. Fred looked a bit embarrassed as he replied, "Well of course, Dr. Brown, you can simply type your attendance report with the word-processing software you bought with the computer, but if you want to do anything with the attendance data beyond printing the day's report, you'll need some specially designed software." Dr. Brown appeared to be quite surprised, as she asked how much that would cost.

Fred began to explain. "The software itself is actually relatively inexpensive— around $200, but unfortunately this model doesn't have enough memory capacity to run that software." Dr. Brown looked blank. Fred continued, "So, you'll need a 64K memory expansion card and a second disk drive so you can have the software run on one drive and your data disks run on the other." By this time, Dr. Brown didn't know whether to be angry at the sales rep or at herself, for being so naive. But she swallowed her anger and again simply inquired about the cost of all this.

Somehow, Dr. Brown found the $900 to buy a second disk drive, a 64K expansion card, the attendance package, and a box of disks. When they arrived, Sally Curtin, Dr. Brown's secretary began to enter the basic information (name, address, telephone, date of birth, date of enrollment) for the students, grade by grade. She found that she couldn't fit much more than one grade on a disk so she ended up using six disks, one for each grade. At that point, Dr. Brown and Sally made an awful discovery: the printer they had purchased did not have a long enough carriage to accommodate the attendance register required by the state. Dr. Brown looked at her budget, cut $1500 from the textbook line, and quietly ordered a new printer costing nearly as much as the original computer.

Finally, Dr. Brown had everything she needed to do the school's attendance on the computer. Unfortunately, she didn't have the funds to buy the expensive software needed to do grades, report cards, and scheduling on the computer. In fact, Fred Pierson had sheepishly suggested that a hard disk might be necessary for scheduling, due to Harbrace's complex daily schedule, involving both regular students and vo-ag students who had to travel to the designated vo-ag school. But the cost of a hard disk exceeded the amount already spent on the entire computer system and Dr. Brown could not authorize such an expenditure without approval from the school committee. That ended that, since Dr. Brown didn't feel she could go back to them and admit how much more this would all cost than she had originally estimated. The school had already spent three times the amount initially approved.

Adding to Dr. Brown's disappointment was the fact that every time a student wanted access to the computer for a math project or in conjunction with some other subject, the computer seemed to be tied up with attendance inputing or processing. Nor was Dr. Brown the only one who was disappointed. Teachers became angry and cynical about broken promises of computer support for instruction and students became frustrated with the difficulty of obtaining access time.

Pitfall #4: Failure to learn and be clear to others about the characteristics and capabilities of hardware and software under consideration.   Dr. Brown had been lulled into an attitude of complete faith in the capabilities of the computer by attractive promotional literature. Too much trust was placed in sales representatives. Dr. Brown, her teachers, and members of the school committee became caught up in the magnetism of technology. There was no research and no planning. The computer was brought into the school without proper preparation and without first establishing a knowledge base about characteristics and capabilities of computers. The result was frustration, disappointment, disillusionment, conflict, and unexpected costs.

Pitfall #5: Failure to provide adequate funding and support for implementation.   The initial experience with a computer in this school was not a positive one. Besides being caught by surprise by what the computer required to perform particular applications successfully, there was no supplemental equipment and supplies budget. This meant that other important items had to be cut in order to purchase additional necessary equipment for the computer. Worse, Dr. Brown didn't foresee potential competition for computer access between administrative and instructional applications and so had not created any mechanism for sorting out these conflicts over access time and priorities. Expectations had been created about the use of the computer which were not fulfilled.

Without more informed support for implementation by Dr. Brown and her department heads in the future, the situation can only deteriorate further. By that time, it is likely that attitudes in the school toward computers will be seriously damaged and that a scapegoat will be identified to absorb the blame for the miserable failure of the entire venture.

AVOIDING PITFALLS/
FULFILLING PROMISES

As a school administrator, it is imperative that you and your staff develop strategies to successfully bring computers into schools for instructional and administrative uses. To cast your fate to the winds or subscribe to the notion that technology can bail you out of any traps you may create with noncompatible or nonexpandable hardware or software is sheer folly. To believe that you can keep up with new demands for computer access or support by adding to your computer system in a willy-nilly fashion is truly shortsighted. To have confidence that you will be able to deal with any desired application simply by being creative is setting yourself up for failure—both personally and organizationally.

To avoid pitfalls such as these and to achieve the promises of educational computing described earlier, school leaders must:

1. Plan systematically for computer acquisition.
2. Provide active, visible, and ongoing coordination and direction to the entire planning and implementation process.
3. Encourage and enable widespread participation by staff, community members, and students in planning.
4. Learn about the characteristics, capabilities, and uses of computers.
5. Obtain adequate funding and support for acquisition and implementation.

The computer holds great promise for schools, but there also are considerable dangers and pitfalls which must be avoided. In subsequent chapters of this book we provide practical information and suggestions to help you avoid the pitfalls and to put yourself in a position to harness the promise of the computer for improved school management and instruction.

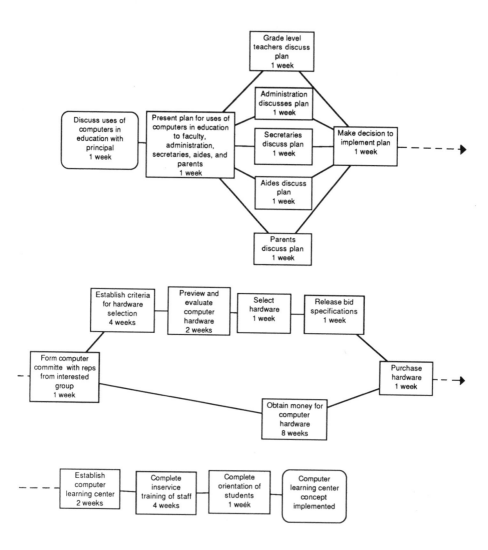

Planning Computer Implementation 2

Doris A. Mathieson arrived at Cameron Middle School on the opening day of school fully prepared for her new administrative assignment. Like most new administrators, her immediate priorities were to insure a smooth beginning for faculty and students. There were new students to enroll, schedules to distribute, supervisory assignments to be made, and a hundred other tasks necessary for a successful first day of school. Computers were not on Doris Mathieson's list of priorities.

Two weeks later, Mathieson's priorities had changed. As she recalls:

> Someone forgot to tell a group of computer-literate ten-year-olds that this impatient technology had not been included in the curriculum or on my list of educational objectives. One sixth grader completed a writing assignment at home on her personal computer. She used a word processor and a spelling editor (a program capable of reading and correcting all spelling errors on a ten-page paper within 30 seconds). The teacher sent the student to the office for discipline. He didn't think this should be allowed. It was unfair to other students and furthermore, how could the student ever learn to conquer cursive writing or basic skills?
>
> While touring the building I found three brand new microcomputers. Purchased the previous year, they were now being stored in the back of the math room waiting. . . .
>
> The PTO offered to raise money to buy additional microcomputers. The message was strong and clear. In spite of tightening fiscal restraints, parents wanted computers to become part of the school experience. They were afraid their children would be deprived of career opportunities and be educationally disadvantaged unless they possessed computer skills.[1]

Doris Mathieson's experience is not unusual. Pressed by day-to-day events

---

[1] Doris A. Mathieson, "Computers: From Confusion to Collaboration," *Educational Leadership*, Vol. 40, No. 2, November 1982, p. 13.

which require their immediate attention, most school administrators unfortunately have little time for long-range planning. Many are simply trying to catch up with the computer revolution, often following the lead of enthusiastic parents or students.

However, school administrators should be leaders, not followers, and a failure to plan is to plan by default. Events occur, things happen, and suddenly there is a system of sorts. The most negative consequence of this catchup game is the lack of sensibly developed long-range goals. Without clear goals for ways to use computers, school districts are forced to fall back on whatever commercial products are available and—oops—the goals have been developed by someone else. Worse, the goals may be at odds with other more established goals of the school. This is where the school administrator can and must play a crucial leadership role, by insisting upon systematic planning and by reminding those involved that computer use in schools must reflect and support the district's stated educational goals.

A SYSTEMS APPROACH TO PLANNING

Systematic planning requires at the outset a systems perspective. School administrators must be able to perceive their school district as a whole consisting of interlocking parts, which themselves are composed of more interlocking parts. Thus a school system can be seen as a hierarchy of nested and interrelated subsystems. Take, for example, the relationships of one classroom to another classroom, a classroom to a building, and a building to the district's central office. The components must work together, not at cross purposes. Such a view can help to provide consistency with respect to the goals toward which the staffs of each classroom and building are moving.

Such a systems perspective is particularly useful when one is considering the purchase and use of computers in schools because computers themselves are most effectively used when they are regarded as a system. Thus, for example, attendance information gathered at the individual classroom level can be passed via computer to the school office and from there to the central office; or information generated by the guidance office computer can be disseminated to parents and students through the classroom teacher; or district student learning objectives can be computer-linked to departmental or grade-level objectives and curricular materials.

Armed with a systems perspective, school administrators can now begin the process of systematic planning and implementation, which may be seen as consisting of three basic phases: strategic planning, management control, and operational control.[2]

---

[2]Robert N. Anthony, *Planning and Control Systems: A Framework for Analysis*, Division of Research, Harvard Graduate School of Business Administration, Boston, MA, 1965.

Strategic Planning

Strategic planning includes making decisions about the goals of the organization, making changes in these goals, identifying the resources needed to attain the goals, and determining policies required to govern the acquisition, use, and disposition of the necessary resources. In the context of planning for computer implementation in a school system, strategic planning might include such activities as:

- Writing a long-range plan for the uses of computers in the school district.
- Establishing citizen and staff advisory committees on the use of computers in the schools.
- Instructing leadership staff on how to write one-year action plans related to implementing computers in the school district.
- Deciding on nonroutine capital expenditures related to effective uses of computers in the schools.
- Making a policy decision to use federal monies, whenever possible, to finance computer implementation in the school district.
- Appointing a top level citizens' committee charged with soliciting funds for the installation or growth of a computer program in the school district.

Most of this chapter and the next, *Politics and Funding*, describe strategic planning for computer implementation in some detail.

Management Control

Management control is primarily concerned with obtaining needed resources and insuring that these are used effectively and efficiently in the accomplishment of the organization's goals. In the context of computer implementation in a school district, some of the activities associated with management control might include:

- Developing instructional objectives for the use of computers in various academic disciplines and grade levels.
- Developing an annual budget for computer equipment, supplies, maintenance, and personnel.
- Planning computer staffing levels.
- Identifying new areas for computer application.
- Deciding on the arrangement of computer facilities.
- Measuring, appraising, and improving the performance of those involved in the computer program.
- Formulating job descriptions for computer personnel.

These and other management control activities for computer implementation are described in detail in Chapter 4, *Implementing and Supporting a One Year Plan*, and Chapter 6, *Management and Operational Control*.

Operational Control

Operational control is the process of insuring that specific tasks are done efficiently and effectively. Typical operational control activities vis-à-vis computer implementation might include:

- Scheduling students and staff to use the computers.
- Implementing computer usage policies.
- Maintenance of computer facilities.

These and other operational control activities for computer implementation are described in detail in Chapter 6, *Management and Operational Control.*

Although the importance of each of these three phases of planning and implementation should not be minimized, the boundaries between them are not always distinct. Strategic planning often continues long after a project has already begun and new management and operational control requirements emerge continually. What is crucial is that all three phases be conducted from a systems perspective that reflects the continuum from strategic planning to management control to operational control and back again.

THE DISTRICT LONG-RANGE COMPUTER PROGRAM IMPLEMENTATION PLAN

Ultimately, successful implementation of a computer program depends upon the creation of a systematically developed district-wide long-range plan. In the remainder of this chapter, we discuss the components of such a plan. Then, Chapters 3–6 discuss the various arenas in which the plan is carried out.

There is no magic to a systems approach to planning and implementation. Simply, it requires that rigorous analytical procedures be used to provide answers to questions such as:

- Where are we going and how will we know we've arrived?
- What are the constraints of the system?
- What are the major events that we want to have occur?
- What specific activities comprise each event?
- What are the alternative ways of accomplishing each activity?

The answers to each question will reveal, depending on the goal, a complex network of interrelationships, which must be addressed if stated outcomes are to be successfully achieved.

The entire process begins with identification of goals. Once these have been agreed upon and the constraints defined, the process continues in successive analytical steps until activities have been identified which may promote the goals identified. At this point the analysis proceeds one step further to investigate alternative ways of accomplishing each activity. The results of the investigation should culminate in the selection of one or more alternate means.

Using the results of the analysis described above, we now can design a systematic plan to get the job done. This requires answers to a new set of questions:

- How can the job(s) best get done?
- What is the sequence of tasks?
- Who is responsible for each?
- What are the most efficient ways to carry out tasks?
- How do we manage to evaluate all the elements of the system?

The answers to these and other questions should then be incorporated into a written document for consideration by all the various people whose opinion and cooperation will be needed for successful implementation of the plan. You should expect your first written plan to undergo substantial revision after you've solicited comments from these people, and you will probably find that the plan goes through numerous drafts before it can be approved. Moreover, even once approved, you would be wise to regard the plan as open to change as circumstances demand.

You may also find it useful to summarize the plan in the form of one or more types of organizational charts, such as a flow chart, PERT (Planning, Evaluation, and Review Technique) chart, or Gantt chart. Such charts sometimes can provide a clearer picture of tasks and their accomplishment than dozens of pages of narrative. Moreover, they can be used by administrators to track progress and make needed adjustments to the plan.

STRATEGIC PLANNING
FOR COMPUTER
IMPLEMENTATION

Dr. Alan Ellis, a leader in the field of school administration and a pioneer in educational computing since 1962(!), has stated that "thinking about computers in education means thinking about education, not thinking about computers."[3] Ellis was neither the first nor the last person to present this point of view, although too many school districts still ignore this advice. Ellis, however, was in a position to act on his own advice, as chairman of the computer advisory committee in a suburban school district. The advisory committee included fourteen teachers, students, administrators, and local residents knowledgeable about education and/or computers. Gradually, over the course of several weeks of meetings and debate, members of the advisory committee came around to Ellis' point of view that

[3]Alan Ellis, *The Use and Misuse of Computers in Education*, New York: McGraw-Hill, 1974, p. 42.

thinking about computers in education means thinking about education first. In its final report to the School Board, the computer advisory committee declared:

> . . . any development that portends such fundamental changes in society as does the computer must become a serious and deep concern of the educators who run our schools.
>
> Determining what ought to be the nature of this concern and the character of its expression have been the committee's principal considerations, in pursuit of which we have come to make the following distinctions among the ways the computer may impinge upon the school district's educational program:
>
> *a. The Computer As a Force in Society*
> Whether or not computers are ever brought onto school premises, and even if the word "computer" is never used in the classroom, the magnitude of the computer's presence in society requires that schools reconsider the content, goals, and organization of their educational programs.
>
> *b. The Computer As an Instructional/Learning Aid*
> Here the question is whether or not computers can be useful in the delivery of educational programs, and if so, the extent to which the educational delivery process itself must change to accommodate such use.
>
> *c. The Computer As Subject Matter*
> Computer programming, systems design, machine operation, electronics maintenance, data processing, or just plain computer literacy are only some of the many things that can be taught about computers. The critical question, of course, is whether or not it is important that the educational program teach anything at all about computers.
>
> Notice that these three distinctions raise concerns that are not primarily about technology. That is, thinking about the role of the computer in education does not mean thinking about computers. It means thinking about education. Thus it is the Committee's strong belief that the process through which these concerns are addressed and resolved, to be of lasting value, must be engaged by the professional educators of the school system rather than by the Computer Advisory Committee alone. Experience shows vividly that attempts to bring automation to schools will fail without the considerable involvement of faculty and building administrators. Indeed curriculum development in general may be broadly conceived as a process for a faculty to grow, learn, reformulate, reconsider, evaluate, and otherwise actively participate in the evolution of their school's educational programs. We cannot expect commitment from teachers, nor the integration of computers into the various curricula simply because we recommend it. We must assist teachers to participate in a process that allows them each to discover computing within his/her own frame of reference so as to make computing a part of the context of each professional life.
>
> Thus while the members of the Committee vigorously support and are committed to the value of the use of computers in schools, still such commitment

must be generated anew by each teacher through the process of considering the uses of computers in his/her discipline.[4]

The advisory committee had developed a simple yet radical view. Rather than determining the goals for educational computing in its district on its own, the committee suggested that teachers and administrators should develop those goals. Rather than relying on scholars and consultants to tell the district what to do, it suggested that those people should serve as resources for faculty and administration members as they developed their own goals. Accordingly, the computer advisory committee refrained from telling the district what to do, and concentrated instead on helping the staff find its own answers.

This experience can serve as a guide to other school districts. Given a commitment to the proposition that thinking about computers in education is thinking about education, and a commitment to the imperative of having faculty and administrators responsible for planning their own computer program, there are six key questions for any district to consider:

1. What are our goals for computer use in education?
2. Who will use computers?
3. How will they use computers?
4. At what age will they use computers?
5. Where will they use them?
6. How many computers do we need and what kind?

What Are Our Goals for Computer Use in Education?

Developing goals is the single most important step in planning the long journey towards the effective use of computers in schools. School leaders must actively work toward the establishment of such goals early in the process of planning, long before any consideration is given to software, hardware, or any other of the many issues in implementing computer use in an educational setting. Important as these other issues are, they are secondary to a determination of the purposes of computer use in education which, once arrived at, will influence all subsequent decisions to be made. Then, with good planning, these subsequent issues will fall into place with relative ease.

One powerful example of the failure to consider goals first is the all-too-frequent attempt to piggyback instructional uses of computers onto a system designed for administration or vice versa. Although it may be tempting to envision a computer system that can be used for both administrative and instructional purposes, the truth is that a district's administrative goals for computing often

[4]Weston Computer Advisory Committee, "Computers in the Weston Public Schools," Weston, MA, 1981, pp. 1–3.

conflict with its instructional computing goals. The best computer system for achieving administrative goals is unlikely to be the best system for furthering instructional goals. Nevertheless, many school systems continue to attempt to justify their instructional needs for computers on the basis of savings that will accrue in school administrative costs. The result is almost always the purchase of computer systems that neither achieve the district's instructional goals nor suit its administrative purposes.

One sensible way around this dilemma is to explore administrative and instructional goals for the use of computers independently, in the anticipation that they will be achieved with separate computer systems. Only if it becomes apparent subsequently that the same computer system will serve both sets of goals in the district's plans should the two be considered together. If the school system makes this decision, it must take great care to recognize and acknowledge conflicts that could arise in implementing both sets of goals. For example, it may be hard to reconcile the need for security of confidential administrative files with the goal that some students learn how to operate the school's computer system as part of their advanced studies.

Instructional goals. In the rush to climb on the computer bandwagon, many organizations or educational institutions are advocating "computer literacy" for students as their primary instructional goal. With rapidly growing support for "doing something with computers" among parents, students, faculty, administrators, and school board members, many school leaders have made such a commitment even before they have considered its implications relative to the other five questions raised earlier, on p. 21.

The truth is that computer literacy as an instructional goal is too vague. The term, which is used in various ways by computer education advocates, demands further definition and exploration before even being considered as an instructional goal by a school system. Andrew Molnar of the National Science Foundation has remarked that "defining computer literacy is like aiming at a moving target." The first shots were fired well over a decade ago. As early as 1972, the Conference Board of the Mathematical Sciences, defined computer literacy and recommended that it become part of the required curriculum for junior high school students. In 1980, universal computer literacy also was defined and recommended by the National Council of Teachers of Mathematics (NCTM) and others.

In 1982, the International Council for Computers in Education (ICCE), surveyed a number of states and national groups and found agreement on the following goals for computer use in education, goals that both include and extend beyond the simple phrase "computer literacy":

1. All students should become computer literate. This means that they should gain a substantial level of computer awareness and develop a reasonable level of skill in using computers as an aid to problem solving in a variety of disciplines.

2. The use of calculators and computers as an aid to problem solving should be integrated into all levels of the curriculum and into both math and a variety of nonmath courses.
3. Teaching using computers should gradually grow in importance and use. Teaching using computers should occur only when it is an educationally and economically sound aid to the current instructional program.
4. All aspects of the current curriculum should be reconsidered in light of the existence and wide-spread availability of calculators and computers. Modification should be made to take into consideration the capabilities and applications of these machines.[5]

Although still rather general, these recommendations for the uses of computers in education do specify several key points. They define computer literacy as a skill required of *all* students, not just those interested in computers. They describe the appropriate uses of computers as problem-solving tools and stress their applicability in all curriculum areas.

Each of the four ICCE goals has somewhat different implications for the questions posed earlier. Taken by itself, computer literacy as a goal could be comparable to the classroom component of a driver's education program. The "hands-on" component of developing skill in using computers might then be analogous to the on-the-road component. Conceived in this way, the number of hours of hands-on experience can be prescribed and then used to calculate the number of computers needed, rooms required, and instructional staff to be trained. In fact, a school district whose only goal is computer literacy and which has a minimal requirement of hands-on experience to meet that goal could organize its program with very little investment in computer hardware and software.

The second ICCE goal, integration of computers into all levels and all areas of the curriculum, has very different implications. First, the school will have to offer opportunities within its curriculum for students to learn the skills necessary to use computers as problem-solving tools, such as word processing, data processing and programming. But more significantly, this goal suggests that responsibility for using computer applications will fall upon the shoulders of the entire faculty, and not just on one or two "computer teachers." Furthermore, computers will need to exist in sufficient numbers, be accessible to students and teachers in different departments or grades, and be capable of running a wide variety of computer software. To insure that these goals are achieved, a school district will undoubtedly need to have at least one person on its faculty designated as a computer coordinator. Moreover, administrators will need to be active in planning for such widespread integration of computers into the curriculum, including making provisions for teacher training and working with the instructional staff to identify appropriate computer applications in each curriculum area.

---

[5]David Moursund, *School Administrator's Introduction to Instructional Use of Computers*, Eugene: University of Oregon, 1982, p. 36.

The third ICCE goal, which is usually called computer-based instruction, has still different implications. Its implementation on a wide scale implies a complete reorganization of the teaching process, perhaps with drastic changes in cherished institutions such as the length of the school day, class sizes, even the location of schools. However, at the present time, romantic visions of computer-based schooling described by futurists like Alvin Toffler[6] and J. C. R. Licklider[7] are not economically or politically feasible. Nor has the quality of most computer-based instruction reached the point where computers can assume the traditional roles of teachers. But, on a limited basis, many schools are already making successful use of instructional software for remedial education and for special topics throughout the curriculum. (See Chapter 7, *Instructional Applications of Computers*, for descriptions of computer-based instruction.)

The fourth ICCE goal at first may not come to mind to the administrator making plans for computer-based instruction. Yet, whether or not a district adopts any of the first three goals, the widespread presence of computers in our society has implications for the school curriculum. For example, even if a school district has no computers available to its students, administrators and their mathematics teachers would do well to reconsider the extent to which they emphasize possibly outmoded calculation skills in their mathematics program at the expense of more useful problem-solving skills (such as estimation). In today's world few adults need to tackle long-division problems with a paper-and-pencil algorithm, and hammering away at this skill year after year with some students may hinder development of other mathematical skills now needed, as well as discourage their interest in mathematics.

Identification of some or all of the goals described above is an important first step in developing a school district's plans for instructional uses of computers. Equally important is the need to translate these broad goals into more specific objectives which apply at each level of the school system. Below is an example of how one district further delineated their goals for computer literacy and integration of computers into its curriculum.

Elementary School
1. Students will use computers in their course work.
2. Students will become familiar with the mechanics of the computer keyboard.
3. Students will understand and apply the vocabulary necessary to operate computers in the classroom.
4. Students will use computers in different areas of the curriculum.

Middle School
1. Students will read and understand computer programs using a computer language.

---

[6] Alvin Toffler, *The Third Wave*, New York: Morrow, 1980.
[7] J. C. R. Licklider, *Social and Economic Impacts of Information Technology on Education*, 1981.

2. Students will write and modify programs.
3. Students will use computers as problem-solving aides in different disciplines.
4. Students will identify advantages and disadvantages of the proliferation of computers in society.

High School
1. Students will become computer literate, including the ability to write and modify programs in a computer language.
2. Students will use computer graphics, word processing, and information retrieval techniques in their studies and in the preparation of written reports.
3. Students will extend their thinking and problem-solving skills by developing algorithmic solutions to problems in mathematics and other disciplines. They will translate these into well-documented computer programs free of logical and syntactical errors.
4. Students will distinguish problems which are not amenable to solution by computers; they will use computers to solve problems in their course work.
5. Students will be able to discuss moral and ethical issues that arise from the impact of computers on our society. They will be able to make responsible decisions about computers and their uses in their own school environment.[8]

Note that this set of goals goes far beyond computer literacy. In fact, these goals assume that by the middle school years, students will begin to be able to use the computer as a problem-solving tool and that most computer use among high school students will be in this mode.

Administrative goals. There are four major goals that are generally cited for the administrative use of computers. These are:

1. Decrease costs of administration.
2. Increase efficiency of operation.
3. Increase output of an office.
4. Support the instructional program.

While it is true that some of the tasks of school administration can be accomplished faster and with far greater efficiency when done with the assistance of computers, it is a mistaken belief that the introduction of the use of computers will reduce educational costs. Experience shows that it takes substantial time to learn how to use computers effectively. During this period the school district will probably have to make additional investments in training programs for its staff and administrators. Moreover, although ultimately greater efficiency in carrying out administrative and office tasks will accrue, computers are not likely to replace personnel in schools. Rather, they may permit busy administrators to reduce the

---

[8]Weston Public Schools Computer Workshop, "Summer, 1981 Report," Weston, MA, p. 3.

time they spend on collecting and handling routine information, thereby allowing them to spend more time on substantive educational issues. Also, administrators may use computers to increase the school district's output of information to the community and the public, thereby actually making more staff necessary. At present, all too often school offices and school administrators are seen as unresponsive because of a failure to respond quickly to parents with seemingly routine requests for information, or to applicants for teaching positions, or even to local school boards with requests for data and reports about school operations. Computers may dramatically improve such communication.

Despite our previous warning it should not be assumed that instructional and administrative goals for computers will always conflict. After all, one of the principal goals of school administration is to support the educational program of the schools and many administrative tasks capable of computerization are designed to do just that. These include attendance reporting, grade reporting, maintaining student records, student scheduling, and providing updated curricular budgetary information. The use of computers in schools can provide administrators, teachers, parents, and students with almost immediate access to this kind of information. For example, using computers to process daily attendance data may allow teachers to have lists of absentees early in the day, and make it easier for administrators to complete attendance reports for the whole school. As a further example, most large high schools use a computerized service to develop student and teacher schedules on an annual basis. But doing this in-house rather than by subscription to a computer service would mean that schedules could be updated and reprinted on an almost daily basis, thereby avoiding some of the confusion in records that inevitably accompanies student schedule changes during the year. And as a final example, some districts will want to use computers to maintain detailed records of students' performance on instructional objectives for purposes of reporting to parents. Teachers, too, can make use of this sort of information in their planning and managing of individual instruction for their classes. Teachers might also want to use computers to keep track of and compute grades. Such uses of computers may go far in winning over computer-shy teachers.

Who Will Use Computers?

Troublesome questions may arise over who will use computers, questions which must be addressed in the process of planning computer implementation. For example, assuming that computer resources are limited, who has priority? Can a teacher during a free period walk into the computer lab and commandeer a terminal, or does a student have the right to use that terminal to finish working on a problem in biology? Can an administrator from the school's office use a terminal to run a simulation of the budget or do scheduling during classroom instructional time, if that use diverts some of the computer's capacity from instructional to administrative uses? And who will referee these disputes? Most often it is the hapless computer coordinator who is suddenly besieged by conflicting demands from students, teachers, and administrators with little guidance or precedent to help.

If the influence of computers increases and spreads throughout our society—as virtually everyone now assumes it will—then it would seem that computers should be accessible to all students in all schools. This is a significant change from the view of the proper place of computers in society only a generation ago, when most of the population was ignorant even of their existence and when skill in the use of computers was limited to a handful of "high priests." However, at least for some time to come, few schools will have sufficient computer resources to provide unlimited access to all.

Thus administrators will need to help their school districts establish priorities among competing users. These priorities should reflect the explicitly stated educational goals of the district. For example, if computer literacy is defined by the district as a primary instructional goal for all students, then small amounts of hands-on experience will be needed for all and equity issues may not arise. If, on the other hand, the district plans to teach its students how to program and expects this skill to be used widely throughout the curriculum, or if it foresees substantial use of computer-based educational materials or other kinds of applications software, then these goals may be difficult to accomplish unless a sufficient amount of hardware and software is obtained to provide equal access to all students.

How Will Students Use Computers?

If computers are viewed as means for using intelligence, solving problems more effectively, and extending the capabilities of human beings—rather than as ends in themselves—then there are many different ways in which they can be used. Many of these are described in Chapter 7, *Instructional Applications of Computers*. For each application, however, the administrator must ensure that teachers ask whether the proposed usage is both possible and worth doing. Such questioning may even lead to a reexamination of basic educational goals and strategies, as illustrated in the following account:

> A group of teachers was developing plans for the integration of computers into the high school mathematics program. The superintendent of schools joined one of their meetings at which these teachers were discussing activities to teach high school students how to write computer programs which would invent games or simulate existing games. The superintendent questioned the value of high school students using computing for the purpose of creating computer games. In the ensuing debate, the faculty distinguished clearly between the teaching—and learning—necessary to write a computer program for a game and the end product of that activity, the game itself. Just as the result of an elementary student's first writing activity might be a rather simplistic paragraph or illustrated comic book, so the result of a beginning programmer's activity might be a relatively unsophisticated activity.
>
> This group of teachers even went one step farther. As one later recalled:

"As we pursued this discussion, we began to reexamine the value of games in general. In fact, teachers do use games as one of the techniques to motivate students in their academic work as well as to promote logical thinking skills. We recalled the important role that children's games play in education, as pointed out by many learning theorists. In short, starting out by thinking about whether computers ought to be used for games at all led us to a more profound look at the role of games in education. The discussion was valuable—it gave us more insight into the purposes of games and the materials we use in the schools, yet it did not suggest that it was important to use *computer* games in the classroom."

The question of how students will use computers extends beyond the relationship of the student to the technology. The following related questions are also important for administrators to consider in formulating their plans.

Will students use computers solely in their classes or also as tools outside their classes? The answer, of course, depends on the district's educational goals. If, for example, the goals are merely to teach students how to operate the technology and then to use computers as tutors of traditional curriculum content, then it is likely that students will use computers in class only. By contrast, if the goal is to have students use computers as general problem-solving tools, then most likely they will begin by learning about computers with their classmates, and rapidly progress to individual use whenever they need the tool to solve problems or to do assignments. If this latter approach is to become dominant in a school, one of its implications is that there must be a drop-in center or similar place where individual students can use computers whenever time is available to complete assignments. These space requirements have implications, in turn, for staffing, budget, hardware, and software.

Will students use computers for mathematics work and computer science only or in other curriculum areas as well? By now, our bias should be clear: computing and the computer have potential application in every curriculum area. Equally important, to assume that computers will be initially or more frequently used in the mathematics program would be a great mistake because a plan developed on that premise will become a self-fulfilling prophecy. It follows that computers should be located so as to be equally accessible to all curriculum areas, that faculty from all disciplines should be involved in developing goals or receiving in-service training, and that money for computer support should be allocated for all disciplines consistent with their goals.

At What Age Will Students Use Computers in Schools?

The use of computers in education began at the university level, typically as graduate students worked with professors in the development of early computer applications. Gradually the use of computers extended downward, first to the undergraduate level—Dartmouth College was an early pioneer in the establishment of computing facilities for undergraduates—and then to the high school level.

With the more recent explosion of microcomputer technology, familiarity with computers is now working its way up from the earliest elementary grades. In a few communities, a sizable number of students have access to microcomputers at home and are already familiar with their use even before beginning elementary school. They, and their older brothers and sisters, often know more about computers than do their teachers.

This piecemeal pattern makes the school's job more difficult. Thus, it is especially important that administrators lead their staffs in addressing the question of the appropriate age for students to use computers for various purposes. As with any curricular area, the goals for computing at any given grade level will have to account for differing levels of students' interest, skill, and ability. Equally important, the goals for computing at any particular grade level will have to be compatible with the goals and activities for the rest of an already crowded curriculum. This is particularly true if one goal is to integrate computers into all curriculum areas. In that case, administrators must ensure that discussion of goals for computers comes to mean discussion of goals for the mathematics program or the English program and how computers can help reach those goals.

Where Will Computers Be Used?

Where computers are used should also reflect the goals for the use of computers in education. If, for example, a goal is to integrate computers fully into all areas of the curriculum, but there are only a handful of terminals located in a computer center in the mathematics wing, then it is unlikely that faculty or students in departments such as foreign languages or business education will use them. By contrast, a computer center located in a central place can provide equal accessibility for all departments, so that there is greater likelihood of achieving the goal of integration into all curriculum areas. Similarly, if computer use in administration is an important priority, then several terminals, if not the entire computer center, will probably be located near the administrative offices. But such a choice may deter students and teachers from making wider use of the computer, particularly if those offices are not in a central area of the school.

Implicit in these examples is the assumption that a mix of centralized and decentralized locations may be most flexible and best suited to the school's long-term needs. A centralized location, with terminals in one place, offers many advantages: it is easier to staff and to control the use of equipment; students can drop in at free moments knowing the computer center will not be in use as a classroom; and there are greater opportunities for sharing among both students and staff. But a decentralized system, with terminals scattered over several locations, such as offices, classrooms, the library, and perhaps a small drop-in center, also offers advantages: the closer the terminals are to their principal users, the greater the chance of their being used by them; if the goals for the use of computers involve only a few students—for example, to provide individualized instruction for special needs students—then the location of terminals should provide accessibility to those students. The best mix of centralized and decentralized terminals should reflect the school's goals for computing, with additional emphasis on creating as flexible a system as possible because needs and usage will change so rapidly. The issue of computer location is discussed in greater detail in Chapter 6, *Management and Operational Control.*

How Many Computers Do We Need and What Kind?

The question of how many computers are needed and what kind to purchase is discussed more fully in Chapter 10, *Choosing Your Computer System.* But it is important to say a few words here about the complexity of this issue for a school administrator. Not surprisingly, the answer to the question again should depend upon your statement of goals for computer use in the school district. From those goals and the assumptions they contain, you can calculate an estimated number of computer stations needed to attain those goals over a period of time. But to answer the question of what type of computers or computer stations to purchase, you must also factor in such matters as price, reliability, software availability and the compatability of different computer specifications with the school system's needs.

Table 2.1 depicts a scheme in which the educational goals of computers become the central determinant of the type and number of computing stations to purchase. The table provides for selecting a single goal or multiple goals for the equipment and identifies which groups will be predominant users of the system. It also allows for the selection of the location in which the service will be provided. For example, Table 2.1 is completed for a school system in which the instructional goals are to provide for the use of computers as a tool for a variety of users in a number of different locations, and for management activities, primarily for staff, but also selectively available to others. The locations for these managerial activities are envisioned to include classrooms and beyond.

Table 2.1   Worksheet listing user group and location of computer services.

Educational Intent	User Group				Location*		
	Student	*Staff*	*Parent*	*Citizen*	*Classroom*	*Building*	*District*
Instruction:							
Object of	Y	Y	Y	Y	Y	Y	Y
Tool	Y	Y	Y	Y	Y	Y	Y
Management:							
Materials	Y	Y	Y	Y	Y	Y	Y
Students	N	Y	N	N	Y	Y	Y
Staff	N	Y	N	N	N	Y	Y
Administration	N	Y	N	N	N	Y	Y

*Classroom means providing the service at the teacher station.
Building means providing the service by interconnecting the teacher stations.
District means providing the service within and among buildings.

From this initial analysis, you can then calculate the number of stations required. Assume for the moment you are an administrator of a small high school with declining student population, not unlike the majority of high schools across America today. Assume also that you have established goals for the use of computers in a broad range of courses. You can now calculate the number of stations required, given one or more assumptions about the number of student contact hours per week and the number of available hours per week. Table 2.2 illustrates these calculations for two different assumptions: five student contact hours per week and three student contact hours per week.

From Table 2.2, you can predict that this high school can be served by as few as 25 stations, assuming 3 student contact hours per week and 80 available hours per week. If only half as many hours per week are available, however, then the number of computer stations required doubles. Here you would need to analyze the tradeoff in cost between purchasing twice as many stations and having to create space to house them versus a smaller number of stations with

Table 2.2   Senior high school system requirements, non-specific[9]

Year	81–82	82–83	83–84	84–85	85–86
Population	765	729	734	699	655
Station hours required per week assuming:					
5 contact hours/week	3825	3645	3670	3495	3275
3 contact hours/week	2295	2187	2202	2097	1965
Stations required assuming 5 contact hours/week and:					
40 available hours/week	96	91	92	87	82
80 available hours/week	48	46	46	44	41
Stations required assuming 3 contact hours/week and:					
40 available hours/week	57	55	55	52	49
80 available hours/week	29	27	28	26	25

[9] Weston Computer Advisory Committee, op. cit., p. 21.

the requirement of providing staffing and security for a computer center open 80 hours a week.

This table illustrates the general, school-wide requirements for a small high school. Similarly, you can calculate the computer needs for different program areas. You can ask the mathematics department, for example, to estimate the number of hours per year students of different mathematical skill levels would require for computing. In a hypothetical freshman class, the department might estimate that 20 hours per year per student are necessary for the bottom and average math groups, while the above-average group should have 25 hours per year and the accelerated group 30 hours per year. You can then translate this calculation into a table illustrating the number of stations required for students, if access is provided 40 hours per week or 80 hours per week. Finally, you can prepare a summary table for all departments in the school. In doing so, you should not assume 100 percent utilization because at any given time a certain number of terminals are likely to be inoperable. The program requirement for the high school illustrated in Table 2.2 might then look like Table 2.3.

Table 2.3   Senior high school system requirements, by program[10]

Stations required at the senior high school

Year	81–82	82–83	83–84	84–85	85–86
Population	765	729	734	699	655
At 70% utilization factor and 40 hours/week availability					
Math program	16	16	16	16	14
Science program: biology, chemistry and ninth grade science, 70 students, 3 contact hours/week, throughout the year	8	8	8	8	8
Physics program, 80 students, 3 contact hours/week throughout the year	9	9	9	9	9
Word-smithing, each student 3 contact hours every two weeks	41	39	39	37	35
Total	74	72	72	70	68
At 55% utilization factor and 80 hours/week availability	47	46	46	44	43

[10] *Ibid.*, p. 23.

Finally, the question of what kind of computers to purchase will depend in part on the outcome of the debate over a timesharing system (minicomputer or mainframe) versus microcomputers or a microcomputer network. The issues here are complex and Chapter 10 discusses at length the advantages and disadvantages of each approach.

MANAGEMENT AND OPERATIONAL CONTROL

Once the school district has finalized its strategic plans, which may be a lengthy process in itself, administrators will face the many ongoing tasks that must be carried out over a period of years in order to bring these plans to fruition. A comprehensive implementation plan for computers in education should anticipate and provide for at least the following elements of management and operational control.

1. Coordination
2. Training
3. Support
4. Communication
5. Computer system development
6. Software development and evaluation
7. Operation and maintenance
8. Evaluation

The school administrator with principal responsibility for computers in the schools must participate actively in developing long-range plans for carrying out these tasks. Ideally that person would report directly to the superintendent. In this way, the school system is more likely to maintain the necessary long-range commitment to its computer education goals.

Coordination

Because the range of tasks associated with a successful computers-in-education program is so great, most school systems will want to have at least one person who assumes responsibility for coordination of computer activities. That person will need to devote considerable time to the numerous tasks associated with computer implementation. The selection of a computer coordinator will be a critical, and sometimes sensitive, issue. The coordinator must be responsive to the needs of students, teachers, and administrators as they struggle to learn new ideas. The coordinator should also have the technical expertise to address hardware and software problems quickly and efficiently, and to help the district develop its computer system. The coordinator should be a quick learner who can keep up with rapidly changing developments in the computer field. And the coordinator should be able to exercise good judgment about what can realistically be accomplished and what cannot.

It will be difficult for any district to find all these virtues in one individual. The most knowledgeable computer person may not be well suited for this role! Moreover, the success of a district's plans could be doomed if the selection of coordinator is perceived as making computers the domain of one department or one group of faculty, students, or administrators. This danger is so great that it might be wise to set up a selection process which involves a good cross section of potential computer users. The selection committee should include computer novices as well as experts because it is important that the coordinator communicate well with those who will be new to the use of computers in education. Chapters 4, 5, and 6 all include descriptions of various tasks which might be performed by computer coordinators and their staffs, if any.

Training

We are at an interesting juncture in educational history. Our goals for computer education for the present generation of students may leave our faculty in the dust! By and large, our current teachers are untrained in the use of computers or in their applications to education. Although this situation will gradually change as members of the computer generation grow up and become teachers, in the meantime, we have a responsibility during this transition period to provide in-service training for today's teachers. Without such training, many faculty members will shun the use of computers in the classroom and for their students the computer's role in school will remain peripheral.

We suggest that school districts establish as a goal that all faculty members, administrators, and staff become computer literate and that the necessary training to achieve this goal be provided by the district. Teaching and learning go hand in hand, and teachers can generally be expected to respond enthusiastically to a district's plans for training in the use of computers.

In-service training is discussed in greater detail in Chapter 5. For now, suffice it to say that a district's plans for training should be comprehensive. It should include all potential computer users, staff as well as faculty and administration. It should anticipate that adults will start with different backgrounds (although the majority will be beginners) and that many will want to continue their learning beyond the introductory level. The district's long-range plans should take into account such questions as who will provide the training (probably partially, but not necessarily, the computer coordinator), when the training can be delivered, and for what duration the training program will be continued. It is likely that the training program itself will extend over several years in most districts. A related issue is the extent to which the district wishes to invest in the training of its computer coordinator. The district must also decide whether it will make a long-range investment in specialized training for a small group of individuals who will continue to provide technical expertise as long-range plans unfold.

Support

One important role that should be assigned to the computer coordinator or other knowledgeable staff is support to teachers and students and nonteaching staff in the use of computers. This may include working with whole classes or with small groups of students in a classroom on topics in a computer-based curriculum. It may also involve helping some students carry out independent projects at the computer which require more advanced or more specific knowledge than the regular classroom teacher can provide. If the coordinator's responsibilities include administrative uses of computers, then similar tasks will be carried out with administrators and their staffs. Probably most significant is the work that a coordinator and others should do with faculty members, again either individually or in groups such as departments. While the faculty must ultimately decide for itself whether a particular application of computers is appropriate for the curriculum, knowledgeable staff need to introduce teachers to new ideas which may have possible applications in their classrooms and to demonstrate them in a way that makes the pedagogical issues apparent. The coordinator must also be prepared to support teachers as they experiment with new applications in their classrooms. Simply feeling that they are not at the mercy of technology can provide some teachers with all the impetus necessary to experiment with new educational strategies in their classrooms.

Communication

Assuming that a district has made a major commitment to computers in education, a successful program will require regular communication with a variety of groups. First, teachers need to know what software is available for them to use on the computers. As new software is obtained by the district, its appropriateness for use at different school levels or in different subject areas needs to be made known. Teachers will also want to know about other teachers' experiences using computers in different ways in their classes. The district's implementation plan should make provision for such communication, say, through a newsletter.

A second, equally important arena for communication is with the community. The school board should have ownership in the district's goals, and the school administration should be accountable to the board for achieving these goals. The board should receive an annual report covering such items as the number of students using computers and the amount of time they spend with them, the percentage of teachers who have been trained in the use of computers and the depth of their training, the curriculum areas in which computers are employed, priorities for the coming year, budgets for computer operations, and specific information in relation to the system's goals and how they are being achieved.

Just as the continuing support of the school board is essential for the district's computers-in-education plans, so is the support of the community as a whole. As the use of computers expands, it is likely that further expenditures will be necessary, either to increase the number of computers or terminals or to introduce more sophisticated hardware and software, as they become available. The community should be confident that the school district is making progress so that the budget for computers does not become prey to an uninformed public. The school administration should strive to keep the public informed through community newsletters and invitations to visit the schools to learn more about how computers are being used in the educational programs. An evening spent demonstrating the kinds of activities that students do in class could go a long way toward convincing the public that the district's endeavors in computer education are worthwhile.

Computer System Development

In developing the district's long-range computer plans, the administration must anticipate a sequence of hardware and software acquisitions that will help implement the district's goals. Administrators should review these acquisitions on an annual basis and modify future acquisition plans in light of actual experience. Because the course of events following the introduction of computers is somewhat unpredictable, administrators should be prepared for two quite different possibilities. They may find that progress in implementing goals is slower than anticipated; for example, if it takes longer to train faculty and staff than originally planned. But, just as likely, the demand for using computers and incorporating new applications may come faster than anticipated and cause administrators to rethink the rate at which their plans move forward.

It is important that the faculty be involved in the process of setting instructional priorities, based on its own considerations of the role of computers in the school's curriculum. In planning for computer system development, issues will inevitably arise about whether to purchase one particular piece of software or another, or whether to locate new computer stations in a central location, in particular areas, in certain departments, or in various classrooms. A standing committee composed of students, teachers, and administrators might be established to oversee the general development of the computer system and its availability to students and staff for educational purposes. This committee could make recommendations for hardware and software purchases to the administration, determine the need for in-service workshops, and determine policy regarding access to and priorities for the computer system. The committee should be representative of all areas of the school system, including people who traditionally have not been involved in the use of computers. As needed, the committee might draw upon the expertise of community members or other technical consultants to assist it in the development of the computer system.

Software Development and Evaluation

Another important task for which someone must assume responsibility is the acquisition or development of new software. With respect to in-house development of software, the most important administrative decision to be made is how much resources (both human and budgetary) to commit. Of course, it is desirable to have software which is tailor-made for the district's curriculum or administrative needs. But the system may have too few people available who can write such software quickly. While a large system may be able to hire specific individuals for just this task, a smaller district may not want its computer coordinator to take time away from other responsibilities in order to work on a piece of software that will have only limited use throughout the system. It is certainly far more efficient for the computer coordinator and teachers to review existing software and purchase those pieces deemed appropriate for the system's instructional goals.

Operation and Maintenance

Failure to provide support for the operation and maintenance of equipment has been the death knell for many promising educational technologies in the past. The same fate could befall computers. Teachers will shy away from the use of computers if they are undependable. The school's annual plans must anticipate both the costs and time involved in operating, maintaining, and replacing computer equipment, including provision for service contracts, security arrangements, and electrical wiring needs. The computer coordinator or other appropriate individuals should have responsibility for providing for the quick repair of defective hardware and software. This may include providing for backup systems to avoid disruption of planned instruction. In a microcomputer-based system, teachers and students probably can assume full responsibility for operation of computers, once appropriate training is completed. In a minicomputer system, particularly one with a large number of terminals, there is likely to be a need for ongoing professional support of computer activities. This support might include creating new systems files, writing systems software to enlarge the capabilities of the computer, running backup files, and monitoring or managing the use of the computer system by a large number of students and teachers. This role could be filled by the computer coordinator or by a systems manager with specialized training.

Evaluation

Administrators must see that the effectiveness of an undertaking of the scope we have described for computers in education is properly evaluated. We will not outline a thorough evaluation plan in this book. Other sources handle this topic in great detail. We will only point out that a good evaluation plan flows from a well written set of goals and objectives. Those goals and objectives should be as specific as possible and measurable. Few districts will be able to afford the services of an evaluation specialist, although that is clearly desirable. Nevertheless, administrators must consider program evaluation at the same time as goals are defined, so that plans for evaluation may be built into the early stages of the planning process.

AFTERWORD

We began this chapter with the story of Doris Mathieson discarding her plans for the opening of the Cameron Middle School in order to cope with the unexpected introduction of computers into her school. We then suggested that systematic planning was required for the successful implementation of computers in schools. We spent the remainder of the chapter describing such an approach to planning.

However, even with planning of this type, Doris Mathieson might end up in exactly the same dilemma as she did on the opening day of school. Herein lies the trap: the effective use of computers in schools requires knowledgeable and careful planning, but, like any significant innovation, it may be strongly affected by a series of random, unexpected events. The danger lies in trying to organize too tightly a plan for implementing goals for the use of computers and in attempting to evaluate progress according to narrowly determined goals, at the expense of following progress in unanticipated directions. Just as a seedling requires time to develop firm roots, so a new technology like computers requires time to evolve and grow in ways specific to the needs of teachers and students. Most good school systems try to strike a balance between adherence to established district-wide goals and the provision for flexibility and adaptation in each classroom, according to the needs of students and the skill or interest of teachers.

This same balance is required for the successful introduction of computers. When achieved, it can lead to scenes similar to the following one, in marked contrast to that experienced by Doris Mathieson:

> Sam Slater, a central office administrator, walked through the new Computer Center at Oak Grove High School. In one room a class of ninth grade students was seated in pairs at a dozen computer terminals. The students were learning programming as part of a required nine-week module in their Algebra I course. In the adjoining room, called the Drop-In Center, an additional twenty students were working or kibitzing at another twelve computer stations. Some of these students were doing homework assigned in their advanced computer literacy class. Others were engaged in different activities: sending electronic mail, graphing mathematical functions, or writing papers for their courses. One ninth grade student stopped Slater to show him a program he had just written which plotted epicycles such as those used by the astronomer Ptolemy in calculating planetary orbits. In a guest lecture a few days earlier, Slater had suggested to this student's world history class that such a project would be feasible for anyone who already knew how to program. Another student was just completing a paper, written

with the aid of the computer system's word processing software, for her electronics class. A third was using the *Geometry Supposer*, an experimental piece of software that encourages students to make conjectures about geometrical theorems. This program allows the student to draw triangles and make different constructions upon them, then instantaneously repeat these constructions over and over on different triangles. The author of this program, a graduate student at a nearby university, was sitting at an adjacent terminal debugging the latest version of it. One teacher, whose supervisory assignment was to monitor the Computer Center, was assisting a beginning student while another teacher ran some trial programs for her next class's lesson.

The computer system on which this was all happening had been installed five months earlier. It consisted of a minicomputer with 23 terminals at the high school and another 9 terminals connected to the middle school. Slater felt a sense of deep satisfaction as he looked around before resuming his tour of the rest of the high school. The terminals were used from 7:30 to 4:00 p.m. every day and plans for evening use were in process. Oak Grove was moving forward with plans first developed over two years earlier. The district had come a long way from that moment when there had been just four high school terminals and a single computer literacy course that reached less than 20 percent of their students.

And yet, Slater realized Oak Grove had a long way to go. Getting students and teachers involved in computing was an important plateau to attain. But Slater knew it had been essential to accomplish this goal only to insure that computers could have an even greater impact on teaching and learning in Oak Grove's schools in the future.

Politics and Funding **3**

Even the most impressive plans for computer use in schools are virtually useless without the ability to translate these plans into reality. The first step in such translation is usually a political one: martialing support from the right quarters. While local conditions will vary greatly, we have identified three basic political approaches to implementation of computers in schools.

The Centralized Approach

The *centralized* approach is used most often in larger school systems or organizations which operate in a highly centralized, top-down fashion. The following vignette illustrates one of several variations of this approach.

> The Office of Management Information Services (OMIS) of a large, western city school system that has taught programming as part of the mathematics curriculum since the sixties was considering switching from a timesharing system to stand-alone microcomputers. As a result of 15 years of experience working with computers, the school system had a cohesive group of teachers, technical staff, and administrators who were able to work as a task force with OMIS to develop a well conceived plan for implementing this change. OMIS coordinated a three-phase process, beginning with a pilot project in which one microcomputer was used in one classroom. What was learned from this project, as well as from extensive teacher interviews within their system, enabled OMIS to write an extremely detailed Request for Proposal (RFP), which was sent out for bid to all microcomputer dealers in the metropolitan area. Based on the bids received, which included hardware, software, maintenance, and security information, one microcomputer system was chosen and several units of this make were purchased. After a trial period with these machines, a second RFP was sent out, reflecting new lessons learned.
>
> As a result, the school system bought 30 units of a different make that apparently was better suited to their needs. Currently, reports from that city indicate that teachers and students are very pleased with the switch from timesharing to micros and that the centralized planning and implementation strategy appears to have given the teachers information and the administrative support they felt they needed.

A centralized approach, such as this one, offers several advantages: cost savings are possible through purchase on a bid basis and there is the potential for greater coordination and compatibility with educational goals of the school system as a whole. There may also be advantages to the central storage and distribution of software and hardware and to centrally-directed courses for teachers. Consistency and accountability are likely to be high, as well.

But there are also disadvantages: teachers tend to be isolated from decisions about how computers will be used and therefore the goals may not relate effectively to the curriculum. Because equipment, training, and software may be located away from individual school sites, there is great danger that they will be ignored by faculty or simply not be available when needed. Expensive equipment may not be used effectively or it may be used in ways designed to achieve goals which look good on paper or in a curriculum guidebook but which, in practice, are not attained.

The Decentralized Approach

The *decentralized approach* was extremely common during the first few years after microcomputers became affordable to individuals. It usually began with parents or teachers bringing their own microcomputers into the classrooms for a few days. Often this loan arose from a sense of frustration that such equipment was not available otherwise. Subsequently, an enthusiastic teacher or parent group would raise money to contribute equipment on a permanent basis.

In fact, in a series of reports issued in 1983 and 1984, Dr. Henry Jay Becker of the Center for Social Organization of Schools at the Johns Hopkins University reported that in 50 percent of surveyed schools purchasing microcomputers in the early years of the educational computing "revolution," a single teacher was credited with first suggesting that a micro be bought for the school. However, since that time, the national bandwagon of computer use in schools and at home has caused a shift in this initiator role heavily toward the school or central office administrators.

Nevertheless, there are still schools, particularly in poorer districts, where central administration support for computing is weak or nonexistent. Here, we are likely to see replays of the sort of implementation story that follows.

> George Russo, an elementary school teacher in a working-class suburb, became excited about the potential of the computer to help him keep track of student progress in his individualized approach to teaching basic skills. However, his enthusiasm was not shared by his principal or by most of his colleagues, none of whom addressed basic skills in a systematic fashion. So George approached the Gifted and Talented Committee for the school and persuaded them to include a microcomputer in their Title IV-B proposal for funding a Gifted and Talented program. The program was funded and when the Apple microcomputer arrived, George volunteered to oversee its use. Since no one else in the school knew anything about computers, they were only too glad to take him up on his offer. So, George

got a microcomputer in his room to use for his individualized program, as well as for the gifted and talented kids in other classes who came there in their elective periods.

Lone wolves, like George Russo, appear to be a disappearing breed, which may be just as well, since often the ending to the story is not quite so happy as the beginning. George, like many such educational computing entrepreneurs, left his school after a year, in his case to enter a graduate program in computer science. The barely tarnished Apple now sits on a shelf, since no other teacher in the school developed any interest or expertise in working with it. The message seems clear: computer programs that depend on the energy, enthusiasm, and presence of one person are unlikely to survive.

In fact, the Johns Hopkins survey revealed that "almost without exception, elementary school teachers who report that a single teacher (in many cases, themselves) played the dominant role in talking about, working for, or implementing their school's first microcomputer, also report that their micro(s) have had a less positive impact on a variety of student outcomes than do other elementary school teachers."

Even when two or three teachers join forces, without administrative and collegial support their efforts are unlikely to pay off for very long. Witness the following vignette.

Sally Oakes, the junior high school science teacher at the Greenville School, a small rural K-12 school, and Libby Peterson, the school librarian, were turned on to microcomputers at a regional teacher center-sponsored workshop. But their school ran on a bare-bones budget and badly needed a new gym before investing in any newfangled educational gadgetry. The townspeople were very proud of their basketball teams, especially the girls' team, which had been state champion in its class for two years running. As a result, there was little inclination to spend money on anything other than a new gym. Nevertheless, Sally and Libby were able to interest a number of their students in the prospect of having a microcomputer. Together, the women and the students raised nearly $500 through bake sales and car washes, and in an imaginative move, they revived the defunct Parent Teacher's Organization and got them to contribute $200 from their inactive treasury. They immediately bought a new TRS-80 and purchased some software for it through the regular library book budget. Within days the computer was in constant use by students in the library during unassigned periods, and Sally and Libby wondered where on earth they could get enough money to buy the three or four additional microcomputers they clearly needed.

However, their success was short-lived. Student expectations at Greenville ran high and consequently were almost fated to be shattered. First, one micro-computer was totally inadequate to meet student demand. Second, when the microcomputer broke down and was at the repair shop for two months, there were a lot of disappointed customers. Third, the repair bill ate up the entire library budget for the rest of the year. Fourth, neither Libby nor Sally knew enough about software evaluation to select good materials, so they wasted a lot of their meager budget on poor software. Fifth, and as a result of all the above, students soon lost interest in the computer and Libby and Sally's colleagues thought they had wasted their time and the library budget.

The Shared Planning Approach

There is an important middle ground—a *shared planning approach*—that lies between the centralized and decentralized planning and implementation process. In this shared approach, administrators and faculty members, with the support of the school board, work together, usually in the form of an advisory committee to oversee the planning for computer implementation in the schools. Often the advisory committee includes parents as well, some perhaps with expertise or special knowledge about computers or education and others representing the general public. Some communities have included students on advisory committees, and most have drawn upon the services of a university-based consultant or other expert to assist the advisory committee in its deliberations. If a local resident, this consultant may contribute his or her time as a service to the community. A shared planning approach, if properly executed, produces a plan developed by faculty and parents, those with the most direct involvement and responsibility for the education of students. It incorporates other key constituencies to insure a broad base of support for its recommendations.

According to the Johns Hopkins survey, this approach of central administration initiation and leadership, followed by teacher and parent group participation, is becoming the dominant pattern in computer acquisition and implementation.

There is one great trap in this approach, however; a trap shared with the decentralized approach. Most educational institutions are hierarchical in nature, with power concentrated at the top of the organization. Often this hierarchical structure is tempered by a facade of collegiality, but when the institution is debating expenditures as large as those for computer technology, this facade can crumble quickly. It is absolutely imperative to have the active, committed support of those with power—the superintendent and school board, in particular—if the school system is to succeed in introducing a major new program in computers. This support is necessary but not sufficient; individual school administrations and staffs can probably thwart, or at least delay, most mandates from the top, so their support is also needed. But without commitment at the highest levels of the institution, there is unlikely to be a system-wide priority for computing and there are certain to be serious problems obtaining the necessary funds and other types of support necessary for success. The key role played by the school board is illustrated by the following vignette of the shared approach to planning and implementation taken by one school system:

Pleasant Valley, a small suburban school system, increasingly found itself criticized by parents, students and faculty for its inadequate computer capability. A small computer at the high school with four terminals served nearly 1,000 students inadequately at best; the vast majority of faculty and students had no exposure to computing whatsoever and those who did have access to the equipment had to compete with colleagues and peers. The School Board decided to establish as a priority for the coming year the investigation of new computer programs, and developed a process to attain this priority. Through newspaper advertisements and articles, it solicited interested residents and faculty to serve on a computer advisory committee. Applications were carefully screened and a committee appointed, divided approximately equally between faculty and residents and including some with expertise in the area of computers, others known for their insight about education, and still others representing the general public. Two students served as members.

In its year's work, Pleasant Valley's computer advisory committee assessed the current state of computing in its schools through various activities: a review of its educational goals, visits to the schools, conversations with faculty and students, a systemwide survey of teachers, and discussions with experts in the field. The committee found the faculty interested and enthusiastic about computing, but largely untrained. Current computer equipment was mediocre at very best and less than minimal for a school system of the district's intended quality. Great inequities existed, with only a handful of students and teachers able to use the high school's terminals.

Confronted with these findings, the computer advisory committee determined that it could best help the school system by teaching faculty and administrators about the possible applications of computers in education as a prior step to developing their own goals for computing in the school system. To accomplish this end, the advisory committee helped organize several events, including a series of lectures by eminent authorities on computers from nearby colleges and industries. The committee also sponsored a series of after-school workshops attended by over half the faculty from all grade levels, and the school system itself sponsored a subsequent course in BASIC programming using rented microcomputers. Teams of faculty visited computer facilities in nearby schools and colleges, while others held an open house in the high school at which students and faculty demonstrated their work. As a result of this activity, the school system developed great commitment to the use of computers in education.

The advisory committee's report included four recommendations:

1. That the School Board make computers a system-wide priority.
2. That K–12 curriculum goals for computer literacy and computers in education be developed.
3. That a coordinator be appointed to carry out plans for computer education.
4. That a standing committee of parents, teachers, students and administrators be established to evaluate progress and make recommendations.

The School Board endorsed these recommendations and funded a summer curriculum workshop at which teachers and administrators developed and wrote up two major goals—computer literacy and the integration of computers in the curriculum—and more specific goals for each level of the school system. The School Board endorsed those goals as well and subsequently appointed a computer hardware committee of faculty, administrators, and technical consultants to recommend the equipment which would best fulfill those goals. The district continued to sponsor courses and workshops in computers for interested faculty, and the School Board obtained funding for its hardware requirements through a special bond issue approved by the community's voters. Essential to the community's support was confidence, gained by the public's participation, both in the specific goals developed as well as in the planning process which had produced them.

The experience of Pleasant Valley and other systems like it suggest several distinct advantages to a shared planning approach.

• A broad base of support for computing in the schools.
• A concentration of financial and human resources on designated projects.
• A range of expertise, point of view, and experience applied to issues of school computing.
• A forum for communication among various constituencies in the school system.

This should not suggest that a shared planning approach is without its potential problems. Committees can stifle action as readily as they can take action. One school system had a committee studying computing for three years without any concrete decisions. In the meantime, several impatient teachers obtained microcomputers for their classrooms via various back-door methods.

A second problem with shared planning occurs when key decision makers are excluded from the committee and its proceedings. Great care must be taken in constituting the committee to include crucial department heads, influential teachers, appropriate administrators and key citizens. One school system computer committee made a serious error when it failed to involve the high school librarian and the director of vocational education in its deliberations. By doing so, it lost two valuable sources of ideas, internal funding, and political support. Later, the committee was forced to go, hat-in-hand, to these important people to ask for help. These belated requests were not received kindly.

THE POLITICS OF IMPLEMENTATION

Based on our analyses of dozens of case studies such as the ones just described and on our own experiences, we have arrived at three fundamental conclusions about the politics of implementing a computer program in a school district. These are discussed in the following sections: Building Coalitions, Making Your Case, and "Putting on the Knobs."

Building Coalitions

Our first conclusion is that successful political support requires building coalitions from the outset among key individuals or groups in the community and the institutional political landscape. This holds true whether the organization is a large corporation, an institution of higher education, an urban school district, or a small rural school district. While there are enormous differences among these organizations, there are likely to be relatively few individuals or groups who, if not joined in an alliance based on perceived common interest, can generate the support necessary to achieve their goals.

As an educational leader, your first challenge in the process of coalition-building is to identify those people or groups who hold power, who can influence decisions, who can make or break successful implementation. Then these people should be joined together in a coalition to develop and support the school district's goals for computer use in the schools.

You will probably be tempted to assume that you already know who the potential supporters are. After all, they are probably visible and active and have been pressed into service to help gain approval of past projects. Indeed, these people may also end up being members of the computer wedding party, but we urge a few moments of cautious thought before acting on that assumption. To begin with, computers may bring a host of new characters out of the woodwork; some in favor, others opposed. There are bound to be local experts who may not have cared much about the last bond issue for a new high school or the community debate over vandalism but who have definite opinions about what is right—and wrong—to do with computers. And past supporters of school proposals probably will not know a great deal about computers; as a result, they may be less confident and less active than in the past.

To aid the process of cautious thought, we recommend spending a little time mapping your community and school system, by asking yourself questions such as the following:

1. What printed material (e.g., newspapers, policy statements from the school board) is available to help you ascertain the nature of the community and its school system?
2. Who runs the community and how, now and in the past?
3. What is the ethnic, religious, and economic mix in the community and how might that be important to your goals?
4. Who are the haves and the have-nots in the community and how do they each interact with the schools?
5. What is the community's image of itself and of its schools?
6. Who owns the news sources and covers the workings of the city or town government?
7. What are and have been recent demographic figures and shifts in the community?
8. How are local powers-that-be in the community tied into control of the school system?
9. Who runs the school system and how, now and before—both formally and informally?
10. How do the norms and structures of the schools reflect the socio-economic structures within the community?

11. Where do the school staff come from and how might they be involved in a community coalition?
12. What immediate, major issues does the school system face which might detract from your computer plans?
13. Is there a history of experience with computers in the school system and if so what does that history reveal?

Inquiry through questions such as these should produce understanding of the power and influence relationships both in the community and the school system, as well as a preview of the likelihood of gaining support. But pursuing these, or similar questions, will require vigor and self-discipline; it is only too easy to yield to the assumption that you already know the answers. While that assumption may be true, we urge that you test it first. There is a great difference between successfully managing an organization and successfuly *changing* the organization. The understanding of school and community norms which allows one to manage well may not be sufficient to bring about significant change— particularly if the desired change involves significant expense for computers.

Making Your Case

Our second conclusion is that successful political support occurs most easily when members of a coalition are convinced that goals are worthwhile in general and serve the interests they represent specifically. Local political leaders and key educators need to believe in a school district's goals for computer use in education in order to support the funding and other steps necessary to attain those goals. To believe in those goals, these people must first be convinced of their general value by a persuasive case based upon clear thinking about education, careful analysis of needs and objectives, and sound technical data. If you and your colleagues have successfully developed a system-wide long-range plan, along the lines discussed in Chapter 2, you will have provided this.

Now comes the second and more difficult task of obtaining support for this plan from the leaders of disparate interest groups. This will not always be possible. However, the key to success is to highlight different elements of the plan for different constituencies. Each group must be able to see what the plan offers them and their educational goals. If the plan has been drawn up in anticipation of this political imperative, there should be something attractive in it for every key constituency. It may be a curricular benefit or a labor-saving one, or even a purely political one.

Nevertheless, you should be prepared for resistance and even resentment from those who will not share your enthusiasm for the plan. While some of these detractors may be computer-enthusiasts who do not like a particular aspect or emphasis of your plan, most will be those who do not see educational computing as a desirable way to spend limited district funds. It is important that you anticipate this and develop a dialogue with these potential antagonists. Perhaps you can offer to support their special interests in the future. Maybe they can be persuaded that the computer will benefit the kids and the school in general and thus indirectly will help them in their efforts. However, it is probably realistic to anticipate that there will always be some staff and citizens who are antagonistic, or at least skeptical, about computers, perhaps for very good reasons, and who may resent the allocation of funds for them. A continuing effort is needed to communicate with these people about computing in the school, their concerns about it, and their ideas about educational innovation.

"Putting on the Knobs"

Our third conclusion about the politics of implementation is perhaps best illustrated by a story:

> An eminent scientist tells the story, probably apocryphal, of a group of scientists in the 1950s working to develop a radar detection system for the Arctic Circle to warn of enemy attack. After many months of design and tests, the system was perfected and finally ready for presentation at a briefing for the United States Joint Chiefs of Staff and other top military officials.
>
> At the dress rehearsal, everything worked perfectly and the scientific team was elated. But the scientist in charge of the project suddenly insisted, apparently inexplicably, that all the large knobs on radar screens and other instruments be removed and replaced with much smaller knobs. The scientific staff objected; there was no need to change a system that had proven its effectiveness in a complete runthrough. The senior scientist prevailed and the knobs were changed. A week later the military brass arrived for its briefing. The scientific team conducted the briefing and, at its conclusion, there was a moment of silence. The system had performed flawlessly. Then a crusty old admiral in the back of the room raised his hand and said: "You scientific boys seem to have got everything exactly right, except for one thing. This is a radar detection system for operation in the Arctic, and you boys have never been up there and don't know how cold it gets. Men with heavy mittens under those condition will never be able to handle those teeny knobs on these machines, so you ought to replace those small knobs with big ones."
>
> The senior scientist looked at him, smiled and replied: "Sir, you're exactly right; we never thought of that." From that point on, the military behaved as if it had designed the entire system itself and the scientific team understood why their leader had insisted on making the knobs small.

The point of the tale is that local political leaders and key educators need the chance to 'put their knobs on the machine' as it is being developed, both because they may have important contributions to make and because doing so will increase the likelihood of their active, committed support of the project. While we do not suggest you engage in as manipulative a strategy for obtaining high level support for your plan, as did the chief scientist in this story, you would do well to leave some aspects of your plan undefined until you can involve all the key decision-makers in your district.

Your community mapping exercise should enable you to identify these important individuals. You can then involve them in whatever ways seem most appropriate for your situation. This might mean asking them to be on your computer advisory committee or simply soliciting their reactions to your written long-range planning document. The important point is that they feel they have exercised influence on the planning process. In general, the earlier this is done, the more enthusiastic will be the support of these key individuals.

SOURCES OF FUNDS

Inextricably connected to the politics of implementing a computer education program is the seemingly overwhelming task of obtaining funds for it. School budgets are under pressure from the effects of inflation and new demands for service, on the one hand, and taxpayer concerns on the other. Cutbacks in federal support for education are matched in many cases by reductions in state support as well, or even voter supported statutory limitations such as Proposition 13 (California) or Proposition 2 1/2 (Massachusetts). But despite the bleak picture, there are at least six potential sources of funds:

1. School budget
2. Bond issues
3. Educational collaboratives
4. Federal or state funds
5. Corporate grants
6. Private gifts.

School Budget

The first place to begin looking for funds to support plans for purchase of computer equipment or materials is in the local school budget, not only because funds might be found there, but also because other potential sources will ask whether the project can be supported from the school district's budget. Indeed, the Johns Hopkins survey reports that 30 percent of secondary school computer funding and 23 percent of elementary school funding comes from the general school system's budget.

Moreover, while budgeting practices vary from one district to another, most operating budgets provide funds to individual schools in various categories for the purchase of equipment, materials, and other supplies. So for relatively small purchases, such as a few microcomputers for an elementary school, it may be possible to obtain funding from that school's allocation of equipment money. Again, the Johns Hopkins survey reveals that individual school budgets provide about the same percentage of funds for computers as do overall system budgets. For larger purchases, such as a minicomputer with several terminals, it may be possible to combine equipment budgets from more than one school.

However, many school administrators seem unwilling to scrutinize their school budgets to find possible funds for computers because doing so forces them to take a stand in favor of computers at the expense of other priorities. This is likely to arouse the opposition of those faculty or administrators who do not support the goals for computer implementation in the schools or who are facing lay-offs due to declining enrollments and budgetary limits.

Further, even if local school leaders come out clearly in favor of a computer program, many school districts are unlikely to have sufficient funds available within their annual operating budgets to support large allocations for the purchase of computer hardware or software. There will be competing priorities and any available funds generally have already been diverted to cope with the rise in energy costs, collective bargaining increases fueled by inflation, and other program priorities such as special education or bilingual education.

The difficulty of finding adequate funding for computing within the budget of a single school or school district is made more difficult by the secondary costs associated with a major new program in computing. These costs include maintenance or service contracts for equipment purchased, which can be sizeable, as well as the costs of software, materials, and other supplies associated with the equipment. There will be additional costs for training of faculty and, depending upon the type of computer system purchased, costs for the operation and supervision of the equipment and perhaps even for construction and maintenance of a computer center. By law, in most states such operations cannot be funded as a capital project or by issuing bonds, but must instead become part of the school district's operating budget. Therefore, whatever funds can be made available within the school district's operating budget are most likely to be consumed by operating costs rather than being available for capital expenditures such as the purchase of major pieces of equipment.

Bond Issues

There is hope, however. While laws and regulations vary from one setting to another, school districts often have a capital budget which is funded separately from their operating budget. The capital budget provides funding for major projects, such as construction of a new school or other facilities, major repairs or renovations, or the one-time purchases of unusually large equipment which may be amortized over a period of years. Capital projects may be funded directly through tax revenues received in the city or town, or by floating bonds for the same purpose. There will probably be local regulations which limit the purpose of bond issues, and there will certainly be the difficult job of coordinating a request for purchase of computer equipment with the attainment of other municipal needs ranging from sewer or road repair to construction of other municipal facilities. Nonetheless, the school district should examine the possibility of funding its equipment purchases through the community's capital budget. The advantage of obtaining a sufficient level of funding through bonding, with the cost to the community spread over the term of the bond itself, often outweighs the extra effort and stress of trying to obtain local political support for this bond issue.

Educational Collaboratives

Increasingly, school districts or other organizations are joining forces to provide funding for computing as well as to share information and expertise. Under the banner of the National Governors' Association, chief executives of several states have formed a special task force to explore technological innovation and possible collaboration in order to raise the funds needed for new technologies and to provide better instruction for students and residents of their states. Other collaborative organizations already exist and are pooling their long-range planning efforts for the implementation of computer technology in the schools.

Some states have followed New York's example and have established boards of cooperative educational services (BOCES), which historically have provided the benefit of collaboration in educational programs, purchasing, and staff development to local school districts and which are now moving towards collaboration in computer technology. The Northern Colorado variation (BOCS) enables thirteen different school districts to participate on a timesharing computer program which handles student records, financial information, and similar administrative needs.

The Minnesota Educational Computing Consortium (MECC), created in 1973 by the University of Minnesota, the state and community college systems, and the State Department of Education, is perhaps the best known of the state-wide collaboratives engaged in computer technology. Almost all of the 432 school districts in Minnesota participate in MECC which has also established collaborative arrangements with over two-thirds of the other states in the country, individual school districts in other parts of the country, several regional service agencies, and the education offices of several foreign countries. By purchasing several thousand microcomputers from a single vendor for local school districts, MECC can obtain excellent price breaks for its member schools. By 1983, MECC had helped Minnesota educational institutions purchase over 6,000 microcomputers at a total savings of more than two million dollars below retail costs, and had provided these same schools with software, developed by MECC staff, member districts, or others. This courseware development has become a major MECC service, with over 100 different educational packages—each encompassing up to 10 programs for students—available for several brands of computer available in the schools. With courseware development has come an emphasis on teacher training as a third area of major activity. A number of MECC trainers are "on call" by telephone, site visit, newsletters and conferences for participating districts across the state.

Similar collaboratives are being formed in other states or, as in the case of New York's BOCES, already exist and are now turning their attention to the pooling of resources for computer technology in local school districts. One example of a strong local collaborative of many years' standing, which is now developing new capabilities in computers, is the Education Collaborative for Greater Boston (EdCo). Relying on modest dues from member school systems, as well as funds from public and private grants or contracts, EdCo has developed several initiatives involving computers. Courses dealing with computers and computer software have filled a great need in the area of staff development, while also providing the chance for teachers to work with, and learn from, colleagues in neighboring school districts. EdCo also has established its own computer center, and some of its participating districts have used EdCo as a vehicle for gaining access to a software distribution system which makes available programs at far lower cost. Member districts have also undertaken shared development of computer courses for students, such as an introductory course for middle school students in BASIC and an intermediate course in Logo for elementary students.

Federal or State Funds

Surveying the national scene in the late 1980s, it does not seem to be an opportune time to look to federal or state governments for financial support of computing in the schools. Federal and state budgets are being cut, and educational programs often bear the brunt of those reductions. However, there is growing evidence of a new national concern for the improvement of education in general and for the support of new initiatives in computing in particular. Several reports and recommendations of national commissions, or privately funded studies of American education, sponsored by such organizations as the Association for Supervision and Curriculum Development (ASCD), the National Institute of Education (NIE), the Carnegie Foundation for the Advancement of Teaching, and the College Board have generated a national debate similar to that which followed the launching of Sputnik in 1957 and publication of the Conant Report in 1960. The 1983 report of the National Commission on Excellence in Education, and studies by the United States Office of Technology Assessment, express increasing concern about "a technology gap" between the United States and other advanced countries, notably Japan. Other studies have established that school children in several countries— Japan, West Germany, the Soviet Union—spend considerably more time than their American counterparts in school, and spend a higher portion of their school time in the study of mathematics and science. Some observers feel that the United States may lose its place as the world's foremost technological power.

Whether such concerns are valid or not, it now appears likely that they will be translated into federal or state funding for educational programs aimed at improving the use of computer technology in the schools or upgrading standards of education in general. At the federal level, Congress considered and nearly passed the Technology Education Act of 1982, introduced into the House by Representative Fortney H. Stark (D-California) with the active support of Apple Computer, Inc. The bill would have allowed computer companies to donate computer equipment to the schools. These gifts would have qualified for up to a 10 percent deduction on Apple's corporate taxable income, much as donations of scientific equipment to colleges or universities are currently treated. Apple Computer, Inc. has stated that if such a bill were passed it would donate a microcomputer to each of the elementary and secondary schools in the country, a gesture whose value is worth approximately two hundred million dollars. While the bill did not pass in 1982, due to its potential drain on the federal treasury, as well as questions about a "tax giveaway" to computer companies, it is likely that some form of direct federal support for computing will become available in the near future.

States also are beginning to establish their own legislative initiatives for support of educational computing. In 1982, the California Legislature established fifteen regional teacher education centers (TECs) which provide funds for teacher training and workshops in a variety of areas, but with an emphasis on educational computing. These regional centers distribute funds to California school districts to conduct their own in-service training for teachers, and they also provide teachers with a place to attend courses or workshops in computing or just to come for hands-on experience with microcomputers. Other states are following California's example, particularly states with a high percentage of jobs tied to high-technology industries dependent upon a future labor pool of adults educated in mathematics, science, and computers.

Regardless of future legislative initiatives at the federal or state level, some funds already exist to support new programs in educational computing. Chapters 1 and 2 of the Education Consolidation and Improvement Act provide financial support to schools with students from low-income families, while Public Law 94-142 provides assistance for special education programs, and block grants now provide districts with funding formerly available under Title IVB and Title IVC of the Elementary and Secondary Education Act and other sources. In addition, Public Law 94-482, in support of occupational education and training, is one of the largest federal programs which can be tapped to support the use of computers in education.

Each of these federal programs has become a major source of funding for computers and should be examined as a potential source of money for new hardware, software, or training programs in educational computing. However, any plans for the use of such funds must be consistent with the purposes and regulations of the act which provides that support. PL 94-142 funds, for example, could be used to support educational programs in computing for the benefit of special needs students according to the law's regulations, but could not be used to provide financial support for computing for all students. Similarly, many federal programs require that federal funds not "supplant" but supplement local funds, so the receiving school district must demonstrate that its use of funds will not replace an initiative which the district has taken or would take in future years.

Corporate Grants

Many corporations, particularly larger companies with substantial revenues, provide corporate grants for various worthy purposes. Like a private individual who contributes to charity, the company receives a tax deduction for its gifts, as well as the satisfaction and public relations benefits gained by helping a worthy institution accomplish its goal. While corporations are allowed to offset up to 10 percent of their income through corporate contributions, the average level of corporate contributions in the United States is closer to only 1 percent.

Many corporations provide discounts or special financing arrangements for educational institutions which purchase computer hardware or software manufactured by them. Other corporations have a corporate giving program, or a corporate foundation, which disperses funds at scheduled intervals to qualified organizations or individuals whose requests are approved by the company. A high technology company may give discounts on equipment purchases of up to as much as 50 percent of the list price, or even donate equipment or software in limited amounts to a district still exploring its needs. Often such corporate grants are awarded in geographic areas where the company has manufacturing plants, or where large numbers of employees reside, as a gesture of support and good will to its local neighbors. On a less altruistic level, corporations know that such grants are a form of product promotion because the school is likely to return to the same manufacturer in the future as needs expand. Similarly, students and teachers who learn on a particular donated machine are likely later to purchase the same machine for their personal use. Product loyalty is as true for computers as it is for typewriters, which for years have been contributed or heavily discounted to schools.

The rules for corporate grants vary and should be explored with a representative of potential donors long before final plans are developed. In general, corporate discounts are available as part of a company's established policy and require little in the form of submission of elaborate proposals for funding. However, a public agency probably has to conform to whatever local bid regulations govern the purchase of any type of equipment or material, so bid documents must be constructed which give all potential competitors an equal chance to make the best offer. Companies which provide funding through a corporate foundation may require a more elaborate proposal for financial support and may have a more rigid timetable for the award of funds.

Some companies or other organizations provide grants-in-kind, instead of direct cash awards, or discounts on the purchase of equipment. The type of contribution may vary: the donation of services by an employee who is a local resident and an expert in the area of computers, or donated services from small businesses which may be involved in the installation of computer equipment, or the provision of related supplies such as tables, chairs, paper supplies, air conditioning equipment, and the like. Grants-in-kind may qualify for deductions as charitable contributions, although the donating individual or organization should check this carefully.

Private Gifts

The final source of financial support for educational computing are private gifts. These can come from many sources: parent-teacher organizations, civic groups or individuals, or special fundraising events organized explicitly to support school districts' plans for computing. Many parent-teacher organizations are now sponsoring computer fairs or similar activities in order to raise funds for the purchase of microcomputers for local schools. Often, manufacturers will assist in the development of these fairs by providing equipment and programs since the fair gives them the chance to exhibit their wares and reach potential customers. Other types of organizations have discovered that their goals may be attained by hitching their star to the computer bandwagon. In one example, a local division of the American Heart Association, in conjunction with a national educational computing magazine sponsored a programming contest for health education in the schools. The contest awarded cash prizes as high as $1,500 to a dozen students who wrote programs in BASIC to run on a variety of microcomputers. Their programs explained the nature of heart disease and ways it can be prevented. Many similar types of organizations currently sponsor 'walkathons' or 'bikeathons' in local school districts in support of such causes as the American Cancer Society, the Muscular Dystrophy Association, the American Legion and so forth. With a little persuasion, these organizations might be convinced to use a computer activity to reach their goal or to provide prizes in the form of support for purchase of computer equipment or software. According to the Johns Hopkins survey, as much as 19 percent of computer expenditures for schools are provided by privately organized fund-raising.

CONCLUSIONS

Suppose that by now, you have developed a long-range district-wide implementation plan as described in Chapter 2: you have built a coalition of citizens and educators to support your plans; and you have identified potential sources of funds. You are now ready to launch your educational computing program.

Each such program will look different. What might work for the State of Alaska could be an inappropriate approach for a farming community in the Midwest, a large city in the Northeast, a dispersed rural district in the Southwest, or a suburban district on either coast. For this reason, we have emphasized the importance of taking a fresh look at the local community in order to understand how things get done and the importance of involving local leaders in the development of plans and a strategy for attaining them.

Nonetheless, certain generalizations seem in order based on the experiences of school systems who have implemented computer use in recent years. First, our assertions about community politics generally hold true. Obtaining support for a major, expensive new school program usually depends on the formation of coalitions within the system and within the community; for prospective partners to come together, there must be clear goals and a common purpose viewed as worthwhile and of benefit to each member as well as to the larger group. Allegiance to the coalition is likely to increase if local leaders participate in the development of plans and, by so doing, feel ownership of those plans. Except in those rare settings where an individual or handful of key people hold enormous power, it is likely that carrying out plans for a major new program in educational computing will require effective coalition-building.

Second, support from the very top of the organization is a crucial ingredient for success. Without the active support of the superintendent and school board, the district's plans for computing may never attain the priority status necessary for success. Support from the top is also essential if the myriad requirements for implementation are to be obtained: time and funds for in-service training, money for software and course development, necessary allocation of space and likely renovation to accommodate the new equipment, and so forth.

Third, plans for educational computing must provide adequate lead time at each step of the process from the development of goals to the purchase and installation of equipment to the development of courses and software to the training of staff, and finally to the evaluation of results. Chapter 2 describes the planning process, and later chapters explain in detail the selection of equipment, staff development, and evaluation. However, you should note here one critically important issue related to program evaluation: whenever a large financial commitment has been made, there will be pressure for premature evaluation of the results. This pressure must be resisted; achieving full integration of computers into a school system is a process which will take many years. While it is possible to evaluate success at several steps along the way, it is essential not to draw premature conclusions. It is especially important that adequate time be made available for the training of faculty and staff and their trial-and-error experimentation with computers in their classrooms and offices. Unfortunately, this 'messing about' step is often cut short, with the result that attainment of the district's goals for computing becomes impossible.

Finally, the process of getting what you want takes time itself. We know of no school district which decided in September that it wanted to develop a major new initiative in educational computing and was able to achieve approval of its plans by April, only eight months later. We know of several districts where the process consumed at least two years, and it can take even longer. Obtaining school board support for study of educational computing can, itself, take several months. A computer advisory committee may need a year or more to develop recommendations or goals, hardware and software priorities, and an implementation schedule. The training of faculty, which can occur simultaneously, will also extend many years into the future. Local support is difficult to organize quickly, and competing municipal priorities may require delay in achieving support. Finding potential sources of funds and following the necessary application procedures takes time, as do the requirements for public bidding and the actual installation and testing of equipment. A major new program cannot be realized overnight, and unless this fact is made clear at the outset, it will be easy for some to become discouraged along the way.

Implementing and Supporting a One-Year Plan

4

A school district's long range computer implementation plan should provide the foundation for various strands of activity, each of which can be extended, step by step, until the goals established by the overall plan are modified or attained. Often this will take several years of effort. Each year, school administrators must insure that a new one-year plan is created to outline the goals and activities to be accomplished that year. They must then provide the support needed by the participants in these various activities.

The task of developing a one-year plan for computer implementation can be quite complex or as simple as assembling into one document many separate action plans from various groups, buildings or programs. In each one of these small action plans, the participants describe some activity to be undertaken in their efforts to achieve the overall system's long-range goals. The administrator in charge of computer implementation may then present these individual project action plans under a single unifying theme or simply combine them into a plan that is the sum of its parts.

Computers affect so many different aspects of the school system's operation that it will probably be impossible to make the overall one-year plan neat or unified. For example, a plan might include a variety of projects, pilot uses, development tasks, and implementation activities during a particular year, such as:

1. Develop an on-line system for cataloguing software.
2. Begin a model program at the junior high level to work out how best to use word processing for writing instruction.
3. Integrate some computer programming assignments into calculus classes.

4. Support the fifth grade teachers who will implement the Logo curriculum for the first time.
5. Work with several primary teachers to develop some activities to develop procedural thinking skills using Big Trak.
6. Coordinate with neighboring districts during monthly meetings in an effort to share information and resources.
7. Work with guidance, central office, and district personnel to create an integrated student database management system.
8. Work with mathematics specialists to integrate computer-based exercises and games into their resource lists for each unit of study.
9. Solicit teachers' recommendations for improving existing public-domain software and monitor the work of student programmers as they make these changes.
10. Assist the social studies department in obtaining simulation software for preview and in evaluating its potential for their programs of study.
11. Involve principals and teachers at the elementary level in designing a three-year plan for in-service programs to meet their needs.

The action plans for these diverse objectives would clearly be quite different. Some would involve just one or two people; others could be quite complex to coordinate because of all the actors affected. In the pages that follow, we discuss the role of an educational leader, perhaps a computer coordinator or a principal or a district curriculum director, in creating a single project action plan and monitoring it during implementation. The overall one-year plan for the district might then be the sum of such individual project plans, accompanied by a description of system-wide support efforts and budget.

PLANNING STEPS

There are five major steps in planning a project action plan:

1. Begin with the goals from the system-wide plan.
2. Identify potential participants.
3. Hold an initial planning meeting.
4. Draft the action plan.
5. Make final plans.

Begin with the Goals from the System-Wide Plan

In planning a particular computer project, you, as educational leader should always go back to the overall school district plan discussed in Chapter 2. You should determine what the logical "next steps" might be for each of the long-range goals of that plan. Decide what aspects of the plan you and your staff might realistically address, given equipment and budget limitations. In the ideal case, the long-range planning committee will already have specified some of what they wish to see happen during the year in question and will have planned the budget so that the needed resources will be available. If this has been done, you might wish to volunteer for one of the tasks they've identified or you might propose a variation or modification of one of them.

Flexibility is the watchword. A plan written in stone lives on a shelf. One which can bear minor modifications and can respond to new information or new educational ideas lives in people's hands as a handbook that guides and justifies their actions.

Identify Potential Participants

Depending on your philosophy of leadership, draft people who you need or who express interest in your project. Probably it will be a combination of the two. For example, if one of your goals is to integrate BASIC programming into eighth grade mathematics courses, then the mathematics coordinator must be involved. All mathematics teachers at that level may also need to be drafted, or you may choose to pilot this new strand with only a few of them in the first year, expanding the program in the following year. On the other hand, if the plan calls for a pilot use of three computers and a printer for word processing in the tenth grade, a survey to see who is interested among the teachers of tenth graders may make sense. Or the English department head may wish to choose one or two teachers who are excellent at teaching writing.

Such choices ought to be made early in the spring prior to the year of planned implementation, so that tentative plans can be made and participants can have time to prepare. Some will need training, or at least experience, with the equipment. Orders may need to be placed for software or equipment, as well. Trying to begin all this in the fall often results in the plan getting going around Christmas, instead of in September or October.

Hold an Initial Planning Meeting

It is important that you involve all of the actors in each project, along with their immediate supervisors, at the earliest possible stage of planning. Practically speaking this may mean that you meet with three or four people for an hour or so in April or May to try to envision what needs to happen the following fall and to anticipate any needs or potential problems. The project leader—perhaps you, perhaps one of your staff—should take notes, so that this meeting can form the basis for the formal action plan to be written up early in the fall.

The experience in one school district suggests that at this beginning stage calling something an "action plan" and entering steps, responsibilities, and time lines on a form can be counterproductive. Many people are uncomfortable with systematic planning and find forms to be intimidating. Instead, you might wish to meet rather informally to gather most of the information needed to write the formal action plan later. Then you can confirm the results of the meeting in a memo to all concerned, including with it an obvious first-draft of a proposed action plan for their comments and suggestions. The result of such a low key beginning should be that other administrators and teachers who are involved will feel free to add ideas and make the plan their own. ("Putting on their own knobs" is as important to participants as it is to decision-makers.) In addition, they will probably feel supported from the beginning, since they didn't have to do the work of writing up what may be a rather unfamiliar and imposing document.

Some of the questions to raise at such a meeting are discussed below.

How much time/training will it take for the teacher or administrator to learn the necessary skills to carry out the project? Planning supportive training or internship experiences is very important. If someone nearby is already using computers in the proposed way, the new user should visit that site during the spring prior to the proposed project. If a formal course is needed, be sure it is realistic to expect that the user will have the opporunity to take that course prior to or simultaneous with the project.

In the list of example projects on page 59–60, several might require training if the staff involved has never done the activity before. For instance, principals and teachers on an in-service planning committee need first-hand knowledge of the possibilities for training. Teachers beginning Logo or word processing will probably need training themselves before they can help their students.

How much time/training will it take for other users to learn the skills necessary for this application? In most cases the "other users" will be students who may have to learn how to load and run programs, how to use a word processor or how to write simple programs usable in the science lab. In some cases, the other users may be aides, parent volunteers, or secretaries who will help to type in data or programs or student stories. This question is designed to prepare everyone for the fact that start-up is likely to be slow because getting new users to be familiar with the equipment takes time.

What will the learning process be? Who will help the new user(s) learn? Sometimes teachers or administrators feel the need for personnel support during the early months of a project. For example, if there is just one computer station for many students to use, the job of teaching the needed skills to each student individually may seem overwhelming. Enlisting an aide or parent volunteer or student teacher can be an enormous help. This has often been the plan when very young students are to learn to run a computer for the first time or when a word processing pilot program is starting up. Sometimes devising a means by which students can train one another can ease the teacher's burden. The planning group should think about this potential problem and suggest some possible solutions early, so that anxiety does not kill enthusiasm.

In noninstructional applications, the learning may be that of the central actors. For example, student programmers may need to learn some guidelines for appropriate response formats for various ages of student users. Or social studies teachers may need some experience using software evaluation forms before they can begin on their task in earnest. The question in these cases becomes "Who will instruct them?" If possible, use one or more experienced peers in addition to the person who routinely does computer training.

How much time will each user have on the computer each day or each week? Is this project using computer time efficiently? Are we spreading computer resources too thinly to achieve the intended goal?   These questions are designed to make everyone aware of the need to schedule computer time if it is scarce (as it is most likely to be!). The first question allows the teacher to state early that certain blocks of time aren't available for general unscheduled computer use. The second question, about efficiency, gets everyone thinking about sharing equipment, supervision of computer use during recess/lunch/studies/after school/before school times, and the reality of school schedules. Having the building principal and/or media specialist in on this part of the conversation can help prevent conflicts among various users in the building. For example, in one elementary school the librarian had been counting on using the computer to generate overdue notices during his free period, but a first grade teacher had already arranged with a parent to come in each week to type in students' stories during the same hour. Fortunately the principal knew about both of the plans and could help work out a compromise.

Sometimes, the result of figuring out the maximum time per week per student may suggest that the project is too ambitious, given the present limitations on equipment. In one system, an elementary school word processing project had to be cancelled for just this reason. Suddenly the committee realized, upon adding up the needed hours, that this project would interfere with fifth graders getting enough keyboard time with Logo. Since Logo was a higher system-wide priority, the other project was postponed and the committee made a note to try to obtain more equipment so that it could be implemented the following year. Thin use should be avoided. If a student only touches the keys once every three weeks, not much will be learned since reinforcement is so infrequent.

To whom can the new user turn to ask questions or solve problems?   Technical support is absolutely necessary for new users. A bug in the software, a glitch in the scheduling, a connecting cord that doesn't fit, paper that runs out too quickly, a menu which is not clear—these can stop the project if the user has no one knowledgeable to go to for help. Knowing ahead of time that this kind of support will be available will help to reduce anxiety. The answer-person could be anyone— a parent, expert student, principal, or computer specialist. Some elementary schools have been served very well by junior high school students who stop by one afternoon a week on their way home to answer their former teachers' questions or to make minor software modifications. On the other hand, the principal might be designated as the red-tape-cutter for a project in his/her school.

What materials or software are needed? What budget will be used? Who will take responsibility for seeing that the purchase orders are written and signed? Especially if the impetus for the use is coming from the central administration, there may be an expectation that the budget of the individual school will not be used to buy the needed materials. It's wise to get the true situation out in the open at this first meeting, so that no one starves the project to death, intentionally or unintentionally. Such items as printer paper or blank disks or student log books or an RF modulator can easily be forgotten in the spring, causing delays in the fall.

   In the case of a noninstructional application, money might be needed for materials such as books or journals, or for printing costs for the finished product, or for professional release time to go visit another school system or work at a software preview center. For example, after creating a curriculum resource book revision, by adding computer-based activities to existing ones, the person in charge might find that the major expense will be to reprint the revised book for dissemination to teachers.

How will we know if the project is succeeding? Another way of stating this is, "What criteria will be used to evaluate this project?" However, unfortunately terms like criteria and evaluate produce anxiety, even when formative evaluation is all that is anticipated. It is probably wise to use the less precise question above in initial conversations with participants, since it may be less threatening but gets everyone thinking about the educational goals of the project. Generally, the information discussed in answering this question ultimately provides the basis for an evaluation design that everyone can live with.

   Being specific about goals is terribly important, so that everyone's expectations are the same. If a teacher feels that the idea is to see if students can learn to use the word processing program effectively, but the language arts coordinator is looking for clear improvement in sentence combining skills, there will be a conflict both in their classroom practices and in their evaluations of the project.

   Likewise for a noninstructional project, the participants should be clear about exactly what product is expected. For example, does planning in-service include such nitty-gritty details as arranging for schedule, rooms, and instructors for the next year, or is an outline of tentative courses sufficient?

How will the ideas developed be disseminated? Will the project leaders be willing to share what is learned with others in the system and with visitors? Will they be comfortable having people observe, once the project gets going? Will they write a report, or is an interview preferred? How about working with someone later in the year to get that person going with the same application? Will there be a need to demonstrate or run a workshop about the project next year?

Bringing such questions up clearly at the outset conveys the expectation that, in exchange for support during the initial months of the project, the project leaders should plan to help disseminate information and expertise later. It's honest to air these expectations early to avoid misunderstandings later.

For the nonclassroom project these questions can translate into a different sort of sharing. For example, the social studies teachers who are evaluating simulation software might commit themselves to sharing their experience with teachers from neighboring systems, or they might be asked to work with the science department the next year when the latter is studying simulation software.

What are the project's highest priorities? If we must cut down this project, what gets trimmed? Again, here we accentuate the importance of goals, while at the same time conveying a flexible attitude toward the plan and what is really possible. Realistically, many new computer uses get delayed or reduced in scope by unforeseen circumstances. Letting participants know that you recognize this possibility may help them with any anxiety they may feel about over-ambitious goals. But at the same time, this question does not imply cancellation of the plan, only reduction of its scope, so you have not undermined the importance of achieving the major goals.

How frequently will the planning group meet during the year to monitor the project? One value to this question is that it conveys the dual ideas of responsibility and support. In addition, it allows each person who will be involved to think about the time commitment. No one should be surprised in the fall when they're asked to mark their calendars with monthly meetings.

Draft the Action Plan

Right after the initial planning meeting described above, whoever is in charge of writing up and monitoring this particular project should summarize the results of the meeting in a very informal action plan document. Putting participants' spoken words into a written form that approximates the format of the final action plan shows them that they have shaped the project. Further, leaving some blank spaces for people to fill in may help them to see that it is just a draft.

This draft document should be sent to all participants with an invitation to them to change or add anything they would like. Getting it in writing makes the commitment real; having them reply as to whether this plan accurately reflects their expectations forces them to sign on.

See Fig. 4.1 for a sample of an initial rough plan and Fig. 4.2 for the final action plan that eventually resulted from its acceptance. The objective, steps, responsibility for each step, and time-line are common parts of most plans. Note that some teacher-oriented details which appear in the informal document such as hours of use, schedules, and planned training sequence may not be mentioned in the final action plan, so as to keep the plan as flexible as possible.

Judy Brown   20 students
Ridgewood Elem.   Gr. 2–3

Title: Text Editing to Improve Writing Skills

Objective: To increase students' use of specifics and elaboration in creative writing and to increase students' interest in writing

Duration: November 1986–June 1987

Times: 8:30–11:30 every morning, one Apple (two, if available)

Classroom use: The procedure will vary according to the child's needs. In many cases, parent volunteers will type into the Apple the original version of a child's story. It will be saved on disk. (In cases where the child has fine-motor coordination difficulty (few), the student will type his/her story directly into the Apple, to avoid use of the pencil.)

From a printed copy, the teacher will indicate places in the story that need improvement. The child will then load his/her story into the computer and use the text editing commands to make changes in it. He/she will then print out two or more copies of the revised story (and save it on disk.) This editing will at first be monitored by the student teacher, teacher, a specialist, a parent or an older student. Ultimately, the student should be able to edit by him/herself.

Needs: One or two Apples; printer; specialists' assistance to teach editing; parent volunteers to type and help edit.

Evaluation: Teacher and L.A. Specialist judge results from folders. Results will be reported to Ridgewood faculty. Judy will help other teachers learn this model, if evaluation warrants.

Figure 4.1   Initial rough plan for a one-year project

Be sure that both the principal actors and their superiors sign on. If there's backpedalling now, there will be a lot more later. At least in the spring there is still time to persuade, employ clout, or change the plans gracefully.

Specific objective/action plan

Objective: State objective explicitly; indicate desired outcome; state how results will be measured.
To work out strategies that can be employed by the classroom teacher to encourage writing and editing by students through the use of a text editing or word processing program with a printer.

Action plan: List tasks or activities to be carried out to achieve the objective.

	Responsibility	*Event schedule to be completed by* J	A	S	O	N	D	J	F	M	A	M	J
Smith will meet with two interested teachers to develop a plan consistent with Betty's goals.	Smith/Jones/Brown	X	X										
Smith will arrange to have the word processor modified as required.	Smith/Harrison	X	X										
Smith and Craig will provide support for the teachers on a weekly or biweekly basis.	Smith/Craig			X	X	X	X	X	X	X	X	X	X
Teachers will use the word processor in class.	Teachers			X	X	X	X	X	X	X	X	X	X
Evaluation will assess the effect of this method on writing skill and students' attitudes.	Smith/Teachers								X			X	
Smith and/or Craig will apply for funding for more printers if the evaluation warrants this effort.	Smith/Craig/Asst. Supt.								X	X	X	X	X

Figure 4.2   Final action plan for a one-year project

Make Final Plan

During the first week of school, the person monitoring the project should contact each actor, go over the plan once more to make last minute adjustments, and set up a sequence of dates for meetings or training sessions to get the project off the ground. The person monitoring the project needs to convey the message that he or she will be in regular contact with the principal users throughout the year. It is not unwise to arbitrarily set dates for monthly or bi-monthly meetings at which information about progress can be shared.

When each of the project plans for the current year has gone through this final step, the administrator charged with computer planning can have them typed up and assembled as a single document, representing the school system's one-year plan. All district administrators should have a copy of this document as should the school committee. Because each of the parts of this system-wide plan took into account the district's long-range plan, administrators should be able to defend it easily and to show how it leads toward the district's goals.

SUPPORTING/MONITORING EACH PLAN

Support for participants in emerging computer implementation efforts comes in two major forms: general mechanisms set up to aid all computer users in the system and specific responsiveness to the needs of particular users or projects.

General Support

Some of the general kinds of support to consider are local or regional users groups, professional development courses, release time to attend conferences, sabbatical leaves, reference materials, and newsletters. These create a climate which encourages computer users in the system and reinforces the idea that they are appreciated. Such support combats isolation by getting people to listen to new ideas and share their own discoveries. Support may be as simple as designating one afternoon a month as the time when any teacher or administrator who wants can bring a computer to a central location and expect to find others who can answer questions, trade homemade software, and share techniques.

There is a great deal to learn about computers and their possible uses in education. This is a wide-open, developing field, and the sharing of ideas helps it in its struggle toward maturity. We are beginning to learn to use a new educational medium, taking the first steps toward harnessing its potential as a learning tool. Teachers and administrators who have not been excited about their jobs for years are suddenly "turned on" again. One of the administrator's roles must be to bring these excited professionals together so they can learn from one another and make creative sparks fly.

Computer Support Person

We said earlier that new computer users should have someone to whom they can go to ask questions and get help. We also suggested that someone needs to monitor the progress of each project. The monitor and the question-answerer might be the same person, or they might not. Let us make the assumption for now that one person fills both roles. What kind of support might this person anticipate providing?

Someone to talk to.   This is the simplest form of help. Teachers who have never worked with computers before may welcome assistance in deciding where to locate computers, how to make the mechanics of scheduling work, how to get students to help each other, and so on. Principals putting word processors in their offices probably have similar concerns: Where do we store the disks? What's the best location for the monitor? Should we leave the computer on all day? These are small issues, but uncertainty about them contributes to anxiety. So the computer support person should try to make the first meeting with the new user during or just prior to the first days of use.

Arranging for volunteers.   This is another burden which the support person can take on for the new user. Often initial training of students is eased by the presence of a second adult (or expert older student) who can monitor the training process. However, many teachers may feel unsure how to identify an appropriate volunteer to fill this need. Through the parent teacher organization or computer advisory committee, the support person can probably make the needed contact. This is one example of the way the person in the support role needs to be aware of resources and how to tap them.

Arranging inter-school visits.   Another example of assistance to participants in computer implementation projects is the potential for interschool visits. The support person should become knowledgeable about all of the computer uses going on in the school system, and in neighboring ones as well, if possible. Then that person will be able to see parallels and suggest a visit when one teacher or administrator could benefit from observing or talking with another. Usually teachers are unaware of happenings outside of their own building; often even department heads are unaware of the projects going on in other departments. Yet, visiting others engaged in similar activities provides one of the best ways to reduce the new user's sense of isolation and to give that user a boost in morale. In addition, such help takes none of the support person's time. Instead it encourages networking and the use of many people in the system as resources.

Clout and red-tape cutting.   This is another service which the support person must provide. Often a planned computer use will stall because of repair problems, or too little money in the budget, or an order which is slow to come in, or a meeting that keeps getting delayed. The person in charge of supporting and monitoring the implementation of the computer plans should have resources to combat such problems when they are holding up high-priority work. A call to the dealer from the superintendent, or a quiet budget transfer, or personal pressure applied to the department head who is putting off that meeting—all of these can work wonders. In most cases, the support person just needs to forcefully remind those who are backpedalling that the central administration considers this a high priority.

Answering questions promptly.   This is another important form of support. Getting used to complex computer equipment and learning to use all of its capabilities is a difficult task. How can I get the printer to work with that program, too? Why does the computer keep crashing when we enter more than thirty lines? Is there a way to hook two monitors up for demonstrations? How do I order more disks or printer paper? Jim seems to have lost his file on the disk; is there any way to get it back? I wish this program gave three tries instead of two; can you help me change that? We'd like to plan to buy another disk drive next year; what approvals do we need? Is there a way to learn to do simple repairs ourselves to save money? Have you seen any articles about how to teach the concept of "files" to students? The questions are multitudinous. If the support person doesn't know the answers, he or she ought to provide the resources from which to find out.

PLANS AND REALITIES

Once the plan is "official," teachers or committees involved in the project may feel that they must follow it to the letter. Since the support person is the participants' link with the planning authority, it is that person's role to recognize the need for adjustments and to make the actors aware that changes can be made. For example, sometimes a person finds that having students come in from other classes to use the computer is just not possible because of scheduling changes. Or perhaps a new piece of software has come out which needs to be added to the plan. Or a parent volunteer on which the person was counting has moved out of town. In the case of a nonclassroom application, the hangup may be the need for more training than the group originally thought would be necessary or perhaps a book they were counting on using is late in being published. The regular meetings that the support person has with each person or group allows them to discover this sort of difficulty promptly and either work out other alternatives or amend the plan to jibe with reality.

The action plan sheet is not meant to be filed away until next spring. If it contains enough detail, it can act as a guide to what should be done next. At intervals during the year, the teacher or administrator along with the support person should fill in the "dates completed" column and make any notes about results or minor variations in what was done.

The action plan sheet will also remind everyone to begin collecting evaluation data as the year goes on. Unless the actors have set up a formal summative evaluation design, the data will probably be formative—attitudes, observations, records of how long learning takes for each step, sample schedules, printouts of work accomplished, copies of posters or worksheets used, and so on. Without such data collection, come June, it will be impossible to reconstruct all of this, except in a general way which will not be very helpful to another user. Yet, the present user is not likely to save such items or to keep a running commentary on the project without the computer support person's help. At each meeting, the support person should gather all the information possible, take notes about the conversation and issues that come up, date each piece of paper, and file it away.

Final Report

At the project's end, sometimes the main actors prefer to write a report and sometimes they would like the support person to do a first draft to which they can add details. Whichever is the case, some kind of written document should come from the project, in addition to the completed action plan sheet. The report should be practical, helpful and honest. Not every project tried will succeed. Remember, it is the computer use or the project which is being evaluated, not the participants!

When the report is completed (see Fig. 4.3), the same group which planned the project in spring should come together to review what happened and its implications for the district's overall plan. Several copies of each report can be made. One is to be put in each participant's personnel file with a letter commending the effort expended. One should go with similar reports from other projects into a document which is sent to the computer planning committee, to administrators in the district, and to the school committee. Several more should be kept on file for people who want to undertake similar work in the future. Sometimes the main actors even put on a "show-and-tell" workshop where they can demonstrate to their peers what they have done, as part of their final report.

FINAL REPORT

Judy Brown
Ridgewood Elem. Gr. 2–3
Text Editing to Improve Writing Skills

Documentation

At first, Judy tried having the Apple for only half days. She discovered she needed it in the room all the time in order to give students concentrated practice in using it.

Judy wanted first to have children learn to enter stories, without editing or being able to go back and correct errors. We made a chart of directions for them to follow.

The idea of using parent volunteers did not work well. They needed too much training.

At several critical times in the year, as progress was beginning to be made, the equipment broke down. This caused a break in momentum.

Toward mid-year, Carol Smith spent a significant amount of time in the room in an attempt to be the needed expert and to teach students how to edit, rather than just how to enter their stories, as they had been doing up to that time.

Because the large keyboard for Judy's room was never ordered, Ann Craig did not spend a significant amount of time with this class and its word processor. Thus, she feels unable to contribute significantly to the evaluation.

Evaluation

Judy Brown feels the children at grades 2–3 are too young to learn to use the word processor independently. Only 4–6 of her class achieved some measure of independence.

Judy found it distracting for children to ask her for help during her teaching activities. She felt the need of some outside expert.

One student who finds it difficult to write with pencil and paper used the Apple word processor as "more of a resource" than the others, according to Judy.

Students enjoyed using the Apple, but found it frustrating not to be able to correct errors and disappointing to lose stories (because they did not correctly save the stories on disk). The word processing program should be more "child-proof."

It takes a lot of teacher time to help children learn to use the word processing program and to organize the use of the Apple so that stories are not just typed in, but are also edited. Judy found this time commitment too heavy and feels she can achieve motivation for writing more effectively in other ways.

There is no indication of any significant increase in writing ability for the independent users of the word processor.

Carol Smith, Ann Craig, Judy Brown, and Peter Palmer agree the printer should move to a higher grade level next year.

Dissemination

Judy Brown and Carol Smith will demonstrate the word processor to a Ridgewood staff meeting in the fall in an effort to interest an intermediate-level teacher in using it.

Figure 4.3   Final report for a one-year project

The computer planning committee thus receives feedback on the results of each year's efforts so that it can revise the overall system plan as necessary and suggest follow-up projects for the following year. Successful efforts can be extended; less than successful ones may signal the need to modifiy goals. The planning and monitoring model works when it supplies administrators with honest qualitative and quantitative data on which to base educational decisions in this fast-changing computer age.

Staff Development 5

One of the clearest lessons to be learned from the various attempts to reform American education over the past 30 years is that teachers and other educational personnel need some formal preparation if they are to participate effectively in a reform. Perhaps nowhere is this likely to be truer and more critical than in the current attempt to infuse computers into the K–12 curriculum. Not only are most professional staff unfamiliar with computers but many are actively hostile toward a computer presence in schools. To some they represent a further dehumanization of the learning process. To others, they appear to be a threat to their jobs. Clearly, educational leaders charged with implementing a computer program in a district face a formidable challenge in preparing their staff for the change.

As discussed in previous chapters, planning for computer-related staff development should be done as part of district-wide long-range planning for computer implementation. Indeed, the goals and implementation steps of your district's long-range plan in large part will shape the content, scheduling and delivery mechanisms of staff development efforts. For example, if your plan calls for the English department to begin using word processors in year three, teachers who need to develop word processing skills must be identified and prepared ahead of time. Or, if you are planning for all tenth grade geometry classes to begin using Logo in January of next year, again appropriate training for the teachers must be planned.

But staff development efforts must include more than just specific training of directly affected staff on particular issues. Everyone who works in the school—secretaries, custodians, paraprofessionals, teachers, administrators—will be affected by the presence of computers in their workplace. Even in the unlikely case that a particular staff member will not use computers directly, he or she will need to understand what co-workers, colleagues, and students are doing with computers. Thus every employee in the school and district will need to be prepared in some way for the coming of computers.

Perhaps the most important single group to receive staff development in the beginning stages of a computer implementation program are you and your colleagues, the educational leaders in the district: department heads, team leaders, principals, central office administrators, and district curriculum personnel. This group needs a specially planned program of in-service, designed to help them develop the expertise and the vision needed to guide their staffs in the coming years of computer implementation.

GOVERNANCE

Like computer implementation, establishing effective staff development requires a recognition of the political need to involve those who will be affected in planning and governance. The research on staff development indicates that if staff is seriously involved, the goals of a staff development program have a far greater chance of being achieved than if a program is mandated. Thus the broadest range of personnel need to be involved in planning staff development from the earliest stages and should remain involved as these plans are brought to fruition.

The Role of the Computer Advisory Committee

If a school district has established a computer advisory committee as part of its long-range planning for computer implementation, it has already begun the staff development process. Most of the staff who are on the committee will initially have only the vaguest ideas about what educational goals can be achieved with computers. So the opportunity to discuss and establish such goals will help them learn some valuable lessons, both about computers in education and about the process of change in educational institutions.

Moreover, the insights of these computer novices into their own needs for information and training will provide guidance in planning actual staff development programs. Such planning might start within the advisory committee, but ultimately responsibility rests with the district's established mechanisms for staff development. Members of the advisory committee must be clear about this, lest they be perceived as preempting the rights and responsibilities of others, thereby causing antagonism toward their larger efforts.

Nevertheless, it is appropriate and necessary that the advisory committee develop some general statements concerning staff development for computer implementation and that its members offer their services to the established staff development committees and staffers. Thus the advisory committee should provide the various staff development committees with copies of their long-range and one-year plans, clearly identifying what sort of staff development efforts would be needed. Further, the committee ought to be prepared to provide information, personnel, and material resources that may be needed to carry out such staff development.

Staff Development Committee

Most school districts have a standing committee or an administrative office whose responsibility is to design in-service education each year. If your district does not have such provisions, the computer advisory committee might do well to propose the creation of a standing committee whose sole function would be to establish and monitor in-service programs for computers. In either case, the people charged with providing staff development for the district should consult with some experts in the field of educational computing. Although teachers and administrators on the committee are likely to be eager to learn new applications and think creatively about computers, they often will not know what questions to ask or what they need to know. Administrative leadership is needed to connect them with some outside knowledgeable source of stimulation and new information.

However, the role of outside experts should be carefully defined. They may know the field of educational computing, but the members of the staff development committee know their colleagues. This is especially true if the committee is broadly representative of teachers and administrators in the district. Local educators are, in general, quite aware of their own learning styles, even if sometimes this awareness doesn't have a label attached to it; and they are aware, again perhaps unconsciously, of where they are in their own developmental growth cycle. Most can also articulate where they perceive the school district or school to be in its historical cycle. This self-knowledge on the part of committee members, combined with the administration's sense of the needs of the school district should result in programs appropriately tailored to the district staff. (See pages 81–83 for an example.) It is not merely a matter of symbolism that teachers and administrators participate together in decisions about staff development; their cooperation is vital to produce an effective in-service program.

Building Level Committees

Not all staff-development will take place at the district level. In fact, if we include support systems, as well as training, as part of staff development, a large percentage of staff development for using computers will be planned and will take place at the building level. In these efforts, the building principal is the key.

Once computer use has begun in a building, the principal should identify a steering committee to set up ways for active parents, students, and staff to share their new knowledge with others in the school community. Clubs, support groups, parents' nights, team teaching, demonstrations at staff meetings, and voluntary hands-on opportunites can all help to disseminate both knowledge and enthusiasm.

CONTENT

A number of educators have begun to think about what computer-related competencies are needed by teachers. Similarly, the Educational Testing Service has been thinking about what computer competencies high school graduates should have. The two lists are likely to look remarkably similar. Fig. 5.1, for example, contains one district's compendium of staff competencies broken down into three major components: learning about computers as an "object of study," mastering the use of computers as an "instructional tool," and learning to use the computer

Competencies

1. An awareness of computer applications in education and educational research.
2. Knowledge of computer applications in industry.
3. The ability to explain computer applications in simple terms.
4. An awareness of software evaluation issues and procedures, and experience reviewing software.
5. A perspective on the range of software possibilities gained from much review experience.
6. Knowledge of CAI and CMI applications.
7. The ability to load and run programs.
8. The ability to operate specific pieces of equipment and to use more than one type of computer.
9. Knowledge of the capabilities of the operating system of the school.
10. Knowledge of communication and networking software and hardware.
11. Knowledge of such tool programs as databases, word processors, and spreadsheets.
12. Knowledge of problem solving techniques.
13. The ability to modify existing software.
14. The ability to write a simple program.
15. The ability to copy programs or files from disk to disk (or tape).
16. Knowledge of a wide range of algorithms commonly employed on computer systems.
17. The ability to write programs and the ability to teach programming, including the understanding of how a well-executed program should be structured.
18. Knowledge of educational/computer research efforts and their implications for practice.
19. The ability to write a design for software which a programmer can understand.
20. The ability to help a teacher write a design for software which a programmer can understand.
21. Knowledge of the history of computers and an understanding of the social and moral issues involved in computing.
22. The ability to explain how a computer works and the mastery of the accompanying technical vocabulary.

Figure 5.1   One district's list of computer competencies for staff

as a "management tool." The first is the hands-on study of computers themselves: how they operate, the languages that can be used to communicate with and to program them, and perhaps even some discussion of their history and the social and moral issues surrounding their use. Some people call this study *computer literacy*. The second component refers to the use of computers in the classroom as a strategy and method for teaching the skills and content of other disciplines, as an extension of what the teacher does and what the student does—a teaching and learning device. The last component deals with computers as recordkeepers, test scorers, and even prescribers of instruction.

Fig. 5.1 is a list of competencies toward which various staff members in one district are working. It is not expected that every staff member will exhibit all of these competencies, but that among the entire staff these competencies will be met. You should note the heavy emphasis this district has placed on staff being able to program, and be aware that this is an issue about which there is no widespread agreement. Indeed, as educators gain experience with computers, most are placing less and less emphasis on the need for teachers to have programming skills and more emphasis on their need to master basic computer tools which can be applied to many kinds of tasks, both instructional and administrative. Comfort using a word processor, experience setting up a spreadsheet template, skills in designing simple database records, knowledge of how to use a graphing program to present data, the ability to use a graphics utility to produce visuals: these skills, many say, are proving themselves to be more valuable to teachers and administrators than programming.

Yet not all computers-in-education specialists agree. You, as an educational leader in your district, need to be aware of the controversy and need to develop some perspective about this issue. Although each district will differ on the emphasis its leaders give to particular computer skills or knowledge, it is important that district leaders define some basic core of competencies needed by all staff and additional skills needed by those involved in particular programs. Then training must be provided so that staff may develop these competencies.

PHASES OF A STAFF DEVELOPMENT PROGRAM

Staff development is an on-going process which you, as an educational leader, must nourish and encourage. When it deals with a new area, such as educational computing, the first phase should probably be informal, providing awareness, motivation, and some very general knowledge. All staff members must have the opportunity to consider and discuss how educating students in the information age is, or should be, different from what it was in the industrial age.

Administrators must ensure that support systems are established in each building to serve such informal learning needs on an on-going basis as the long-range computer plan unfolds. Then, as equipment is procured for the implementation of each part of the plan, specialized training will be needed so that staff members may learn about the applications of computers to their fields and management tasks. For example, administrators and teachers should all have opportunities to learn to manage information more efficiently and effectively by employing word processors, databases, spreadsheets, and graphics and communications tools. Prior to the implementation of each new aspect of the long-range plan, administrators must be sure that equipment levels are adequate to provide both hands-on training and subsequent frequent access to the targeted groups.

In our opinion, the introductory or consciousness-raising phase of a computer in-service program ought to be mandatory. Every teacher and administrator needs some exposure to computer literacy—awareness of how a computer functions, how it can be used in a classroom and a school, what the district's plans are for implementing computer instruction. Even though faculty meetings are usually seen by many staff members as a less desirable setting for in-service education, for this phase such a method may be useful. It is important that every teacher see that every other teacher is involved in learning about computers. However, this phase works best if it is more than mere talk. A mini-fair with computers available for hands-on experience in rotating 15 minute segments can be very instructive. And since there will always be staff members in a district who already have more computer experience, these people, as well as members of the computer advisory committee, can be facilitators at the various hands-on demonstration stations.

In planning the next phase of in-service training, administrators should attempt to establish a beachhead of vision, support, and knowledge in each school building.. Most teachers who are contemplating the "perilous" step toward the future by trying to use computers need to know that someone in their building can assist them if they meet a problem. Moreover, these leaders need to be prepared to work with teachers who may be reluctant to plunge into computer use. Thus, at minimum, the principal, the media specialist, and one or two teachers should be given some general hands-on experience first. Once a core of knowledgeable staff exists in a building, others will feel less hesitant about becoming learners.

It is crucial that the principal, as instructional leader, be one of the first who is trained. Writing memos by word processor, expressing interest in particular instructional applications, arranging demonstrations, facilitating sharing—all of these are ways that a knowledgeable principal can lead his or her staff toward appropriate implementation of computers and, perhaps, a new vision of the future.

The third phase of staff development should broaden in-depth training to include more staff than just building leaders. All staff can benefit from having a deeper understanding of software and applications which can be used in their particular fields. In other words, staff need to begin to develop a basic core of competencies such as those listed in Fig. 5.1. How soon in the implementation process you can take this next step depends on how much hardware is available in your district. There is very little point to teaching staff how to use computers unless they have machines to use and to practice on. There must be access time during which they can begin to experiment and then use computers fully. Similarly, there is little point to a PTA's generosity in giving a school a computer, unless administrators arrange for some teacher training to be simultaneously provided. Many teachers who learned programming in college on mainframe computers in the early 1970s had to relearn it when microcomputers began to appear in schools. Computer competencies are frail and need constant practice. It is frustrating to be taught skills which one cannot use almost immediately.

The question of mandating such in-depth learning is complex. It depends upon the particular plan adopted by your school district. Usually the most intensive need for training occurs for teachers who are to teach about computers as objects of study. If the district plans to have all fifth grade teachers present Logo to their students, then all fifth grade teachers must be given Logo training before they start to teach it. If, for example, BASIC is to be taught by junior high teachers of industrial arts who have volunteered because they are interested, then these teachers will need instruction in BASIC and methods of teaching it! If a district plans to establish a department for the teaching of computers as an object of study, which might be called an Information Science Department, the people who might move into that department would have a high priority for training and on-going in-service support.

The implications of such large scale efforts in training staff for computers, will be regarded by some staff as negative. Some people will argue that computers are getting the major portion of in-service monies and that this implies that all the other tasks a school accomplishes are unimportant. Indeed, major in-service efforts in computers are bound to trigger a raft of anxieties about the role of computers in the curriculum. Some concerned people may predict that eventually teachers won't be needed, with computers "taking over." To combat this negative attitude, you must provide more realistic visions of the future and plenty of opportunities for staff to discuss their implications and the steps which schools must take to realize the best future possible. Leadership and participation are the keys to relieving anxious thoughts about computers.

A ONE-YEAR MODEL STAFF DEVELOPMENT PROGRAM

In this section, we discuss one example of the content that might make up an in-service program for one year. It is based on the staff development program of a school district already highly committed to educational computing and with a majority of "mature" teachers on staff. It is included to illustrate the wide range of possibilities for in-service content in this field. This extensive in-service program is tied very closely to the district's long-range plan.

Of two district half-day releases, one is devoted to technology, the other to the humanities. On technology afternoon, each teacher, K–12, selects a two-hour workshop on computers and other technologies from a panoply of offerings developed by a committee of district staff members. This is a required in-service obligation in that each teacher must attend a workshop which closely relates to his/her level of competence in computers and to the role he/she plays instructionally in the system. In addition, there are two K–12 departmental release days. On these afternoons departments engage in computer-related activities, such as the following, planned by their department leaders in response to district plans and goals.

- Instructional Media. An afternoon spent practicing how to use the networking capabilities of the district's computer system, so they will be able to assist teachers who need it.
- English Department. An afternoon of curriculum planning, following up previous exposure to word processing as a way of teaching composition.
- Home Economics. An afternoon pursuing computer applications for the pre-school classroom they run.
- Industrial Arts. A field trip to look at ways computers are used in vocational classrooms by teachers in the local regional vocational school.
- Science. An afternoon of "computer round robin" where several knowledgeable science teachers share with their peers experiences, techniques, programs which they have developed over the past two years.
- Foreign Language. A trip to a local software preview center to evaluate the available computer-assisted instruction.
- Business. Two afternoons honing skills using programs such as spreadsheets, word processors and accounting packages.
- Information Science. Monthly sessions to evaluate the newly created/organized curriculum and to plan for new courses to be added.

In addition to these activities, designed specifically by these departments for their own education, the elementary computer specialist offers the following courses on the weekly release afternoons for elementary school teachers:.

- Logo and Mathematics—Crosscurrents. A one afternoon workshop for fifth and sixth grade teachers to instruct them in the uses of Logo in mathematics in such areas as graphing, polygons, geometry, estimating, variables, and problem solving.
- Word Processing. Two two-hour sessions (during release time for elementary teachers and after school for secondary teachers, secretaries and administrators) to teach interested staff to use a simple microcomputer word processing system.
- Computer Literacy for Fourth Grade. Two afternoons to prepare fourth grade teachers to teach computer literacy and to use turtle graphics programs and Big Trak.

- Logo Programming. A required five-day plus five half-day training session for sixth-grade teachers, any new fifth-grade teachers, librarians, and specialists in other fields to prepare them to teach Logo 2. (For about half of this time, substitutes are provided; the rest is during regular released afternoons.) Hands-on experiences are provided by the computer specialist and two experienced fifth-grade teachers. Teachers learn to define and modify procedures, handle disk files, write procedures, do simple interactive programming, and debug.
- Overview of the Grade Five Computer Curriculum Revisions. One two-hour session for fifth-grade teachers to become aware of the changes made after the program's formative evaluation.

The computer specialist also assists several experienced teachers to provide for their colleagues an introduction to the microcomputers in their own buildings!

Finally, one of the elementary librarians, who had been on sabbatical to study computers, team-teaches with an elementary teacher a course called "Teachers and Programmers Together Get Results." During the four one-to-two hour sessions spread throughout the year, participating teachers bring to the instructors the teachers' ideas of time-consuming repetitive tasks and discuss how to transform these into programs. The programs are then produced by high school students. The teachers use the programs thus developed before the end of the year.

In addition to the release-time workshops, there are several after-school classes/courses offered:

- Using Microcomputers for Filing Information in the Classroom. Three one-and-a-half hour sessions to encourage teachers to use databases in the classroom.
- Software Evaluation. Three one-and-a-half hour sessions to prepare supervisors and consultants (librarians, department heads, specialists, program managers) to train teachers to look critically at computer software.

The collaborative to which this district belongs also offers a course in BASIC and in Pascal for those who need to teach those languages at the high school level. And the district's Academic Planning Committee (a committee of faculty and administrators whose role is to lead the way for teachers in the district to use the computer as an instructional tool) meets with a number of distinguished speakers to discuss how to develop their vision of the future uses of technology in learning.

This school district has a consulting specialist in computers for the elementary grades. A significant part of her job is to train teachers, at first all fifth, and now sixth and fourth grade teachers, in the use of Logo. Even more important, after the initial workshops, she visits teachers regularly to model lessons and coach them, thus helping to tailor the theory they learn to the practice they use in their own classrooms. This is another form of in-service training.

If a school system cannot afford to fund a position for an elementary school computer specialist, it can encourage teachers to team up and observe each other as they use computers in their classrooms. Such an arrangement may even be less threatening and more rewarding in the long run since one specialist divided among one hundred teachers cannot have the effect that several groups of two or three teachers working together can produce. Of course, both practices can occur side by side.

INCENTIVES FOR STAFF

In every school district there are a small number of innovators who latch on quickly to changes, who enthusiastically approach new ways of teaching, and who constantly seek self-renewal as teachers through these processes. These are likely to be the people, both teachers and administrators, who learn first about computers and who play active roles in planning.

The rest are not so quick to change or so easily motivated to try something new. They must be sold on the idea and be given some reason to go to all that trouble. These are the second and third wave of computer learners—reluctant, often frightened, and skeptical.

While this section speaks matter of factly about tangible incentives, we don't want you to forget the enormous importance of inspiring leadership and flexible support systems. Train your leadership team first, with these reluctant staff in mind. In many cases only a very personalized approach by their local leader whom they know and respect will bring them willingly into computer training sessions.

If your district expects or requires teachers to use the computer in any of the three ways already described (object of study, teaching tool, or manager of instruction), it must bear the financial responsibility for the professional development of the staff—either by providing in-house in-service training or by providing outside learning opportunities.

Some communities have been talking about giving higher salaries to teachers of high priority subjects as a way of attracting and retaining qualified staff. Certainly computers fit into that category. However, this suggestion has not met with tremendous warmth by teachers' unions and may work counter to political objectives of computer advocates. Nevertheless the issue of payment for computer education is very important to consider.

Where there are young teachers still in search of higher degrees and the next level on the salary scale, a workable incentive, in addition to paying for in-service training, is to allow them to obtain credit toward the next salary step by participating in approved in-service programs. This is less difficult in most school districts if the training activity is offered through a university or college, and more problematic if offered internally. However, many school districts have developed formulas for translating in-house in-service into salary schedule credit (e.g., 15 hours of contact time may be considered the equivalent of one credit). Depending on the district's contract with the teachers' association or union, courses may be paid for, entirely or in part, by the school district, if it suits the needs of the school to have a particular teacher take a particular course. The master contract should be checked before an individual makes any assumptions about such payments since each school district handles these benefits differently.

Knowledgeable educational leaders should offer to help teachers think through their own educational plans vis à vis the school district's goals and the teacher's own ambitions. This kind of guidance, at no cost to a teacher, is a motivating factor which should be seen as an integral part of computer in-service programs.

An example of a motivational strategy used by one school district is the following: An experienced social studies teacher, after a sabbatical spent studying computers, decided that he wanted to learn how to use SPSS (Statistical Package for the Social Sciences). He needed to attend a series of conferences which were held out of state. In order to get the school district to pay a part of the rather large fee, he agreed to teach the use of the SPSS package to the rest of the social studies department during its staff development time, and he offered to consult with any other teacher on staff who might be interested in using the package. Thus his effort contributed not only to his own and others' training but also to curriculum evolution, as other teachers began to modify their courses to incorporate SPSS. Thinking about computers in education often leads not only to thinking about computers but also to thinking about curriculum and education in general.

Another district provides a system whereby teachers can earn an extra day off during the year by attending 30 hours of in-service training. This same district also allows teachers to earn either money or credit toward days off if they agree to teach in-service courses after school.

For some, the promise of having a computer in their classrooms will be enough incentive either to attend or to teach computer in-service.

MODES OF DELIVERING STAFF DEVELOPMENT

There is a great deal to learn. One estimate suggests 1000 hours of training and/or experience are necessary to produce a truly computer literate teacher! Even if this estimate is overblown, and our experience suggests it is not, this figure makes clear that a two-hour after school workshop is just a drop in the bucket. Thus, in addition to the kinds of in-service training described earlier, many other strategies and modes of delivery are needed.

College Courses

The traditional method of acquiring learning while on the job is to attend school— a college or university. A cursory glance at most university course catalogs will indicate how much a part of the fabric of our lives computers have become.

Courses are generally available both in computer literacy and in many of the computer languages currently in use. Staff members can take isolated courses, with or without credit, enroll in degree programs at nearby institutions, or attend intensive institutes during the summer at more distant locations, either following their own interests or pursuing the school district's stated goals. Some districts contribute to the cost of such courses; others do not.

School-Site College Courses

Another version of the "traditional" approach to in-service training is for a district administrator to arrange for a nearby college or university to offer a course off-campus, say, at the school district's site and/or in collaboration with a neighboring school district. The instructor of the course might even be a teacher from the school who then becomes an adjunct faculty member at the college. The beauty of this approach is that students can watch their teachers learn. Moreover, such courses can emphasize projects that relate to specific district priorities.

When a teacher of computers at one high school was contracted by a nearby college to teach BASIC at the high school after school one afternoon a week, about 15 staff members from that high school and the high school in the adjoining town enrolled. The "students" included the superintendent, the high school principal, the director of curriculum, the high school librarian, several elementary school teachers, the junior high school psychologist, the Industrial Arts department head, and a member of his staff. As they began to come to the computer center in between classes to do homework on the school's computers, their teenage students wandered into the center, and both sets of "students" learned from each others' experiences and assignments.

Projects submitted for credit in this course were designed to meet the needs of the school district. For example, the Industrial Arts department head became fascinated by the graphics potential of the computer to teach mechanical drawing and was soon using the computer as part of the course he was teaching, even while he was himself still learning. Two of the elementary school teachers went on during the following semester to offer courses to other teachers in their schools.

One irony of this course was that the superintendent left education to work for a computer "think tank" designing computer-based curriculum! This should not suggest that one can become an expert by taking one course, but it should indicate that one course can excite staff to consider how to use computers as professionals.There is certainly a danger that in helping teachers to acquire computer competence we will motivate them to move out of the field of education. Examples abound of teachers who reviewed their professional goals and decided that they preferred to work in industry once they understood and could use computers well. This is a reality which must be faced, but which should not deter a school district from providing staff training of the highest quality.

After School and Released Time Workshops

One of the most effective forms of in-service training is the one or two hour workshop, usually held after school or during allocated professional development days/afternoons for longer periods of time. If members of the English department at the high school want to teach writing using word processing, they must know how to do word processing. If members of the art department wish to use graphics printers in their classes, they need to know how to operate the equipment and to think about how to integrate the technology into their courses. Workshops on such topics can be one session or they can be multiple sessions. Some school districts even allow teachers to be released from classes for a few days to take specifically designed workshops. One school district found the latter financially more attractive because paying substitutes is less expensive than paying teachers' summer salaries.

Perhaps because released time only occurs occasionally, usually no more than six times a year, you should reserve it for widespread staff exposure. Thus instead of using the released time for in-depth learning activities, your committee might decide to use the time to show that computer education is valuable across the board and that everyone needs to be engaged in its pursuit in some way. The message is that the school district thinks computers are so important that it is giving the entire staff time to learn. For example, if new equipment has just been procured for the school district, this kind of time is perfect for explaining to staff how to use it and what applications are available with it. Often hardware distributors will provide these workshops gratis or as part of a bid.

Teaming Together at School

Assuming that some classroom uses of computers are already occurring in a school district, an excellent way to help staff learn about computers is to team up teachers engaged in such use with colleagues who would like to know how. Usually such events do not occur spontaneously, but require some leadership to facilitate. In one school, a social studies teacher offered an experimental course, "Computers and American History," in which students learned to write programs for teaching the subject matter, evaluated each others' programs, learned how to manipulate statistics, and used a variety of other problem-solving techniques. A well-respected but somewhat conservative history teacher on the staff audited the class alongside the high school students.

Another teaming arrangement which can be extremely beneficial is between a teacher and an administrator whose job includes scheduling, attendance, and budget. Together they can learn about computer-based management of administrative tasks and classroom tasks. Many of the basic principles of management are the same for both settings. And as an unintended outcome the teacher might come to understand and appreciate some of the problems of administrators and might explain these to other teachers!

After a sabbatical to learn about computers, often a teacher returns with a great desire to share his/her knowledge and enthusiasm. One day in the lunchroom, one such teacher offered to work after school one day a week with any teachers who were interested in learning about computers. She said she thought she could handle four teachers, one for each of the school's four computers. For the first semester she worked with three teachers, the next semester with four more, slowly and gently introducing her long-time colleagues to computer-based instruction, word processing and computer graphics.

This same teacher found herself teaching next door to another fifth grade teacher with less than adequate self-confidence about teaching Logo. To help him become more comfortable, she offered to present some all-class Logo lessons to his class in return for his doing a weather unit in science with her class. Watching her teach Logo for a term was just what he had needed, and now he is working confidently on his own.

School District Users' Group

In one district, where all third grade teachers began teaching Logo to their classes in one year, they formed an in-district user's group. They met periodically to discuss how their work was proceeding and to share with their supervisors any needs they had or any new discoveries they had made which they felt others could benefit from. The elementary specialist in computers was on-call for these teachers at all times to provide them with model lessons and to help them think through new ideas or problems they had encountered. The specialist also met with them as a group to support their efforts. This core of third grade teachers was then available the next year as a support group to the second grade teachers when Logo was implemented there as well. This is an example of peer teaching, frequently a most effective informal method of training.

Working Alone at Home

In another school district there was much controversy about whether microcomputers should be taken home by staff during weekends or on vacations. Everyone agreed that a few hours alone with a micro and a spreadsheet program, or with word processing could make a believer out of any teacher. So a policy decision was made to allow such transport of equipment and software. On Friday afternoons or just before a holiday, teachers at all levels of the district could be seen carefully carting keyboards and disk drives to their cars. Teachers and the school district were at first nervous about security. What would happen if the machines broke down or were stolen while in a teacher's possession? The superintendent allayed everyone's anxieties. The district's maintenance contract covered breakage and the insurance policy covered theft. Instead of the usual $1000 deductible designed to save money on premiums, the superintendent asked the business manager to purchase a policy with a $250 deductible, considering the extra cost an investment in teacher training.

Summer Opportunities

Summers have traditionally been curriculum development time for schools. The development of curriculum can be viewed as an important staff training function, an extremely involving and specific method of familiarizing teachers with what they need to know. The arrangement is especially fortuitous if the curriculum development team mixes several veteran teachers along with some teachers who are new to the subject or to the school district. Such mixed teams become mutually beneficial for all concerned. In addition to creating course content, this approach allows the new teachers to learn the expectations of the subject and become socialized as well. Veteran teachers are often rejuvenated by the enthusiasm of the recently trained who look at what is happening in the school district with fresh eyes.

Summer computer courses at the high school level are quite popular with students. Teachers, too, can take advantage of these. In one school district, the first summer computer course was open not only to students from all levels of the district, but also to parents, community people, and staff (the latter were not charged tuition). A foreign language teacher, the school nurse, and a social studies teacher enrolled!

Summer institutes or university courses are, as mentioned earlier, another form of summer opportunity. Many universities run summer programs on computers, some of which are designed especially for educators.

Interning in Business or Industry

Occasionally, a company, agency, or institution will allow a teacher to intern there. In one school district a guidance counselor felt that learning about computers would be useful to her job. She approached a nearby hospital's data processing center and asked if she could work a few hours a week at the center. (She had taken a course in COBOL given by one of the staff members of the center at a local community college.) The hospital agreed. At first she received no pay, only the experience. After six months, she began to be paid and worked at the hospital computer center in the evenings while continuing to be a guidance counselor.

Two large and well respected school districts worked out an unusual interning relationship with one of the large computer manufacturers in their area. Five staff members from each district were selected to become "experts" in programming and in using that manufacturer's equipment. After an initial school-day investment by the districts, the time was entirely contributed by the company and the school staff. The staff spent a total of 120 hours after school and on Saturdays between February and June at the computer company. The objective was to have district staff members who could take leadership in applying that particular equipment and software to educational tasks. The staff members were also expected, through training and consulting, to help other staff members do the same.

Sabbaticals and Leaves of Absence

In some school districts, sabbaticals and even unpaid leaves are part of the contractual agreement between the teachers' union and the school committee. When this benefit exists, a teacher who is very serious about computers in education can take either a half year or a full year off to study, in a formal manner, computers and education, perhaps expanding even to other allied technologies. In one community, which has a sabbatical policy, recently five out of twenty-one sabbatical proposals were in the area of computers, including: a librarian wishing to know how to direct teachers to use computers as part of instruction; a sixth grade teacher wanting to explore Logo further to be able to teach it in more depth to students; a science teacher wanting to apply computers to biology and chemistry; and a special needs teacher wanting to use computers to meet individual youngsters' learning needs. Obviously, this is an expensive staff development mode. However, the benefits to the individual and to the school district may be incalculable. The teacher returns to work refreshed and knowledgeable after time away from the classroom in which to think about computers. The teacher is then able to be an in-house "expert," consulting with other teachers, providing leadership, and establishing model programs for others to emulate.

Remaining Current

Probably the most difficult part of computer in-service training is helping people to stay current. They have such different needs as they learn to use computers at their own rate.

One useful source of knowledge, which is independent of the school district, is geographical users' groups. Often emerging from computer stores, these groups are generally run by individuals with support from the store. The groups usually meet once a month to hear from a member who has something new to share. Agendas go out a week ahead to members who pay a small membership fee. Members can often buy special disks at savings and can meet other interested people with whom they might share some task, project or problem. A teacher from a local regional-vocational technical school became involved in one such users' group and started offering mini-courses, for a small fee, which were advertised in the store and through the users' group. These courses were offered on Saturday mornings and employed the equipment on display in the store.

However, while it is nice to know that teachers are learning on their own time, the school district also has a clear responsibility for helping teachers to keep their competence in computers up to date. A costly but extremely effective way, which has been discussed previously, is for someone in the school district to be designated as a computer resource person. Part of his or her job is to keep staff informed about resources and also about the latest developments in the field. This person can be a librarian, a computer specialist, or the head of the computer science department. He or she can stay in communication with centers for research and training connected with universities, with nonprofit service organizations and with government service or advisory groups.

The district's designated computer resource person ought to be aware of funding possibilities for teacher training, such as NSF grants or state in-service grants which are earmarked for teachers to create their own in-service programs. This person, working closely with the principals and other administrators responsible for supervising teachers, can recommend specific ways in which teachers can develop individual educational plans for remaining current with the field. The more individualized the program for a teacher at this point in his/her development, the better.

Self-Education

Learning to use computers is not like learning to ride a bicycle. One forgets easily, if one does not practice. And keeping abreast of this constantly changing field is not a simple task. But it is an important one since the technology is developing so swiftly and the implications of each development are so vast. Equipment can become outdated and incompatible easily. While a school district must go about the task of staff development in an organized way, individuals cannot depend solely on the school system for their continuing education. Reading magazines and books on computers is one way to remain informed about new developments. Another is to haunt computer stores, because many salespeople are rich sources of the latest details. Still a third is to attend computer shows where the industry displays its latest technological advances. And of course, there are the old standbys, conferences.

CONCLUSIONS

Staff development in the computer area is a long-term, ever-changing task. Over the next two decades, training needs will change almost as rapidly as will the technology. The keys to success will be keeping current, planning in-service components to support each new initiative, and remaining flexible in the face of rapid mind-boggling changes. In this chapter we have outlined the importance of governance—involving staff in identifying training needs; content—setting some guidelines so that both you and your staff know what competencies they need to acquire; incentives—including ways to limit anxiety; and modes of delivery— the large variety of ways that staff can acquire computer skills.

Your leadership, which is needed to formulate and implement a staff development program for computers, must be aimed *toward* some vision of the future. It is in helping your staff envision and discover a new future for teaching and learning that you will motivate them to acquire the technological and pedagogical skills to realize the goals of your computer plan.

Management and 6
Operational Control

All educational endeavors have their mundane side. After the planning and politicking, beyond budgeting and letting out bid specs, apart from the on-going visions and revisions embodied in project action plans, administrators must create a system to manage and control the use of equipment, materials, and supplies. Where will the computers be housed? Who will be responsible for determining their schedule? Will they be moved around or stationary? Who will check them? Maintain them? The basis for these and many other decisions must again be the educational priorities determined by the overall district implementation plan developed previously.

Someone, or more likely, several people in a school need to take responsibility for scheduling equipment use, moving microcomputers or terminals when necessary, maintaining the equipment, checking out and marking new equipment prior to use, supervising use, setting up a system for cataloguing and storing software, seeing that needed repairs take place, keeping abreast of new developments in the field of educational uses of computers, choosing new software, hosting visitors, and planning publicity. This is a big job. More accurately, it is really many new responsibilities which must be more or less officially added to one or more staff members' role descriptions. In smaller districts and schools, discussing these needs with staff ahead of time and dividing the burden will mean a smoother running system later. In larger schools and school systems, it is essential that appropriately skilled full-time computer coordinators be appointed to handle these tasks, as well as other duties previously mentioned such as; evaluating and even debugging software, providing in-service training, overseeing staffing of computer service centers, acting as a resource to teachers and administrators, and teaching advanced computer science courses.

When making such practical nuts and bolts decisions about computers, administrators should ask themselves three more fundamental questions:

1. What choices will be most consistent with and supportive of the general philosophy and goals as stated in our plan?
2. What are our highest priorities this year for using this equipment? Which choices will best enhance those priorities?
3. Can we afford (in terms of personnel time and money) the decisions which are most consonant with our goals?

At first, answers to these three questions may seem to lead to different conclusions. For example, it may be most consonant with goals and priorities to keep equipment in constant use, eliminating down-time through an on-site service contract; but the price may be prohibitive. Compromise is then necessary. Go back to the first question and try to identify alternatives which will produce almost as desirable a result. See if it satisfies the priorities in the second question. Try the third question again.

We placed the cost question last for a reason. Each alternative considered should first be tested for educational soundness. There is no sense in first making cost decisions which may prevent achievement of desired goals. Nevertheless, financial considerations ultimately must be applied.

In this chapter, we present a number of alternatives for the major management and operational control decisions you and your staff will need to make. However, the enormous variety of possible applications precludes outlining every eventuality.

LOCATION OF COMPUTERS

There are a number of important educational and practical issues surrounding the location of computer equipment. Access by students and teachers is probably the most important of these in educational terms. Computers have a history of being used only by the "high priests" of the scientific community. And in many high schools, the computer lab is still peopled by an elite group of students and teachers, usually white males, sometimes called by others "computer freaks." With the widespread growth of computer use in our society, this stereotype is being challenged by other students who are knocking on the computer room door. Yet past practices are fresh in everyone's minds, so promoting the idea that computers are for anyone is an important role of the school.

The access issue is further complicated by the limited quantity of computer equipment available in most schools. Taking turns is necessary, yet it is often when a student has an unlimited amount of time—to work on an exploratory Logo programming project, for example—that the deepest learning takes place. For other uses, such as skills practice, schedules work nicely, and the more rapidly one student can leave the computer and have another take her place, the more access the class as a whole has. For this type of use a classroom station is probably the best location for computers, since having each individual student walk down the hall to some central computer lab can take a lot of time.

Scheduling also works well in a setting where various teachers need one or two computers periodically for classroom demonstrations, simulations, or lab instrumentation. If Miss Allen knows she can count on having the equipment for her third through fifth period classes twice a week, she can plan to use a simulation during that time; then Mr. Meyers can use the computer to demonstrate sentence combining during the last two periods of the day.

It is also important for teachers to have access to computers in their unassigned and planning time. Educators need time to try out new software, time to plan classroom uses of the computer, and time to review their students' programming projects. They also need time to obtain a printout of results from a skills program that keeps a record of their students' performance, or to update grades in the computer's files, or to use the word processor to generate new activity sheets. Administrators should be aware that the more ways a teacher uses the computer, the more computer literate that teacher becomes. Whisking the computer out the door when the class leaves for lunch not only leaves the teacher high and dry, but also prevents that teacher from developing better computer skills. Or, if computers are in a lab, scheduling their use so tightly that teachers have no time to use them can also be counterproductive. One nice solution to this problem is setting up a computer corner in the teachers' room or other faculty work area, so teachers can work in privacy. This provides a comfortable alternative to the teacher who is frightened, but curious, and is unlikely to willingly walk into a lab seething with young computer enthusiasts.

There are more subtle kinds of access, too. For example, how easy is it for the computer user to share his or her triumphs with peers or get an answer to a roadblocking question? Despite many expressed fears to the contrary, computer use has been observed to be a very social experience, often promoting cooperative learning. Locating computers to encourage this phenomenon seems important.

In addition, one must consider access to software and support materials. These must be catalogued and controlled by a librarian, yet easy access for computer users is also a must. Manuals, software lists, directions, and at least some programs should be located at computer stations, not on reserve shelves. If possible, an on-line catalog of available resources should be available to users right at the stations as well.

Let us consider the pros and cons of the most common locations for computer equipment in schools.

The Library

One of the main advantages of locating computers in the library is psychological. Libraries are for everyone, so if located there, computers must be too. The entire software and support materials collection of the school is likely to be right there, too, which is a great convenience. Libraries can even serve as a checkout station for the school's supply of hand-held computers. And stationary computers under the care of just one person and her staff are less likely to develop repair problems than those which are wheeled from place to place, from user to user. Since libraries are more or less constantly staffed, they also provide some supervision of computer use. With training, librarians can answer users' questions and help them over the hump of becoming familiar with the keyboard. If librarians become knowledgeable about the school's collection of software and support materials, they can consult with teachers and students on these issues, too. This, of course, presumes that the librarian is not already "out straight" keeping up with normal duties.

Figure 6.1   Computers in the library

At the national level, many librarians and their professional associations are viewing computers and software collections as a natural extension of their traditional roles. In many schools, librarians for years have been called media specialists, and libraries have housed the audio-visual collections, if not the equipment.

In one elementary school, Miss Jones, the library/media specialist, has accepted two terminals (hooked up to the high school's minicomputer) and a number of microcomputers into her domain with enthusiasm and dedication. Because she knows what the classroom teachers in her building do in their curricula, she is able to interest them in coming down during free half-hour time slots to try out software appropriate to their grade levels and to learn to tailor programs to their curricular needs. One-to-one consulting like this has paid off in increased teacher involvement. Similarly, Miss Jones schedules small groups of students at different grade levels to come down to the library to learn how to use the computer terminals as word processors or how to write simple programs in *Kidstuff* or Logo. Parent volunteers and student helpers assist users when Miss Jones is reading a story to the first graders or teaching research skills to ten-year olds.

The potential for exciting uses of computers in secondary school libraries is even greater. Students with diverse interests may sign up to use a computer for research (perhaps using a modem to gain access to distant databases), to rerun a simulation used in class, to write a program, or just to improve skills prior to the SAT exams. Libraries are often the location chosen by students who need to write a paper; a word processing mini-lab is therefore a natural addition to the library's resources. Because secondary students tend to have more "free" time to spend in the library, the computer area in the library can also become a natural gathering place for students to exchange ideas about their computing projects. One student can help another with his program, or share her knowledge of how to use a database, or exclaim over the marvels of revising text on the screen.

What are the disadvantages of placing the computer in the library? One is that if computers are not in a teacher's own domain, she needs to make extra efforts to keep in touch with (and in control of) students' learning experiences with them. Whether the students are programming or running packaged software, the result is similar to what happens when any other curricular or extra-curricular activity pulls students out of class. Integrating the learning that has taken place at the computer with classroom experiences is part of the teacher's role, but it is often difficult to do this when the computer work takes place far from the teacher's supervision, especially when the students are of elementary age.

Having students fill out record sheets or keep logs about their computer work can help overcome this information gap, but it can't completely close it. A printout of work, shared with the teacher by each student can also be effective, if the school has enough printers. Also there are some kinds of skill drill programs which keep records of students' performance so that the teacher can later come see it. None of these, however, can take the place of observing the students' efforts first hand. In a secondary school, where students are more responsible for their own learning, this is not as significant a problem, but at the elementary level most computer-based activity needs to take place under the primary teacher's supervision.

A second disadvantage of computer location in the library, again one most applicable to elementary and middle schools, is that Mr. Thomas in room 109 cannot see whether or not the computer is free at any given moment. He'd like to put Josh on the computer now, since he's finished the test early, but he doesn't know if the computer is available. This problem can be partially overcome by a librarian who aggressively disseminates up-to-date information about the computers' scheduled and free times. This situation has another side, however. While it is true that if a computer were in Mr. Thomas' classroom rather than in the library, it would be better for *his* students, it likely would be much worse for students who had no computer in their room, and it is unlikely that most schools would have enough computers to have one for every classroom.

Another disadvantage of the library setting for computers is that flexibility in the lengths of users' turns may be lost because a sign-up schedule will probably be necessary to govern the computer's availability. If Ed is scheduled to use the computer at two o'clock and Debbie is not quite done with typing in her story when he comes, Debbie may have to wait until next week to finish. In future years, as access becomes less and less of an issue with the influx of more equipment, scheduling equipment for full use will be less important, but until that time, schools with limited resources (nearly all schools!) will find this to be a problem.

Perhaps the biggest disadvantage of placing computers in the library is the difficulty this presents for creating a cooperative learning environment. In an elementary school building such an environment is most easily created when the computer is in the classroom itself. One of the beauties of kids and computers has been how naturally students of all ages help each other with the computer task at hand. Whether it's a kindergartener seeking the right letter on the keyboard or a ninth grader trying to correct the syntax of a BASIC statement, learning from other learners is the name of the game. Students build on each other's ideas, especially in a programming class, in wonderful and unexpected ways. If the elementary school's one computer is located in the library, and students are scheduled to use it for half-hour slots away from their peers, much of this educational interaction is likely to be lost. Pairing users helps, but doesn't eliminate the problem.

On the other hand, because of the tighter structure of most secondary classes, the high school library might actually be a better place than the classroom for collaboration at the computer to occur. Students of all ages and interests are around, so they naturally tend to feed into each other's work at the computer. However, here the "computer culture" runs smack into the "library culture." Libraries are by tradition and necessity quiet places. Computers generate all sorts of noise—machine noise, software noise, excited people noise. To insist on quiet around a computer is to ask the impossible. Thus a noisy computer lab may be a more appropriate location for secondary school computers in which a collaborative learning environment is a desired outcome.

Classroom

The advantages to placing microcomputers or terminals more or less permanently in classrooms are several. First, they become a permanent and accepted part of the entire learning environment, encouraging teacher and students to think of the computer as an ordinary teaching and learning tool.

Flexibility of schedule is relatively easy to achieve, since the teacher can make adjustments according to students' needs, allowing Bill to complete his term paper or Sue to try running her program once more before turning the keyboard over to a classmate. In addition, the teacher can take advantage of the "teachable moment," using what's happening at the computer as an example for everyone to learn from or giving the limelight to a poor reader who has just completed writing a spectacular program. Cooperative learning, too, can be easily encouraged by asking one student to help another who has a question.

Classroom-based computers also permit the teacher easily to monitor what various students are doing with the computer. If the teacher knows that when

Figure 6.2   Computers in the classroom

Barry and Keith go to the computer, Keith takes a novel to read, is aware of how much trouble Marge is having with word processing, and has observed that Julie is designing creative programs but never saving them, then the teacher can constructively intervene to maximize learning. Conversely, if the teacher were not present when these students are at the computer, it would be difficult for her to diagnose why they're having difficulty.

Another advantage to classroom location of computers is that no matter what the grade level, like any other piece of audio-visual equipment, a computer that is in the room is more likely to be used frequently than one which must be specially brought in for a particular lesson. An inventive teacher will constantly take a few free moments to work out a new use for the computer while students are out of the room. Students in the class or classes that use that room will get a much more concentrated computer experience than those who don't have such access.

And this, of course, raises one of the major disadvantages to classroom location of computers already alluded to. Presuming that equipment is relatively scarce in most schools, students outside the lucky classroom have little or no access to the computer. So if your goal is for everyone in the school to have occasional access to the limited amount of equipment available, semi-permanent classroom location of computers is not the best solution. Even though teachers whose rooms are near one another have been known to share a computer quite successfully and teachers in whose rooms the computers "live" might offer to let other students use them when no class is in the room, both of these solutions require compromise and very careful planning.

Another limitation of the classroom location for computers is that teachers without computers in their classrooms have little or no opportunity to get used to using the computer (unless host teachers tend to rather aggressively share their computer excitement!). Moreover, the principal or librarian is unlikely to enter a teacher's room to use the computer for administrative purposes, even if the class is letting it sit idle. There is an unwritten rule of privacy which very frequently keeps one educator out of another's room.

Again, as with the library, a computer's presence in a classroom can be disruptive to the other business of the class. Students tend to congregate around it to see what the user is doing. Sometimes a program makes noise; often student-users make noise. And teachers who do a lot of whole-class lessons find that always having one student at the computer means someone always has work to make up. This is generally a matter of teaching style. There are, of course, some ways around these objections. Screening the computer from the view of the class (but not from the teacher's view) can limit distractions as well as the tendency to congregate. Careful scheduling, so that good readers work at the computer during reading and good spellers during spelling, can help ease make-up problems. Putting the onus on the students to take responsibility for making up missed work may also be a good idea. Give them a choice of scheduling their computer work during mathematics class (which will surely mean making up missed work) or during some more open time period when they won't have that worry.

Moving Carts

If several teachers in a school are to share one microcomputer, bolting it to a computer cart may make sense. Be sure the cart has room for manuals, programs, and directions, and be certain the computer is securely fastened down, to avoid accidental falls on the way down the hall.

This arrangement marries the advantages of classroom use with the kind of broad access achieved in a library setting. It also makes possible some of the most efficient uses of the computer: demonstration and simulation, when only one computer is used for the whole class. The main disadvantages are to the computer's health. Constantly moving a computer around tends to loosen electrical connections, collect dust inside, and subject the computer to the varied habits of a wide variety of users. Careful supervision by one adult is forfeit to the advantages of broad use. Unfortunately, some teachers will be less careful than others in their supervisory role, and a computer that "belongs" to no one teacher isn't likely to receive the tender loving care that teachers give to their own classroom equipment.

If computers are to be located on carts and moved around the school, you should institute a very regular program of maintenance. Train some students or a staff member to check the computers' functioning and blow the dust off their components frequently. Attach clear simple guidelines for care, and perhaps some hints for troubleshooting.

In addition, there must be a clear statement of procedures stating how the computers are to be moved around. These procedures need to identify the persons responsible for putting the computers away at night and getting them out in the morning. You should specify that two people would be assigned when a computer is moved from room to room—one to hold the door open. If students are given this task, be certain they are responsible and are well cautioned to push the cart slowly and observantly. For the computer's safety, use a secure cart with a rubber mat, raised edges to prevent sliding, and large wheels to negotiate bumps more easily. Avoid wheeling a computer over rough surfaces, since the vibrations can loosen connections. And beware door jambs or other obstacles that could cause the cart to tip over. Obviously a cart should not be used in situations where the computer must be moved up and down stairs.

Computer Lab

As pointed out in discussing the library as a location for the school's computers or terminals, there are distinct advantages to placing all the school's computers in one place. They don't have to be moved; they can be easily supervised by one expert, eliminating the need to train all the teachers; larger groups can use them at once, which often makes scheduling less complex and disruptive. In addition, there may be some cost benefits, since networking can allow all of the stations at one location to share a printer or hard disk drive, eliminating the need to purchase many of these expensive peripherals. Moreover, costs associated with electrical wiring and security can be minimized if all or most computers are located in one place.

The advantage of a computer lab over the library is that in a lab, computer use does not disrupt other educational activities. This sort of arrangement makes class interaction around computers possible, since a group or even a whole class accompanied by their teacher can come to the lab all at one time. Unlike a

Figure 6.3   Computer lab

library, the atmosphere in a computer lab is typically noisy and excited. Students and teachers with computer interest and skills tend to congregate there and be available to help fellow students and teachers in their efforts. Staffing of computer labs tends to take care of itself; there's no need to train a reluctant librarian when computer enthusiasts would gladly monitor activities in the lab.

The negative aspects of a computer lab are subtle, but can be very important educationally. Instead of integrating computers into the normal life of the school (classroom or library), the lab keeps them separate from it. In this sense, the computer has much less potential for making an impact on how all students learn. Computer literacy education may take place very effectively in a lab, and even some whole group computer-based activities may work (each student or pair of students at a computer station during a class visit to the lab), but the computer is less likely to be used by many students and teachers on a daily basis in a tool-like way, for real information processing.

Second, a lab often becomes the province of a small group of "experts." During free time they congregate there, and the teacher experts are likely to encourage this extra computer time for their best students. The problem is, as when any group sticks together, others can feel excluded. This tends to support the old stereotypes about computing and "computer freaks" and to limit use by other students, particularly girls.

Moreover, in this situation teachers have much less opportunity to become truly comfortable with computers. They tend to leave responsibility for them to the "experts." If teachers of all kinds are not invested in using computers to enhance all parts of education, computers are likely to have very little impact on schools. It is people who know both education and computers who will make the difference.

On the other hand, in a secondary school setting, it may be very appropriate to plan for several computer labs, located in various departmental areas and each devoted to particular uses. Each of these should be equipped according to the need. For example, a lab designed for programming classes might be located in the mathematics or computer science area and might contain a class set of hand-held or other inexpensive computers to be used for learning BASIC, plus some terminals to a minicomputer (or a network of larger micros) which allow students to use other, larger computer languages such as Pascal, COBOL, or Logo. The programming lab should also contain several printers for printing out programs and peripherals such as a graphics tablet or speech synthesizer to demonstrate the wide range of computer capabilities. The word processing lab would probably contain networked micros, sharing a hard disk and a high quality printer. The quality of the keyboards, the ease and versatility of the software, and monitors chosen to limit eyestrain are most important here. A lab for use in science and social studies needs to be equipped with a brand of computer well-supported by applications software and with enough memory to run sophisticated simulations. Color graphics are desirable since teachers and students in these areas should be learning to represent concepts graphically. Demonstration-sized monitors also are needed, but fewer stations in all might suffice, since small groups might be expected to work at each station. The business education department would also need a lab for accounting and word processing.

In the high school, then, the existence of many labs may serve to increase access to computers for all kinds of classes and to truly integrate their use into existing subjects. Only a high school with just one computer lab would be subject to the disadvantages described previously.

One final advantage to setting up computer labs is that they are then available as sites for teacher training or adult education classes after school and on weekends. Having equipment scattered around a building, with no group of stations in one room, can discourage these important activities because moving and setting up the equipment for a workshop is so time consuming.

Office

So far we have discussed the location of computers in the context of instructional computing. Let us turn now to their location in the context of computing as a support service for educators. A perfectly legitimate place to put one or more computers with printers is in the school office or teachers' work room. These could be stand-alone micros at first, but eventually most schools will want the advantages of a hard disk and letter-quality printer which can be used from a number of stations (e.g., guidance, principal, secretary, librarian, or teachers). To provide these efficiently, you will probably wish to consider some kind of networking system. For example, these stations could all be connected to a time-sharing system which supports administrative uses, or they could be microcomputers, linked through a local resource-sharing network, or they could even be micro-computers connected by modem to a timesharing system, so that they can have access to central data, but then be disconnected for use in local processing. The key again, if one of the established goals is a computer literate staff, is to encourage all the adults in the school to use whatever stations are available for a wide variety of purposes. Integrating computers as tools into the life of the school will not only make the school somewhat more efficient, but also demonstrate to all the role computers can play in our working and learning activities.

The disadvantage of a computer being located in the administrative office is simply that students and teachers are unlikely to use it there. This is acceptable, if they have access to computers in their own work areas, but if equipment is still scarce and they do not have such access, the efficiency gained may not justify the educational loss.

Making the Location Decision

Clearly, there are advantages and disadvantages to every possible location for computers in the school. Your decision about location must be based on your system's educational goals and priorities. Besides the ways these goals affect

Figure 6.4   Computers in the school office

location decisions that have been discussed already, they may also influence computer location by determining what kinds of computers are purchased. For example, if you determine that a network of microcomputers all sharing a printer and hard disk best meets the needs of your plan, then placing computers in a central location may be necessary. For any kind of locally networked or resource-sharing system, the cabling is costly and in some cases cannot be run over long distances, so a laboratory set up may make the most sense. On the other hand, timesharing does not place such stringent restrictions on proximity of equipment, so it will permit you to spread terminals around a building wherever there are phone lines, if that fits your educational goals.

In making the location decisions, the type of equipment chosen and its associated costs, as well as ease of access for users are the primary concerns. Another concern is personnel strengths and weaknesses. If the librarian really has no interest in computers, it would be foolish to station equipment in the library and hope the librarian will come around. Similarly, some excellent teachers are very uncomfortable with computers in their classrooms. Others would much rather have one in the room than send their students out to use it, thereby losing touch with their learning.

The keys to making a good decision about location seem to be: 1) specify your long and short-range goals, and 2) involve the school staff in determining how best to meet those goals with the available equipment. Armed with the above pros and cons, as well as the cautions about personnel, the school administrator should be able to present the alternatives and lead the staff to an appropriate decision.

SCHEDULING USE

The task of scheduling people's use of a school's computers is tricky. The person charged with this responsibility must be diplomatic but firm and must have a good grasp of the goals the school is aiming for. Mediating and compromising should be among the person's strengths. Conflicts are inevitable. Schedules are needed when many users demand time to use a limited quantity of computer equipment. As more equipment is available, one might think this problem would go away, but increased use generally keeps the pressure on equipment high, even in lab situations. With the system's priorities firmly in mind, the highest priority users should be scheduled first, fitting in other users around them as possible.

One danger, in particular, bears mentioning here. Teachers, as well as students, need time to use the computer, if they are to feel comfortable and in control of computer-related learning. Teachers must be made to feel that their personal use of the computer is a responsibility and a necessity, not a luxury.

Two common scheduling conflicts you might wish to be aware of are the following:

1. Administrative use vs. instructional use. The main conflict here is on a timesharing system where the running of administrative jobs may cause long delays in response time for student users at another location. This can often be eliminated by running those jobs at hours when student use is low.
2. Desirable length of a user's turn at the computer vs. school schedule. Especially at the secondary level, it is often hard to fit a number of student turns in before the bell rings.

Because the various ways a computer can be used are so different, no one model for scheduling could possibly work. For example, students using the computer to learn programming may need fairly long (30–60 minutes) turns every day or two to make the best progress. Having paper output (e.g., a networked printer) available can decrease this time somewhat, as a student can then analyze the program off-line, attempting to find bugs and develop corrective solutions before going back to the computer to try them out. The student who is using the computer to drill on French vocabulary, in contrast, needs brief (10–15 minute) daily turns for best results. A class which is using a simulation to understand a complex system may need a computer for an hour or two a day over the period of their study, but not at all later in the year. Notice that in this case the whole class can use just one machine, an economy of resources not possible with many types of uses. For word processing, users need considerable machine time, perhaps in 30 to 60 minute turns. However, as with programming, work away from the computer with paper output can reduce the on-line time needed for editing.

From these examples, one can see that the people who schedule computer time must be sensitive to the variety of uses possible and must be willing to go to the trouble of inquiring about the kinds of time-chunks needed for each requested use.

In most schools, not all requests can be honored due to limited equipment. Beware trying to accommodate everyone and ending up with "thin use," where little learning takes place because each person's turns are so infrequent.

Consider using the computer itself to help develop schedules and to have available for display at all times an up-to-the-minute record of use and availability. A timesharing system or hard-disk local network of microcomputers, with the right software, can easily accomplish this convenience.

STORAGE OF MATERIALS AND EQUIPMENT

Computer materials and equipment represent a costly investment for schools. They are also tempting targets for theft. Appropriate storage can greatly reduce such losses and can help users to find what they need when they need it.

Hardware

The two major factors to be considered in storing computer equipment are safety from theft and protection from dust. In a time of tight budgets, many schools may not feel they can justify spending the money to insure their equipment, so storing the computers and any expensive software or peripherals in a locked area is smart. If possible, put them away or cover them before the custodian sweeps up at night. Chalk dust and dirt can build up on internal computer components, and equipment failures may result. In addition, be certain the responsibility for putting equipment away and getting it out is assigned to an appropriate person who has been trained to dismantle it properly, to keep track of pieces, and to carry everything safely.

One way of "storing" microcomputers is to lend them to teachers and students to take home overnight, on weekends, and during vacations. Despite the obvious potential problems involved in such an unusual arrangement, there are good arguments for doing so, if the primary goal is universal computer literacy among student and teacher populations. Getting used to a computer in the privacy of their own homes is easier for most teachers than trying to do so under the watchful eyes of colleagues. Loaning the computer to students can promote literacy among parents and siblings as well. If, on the other hand, your primary goal is to teach computer programming to all seventh graders and you have just barely enough equipment to do that, you might think twice about taking the chance of having someone's little brother spill juice on the keyboard. Being carried around is not very good for a computer. Accidents may happen.

Let's assume you've decided that equipment loans are OK. Writing some guidelines is then crucial. Here are some suggested ones which you might wish to consider and modify according to your needs.

1. As borrower, you take financial responsibility for loss or major repair of the equipment.
2. You must be able to demonstrate proper set up and use of the equipment before borrowing it.
3. Legitimate reasons for borrowing equipment might include:
   • previewing software
   • learning to program
   • planning a classroom use
   • getting used to a new tool program, such as a word processor
   • writing a program for the school
   • getting used to the keyboard and the experience of running software.
4. Playing video games at home is not a good reason for borrowing the computer.
5. Do not leave the computer monitor on if you need to stop using the computer for awhile, but don't want to turn it off. The computer will not be hurt by leaving it on, but the screen, left with the same image for a long time, can be permanently damaged.
6. Do not allow food and drinks near the computer.
7. Keep the computer clean and free from excessive dust and smoke.
8. Sign out accompanying software and books before taking them, so everyone knows where these items are.
9. Take the phone number of an experienced computer-user, to avoid frustration in case you have questions.
10. When carrying the computer in your car,
    • be sure it cannot fall if you stop quickly
    • cover it and lock the car if you must park on the way home
    • do not expose disks, tapes or the computer to excessive cold or heat for more than a few minutes.
11. Computers must be borrowed after school is over for the day and returned before it begins on the next school day.
12. Duplicating copyrighted software is illegal.

Software

Software is subject to the same abuses as other educational materials: hoarding, loss, separation of the parts of a package. When the first computer is delivered with a half-dozen programs, it may be tempting to simply pile the programs next to the computer so everyone can try them out. As use grows, however, instituting some kind of library system becomes necessary so that different users can find what they need. The budgetary implications of this cannot be ignored. Administrators need to plan for the purchase of appropriate cabinets or storage drawers. Time and blank disks will also need to be allocated to make backup copies of software for archival purposes and to make multiple copies of non-copyrighted or multiple-licensed microcomputer disks for use at various stations. Allowing the school's microcomputer software collection to start accumulating in individual classrooms is asking for trouble!

If one is used to a timesharing system with terminals, the complexity of a system to catalog, control, and house *microcomputer* software will boggle the mind. Of course there are issues surrounding software storage on a timeshared system as well: naming files uniquely, deciding what files need to be kept always on-line and which can be stored to tape to be loaded on request, and especially getting system users to clean unnecessary or duplicative programs out of their files. Timeshared systems have the advantage, however, of central control. Central control is very difficult to establish over microcomputer software collections.

There are a number of practical issues surrounding the storage and control of microcomputer software: how to package it for borrowing, who will back-up the software, how to index and catalog it, where to store it, and how to avoid unauthorized copying yet make legal copying easy for everyone. Then there is the controversial issue of software evaluation, which is both terribly time consuming and terribly important educationally. An in-depth discussion of software selection and evaluation appears later in this chapter. Here we deal only with the practical issues surrounding the existing software collection.

Packaging.   Software comes in different shapes and sizes. Most manufacturers provide a hard case of varying sizes and shapes which holds both the disk or cassette and some kind of instruction booklet. Some software comes in a plastic zip-lock bag, with only a sheet of cardboard to protect the disk. Sometimes a teacher or parent or student will create an original program and simply hand in a bare disk or cassette relaying directions by word of mouth (or not at all).

In whatever form the software is ultimately stored, it must be protected; it should be accompanied by a "library" card; it ought to remain with its documentation (the explanatory papers or accompanying lesson plans); and it must be shelved or otherwise stored neatly, thus requiring a modicum of uniformity in size and shape. A number of commercial products have appeared to try to fill this need.

There are several kinds of heavy plastic pages, which are three-hole punched to fit in a notebook, and which generally have at least two pockets that hold a disk and its paper cover snugly in place. One kind also has a large pocket on its back side to hold a booklet. (The only drawback is that it won't hold one as large as 8 1/2 x 11 inches.) Some have smaller pockets to hold library cards or identification labels. For a small software collection, a large notebook filled with these plastic pages alternated with punched copies of the accompanying documentation works well. A teacher or librarian can easily store such a book safely at night and move it close to the computer for the school day. It can circulate from room to room. This does not automatically provide any control over who borrows a disk or cassette, but it provides a means to do so and it does make a small collection accessible to several users of one computer.

If there are two or more computers located in different parts of a building, the notebook of software becomes less handy. Suppose Mr. Peterson, the librarian, decides to keep the notebook in the media center and use the small pockets for lending cards. Mrs. Yates sends Ginny, age 7, to the media center with a note requesting a copy of *Bumble Games*. Mr. Peterson signs it out, handing Ginny the disk and a small booklet. What will happen to the disk on the way down the hall? Will both the disk and the booklet be returned? How will Mrs. Yates safely store the disk in her room? Although the notebook protects the disk and booklet while it is in the library, it provides no mechanism for keeping them safely together in the room.

A better solution, but costlier, is housing each disk or set of disks in its own inexpensive plastic binder, with the documentation as part of the package. Then it can be shelved like a book (by Dewey number, if you wish); it has protection always in place; and the accompanying materials are unlikely to be separated from the notebook since they are bound in it along with the disk in its plastic page.

An alternative is a clear plastic bag which can hang from a bar, either in a file drawer or on a shelf. Since it can contain disk or cassette, manual or instruction card, it is very adaptable. The librarian can also insert a list of its contents, so users can see what needs to be returned. Some form of stiff protection should be included for disks.

Note that housing a software collection has both budgetary and personnel implications. Funds are needed for the notebooks, plastic pages, and perhaps a new cabinet or shelf to hold them. The librarian's role description must be expanded to include the preparation of new software for lending.

For a timeshared system, packaging translates into organizing software into library accounts so that users can obtain access to various programs speedily. Such accounts could contain instructional software (one account for mathematics, one for science, one for language arts, etc.), or general purpose programs used by administrators to generate reports (one account for fiscal accounting, one for personnel uses, one for inventory purposes, etc.). All of these administrative programs would probably draw on a centrally shared pool of data, but the programs would organize and process the data in different ways for different purposes.

On many timesharing systems, the length of a program name is limited to six or eight characters. This results in the need to name programs carefully and to create an index or catalog to help users find old programs quickly. One computer center manager who runs reports for many administrators in a school system keeps a database of the available system software which he can search, not only by program name or subject, but also by the name of the administrator or department who uses it. Then when Ms. Thompson calls him up and asks for something similar to a report run two years ago, he has a chance of finding it!

Back-up. Because software is both quite expensive and very easily destroyed, you should be sure to keep an extra copy, called a back-up. This holds true for all kinds of software, whether it is for a timesharing system, where backups will probably be on magnetic tapes or hard disks, or for a stand-alone microcomputer. Most software manufacturers have some policy about back-up copies: either they will sell you one for a few extra dollars; or they promise to replace a scrunched disk if you'll send it to them; or they've set up the disk so that it can be copied some small number of times; or they'll actually sell you two copies in the first place, usually at a reduced price for the second one. The number of software publishers and distributors that make such provisions are likely to increase dramatically in the near future. It is essential that a school not have to wait weeks for a back-up disk in case one is destroyed. We suggest you buy only disks which either come with a back-up or allow the user to make a back-up easily.

For publishers who have no such policy and who copy-protect their disks or tapes (making it impossible for users to copy using normal means), the only solution is to buy a sort of super copy program which will break through the copy protection scheme and allow you to make a copy. *This is legal if the copy is for archival purposes only.* Such copy programs can be quite expensive, but may be worth it if there is no alternative. If your school does purchase a powerful copy program, access to it should be very carefully controlled. No school should aid and abet illegal copying by students or staff, by allowing them to use the school's copy program.

Notice that again both budget and personnel time are affected by this situation. A school must plan to have on hand blank disks and tapes, perhaps a super copy program, and some secure storage mechanism for the back-up copies (in the case of microcomputer disks the large notebook may serve very well). In addition, someone must take responsibility for obtaining back-up copies and storing them securely. For a timesharing system which holds a database of administrative information, back-up of active files will probably have to be done on a daily basis to insure that recently entered data is safely stored away in case of a system crash or other disaster. In addition, the entire software library on a timeshared system should be backed-up on tape. However, since programs do not change frequently, this back-up can be much less frequent than data back-up must be.

Indexing and cataloguing. It is very important for the software librarian to let people know what is available and to make it easy for them to locate what they need. One problem in doing this for microcomputers is that one disk can hold many programs each of which can be on a different topic or level. So shelving a disk by Dewey number is not always easy to do, nor can a librarian always easily catalog one disk as a unit. For if a disk contains several programs, each one needs to be catalogued separately (even though they cannot be physically shelved in separate locations in the library). The task is more like cataloguing magazine articles! However, increasingly this is becoming less of a problem, since most commercial disks now contain only one subject.

Where a disk contains more than one subject, the solution seems to be to catalog programs separately (when necessary) or disks as a whole (when that makes sense), but to have an entirely different method for shelving—an arbitrary but unique number associated with each physical unit. For example, each disk might have a number used just as a Cutter number might be used (to determine order of shelving). If a computer-based catalogue is being used (which can sort the entries in any of a number of ways) a list of available software can then be printed by subject or grade or whatever other criteria one wishes. Each entry on such a list, though, must refer to the unique shelf number of the package that contains the program in question.

Catalog entries also need to contain information about the type of computer needed to run the software, including required memory capacity, operating system requirements, if any, and all necessary peripheral devices (such as a printer, joystick or color monitor). Even if the school has only one type of computer now, include this information, because changes in hardware are taking place very rapidly. If the software is copyable (not protected by copyright) this should also be noted. In most cases, this information should also include a brief description of subject matter and mode of interaction. This is necessary because all disks (or tapes) look alike from the outside, and there is no way to leaf through such software to get a sense of what it is about. As documentation has been improving, this problem has eased somewhat, although trusting printed documents to describe accurately an electronic interaction is still risky at best.

Someone needs to start and maintain this catalog. Again, both an enormous amount of personnel time and some small printing costs will need to be allocated. The person creating the catalog will need to reserve considerable time on a computer to look at and describe the software, as well as time to search out reviews and abstract them as part of the filed information.

Actually putting such a catalog on a computer is a sensible idea for two reasons. First, updating the list and printing out a new version is easy every time a new piece of software is obtained. Similarly, descriptions can easily be revised as feedback comes in about classroom uses. Second, if the whole list is typed into a database program that has sorting capabilities, separate lists of software for various levels or subjects can easily be generated, as they are requested.

There is no reason why just microcomputer software should be handled this way. On a timesharing or networked system, the need is just as great to keep users informed about available programs. One school system we know has established a fat notebook, divided into sections by curriculum area and cross-indexed by both grade level and subject matter. The notebook contains a printed "run" of each of the educational activities on the timesharing system. Teachers can thus actually read a program's directions and a sample of the interaction with students in order to judge whether the activity will be appropriate for their classes. There would be no point to putting such a book *online*, but the indexes, with each entry accompanied by a short description, could be put online. Included, as well, would be some instructions about how to call up the program for use from its file. Users would probably use a menu to choose the general subject and level wanted, then search the descriptions until they found an appropriate program.

It is very desirable to keep a software list on-line, so that any user can have direct access to the up-to-date list of resources. Of course, in order for users at multiple stations to have this capability, some kind of networking or timesharing must be in place and large amounts of disk storage available.

Avoiding unauthorized copying. Schools have an obligation to demonstrate and enforce compliance with the copyright laws. While it is impossible to control what a user does with borrowed software, one can at least make a strong statement reminding all borrowers of the requirements of the law. A photocopy of such a statement might be pasted to the cover of all copyrighted packages, for example. Similarly, packages which may be legally copied ought to be clearly marked and contain helpful instructions for copying.

Another related issue is student or teacher use of the school's computers to make unauthorized copies of software which belongs to them. Software piracy is unfortunately fairly widely practiced, with computer users trading pirated copies of games with one another. Since it is illegal, this practice must not be condoned or permitted within the school. The adult(s) supervising computer use must be alert to such practices and be prepared to prohibit them strongly. Penalties might include the confiscation of diskettes until parents come in to school to discuss the situation or a suspension of computer-using privileges for a reasonable period of time.

Summary of procedures. Receiving a new piece of software involves the following steps:

1. Package it with the documentation.
2. Assign a shelf number to the package.
3. Make or order a back-up copy.
4. Look at each program carefully and describe it.
5. Add necessary catalog information to the database, including type of computer equipment needed.
6. Prepare pockets, labels, and cards for borrowing.
7. Mark it with a copyright warning or label it copyable and include instructions.

Manuals and Other Support Materials

As an administrator, you should include in your budget some money to subscribe to computer magazines and professional journals, and to buy books, as well as to purchase software. A teacher who wants to learn BASIC should be able to borrow a book on the subject from the school library. Magazines on educational computing ought to be available in the various teachers' lounges and/or on a circulation system.

While all such support materials ought to be centrally catalogued, it is appropriate for certain of them to be stored near the computers for easy reference. Manuals for the equipment, software lists, master diskettes, and programming manuals are examples of materials which need to be near the computers.

CARE AND FEEDING OF EQUIPMENT

Like all school equipment, computers need to be maintained and repaired. Responsibility for equipment must be clearly assigned and adequate budgetary provisions made for repair.

Checking In New Equipment

Most schools have procedures for receiving new equipment. Perhaps the media specialist sends in the warranty card, files the guarantee and instruction booklets, records the serial number and model number on an inventory sheet (or, better yet, a computer-based inventory program) and puts the school's name on the back. Obviously all of these tasks need to be done for computers, so what's so difficult? The primary differences are that a computer tends to come in detachable parts (monitor, connecting cord, console, disk drive, disk controller card, printer, printer interface, etc.) and that it has many functions, all of which should be checked before use.

The first step must be a performance check. Before the equipment is labelled and put into general use, the person in charge must be sure the components purchased work satisfactorily together. Will the printer accept output from the word processor? Does all the purchased software run well? Is the screen display what was expected? Does the computer make a good connection to the school's large TV for all-class lessons? Will it save and retrieve programs reliably? Warranties are often quite short in duration, so it is a good idea to discover potential problems early.

The second step is to take care of the many parts. Each has its own set of numbers, its own warranty, and its own instruction booklet. So the person in charge of checking in the computer must set aside some real time to do this properly. Each detachable piece should be labelled—p.c. boards and cords and hand controllers as well as the larger components. The first time you do a workshop and begin to trade components you'll be awfully glad for those labels which allow you to get every computer's boards back in properly when the workshop is over.

As an administrator, you must ensure that an appropriate staff member is given time to do these tasks, for the time involved is not insignificant.

Maintaining Equipment

Many schools recruit a group of interested students to do regular routine maintenance such as cleaning tape heads, demagnetizing, wiping dirt from the exterior, and blowing or vacuuming dust off internal components. At the same time, such a crew can also check to be sure all of the keys work, that the computer continues to read and save programs properly, and that it has its full complement of memory. Obviously, an adult needs to train such a crew and to be in charge, but it need not take a lot of adult time. In a secondary school, these roles may be an extension of the responsibilities of the AV club, but even ten or eleven-year-olds are quite capable of these tasks.

Other simple maintenance tasks which someone needs to be responsible for are replacing paper and ribbon on a printer and replacing blown fuses. Also, you should find out from the dealer what maintenance routines are recommended. Summer is an excellent time to perform more extensive maintenance tasks, which may require disassembling, such as cleaning disk drives and printers.

Supervising Equipment Use

Someone needs to be in charge of all of this expensive equipment. That person must know where portable equipment is located at all times. Policies must be developed about safe procedures for moving equipment from one location to the next. But the biggest responsibility is seeing that all computers are properly supervised at all times.

During classtime, whether in a classroom, library or lab, supervision will clearly be done by the adult in charge of that group of students or by some volunteer or advanced student assigned to the task. Whoever is in charge must be able to troubleshoot and assist with the task at hand, to avoid frustration and maximize learning. Common skills needed are how to load, run, stop and re-run a program. If students are programming or writing, the person in charge should also know how to save, edit, and retrieve programs or text.

More difficult is the issue of who will supervise student use of a classroom computer before and after school or during lunch or the host teacher's free period. Because the demand for computer time is high, it is hard to deny students the opportunity to use computers constructively during their free time. Yet a teacher with a classroom computer should not have to remain in the room all day! Again this situation calls for a creative and cooperative solution developed by a group of interested staff (and perhaps parents). Sharing the burden is the answer, but it won't happen without some administrative leadership and encouragement.

Repairing Equipment

Although microcomputers and terminals have few moving parts that can wear out (exceptions are keyboards, tape recorders, disk drives and printers), schools are hard on them, and they do demand repair occasionally. Since computers have only been common in schools since about 1980, most school audio-visual maintenance personnel are only beginning to become familiar with repair procedures. Generally schools depend on a dealer or, if they are lucky, the local vocational high school may have an electronics shop that can help.

As with all of the other functions we have discussed, someone needs to be in charge and to take responsibility for the steps in the repair process.

Determining the need for repair. Because terminals and microcomputers in a school are used by hundreds of different people, few of whom feel any responsibility for their condition, unless a system of reporting problems is introduced, a station may need a minor repair for months without anyone in authority knowing about it. When discussing maintaining equipment, (see p. 115), we suggested a regular routine check of the computer's functions by some group of trained students. This will pick up problems such as keys that stick or functions which do not work. In the absence of such a group, each station might have posted near it or on its exterior a 4 x 6 card where users can note any problems they detect. The person in charge of computer repair can then double-check the machine.

If a computer is not working properly, the person in charge should at least do the following:

- Check fuses (if any).
- Check switches on the terminal or modem to see that they are set right.
- Unplug the machine and open it up to see if any connectors have come loose.
- Press down on all chips to see that they are well seated in their sockets.
- Remove and replace any auxiliary p.c. boards to tighten their connections. Be sure they are in the correct slots.
- While the machine is open, blow dust and dirt away from components using a pressurized can of Super Dry Arctic Freeze or a similar product.
- Put the machine back together and try the function in question again.
- Exchange one component at a time with those from another computer of the same make, in order to isolate which piece is malfunctioning.
- run any diagnostic software which can be obtained from the dealer. (Sometimes these programs can quickly identify a single chip which has failed or can show that the disk drive's timing is off so that a staff member can fix it without sending the computer out for repair.)

With some training, staff members can learn to do minor repairs, as well. They may be able to adjust the head on a tape recorder or the speed of the disk drive, for example.

Once the need for repair has been clearly established, all known information about the problem should be written down. This will save you money, because it will save the repair person's time. Create a standard form to contain this information, along with the date, serial number of the equipment being repaired, and a space for a description of the repairs made and the cost. When the repair is completed, this sheet can be filed by serial number so that the repair record for a single machine is all in one place. This will help identify machines which have become so expensive to keep in use that they should be replaced. It will also alert the person in charge of computer repair to a chronic problem that the dealer has not really fixed properly. This sort of equipment maintenance database is a perfect candidate for computerized treatment (see Chapter 8).

Repair contracts.   Most larger computer systems are covered by a repair contract, and microcomputers can be, too. The provisions vary (as does the price) according to your needs. Again, keep in mind your priorities. One can require that repairs be done on site within 24 hours (expensive), or at a central site in the district when three or more machines need repair at once (less expensive), or at the dealer's site with no time limit imposed (cheapest). It's all a matter of how badly the school needs all of the stations up and running all of the time and how scarce personnel time is to truck machines around the district or out to the repair shop.

If it is decided that school staff will transport the computer to a repair site, it is important to identify the persons who may do so and to write some policies regarding how equipment should be carried. The person doing the carrying will want to know who is responsible if it is dropped, and the administration will be happier knowing that there are clear instructions about protecting equipment in case of rain and about carrying it on the floor of a vehicle, so it cannot jump off a seat.

Time lost.   One of the single most important factors in choosing where to purchase computer equipment should be the quality, speed, and reliability of their repair shop. Months of instructional time can be lost while you wait for a part to come in. Hours of staff time can be wasted trying to track down a piece of equipment that has been sent out for repair (or trying to locate the repair person who was supposed to show up last week).

Some districts keep a central group of spare machines to temporarily replace those that are being worked on. Once warranties have run out, keeping spare parts on hand to do simple repairs can also be smart.

Checkout of repaired equipment. Don't sign the slip until you've verified the repair! If you have a reliable repair person, it is probably alright for the school secretary to sign for the computer's return, but unfortunately in many cases this is not smart (unless that secretary is also the person responsible for determining when machines need repair). Again, here is a situation where the administrator whose budget is being impacted by repair costs needs to clearly identify a person who can be called on a moment's notice to check out a machine returning from the shop to be sure its condition is acceptable.

Who pays?   When schools start to purchase computer equipment, administrators must start to budget for their repair. They must also establish clear policies regarding which budgets these monies come from. For example, in a high school, repairs may be part of a media budget or a department's budget, depending on how the ownership is determined; for elementary schools, repair funds may be budgeted in a district-wide account or in individual building accounts.

GROWTH OF COMPUTER FACILITIES

Once a school begins to use computers, it will find that its needs expand quickly. Administrators need to plan and budget for growth of their computer facilities.

Keeping Up to Date

Every week dozens of new software packages appear on the market, and new computers, printers, and terminals are introduced almost as frequently. Keeping up, so that schools can take advantage of a new educational opportunity when it arises, is a very difficult task.

Periodical subscriptions can help since some editorial staffs of journals try to weed the junk offerings from the significant advances and report only on the latter. But even these can be overwhelming to plow through each month.

Having one teacher or librarian perform a clipping service for others can also assist, especially if the burden is divided among several people. If, for example, it is Ms. William's job to read a particular magazine each month, she would be responsible for sending copies of interesting articles or reviews to the departments and individuals she thinks should know about these. For example, the review of a science simulation would go to the science department head (with a copy also to the central reference file of software reviews). All elementary principals might receive a copy of the article on *Big Trak*, while teachers of BASIC would get the one on structured programming. Copying and sending out such articles is time consuming for the individual, but saves the time of those whose primary responsibility is not in the computer field.

Some districts publish a newsletter for teachers and administrators which is put together each month by persons who keep up with the journals and reviews.

While this is a big job, it may be a good vehicle for distributing information of other sorts, too. For example, it might inform computer users that they can order blank disks at a low bulk rate by contacting the district purchasing office. Or it might detail a new maintenance procedure or announce in-service workshops. Courses in computing at local colleges might also be listed.

User groups are another way to keep up with new developments and get answers to questions. These are organizations formed by people all of whom use the same brand of computer or all of whom are interested in a particular computer application, such as education or *Lotus 1,2,3*. Local computer stores will generally be able to steer you to appropriate user groups. Monthly meetings often offer a speaker as well as an informal opportunity to share information and software. Designate someone in your school to attend and report to the rest of the staff.

Advisory groups of parents and knowledgeable community members can also be invaluable in helping keep equipment and software up to date. In addition, their recommendations may carry considerable weight with the school committee or central administration. As taxpayers (and parents), they have a vested interest in seeing that the schools get the best educational bang for each buck, so they are likely to be hard workers. If at all possible, enlist such a group to help you.

Choosing New Instructional Software

Software is curriculum content, educational philosophy, and teaching strategy all rolled into a (usually) unchangeable package. While teachers can generally modify more traditional print materials simply by skipping a chapter or adapting a worksheet to meet the needs of their classes, software, if it is write-protected (as most commercial programs are), is not so easily modifiable. It is hard to use just part of a program, or to change its pace, or to use the content without the embedded pedagogy. While some programs do allow the teacher to choose a level or rate of presentation, in most programs the programmer or designer has predetermined many of these factors and has left only one decision to the teacher or administrator: whether to use it or not.

This is a great danger that should cause educators to be very careful in their software selections. Yet there is another force driving us to buy, buy, buy—the rush to use computers for the sake of being up to date.

Administrators must provide leadership to their staffs in this terribly important area. If no control is exerted over the purchase of computer software, much money will be wasted on programs which have no logical ties with the existing curriculum, or which do not promote the goals of the district-wide computer implementation plan or which do poorly that which the schools have been doing well until now.

Further, administrators need to provide leadership in a more global arena. Computers have the potential to change the face of education, but it is not yet clear who will decide the direction or pace of coming changes. Administrators need to think especially hard about software, for in it is embedded both curriculum content and pedagogy. Even now administrators can put pressure on software publishers to produce products which are truly helpful to schools. In addition, they can lobby in legislative halls for federal support to develop really sophisticated software to teach the basic skills our students will need in the 1990s. Good computer-based instruction is possible (but very expensive) to produce. Educators need to band together to influence the marketplace to produce excellent products worthy of wide use.

Who chooses?　　Curriculum leaders need to determine whether software being considered for purchase fits with the curriculum and with the teaching strategies adopted by the district. They should decide for what grade levels a program is appropriate and whether it should be a required activity or merely supplemental, perhaps for only a few students each year.

Teachers need to try out the software to find out whether it is usable in their classrooms and supportive of their goals. (Some dealers will loan software for preview, but most vendors require that a school actually purchase the package, with permission to return it for a full refund within 30 days.) If students do not like a piece of software or if they do not understand it or learn from it, then it should not be purchased. This does not mean that every piece of software should be used by a whole class prior to purchase, which is impractical. But it does mean that one or more teachers ought to try out each piece of software under purchase consideration with a few students at the recommended grade level to get some ideas about its value.

In addition, someone needs to make a judgment about whether the software being considered represents a good use of the computer. Any use can be a "good" use if it strongly supports the educational goals being pursued. The questions to ask are, "Does this computer-based activity help (some) students learn better or faster than other methods we are using?" and "Is this use of the computer consistent with our goals for computer use in the schools?" (For example, if the computer advisory committee has placed highest priority on the use of computers as tools, can one justify the use of a fractions game?)

Curriculum leaders, teachers, and others familiar with the computer goals of the schools should all be involved in choosing software.

What is the process for making decisions?　　The structure of the school's decision-making ladder will, of course, partly determine who takes responsibility for software selection. In the fast-growing marketplace for educational software, it is clear that those who take on this responsibility need all the information and help they can get.

As mentioned previously, one source of help is reviews, published either in individual journals or put out in review compilations (see the Resources section of this book). Beginning a file of these makes some sense so that when someone is interested in an advertised program, that person can look in the file to find one or more reviews of the program.

However, one problem with reviews, whether published or done locally, is that educators have widely divergent views about what makes a program good. For some, the fact that it is a drill-and-practice program condemns it to the ranks of useless page turners. For others, that drill may respond to a particular student's need for instant feedback and external reinforcement. Some reviewers pan a program which is not completely "crash proof." Others are more concerned with the educational philosophy embodied in the program. In short, reading reviews is an art; one must be prepared to infer the prejudices of the reviewer and to glean as many solid facts about the program as possible, so that one can make an informed judgment. That judgment needs to be made on the basis of the educational needs of each school, classroom, and even individual student, not on the reviewer's personal opinions.

Locally done reviews are another vehicle for gathering information. If, on the basis of the catalog description and any reviews that could be found, the curriculum leader and teacher decide it is worth the trouble to try to obtain the program for preview, they can then do such a review. A friendly dealer may be willing to obtain a copy for a school to try out for a week or so. As previously mentioned, most software distributors now allow return of software within thirty days, as well. In some cases, a school might need to send a committee to a teachers' center or other software preview location to look at and report on several apparently desirable programs.

There are many software review forms which may serve to guide the review team as they look at software. Each has a slightly different emphasis and format. Appendix A contains a software evaluation form created for the Addison-Wesley series on *Computers in Education*. A school can, of course, make up its own form based on its needs and philosophy.

No matter what form is used, the process of looking at software is a lengthy one and very costly in terms of personnel time. Good decisions will not be made unless time is set aside for this activity and someone is given the responsibility of seeing that such review sessions take place. Administrative support is crucial to this important educational process.

So far we have been discussing commercial software, but two other options exist: educators can write their own and they can obtain public domain programs. Public domain software that may be legally copied is available from a number of sources. (See the Resources section of this book.) These programs are usually available by the disk-full for a nominal charge. They are also the sort of software that one encounters at user group meetings, when people trade their programs. Magazines are another source (you enter the BASIC program listings yourself— a tedious and error-prone process.) Most public domain programs have been written by educators for their own use.

The drawback to these programs is often their poor quality. Most are easy for the novice user to break out of; no one guarantees them to be error-free; and many are quite trivial drill-and-practice activities (the easiest type of program for programmer/teachers to write). These same criticisms can be made about a sizable percentage of commercially available programs, so if teachers have the time to weed through them perhaps they have lost nothing by trying. Remember, though, that the review process is just as important here as it is with commercial software. No matter who made it, a program embodies curriculum content and an educational philosophy that teachers will want to check for consistency with their own. The only difference is that since these programs are not write-protected and are generally written in BASIC, they can be easily modified by a local programmer to meet a teacher's needs.

For teachers themselves to write programs, whether from scratch in BASIC or using an "authoring system," is a very time-consuming process. Even modifying public domain programs takes considerable time. It is important for teachers and their supervisors to determine if the time and effort to be expended will be worth the educational result. Prior to any coding being done, teachers should propose their ideas for programs to their curricular supervisors, who should carefully review the proposals to help shape their learning strategies and the content. This is almost like the software review process, but it takes place ahead of time. Designing software requires that one discuss the same issues brought up on the review forms. One must make decisions about the desired interaction, motivation, feedback, reporting, and a whole raft of other educational issues. Once a plan is outlined, someone must convey the requirements to a programmer. (The programmer might be a student, parent, or another teacher.) Several revisions of the program will probably be needed before it is classroom-ready. Students, by the way, are the best critics.

Hosting Visitors and Planning Publicity

The local paper, parents, a neighboring superintendent, or a state education agency representative may express curiosity about "what you're doing with those computers." Unless visits become a common occurrence, they can be handled on an *ad hoc* basis. But keep in mind that the growth of computer use in schools is going to cost a lot of taxpayer dollars. Putting your best foot forward may be terribly important for obtaining support from the community. Delegating the hosting of visitors to an articulate, enthusiastic, and knowledgeable spokesperson is the best policy.

Plan, too, to let the public know in other ways about your efforts. Parents welcome an opportunity to learn about their children's activities with computers. Remember that computers are very new in the world, and many people have had little opportunity to get over their fear and skepticism about them. Since community support is important to the present and future success of your program, you need to educate the public and the parents about the joys and rewards of computing. A display at the local library, a demonstration at the meeting of a civic organization or PTA, a computer fair put on with the help of students as well as local vendors, a feature article in the paper—all can be effective. Find someone in your school who has a flair for organization and work together to plan such activities.

A third way to obtain community support is to share the computers with them. Sponsor hands-on adult education programs in the evening, on weekends, and during the summer. Taxpayers who don't have children in the schools will more readily support the purchase of more equipment if they see it as a town-wide resource instead of just another expenditure for the schools.

Planning Future Purchases

The one-year plan will be reviewed and revised each year. These revisions will be reflected in new needs for equipment and materials. Administrators must then translate these requirements into budget proposals.

If word processing is going to start at the high school next year, the budget must reflect the cost of the printers to be purchased over the summer. "But how do we know how much to budget, with so many new products coming out daily?" one might ask. The answer is to plan on the basis of currently available equipment at approximately current prices, and hope that improved technology and falling prices will make it possible to buy more or better quality equipment than had been anticipated.

A word should be said here about the joys and dangers of equipment purchased by PTAs or class garage sales. Publicity efforts will tend to encourage such acquisitions, but should also include a plea that groups who wish to donate equipment to the schools check through some central authority about precisely what type of equipment is compatible with the district's plan and needed most desperately by the schools. If the PTA buys an Apple in a district which supports only TRS-80s, it may not be pleased with the long term results.

Translating the plan into budgetary reality means more than simply purchasing additional computers. Peripherals (printers, disk drives, graphics tablets), supplies (paper, ribbons, disks), and software will also be needed. There will, in fact, be a tendency to get caught up in what is known as the "Barbie Doll Syndrome,", purchasing accessory after accessory for each computer station. The key is to know what applications will be used at each station and to plan several levels of computing power, according to the need of the individual application.

CONCLUSIONS

This chapter has been designed to help the administrator be proactive rather than reactive in the face of all of the practical issues of management and operational control of computers in the schools. Administrators should use the district-wide long range implementation plan as a firm guide in addressing these various issues and needs. They should take personality and professional strengths into careful consideration, divide the burden, and put education, not computers, first.

Instructional Applications of Computers

7

When immersed in the day-to-day events of administering a school or school system, it may sometimes be difficult for you, the school administrator, to remember that the primary goal of schooling is children's learning and that one of your most important professional roles is as *instructional* leader. Particularly when faced with the forbidding prospect of purchasing and installing a computer system, many school administrators may tend to focus on the financial and bureaucratic aspects of the situation rather than consider the children and their learning. Indeed, the stampede to buy computers for schools in the name of computer literacy exemplifies the subordination of well-developed educational goals to political and bureaucratic imperatives.

Yet, there is no more important role for a school administrator in the establishment of educational computing facilities than as instructional leader. It is you the school administrators who must guide your staff and community in articulating educational goals and matching these with instructional strategies, staff capabilities, and materials support. In considering computer implementation, you and your staff must be prepared to answer questions, such as:

- How may students make effective use of computers in their learning?
- What skills, knowledge and understanding of computers are necessary for today's students?
- Given limited computer resources, what kinds of uses of computers for instruction should have priority?
- How might using computers for instruction alter curricular content as well as instructional methods?

- How will teachers adjust their methods and attitudes to make best use of computers for instruction?
- How will various implementations of computers affect different groups of students and teachers?

Such questions can be important to administrators who have responsibility for determining the role of computers in the instructional program. However, prior to answering these questions, administrators need to understand the potential that computer applications have for fulfilling educational goals. Knowledge about the capabilities of computers in general and knowledge about particular pieces of educational software are necessary starting points, but each administrator must carefully consider these capabilities in light of the goals of the district's overall educational program before making judgments about the impact computers might have in that school system. It is only in relationship to the district's educational goals that the answers to the above questions have meaning for instructional planning.

TAXONOMY OF COMPUTER USE

Historically, computers were first put to use as "number crunchers," machines with incredible capacities for rapid calculations with vast amounts of data. As the mass storage capabilities of computers grew, and as the costs of these machines decreased, computer scientists and educators began to dream of new roles for computers based upon their information-processing capabilities. Thus in the 1950s and 1960s, interest in computers as "teaching machines" spawned the educational strategy of programmed instruction. But as computers have become more widely available in schools, new applications have begun to emerge that depend more on the interactive potential of computers and thus on the relationship between student and computer.

Various educators have proposed taxonomies for classifying the vast and growing body of educational software. Such schemes are intended to provide insight into the appropriate educational uses of software, although most such classification schemes turn out to be imperfect. Categories tend to overlap, and their distinctions are increasingly blurred as new applications are found for computers in education. To complicate matters, a single piece of software may fit into different categories at different times.

In this book, we have adopted Robert Taylor's classification of computer software according to the principal manner in which it engages the student: tutor, tool, tutee.

Uses of the computer as a *tutor* encompass what is often called **computer-assisted instruction (CAI)** or, more recently, **computer-based instruction,** in which teachers may use computers as teaching methods and materials in pursuit of their curricular objectives. Characteristically in computer-based instruction, the computer directs the students' work on the basis of their responses to a series of questions or tasks. Computer-based instruction ranges from simple drill-and-practice exercises to complex simulations with which students probe the workings of natural systems or historical events.

Tools consist of those applications in which students use computers to accomplish a single purpose or a related group of purposes. Some tools, such as the calculation tools of addition, subtraction, multiplication, and division, may be built into the computer and made available to the student at all times. Other specially designed tools come in the form of programs for purposes as widely different as computing mortgage payments, storing any type of data and retrieving information based on it, graphing mathematical functions, doing statistical analyses of survey data, and producing written reports and letters.

The computer is a *tutee* when the student directs it by writing instructions (**programs**), in an appropriate computer language, which describe procedures the student wishes the computer to execute. Writing computer programs is a form of problem solving that requires students to define procedures to carry out a series of steps leading to a solution. Asking students to solve problems in this way is a means for developing their procedural thinking skills. In recent years, Logo, a new programming language has made it possible for even young children to work in this tutee mode in special environments called computer-based *microworlds*.

THE COMPUTER AS TUTOR

Computer-based instruction is currently the most widely practiced form of instructional computing. Hundreds of pieces of courseware are available for teachers to use with their students. Computer-based instruction involves using computers in any one of the following modes:

- Drill and practice
- Tutorials
- Simulations
- Demonstrations
- Games

Drill and Practice

Drill-and-practice software has received the most attention of any type of educational software over the past decade. As a medium for instruction, the computer can offer endless sets of drill-and-practice problems, and these can be assigned by a teacher according to the individual needs of each student. Commercially available software for this purpose is overly abundant and covers every area of the curriculum.

In most cases, drill-and-practice software provides learning exercises similar to those found in student workbooks. The quality of this software varies enormously. Just as with workbooks, attractive graphics displays can be built into the exercises as motivational aids for students. Or the exercises can even be made into games which require students to produce correct answers in order to gain high scores.

Perhaps the main advantage of drill-and-practice exercises on the computer screen over their workbook counterparts is the computer's ability to give immediate feedback to a student upon completion of a problem. The form of the feedback will vary according to the author's views about the appropriate uses of positive and negative reinforcements. Some programs provide graphic feedback such as "happy and sad faces" or even animation and sound such as fireworks exploding. Others stick to text, although there is a great deal of variability in these text messages. For example:

- "Fantastic!!! Do you want another problem?"
- "Sorry, that's incorrect. The correct answer is 34."
- "Wrong. Try again."
- "That's not correct. Would you like a hint?"
- "That's your third error in a row. Perhaps you should ask your teacher for help."

Many observers have noted that students seem to resent negative feedback less when it is given by the computer and that they are more likely to maintain their interest in drill-and-practice exercises at a computer than in a workbook or on a worksheet.

The usual format for drill and practice is for the computer to present the question and request an answer from the student. Questions may be presented pictorially as well as in writing. One program, which tests students' knowledge of states and capitals, randomly picks a state, draws its outline within a larger outline map of the United States, and then asks the student to type in the state name and its capital. (See Figure 7.1.)

In drill-and-practice software the computer usually accepts answers in one of two ways. Either the student is asked to type in an answer which then must be checked against a list of acceptable spellings, or the student chooses from a list of multiple answers and enters the number or letter of the correct one.

More sophisticated drill-and-practice software may give hints to the students who answer incorrectly or may even attempt to analyze the errors students make. The best (and rarest) drill-and-practice software actually uses such error analysis to direct a student automatically to an appropriate next problem. After a predetermined number of incorrect tries, usually three or fewer, the computer provides the correct answer, sometimes with explanatory material.

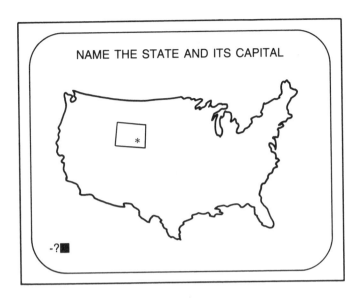

Figure 7.1   Screen from a drill-and-practice program on state capitals

ESTIMATE A VALUE FOR 89 x 111.
950
THAT'S NOT VERY CLOSE. A BETTER ESTIMATE WOULD BE 9000 OR 10000.
LET'S SEE WHY.
FIRST, WHAT DO YOU GET IF YOU ROUND OFF 89 TO THE NEAREST TEN?
90
GOOD! NOW, WHAT RESULTS IF YOU ROUND OFF 111 TO THE NEAREST HUNDRED?
100
GOOD! NOW YOU CAN MAKE AN ESTIMATE BY MULTIPLYING 90 x 100. KEEP TRACK
OF THE ZEROES
9000
VERY GOOD! CAN YOU MAKE A CLOSER ESTIMATE?
9500
FINE! LET'S TRY ANOTHER PROBLEM.

At the end of a drill-and-practice session, the computer can report the number
of exercises a student has attempted and the percentage of correct answers on
the first and any permitted subsequent tries.

Although most educators would find a steady diet of drill and practice an
uninspiring approach to instruction, this type of software appears, at least for
the present, to have a definite role to play in many areas of the curriculum. In

situations where a teacher needs to provide individualized assignments to students or wants some students to spend additional time on reinforcement of a concept taught in class, or recognizes that a small number of students require remedial work on a basic skill, drill and practice offers promise.

One possible reason for the current popularity of drill-and-practice software is its familiarity to teachers. Of all instructional applications of computers, it comes the closest to methods, such as workbooks, that many teachers have used for years. Thus teachers are more comfortable with drill and practice than with more innovative computer-based instruction, such as simulations, or with programming languages. Drill and practice can help teachers to promote traditional student learning objectives more efficiently, via more or less traditional methods.

However, to many educators, computers have far greater potential for instruction than this. They can revolutionize how students learn and what they learn, teaching methods and curricular content. These educators argue that to ignore *these* possibilities in order to cater to teacher conservatism is a waste of a powerful learning tool and runs the risk of computers ultimately falling into disuse, as the latest failed audio-visual fad.

Although it is true that computers can be used in a school for drill and practice *and* in other more imaginative ways, limited computer resources are bound to require school leaders to establish priorities. And these priorities will set the tone for how computers will be viewed and used by teachers and students. Thus school administrators must exercise leadership in helping their staffs to thoughtfully prioritize computer use for instruction. If drill and practice is to play a role in the curriculum, let it be by affirmative decision, not by default to maintain the *status quo*.

Tutorials

Today's computerized tutorials are an outgrowth of the teaching machines of the 1960s. Based on behaviorist assumptions about learning, these products begin by introducing small amounts of new information to the students. Then they allow the students to practice these new concepts, followed by testing them for understanding. Finally, based on this testing, they direct the student to review the material or to proceed ahead to the next concept.

Computers have several advantages over textbooks and other media for such tutorial instruction. It is easier for computers to control the amount of information introduced at one time and to limit the amount of information on the screen so that the student is not distracted from the main concept being presented. Moreover, the graphics capabilities of computers are not limited to static pictures. A student can watch a graph as it develops or shift concentration from one aspect of a picture to another as each is successively highlighted by the computer.

Computerized tutorials have been available for many years. However, until recently their use in schools has been inhibited by insufficient numbers of computer stations and the memory limits of inexpensive computers. Thus, such tutorials have been used primarily outside of schools, particularly in settings where individuals can work independently at mainframe computer terminals such as at libraries or college computer centers. It is for such settings that Alfred Bork and his colleagues at the University of California, Irvine, have developed and tested many examples of tutorial software in the sciences.

More recently, breakthroughs in microcomputer software design have made possible reasonably sophisticated tutorials that will run on most common personal computers with as little as 64K bytes of **RAM** and a disk drive. Fig. 7.2 shows a sequence from one of the programs in the Arrakis Advantage series.

It is not clear whether tutorial software will ever become established in school settings. It carries with it some heavy although contradictory liabilities. On the one hand, even the most sophisticated tutorial design today does not provide the computer with the skill of a teacher to ferret out the sources of student confusion and make appropriate suggestions. On the other hand, the very idea of a computer providing primary instruction is anathema to many teachers who fear being displaced by computers. Thus far, such fearful teachers have seized upon the limited "intelligence" of computer tutorials as reasons for rejecting them. Very little tutorial software is available for, or used in, schools today.

Simulations

A simulation is a programmed model which contains information about a particular environment, either social or natural, and displays the effects of varying any of a number of relevant factors which are under user control. Computer simulations have been used by the military and in industry for years to investigate the possible effects of various actions that would otherwise be impossible or undesirable to test, such as a nuclear attack or the dumping of chemical wastes.

During the late sixties innovative curriculum developers began using simulations with students to provide a more experiential route to understanding concepts they were studying. Simulations of historic encounters, presidential elections, anthropological speculations, and interpersonal situations were designed as board games, paper-and-pencil tasks and role-playing activities. Then, with the increase in the numbers of computers in schools, software designers began to develop computer simulations for classroom use. For example, *Lemonade* is now a classic simulation, suitable for elementary and junior high age students, which measures the daily success of a lemonade stand as students vary the number of glasses made, the cost per glass, and the amount of advertising. This simulation can be viewed as a game which pits students against an unknown economic algorithm, or it can be seen as a vehicle for helping students develop a feeling for the dependence of success on a variety of business and economic factors.

Recognizing that computers in classrooms will, for some time, be a limited resource, Tom Snyder has developed a number of computer simulations for students of middle school age that are appropriate for whole-class use with just

Man has always known about light, but he has only thought about it scientifically for a relatively short time.

Introduction Characteristics of Light

Press RETURN to continue, ? for help

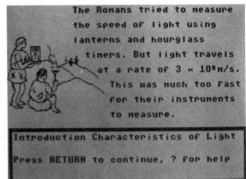

The Romans tried to measure the speed of light using lanterns and hourglass timers. But light travels at a rate of 3 × 10⁸m/s. This was much too fast for their instruments to measure.

Introduction Characteristics of Light

Press RETURN to continue, ? for help

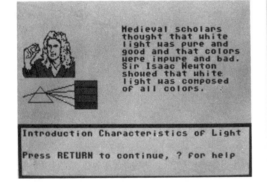

Medieval scholars thought that white light was pure and good and that colors were impure and bad. Sir Isaac Newton showed that white light was composed of all colors.

Introduction Characteristics of Light

Press RETURN to continue, ? for help

Here are some known facts about light. Any good theory of light will have to explain them all.

Introduction Characteristics of Light

Press RETURN to continue, ? for help

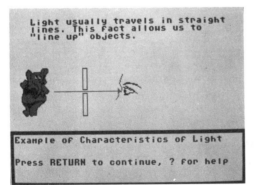

Light usually travels in straight lines. This fact allows us to "line up" objects.

Example of Characteristics of Light

Press RETURN to continue, ? for help

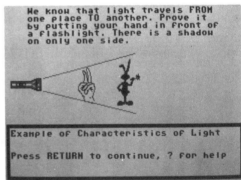

We know that light travels FROM one place TO another. Prove it by putting your hand in front of a flashlight. There is a shadow on only one side.

Example of Characteristics of Light

Press RETURN to continue, ? for help

Figure 7.2   Screens from the *Arrakis Advantage* tutorial series

a single microcomputer. In his *Search Series*, students are divided into teams, and each team is given a short session at the computer during which its members must extract information they need to make subsequent decisions. The activities are designed to reward cooperation, careful record keeping, and the ability to make reasonable inferences from incomplete data. In *Geology Search*, for example, each team manages its resources while it searches for oil deposits on a mythical continent. In each round, the students can invest a portion of their assets to make a variety of tests at different locations on the continent. Each such test produces new information that the students can use to determine their strategy in the next round. The work at the computer screen is correlated with additional information students obtain in a short instructional booklet about geological formations and paleontological deposits.

In part, the success of a simulation depends upon how realistically it models a complex environment. On the other hand, for use with students, simulations must be more interesting than a set of charts and graphs. Software designers like Tom Snyder have attempted to provide simulations that are at the same time, both reasonably accurate and highly motivating. Indeed, one of the desirable outcomes of classroom use of simulations is that students come to understand that simulations are not real, but rather simplified models which highlight the interactions of a limited number of variables. This is an important lesson for citizens of a society which uses simulations extensively for decision-making.

Simulation as an instructional method is strikingly different from both drill and practice and tutorial. The latter are highly convergent methods. The student is directed to learn exactly what they present. Simulation is more open. There are many lessons to be learned from a simulation, both in terms of content and process. Thus it is much more difficult to measure student learning from simulations than it is to measure student mastery of facts learned by drill. This often means that computer simulations may be harder to justify on the basis of student outcomes. On the other hand, simulations like the *Search Series* make highly efficient use of limited computer resources. In contrast to drill and practice, which is pretty much a solo activity (one student at the computer), a simulation can be worked on by the entire class with a single computer.

Demonstrations

One way to increase the efficiency of drill-and-practice and tutorial software is to use them as demonstrations in the classroom. With the full class participating, a teacher can conduct a lesson in which students' responses are the basis of a dialogue with the computer. For example, in a chemistry class, the teacher could use the computer to present graphically, even with animation, diagrams showing the molecular structure and the formation of chemical bonds of various compounds under study, as in Figure 7.3.

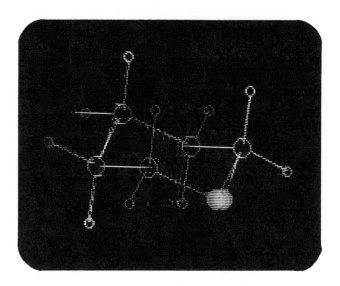

Figure 7.3   Classroom demonstration program showing an organic molecule being rotated

Use of computers as interactive audio-visual devices is both efficient (one computer/class) and comfortingly familiar to teachers. Of course, as with all instructional methods, teachers must learn how to use the equipment and should preview the software before using it. The school media specialist thus has a responsibility for in-service training and on-going support of teachers using computers in this mode, lest the computer join the 8 mm single loop projector, the opaque projector, and the slide/tape projector in the dusty closets of the audio-visual supply room.

Games

The vast majority of software available for computers is in the form of games. Most of these have minimal or even negative educational value. However, there are a growing number of computer games that are well suited for educational settings. Typically these games present students with a goal they must reach by exercising some skill or displaying some knowledge of a particular curricular content. In contrast to other computer-based instruction, many computer games provide feedback to the player in the form of what works better, *not* what is right or wrong. Thus the motivation to do well becomes intrinsic to the activity, rather than requiring extrinsic rewards and punishments.

There are at least three different types of educational computer games. These differ in the principal manner in which they capitalize upon the computer. Games of the first type are really just drill and practice using arcade effects, such as computer graphics and sound or fanciful characters and situations, to motivate students to carry out standard academic exercises. For example, in *Alien Addition* of the *Arcademics Series*, the player shoots answers at descending alien spaceships carrying addition problems. The player loses if any of the spaceships reach the ground before being destroyed. Although the rewards of getting right answers in such games may be more exciting than in traditional drill and practice, the facts recalled or the skills being drilled are not intrinsic to the game play.

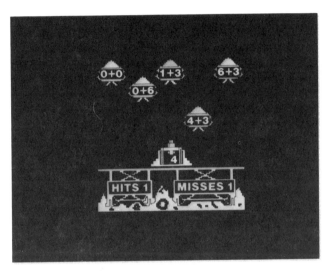

Figure 7.4   Screen from drill-and-practice game, *Alien Addition*, from DLM's *Arcademics Series*

Games of the second type are computerized versions of standard educational games. Given limited computer resources, this use of the computer may seem wasteful, yet there are distinct advantages to the computerized versions of these games. For one thing, having the computer assume the role of opponent may make a game easier to use in a classroom. The teacher can arrange for one or two students at a time to use the game without interfering with other class activities. Further, many of these games permit the teacher to adjust their difficulty levels and even content to the learning needs of individual students.

The best of this second type of educational game require students to apply some knowledge or skill to succeed. The game play is intrinsic to the learning objectives! An example is *Taxman*, in which students identify the multiplication factors of numbers in a changing list in order to compete with the Taxman for a net gain. In each round the student begins by selecting a single number from those that remain on the list. This is added to the student's score. The computer then takes any smaller numbers that are multiplicative factors of the student's choice and adds these to its score. The student is only allowed to select numbers that have factors remaining on the list. When no such numbers remain, the Taxman collects all the remaining numbers. This game places a premium on recognizing the factors of numbers, recognizing prime numbers, and developing a strategy for the order of selection of numbers.

HOW MANY NUMBERS DO YOU WANT?
6
O.K.
1 2 3 4 5 6
WHICH NUMBER DO YOU PICK?
5
OK. TAXMAN GETS 1. THE SCORE IS: YOU 5 TAXMAN 1
THE REMAINING NUMBERS ARE:
2 3 4 6
WHICH NUMBER DO YOU PICK?
6
OK. TAXMAN GETS 2 AND 3. THE SCORE IS: YOU 11 TAXMAN 6
THE REMAINING NUMBERS ARE:
4
THERE ARE NO FACTORS OF 4 LEFT SO TAXMAN GETS THE REMAINING NUMBERS
THE FINAL SCORE IS: YOU 11 TAXMAN 10
YOU WIN!!!

Different strategies yield different results. For example, taking the numbers in the order 5, 4, 6 will result in the player winning 15 to 6, while taking 6 first will cause the player to lose by that same score.

In contrast to *Taxman*, in which the rules of the game are embedded in the mathematical concept of factoring, *Hangman* provides extrinsic rewards to mastering *any* curricular content. In *Spanish Hangman*, for example, students practice their knowledge of Spanish vocabulary and spelling by guessing the translation of a Spanish sentence letter-by-letter.

¡__ _I_ _ **A**, **A** __ __ _I_ __ __ __ **A** __ __ __ __ __ __ __ **A** __ _I_ __ __¡
LOOK, THERE IS OUR FRIEND!

The variations of software based on hangman are endless, with the best programs permitting the teacher or the student to enter vocabulary lists which are to be used in the game. In this way the game can be directly linked with other work taking place in the classroom.

The third type of educational game uses the computer to present learning tasks in a novel format, not easily achievable without a computer. Students solve problems in a special realm which is characteristic of the computer game and of some particular curricular objectives, usually higher level cognitive skills rather than basic skills or facts. Thus, *The Factory* from Sunburst Communications challenges students' problem solving skills and helps them learn from experience in a factory microworld the significance of concepts such as order of operations and reversability. *Rocky's Boots* from The Learning Company teaches fundamental concepts of computer logic, again by the application of these concepts in a microworld. *Green Globs*, developed by Sharon Dugdale and her associates at the Computerbased Education Laboratory at the University of Illinois, promotes a wide range of mathematical skills and conceptual mastery by challenging students to enter equations, which are then graphed by the computer with the object of using the fewest equations to hit thirteen green globs located randomly on a coordinate grid. In *Green Globs*, as a student's understanding of the properties of equations increases, success in hitting the green globs also improves. This is as true for the beginner working with vertical and horizontal lines as it is for the advanced student using quadratic and higher order equations.

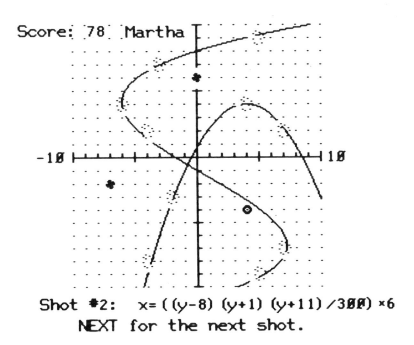

Figure 7.5   Screen from mathematics game, *Green Globs*, developed by Sharon Dugdale and David Kibbey at the University of Illinois at Champaign-Urbana

Games are not new to education. They can play an important role in learning, particularly for young children, and may be strong motivators for students of all ages to apply their developing knowledge and skills. However, recent waves of back-to-the-basics sentiment have included a denigration of the value of such games, resulting in their falling into disuse in many classrooms.

The advent of computer technology and educational computer games offers the chance to reconsider the role of games, in general, in classrooms. Can such games promote the mastery of basic skills? Are they efficient modes of instruction? Can an occasional game provide sufficient motivation for students to become more involved in their other learning activities? Can educational games provide an opportunity for students to apply skills they have recently learned and so reinforce that learning?

If such a general consideration of educational games leads to an affirmative decision by district educators regarding the use of games in school, teachers must then assess whether the use of particular games helps to meet the learning objectives of their classrooms.

In thus evaluating computer games for instructional purposes teachers should ask such questions as: Do the graphics and sound in a game increase students' interest in a topic, or do they distract them from thinking about that topic? Does the game require students to recall factual knowledge, apply knowledge to solve problems, or use skills which are independent of knowledge? Is speed of response an important element of the game and is that an important educational goal? If the answers to such questions are consistent with the teacher's goals, the incorporation of that game into learning activities can add a new dimension to the classroom environment.

THE COMPUTER AS TOOL

Although the pioneers of instructional computing, such as Patrick Suppes of Stanford University, regarded computers as teaching machines which would impart specific facts and concepts to students, more recent leaders in the field have stressed the use of computers as tools for students engaged in the learning process. Thus computers can provide students with powerful calculators, word processors, research tools, and more, for their application to the tasks at hand. Used in this way, the student controls the computer, not vice versa, as is the case with computer-based instruction.

Acceptance of this view by teachers has been slow in coming, however. By and large, education as a profession has avoided overdependence on machines. The traditional tools of learning have been pencil and paper, chalk and chalkboard, books and other written materials. True, in the past two decades audio-visual equipment of various kinds has been added to the repertoires of most classroom teachers, although more often than not this equipment is used to present information to students rather than being used by students. Moreover, much of this equipment has been relegated to school closets, as the audio-visual fad has waned.

Thus if schools are to make computers available to students as tools, school administrators will have to play a major role in helping their staffs to recognize the value of such use. Perhaps the downward pressure from the colleges, which are increasingly requiring students to use computers as tools, will provide the encouragement teachers need to use computers in this way.

Indeed, computers can be a veritable tool kit for students to use, providing a wide range of new possibilities for learning. Not only can students use them to gather needed data rapidly, but they can also use them to carry out many of the laborious tasks involved in the processing of such information. Students can use computers to carry out operations with ease which most of us wouldn't consider doing by hand or even by hand-calculator. Thus computers can free students from forbidding data handling, permitting them to attend to the essential aspects of a problem and to gain deeper understandings of problems by exploring them under a variety of different conditions. Of course, these capabilities aren't always virtues. Sometimes it is valuable for a student to work through the details of a complex task by hand. Teachers must continue to exercise judgment and determine when the use of the computer is valuable in the learning process and when it may subvert a learning goal.

There is potentially an unlimited number of useful tools for learning which could be created on the computer. However, there are practical limits on their availability to us because of the memory limitations of personal computers and the high cost of customized software for most timesharing computers. In the pages that follow, we consider a number of different types of tools that may contribute to student learning. Some are "real-world" tools which can also be useful for various purposes in educational settings, while others are designed specifically with educational ends in mind.

Word Processing

Word processing is the most widely used computer tool in the business world and for home computers. It also offers great promise in education. Word processing software exists in many variations for every brand of computer on the market. All of this software has in common that it allows the user to enter written text into computer memory, recall it as needed, and manipulate it into a final form that can then be printed. The user can add or delete words, parts of sentences, whole sentences or groups of sentences at any point in the text simply by indicating the section to be changed and entering the appropriate command. The user can also change the order of material, moving one section of the text to another location. Most word processing software will also permit a user to define the format in which the text is printed out, including ensuring that lines are right and left justified and that words are not split at the ends of lines. More sophisticated word processing programs provide numerous other capabilities as well, including spelling and punctuation checkers, pre-writing tools such as outliners, and post-writing tools such as variable print fonts.

Word processing greatly simplifies the task of drafting and editing written reports, making it a valuable tool for students and teachers alike. Although term papers are more frequently required of students in secondary school, elementary school teachers are also finding word processing to be a highly motivating way for younger students to learn to improve their written work. Many teachers report that students who have great difficulty writing by hand show marked improvement in their written work when they are allowed to do it with a word processor. This is not so surprising. Some students dislike writing because they do not like the appearance of their own handwriting or because they find handwriting awkward. Many young writers are also reluctant to make changes in what they have written simply because of the tedium or mess involved in erasing and rewriting slowly by hand. Somewhat surprisingly, these students do not seem to be discouraged by the fact that they have not yet been taught to type.

The use of word processing software by students raises some important curricular issues that teachers and their supervisors must address. The most fundamental issue involves access to computers and priorities for computer use. Once students begin using computers for word processing, they wish to use them for more and more of their written work. After all, word processing *is* easier and more rewarding for most people than handwriting or typing their written efforts. Schools making word processing available to students discover immediately that they don't have sufficient computer resources to meet student demands. Indeed, to provide adequate access to computers for word processing alone would probably require no less than one computer for every two students, teachers, and administrators in a school. If computers are to be used for other applications as well, the numbers required increase further. There are few schools today that have, or could, make such a financial commitment to computers.

As has been discussed previously, school leaders must establish both clear priorities for computer use and mechanisms for allocating limited computer resources to a variety of uses and a broad spectrum of students. Because word processing with computers puts a great deal of pressure on such resources, its role in the curriculum must be especially carefully evaluated. Among the questions that must be asked are: What impact, positive or negative, will word processing have on student writing skills, spelling, punctuation, grammatical useage, hand-writing, reading, and subject-matter specific learning? Which students may be helped most by word processing—gifted and talented, handicapped, students with other special needs, or average college bound students? At what age should students begin to use word processing? For which subjects and types of assignments is word processing most appropriate and most efficiently used? Under what circumstances should word processing have higher or lower priority than other uses of the computer?

Needless to say, teachers too will have many occasions to use word processing software for creating worksheets, tests, and supplementary materials, as well as for writing up student evaluations, proposals, and any other documents related to their jobs or professional development. Teacher access to word processing on the limited number of school computers is as problematic as student access, and requires careful planning and monitoring by school administrators.

Numerical Analysis

Spreadsheets.   Spreadsheets are the next most popular real world computer tools after word processing. Initially viewed as business accounting programs, spreadsheets are now used by millions of business and home computer users for a wide variety of purposes, ranging from financial planning to keeping track of sports statistics to running a modern farm. A spreadsheet is quite simply a program which permits the user to enter data and or variables in tabular formats and then press a key to calculate and recalculate values of variables over and over again, as any value is known, or projected, to change.

In school settings, spreadsheets may serve as tools for students, teachers, and administrators. (See Chapter 8 for a description of administrative applications of spreadsheets.) For example, students can use them to manipulate accounting ledgers in business education courses or to do economic forecasting in social studies. They can also be applied to problem solving in science and math. (See Addison-Wesley's *Computers in Teaching Mathematics* for several detailed examples of spreadsheet use in science and mathematics.) The key feature of the electronic spreadsheet is that the student can change any one of the entries on the sheet, and the computer automatically calculates and changes all the other entries which will be affected by that single change. In this way, a student can quickly substitute different values for one variable quantity and try to optimize an important dependent variable, such as profits.

Calculator.   Perhaps the most obvious use of computers as tools is as super-calculators. The capacity to carry out the fundamental mathematical and logical operations (addition, subtraction, multiplication, division, exponentiation, AND/OR) is built into many computers' on-board memory and is available to all computer users through the BASIC language. Moreover, most computers can be easily programmed to do trigonometric, logarithmic, and a host of other special mathematical calculations. Using BASIC, for example, a student can use the computer as a calculator simply by typing in the appropriate commands to give a calculated value as output. For example, the BASIC statement PRINT usually means "print the value of the expression which follows," such as:

PRINT 86*234
20124

(The * is the symbol for multiplication in most computer software.) Or:

PRINT SQRT (A∧2+B∧2)
5

(Here, A and B had the preassigned values of 3 and 4, respectively, and A∧2 means A-squared.)

The student can also define new functions at the computer keyboard. These functions can be stored in the computer's memory and added to its repertoire of tools. For example, the statement:

PRINT MONTHLY.PAYMENT 25000 12 25
$263.31

might calculate monthly mortgage payments on a loan of $25,000 at 12 percent interest to be paid back in 25 years in monthly installments. One advantage of defining new tools like this one is that they can be used to carry out a long series of calculations that would be impractical to do by hand. For example, the command PRINT PRIME 10000 might cause the computer to generate a list of all the prime numbers between 1 and 10,000.

In the last few years, more powerful and more specialized "number crunching" programs, as such software is affectionately called, have been designed for use by engineers and other professionals. Software like *TK! Solver* and *Mu-Math* provide the user with tools for easily solving virtually any quantitative problem, regardless of complexity. With *TK! Solver* users enter the names of the variables in their problem, equations which relate the variables to one another, units for each quantity, any necessary unit conversion factors, and the numerical values of any known quantities. The program then solves the equations for unknown quantities that the user wishes to find. It is unlikely that most physics or mathematics teachers would want their students to use *TK! Solver* in this way, since it would trivialize most of their problem-solving assignments. However, there are numerous physics and mathematics problems whose complexity has heretofore prevented their inclusion in high school courses, despite their relevance and importance. Judicious use of *TK! Solver* could help high school students to solve such problems and allow educators to consider including more sophisticated content in these secondary school curricular areas.

Statistical analysis of data. This is another area in which the calculating power of the computer may make it a useful tool to students, as well as teachers. Most educators agree that today's high school graduates should have at least a rudimentary notion of statistical concepts and be able to recognize when they are applicable. Yet, until the advent of personal computers, the computing power needed for statistical calculations was unavailable to students. As a result, they had to be satisfied with statistical *results* provided in charts and tables in textbooks. They had no meaningful way of manipulating the statistics themselves and thus very little "feel" for their significance. Today, easy to use statistics packages for virtually all personal computers can provide high school, or even younger, students with statistical tools they can use in science labs or social studies investigations. Now, the meaning of a statistically valid result can be understood first-hand. This is an important skill for a citizen of a society increasingly influenced by statistical studies and their results.

Teachers, too, will likely appreciate the convenience of statistical packages that allow them to record student grades, maintain them in storage over periods of time, and later compute student averages.

Graphical analysis. This is another valuable analysis tool. It can aid students to understand data gathered in social studies and science classes, as well as to study the properties of different mathematical functions. For example, *function plotters* produce graphs that show relationships between variable quantities. In Fig. 7.6, a student has asked the computer to determine the slope of the function $y = 3x^3 - 3x$ at the point $x = -1$ and to draw the tangent line to the curve at that point. The computer responds by drawing the complete graph, calculating the slope, and finally producing and displaying the tangent line.

Or, working in the opposite direction, *curve-fitting programs* will find the best equation for a given set of points obtained from laboratory investigations.

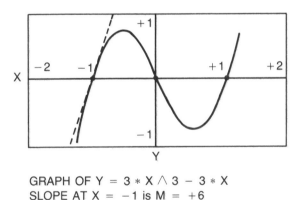

GRAPH OF Y = 3 ∗ X ∧ 3 − 3 ∗ X
SLOPE AT X = −1 is M = +6

Figure 7.6 Output from a function plotter

Information Processing

Along with word processing and numerical analysis, information processing is one of the primary ways in which computers are used in the "real world." For years now, governmental and other institutions have been storing vast quantities of scientific, social science, and other data on computers. These *databases*, as they are called, may then be queried to provide selected information for a wide variety of research and reporting purposes. More recently, with the widespread availability of personal computers, a variety of database management software has been created to allow businesses and individuals to create and manipulate their own, more modest databases.

School applications of database management software range from querying large public databases, such as U.S. census information or election survey data, to setting up much smaller student databases such as books read by members of a class. Database management software can provide students of all ages with the ability to do research more efficiently and more thoroughly than was heretofore possible at the pre-college level. For example, students may be interested in voting patterns in recent presidential elections. Databases are available which include information broken down by state and precinct, about the number of registered voters in each political party, and the number of people who actually voted, as well as percentages of residents who are blue-collar workers, professionals, etc. Suppose the students want to retrieve information, related to one particular variable, such as ethnicity, over the course of several elections. This can be done if the database has been put together in a way that allows students to locate any necessary information with a system of simple descriptors. Such large databases naturally require large quantities of computer *mass storage*, so that they are not maintained directly in the school, but must be obtained from remote databases via *modem*.

Specialized Tools

General tools for word processing, numerical analysis, and information processing have so many applications in school and beyond that facility in using them will likely be seen as an educational requirement in the future. There are, in addition, many specific computer tools used in the real world that can also help students in their studies.

Laboratory simulation. Computers are often used by engineers and industrial designers to test new designs by simulating their actual components with software. Relatively simple laboratory simulation software has also been developed for training technicians. For example, in electronics courses students at some point design and test the properties of electrical circuits. These contain components such as resistors, capacitors, diodes, and transistors, each of which has unique properties. A typical class problem is for the student to determine the amount of current or voltage in a particular part of a circuit. Such problems can be solved with pencil and paper or by actually constructing the circuits in the laboratory and making changes in each of the components as required. But the circuits can also be easily simulated by a computer program and displayed on a computer screen. Then students can indicate a single component of the system and change its value or substitute another component for it. As a result, the computer displays the effects of this change on currents and voltages in other parts of the circuit. Some teachers may object, pointing out that actual manipulation of the components in the lab provides more concrete learning experiences for students in these classes. However, these teachers should also recognize that computers can sometimes permit students to explore values or arrangements of the components that are either inaccessible or too dangerous to test in the laboratory. Computer simulated laboratory investigations may lead to interesting discoveries or new insights into the characteristics of a system under study.

Instrumentation. In contrast to lab simulation, computers are also used in industrial laboratories as tools for recording and displaying data obtained by various measuring instruments. For example, thermometer readings can be converted electronically into small voltages, sent to a computer through cables, and then interpreted as numbers which are displayed on the computer's screen. Such applications are extremely useful in secondary school laboratory investigations since they provide immediate results to students who are often frustrated by obtaining poor data or by careless errors in performing calculations from data. Used wisely, an entire class can contribute data, which together, provide a quick, accurate visual picture of natural laws or hypothesized results.

A number of interesting instrumentation software packages have been designed for classroom use, such as HRM Software's *Experiments in Human Physiology*, which includes a microcomputer interface and a number of probes for measuring respiration rate, skin temperature, heart rate, and response times. With it students can record their own and their classmates' physiological responses in graphic form and so study the effects of diet, exercise, sleep, cigarette smoking, and stress on these biological parameters.

Graphics. As computers became more and more powerful, computer engineers began to design software that could manipulate graphic images as well as words and numbers. Recently, even personal computers have become powerful enough to handle complex graphics information. At their simplest, drawing programs like Reston Publishing Company's *Paint* allow users to do line-drawings and fill in areas with a variety of colors or patterns. More sophisticated programs like Reston's *Movie Maker* even permit users to animate their drawings to create cartoon-like effects on the computer-screen. More serious graphics software, called CAD/CAM (*Computer-Aided Design/Computer-Aided Manufacturing*) is used by engineers and architects to design cars, planes, houses, bridges, etc. Such software permits the user to draw on the computer and then to rotate the drawn image to show its appearance from a variety of angles and viewpoints. CAD/CAM software is just becoming available for personal computers, and soon industrial drawing and art classes will have software to use in this way.

Music Synthesis.   Electronically produced music, once considered esoteric, can easily be explored today with either microcomputers or specially designed synthesizers. Moreover, the computer's ability to produce tones and combinations of tones on a student's or teacher's command makes it an excellent laboratory for the study of music theory. While computer-based music may not appeal to everyone's aesthetic tastes, the computer still offers students, as well as musicians, a rich medium to explore with their creative talents.

Educational Tools

Just as physicists, musicians, architects, and engineers have created tools to explore their fields, so too have educators begun to devise specifically educational tools. However, unlike the former tools which deal with the subjects under investigation, educational tools focus on processes of learning.

SemCalc.   Results from a 1978 National Assessment of Educational Progress Report revealed that students' abilities to solve problems in mathematics were considerably weaker than their abilities to carry out numerical and algebraic calculations. The report concluded that problem-solving as a skill is not developed systematically in schools even though its importance is universally recognized. This finding has inspired educators such as Judah Schwartz of MIT and Harvard to design computer software to aid students in understanding and solving problems. The first of these programs, called *SemCalc* (for *Semantic Calculator*) and published by Sunburst Communications, assists students in using dimensional analysis to solve word problems. To see how this program works, consider how *SemCalc* helps the student figure out the well known puzzler:

> If a hen-and-a-half lay an egg-and-a-half in a day-and-a-half, how many eggs does a single hen lay in a day?

SemCalc is basically an electronic scratch-pad which allows students to record information from a problem in a systematic way and to perform simple operations on that information. The program is unique in that it acts on both the magnitude and the units of each variable. It is the failure to carefully consider units and their implied meaning that often foils students in their problem solving.

Students begin by completing a basic table of information given or implicit in the problem. (The program assigns labels *A*, *B*, *C* . . . to each variable as it is added to the table.)

How Many?	What?
A 1.5	**HENS**
B 1.5	**EGGS**
C 1.5	**DAYS**

Students can then add new variables to the scratch-pad by using the four basic arithmetic operations on the existing variables. The program responds by informing the students of the units the newly caculated variables will have. The students must make a decision at this point about whether the operation has produced a useful result or whether a different operation is what is needed to lead to a solution. *SemCalc* does not tell students whether or not a solution has been reached; it merely carries out each of the students' requests and prompts them with information about units. The students must decide when the solution of a problem has been achieved. The dialogue continues:

OPERATION **B/A**
THE UNITS OF THE ANSWER ARE EGGS/HENS
DO YOU WISH TO CARRY OUT THE CALCULATION?
(TYPE Y) OR INDICATE A DIFFERENT OPERATION? (TYPE N)
Y
1.5 EGGS/1.5 HENS = 1.0 EGGS/HENS

At this point the scratch-pad looks like this:

How Many?	What?
A 1.5	**HENS**
B 1.5	**EGGS**
C 1.5	**DAYS**
D 1.0	**EGGS/HENS**

Now the students can obtain the solution by recognizing that they are looking for "eggs per hen per day." This should result from the division of quantity *D* by quantity *C*.

OPERATION **D/C**
THE UNITS OF THE ANSWER ARE EGGS/HENS/DAYS
DO YOU WISH TO CARRY OUT THE CALCULATION?
(TYPE Y) OR INDICATE A DIFFERENT OPERATION? (TYPE N)
Y
1.0 EGGS/HENS/1.5 DAYS = .67 EGGS/HENS/DAYS

It is important to emphasize again that *SemCalc* doesn't solve the problem for the students, who must still think about the operations and the meaning of their calculated results. Look at the scratch-pad below in which the students have entered some extraneous and misleading information about the number of days in a week:

How Many?	What?
A 1.5	**HENS**
B 1.5	**EGGS**
C 1.5	**DAYS**
D 1.0	**EGGS/HENS**
E .67	**EGGS/HENS/DAYS**
F 7.0	**DAYS**

If the students decide to divide *D* by *F*, the computer will provide the correct units (Eggs/Hens/Days) but not the correct answer to the problem because the units of *F* should have been entered as days/week. If they had been, the students would have seen that *D* divided by *F* was inappropriate, since the units would have been Eggs/Hens/Days/Week.

Because *SemCalc* can handle words and labels in much the same way as it handles numbers, it also has the capability of handling algebraic quantities. Schwartz and his colleagues are completing a variation of this program which will be an aid to students in manipulating algebraic equations.

Writing aids.   Following the publication of the *Bank Street Writer*, as the first real student word processor, educators began to recognize the potential advantages and disadvantages of word processing for students. We have already discussed many of the advantages. Here we will touch briefly on some of the disadvantages, insofar as these have stimulated the development of a new generation of student word processors that have built-in writing aids.

Perhaps the most obvious disadvantage of word processors for students is that despite producing beautiful looking written work, they do not really help students to write better. In fact, the neat appearance of their writing can mislead students into being satisfied with work that is far less than satisfactory and to become demoralized when their teachers return papers with low grades.

Moreover, certain aspects of word processing can even lead to a deterioration in the quality of student writing. For example, it has been observed that many students, knowing how easily they can edit their texts with a word processor, simply plunge into writing without giving it much thought or planning. While this may be an excellent way to overcome writer's block for some, for many others the results may be written work that is so disorganized from the outset that no amount of text editing can fix it.

Further, the powerful text-editing features of most word processors can lead students to focus on fixing individual words and sentences, rather than attending to larger problems of organization and the relationships between paragraphs. Here, too, the limit of viewing a single screen of text at a time can be especially damaging to student writing that has not been well-organized in the first place. Taken together, these disadvantages of word processing have led some teachers to forbid their students to use word processors for schoolwork.

However, several university-based research and development projects have taken a more enlightened view of the problems associated with student word processing. The result has been the creation of several word processing systems, based on the "process approach" to writing, which contain writing aids addressed to these very problems.

WANDAH (*Writing-aid AND Author's Helper*), developed at UCLA, and *Writer's Assistant*, developed at the University of Wisconsin, for example, both include software to help students plan their written work, overcome writer's block, and identify problems in organization, mechanics, and style.

Writing tools like these, which are also beginning to appear in commercial products such as Scarborough System's *Master Type's Writing Wizard* and Milliken's *Writer's Helper*, promise to alter the way student writing is handled in schools. Clearly, instructional leaders must consider such tools and their implications for all areas and levels of the curriculum involving written work by students.

THE COMPUTER AS TUTEE: PROGRAMMING

Although computer programming has been offered as an elective course in many high schools for some years, the advent of microcomputers has led to a dramatic increase in computer use in schools for this purpose. Virtually every survey to date lists programming as by far the most common activity for which school computers are used.

At present there seem to be three major justfications for this emphasis on computer programming in grades K–12. These are: to prepare students for jobs and for postsecondary education; to prepare students for citizenship in a computer-based society; and to use computer programming to enhance a student's general intellectual abilities. As a school administrator, it is incumbent upon you to consider these arguments carefully before commiting significant and expensive computer resources to teaching students to program. The role of student programming in the curriculum is likely to vary with every school and school system, depending on their educational goals. You should not allow yourself to be stampeded by the self-serving computer science establishment and the media into giving any more emphasis to student programming than is appropriate for your students.

PreVocational Training

The traditional argument for students learning to program is preparation for computer-related careers. It is argued that more and more jobs in society involve the use of computers, many calling for actual programming skills. Even for those jobs that do not directly deal with programming, some understanding of how programs work can be very helpful. So, according to this reasoning, most, if not all, high school students should have at least one course in programming. This view has become practically a truism among educators and many politicians.

However, there are those who challenge the notion that schools should prepare students for high technology jobs by teaching them programming. These critics point out that the number of high-tech jobs available is far smaller then imagined, that in fact there is a glut on the market of people with programming skills, that most jobs involving computer use require few, if any, programming skills, and that in any case, technical skills are most appropriately learned on the job, not in schools.

Nevertheless, many high schools and junior high schools now include introductory programming in their curriculum as a required or elective course. Small, very inexpensive microcomputers such as some hand-held computers are well suited for teaching large numbers of students simple programming in BASIC. Some schools have found, too, that older, less powerful micros no longer appropriate for today's computer-based instruction make perfectly adequate machines on which to learn BASIC, for which students don't need color, sound, elaborate graphics, disk drives, or even printers. The cost effectiveness and the simplicity of instruction when using such machines allows almost any school in the country to offer programming courses.

As the name suggests, BASIC is a language developed for the specific purpose of giving computer novices a tool they can quickly learn and use for a variety of purposes. It is a simple enough language that bright elementary school students can be taught its rudiments, while high school students can learn enough in an introductory course to provide them with some ability to create interesting programs. Another strength of BASIC is its availability, in some form, on virtually all computers manufactured today.

A related argument for teaching programming in schools involves preparation for further academic work in computer science, a discipline that is becoming as important as the traditional sciences—biology, physics, and chemistry—to a student's precollege academic career. The Elementary and Secondary Schools Subcommittee of the Association for Computing Machinery has outlined goals and objectives for a computer science course that they recommend be taken by almost all students in the first or second year of high school. The course would be comparable in scope and significance to the type of biology course taken by most high school students today. Increasingly, high schools with strong academic programs are instituting such courses.

Indeed, many schools are going beyond introductory programming courses as they expand their capability to provide vocational and academic training for their students. Schools engaged in serious prevocational training or college preparation are including courses in a number of the more widely used programming languages such as FORTRAN (used in scientific programming), COBOL (business programming), and Pascal (used in training computer scientists). In fact, there now exists an Advanced Placement Test for Computer Science that requires programming knowledge of Pascal.

Schools moving in this direction should be aware of two serious problems they will undoubtedly encounter. Industry and business are changing more rapidly than schools can usually respond to changed needs. Schools going into prevocational preparation should recognize that their courses will need continual review and reevaluation to ensure that they are meeting current training needs. Second, teachers who can teach intermediate and advanced courses in computer programming and computer science are increasingly likely to leave teaching for higher-paid positions in high-technology industries. It is an ironic and disturbing fact that at the same time industry and business are decrying the lack of skilled workers to fill existing jobs, they are recruiting away from schools the teachers who could help train the workers they need. These difficulties should not deter a school from offering introductory programming courses to all students who want and need them, however.

Computer Literacy

A second prominent argument that has emerged recently for teaching programming relates to the notion of *computer literacy*. Although this term has been used by different people in many different ways, we will take it to mean the general range of skills and understanding needed to function effectively in a society increasingly dependent on computer and information technology.

The reason for including programming as part of a computer literacy program is not so much prevocational as it is precitizenship. According to this rationale, so many facets of our lives are computerized that some understanding of computer programming is necessary for the exercise of the rights and responsibilities of citizenship. While such a view may seem rather abstract to some, computer literacy courses and units that include programming have proliferated so quickly that, as of this writing, more computers are used in elementary and secondary schools for this purpose than for any other, by a wide margin.

Elementary school children are being introduced to programming by using programmable toys and by learning a child-appropriate computer language such as Logo, which is discussed below. Junior high, middle school, and high school students are learning enough of programming languages like BASIC, Pascal, or Logo to create programs of their own.

Developers of introductory programming courses in the context of computer literacy programs have found it to be particularly effective to emphasize projects of intrinsic interest to the students, such as graphics, animation, and computer games, as well as real-world data processing or problem-solving tasks. More advanced courses often make a conscious effort to engage students in using computers to solve problems that exist within the school system so that they can carry their projects to completion and actually see their programs implemented.

Some high school computer teachers even have their classes developing simple computer-based instruction programs for other students in the system. Other high schools assign administrative programming tasks to their advanced students or use paid student programmers in their administrative work. Of course, this places much more responsibility on the programming teacher than does a normal teaching load. Nevertheless, it appears that in most cases the teacher is pleased to be involved in such useful projects.

Learning to Think Better

A third argument for teaching programming is the contention that learning to program a computer can enhance a student's intellectual functioning. To educators who hold this view, learning to program offers more than a route to jobs and citizenship. It can help us to learn to think better, more deeply, more clearly, and more profoundly.

This view has been held for some time by mathematics educators and has accounted for the infusion of computer programming activities into high school algebra classes in many school districts. Since the actual behaviors involved in "thinking better" tend to be difficult to describe and evaluate precisely, we tend to lump them into vague categories such as "logical thinking" or "problem solving." Moreover, although programming has been included in some schools' mathematics classes since the early seventies, there is little objective evaluation data confirming the contention that programming promotes thinking skills. Nevertheless, a growing body of anecdotal and observational data does indicate that there are positive cognitive and affective benefits for many students learning programming, however difficult these effects may be to measure. For example, studies at the University of Massachusetts have examined student behavior in solving algebraic word problems. The results show clearly that students attempting the same problems have a much higher degree of success on their first attempt when a problem is expressed as a computer programming task than they do when it is expressed in a more conventional word-problem format.

One of the most prominent and eloquent advocates of the view that computer programming can enhance intellectual functioning, even for young children, is Professor Seymour Papert of MIT. For more than a decade, he and his associates have worked to develop some concrete mechanisms for attaining this goal. The Logo language already referred to, together with a growing repertoire of commercially available features, including "turtle geometry," "sprites," and "demons," have provided children, older students, and teachers with unique ways of being with and learning from computers.

In his book *Mindstorms*, Papert describes how Logo enables children to enter "mathland," a place where they can explore sophisticated, advanced mathematical concepts such as differential geometry, but in terms and ways that they understand and enjoy. For example, programming in Logo involves giving the computer commands and inventing new commands to "teach" the computer, rather than creating a long sequence of instructions in logical order as is done in most other computer languages.

The best known Logo activity is called "turtle geometry." Here, the learner controls a cursor, called a turtle, that can move around and draw pictures on a TV screen. Using common expressions like "forward," "back," "right turn," and "left turn," a student can create exciting geometric designs and cartoon drawings. The immediacy and concreteness of the output—the lines drawn by the turtle—remove programming from the sphere of the abstract, and make it accessible to very young children. When problems occur, learners can "play turtle," placing themselves in the turtle's place and asking "If I were the turtle, what would I do next?" Working with the turtle, students develop a strong intuitive sense of its geometric world, laying a cognitive foundation for future studies in such areas as formal geometry, trigonometry, calculus, and physics.

An important reason for Logo's power as a learning environment is that to use Logo effectively, students must learn the specific subject matter for which they wish to use Logo. For example, if they wish to create an electronic pool game, they need to learn the physical laws of motion governing the behavior of pool balls. The learning process is much like that which a teacher experiences in teaching a subject for the first time. "Teaching" a computer to carry out a task forces a programmer to develop a clear, well-articulated description of the task, which in turn helps build an understanding of the task domain. The fact that a student must create a special language—a set of new commands—to describe each task and its constituent parts makes the teaching/learning/programming process easier, more personal, and more coherent.

Although turtle graphics is the most well known form of Logo programming, it is by no means the only or the most powerful application of Logo. It was developed by Papert and his colleagues to provide even very young children with a context for programming. However, as children become comfortable with Logo and as they develop reading and language skills in school, they can also use Logo's *list processing* capabilities to manipulate words in new and interesting ways.

INSTRUCTION AND TECHNOLOGY IN THE FUTURE

Despite the wealth of instructional applications of computers today, it is probably just a hint of what is likely to become available over the course of the next decade. As computer hardware becomes less expensive and software becomes more sophisticated, the number of pedagogically sound applications in schools should increase dramatically. However, the promise is not just to replace old teaching methods and materials with new ones. The unique interactive nature of computing has the potential to alter the roles of student and teacher in the learning process and to radically change the content of the curriculum.

Several technological advances looming on the horizon promise to stimulate even faster growth of educational computing. The first of these is *voice pattern recognition*, the capacity of a computer to decode information it receives orally through a microphone and to correctly interpret its meaning. When inexpensive computers come equipped with this facility, students will not be required to type instructions and responses at a keyboard, but instead will be able simply to speak to them using an acceptable language for communication. This new development has already been successfully demonstrated in a controlled vocabulary domain. While it will be some time before voice input to computers is economically viable for most applications in schools, it is already finding use with certain handicapped students in special education settings.

A second technology which offers exciting new educational possibilities is the intelligent *optical video disk*. Video disk technology is commercially available today. In combination with computers, optical video disk systems allow storage of and access to a wide variety and a huge quantity of visual and sound images. These can be combined in various ways, including stationary pictures, picture sequences, and moving video sequences at different rates of speed, all under the control of a computer program. A single digital video disk has enormous storage capacity—it can hold the equivalent of thousands of books of text. The entire history of art recorded in pictures could be at a student's fingertips! Or news footage for the past fifty years. Using huge databases stored on such video disks, students could gain unprecedented control over information to be used in their learning.

Another developing technology which has implications for education in the future is *interactive telecommunciation*. With a terminal at home or at some other remote location, students will be able to carry on two-way communications with a centrally located computer system at school. Such communications, already feasible over telephone lines, will be simplified, more powerful, and far less expensive with improved cable and satellite communication. Computer telecommunication makes it easy to send educational material into the home. It also makes it possible for students who are incapacitated by long-term illnesses to participate in a class from their homes. Indeed, some futurists have speculated that schools as centralized institutions may cease to exist in the future! While such a revolutionary change would entail other fundamental changes in society, its possibility is nonetheless inherent in the new communications technologies.

We can also expect significant progress in software capabilities in the next decade or so. This will likely come about as advances in the field of **artificial intelligence** can be incorporated into educational software written for computer systems of the future. Artificial intelligence is a frontier research field in which computer scientists have been exploring the nature of intelligence and human problem solving for the past thirty years. One of the fundamental goals of this field of research has been to devise ways for computers to understand natural language, such as spoken English, so that they can communicate freely with human users. The problem is a difficult one, but its solution could lead to computers which are highly flexible and capable of "understanding" the intentions of students who work with them. Already, primitive natural language processors and a technique called *expert systems* permit computers to interact "intelligently" with users, albeit in highly limited domains. But the scope of these domains will grow as other advances in microtechnology lead to even more powerful computing systems in the years ahead.

We began this chapter with an exploration of the different instructional applications of computers that are available today. We end by imagining where the incorporation of these applications might lead us—what computers in education might look like several years down the road. We will consider three possible scenarios of the future, none of which require exploitation of anything but existing technological capabilities, and all of which would require the active leadership of school administrators for their successful implementation.

Scenario I: Computers Become Everyday Tools for Students and Teachers in Schools

Students have ready access to computer centers or other locations in the school, where they can work and get help from computer specialists as they need it. Typically students spend about an hour each day doing assigned problems, writing papers, or using special databases related to their studies. Some students also use prepared programs to review or study concepts or to do homework their teachers have assigned in their classrooms. Teachers frequently collect homework results in computer files where they can examine them at the end of the day. They also use computers to maintain class records and to monitor individualized assignments for some of their students. In this scenario, although computers are important tools within the school, they are still largely external to the classroom, where instruction is not very different from what it is today.

Scenario II: Computer-Based Instruction Becomes an Important Part of the Learning Process in the Classroom

Advances in software make feasible computer-based tutorial instruction for many topics in the curriculum. Students use computers regularly in their classrooms to learn new concepts, to practice skills, to take mastery tests and, as tools, to accomplish other learning tasks. They also spend part of each day working on higher-level cognitive tasks using programming languages, such as Logo, as tools to help them solve problems. Teachers organize classroom work so that students can work individually or in small groups at computers during part of every day. During this activity, teachers are no longer the focal point of the lesson, no longer the presenters of new knowledge or the leaders of a discussion. Rather they are the facilitators of learning, moving from station to station to assist students as they carry out tasks at the computer. The classroom is, in effect, a series of learning centers where students have access to powerful and flexible learning tools in all areas of the curriculum.

Scenario III: Computer Workspaces Replace Traditional Classrooms in Schools

Students do much of their work each day at computer stations which can communicate with one another and with databases in and outside the school. Through this network, they have access to many teachers, to other students in the school, as well as to other schools and information sources. Students communicate by sending messages and requesting information and help from these various sources. They know how to use the system and its word, number, and data processing capabilities, how to write short programs for organizing information on any topic, and how to use new information for the purpose of learning. The databases they access have unlimited information in the form of still images, maps and diagrams, moving pictures, written and oral text, all of which can be displayed at a learning station. Students spend as much time at the computer as is needed to accomplish their goals for the day. They progress at their own rates, and, in a sense, they are in control of their own learning. Teachers monitor their progress, suggest new directions to pursue, and help them with problems they encounter. Often, teachers assemble small groups of students to work cooperatively on a project, to discuss issues, and to share experiences. The computer system also facilitates learning by interpreting students' questions (using artificial intelligence) and adjusting the presentation of information to students' learning styles.

CONCLUSIONS

There is still a very long way to go before any of these "future scenarios" could be widespread. Along the way, instructional leaders will have to resolve many issues about the use of computers in instruction, including the following:

- Will the availability of computer-based instructional materials create a new impetus for individualized learning?
- Will use of computer-based instruction change the role of teachers in classrooms?
- Will more powerful computer tools open up new domains of knowledge that enhance students' acquisition and understanding of fundamental concepts? Or will they distract from basic educational goals?
- Does work with programming languages, like Logo, strengthen students' basic thinking skills?
- Can we develop systematic curricula which use the computer as a medium for learning?

It is too early to state with certainty the answers to any of these questions. The research on computers and learning is meager. Until recently few schools have had adequate computer resources to test these questions. And likewise most of the software available to schools has been inadequate for realizing anything but isolated fragments of curricular goals. As this situation changes, the answers to these questions should unfold, particularly if we are vigilant and do not lose sight of our fundamental educational goals. Meanwhile, we can expect the number of computers in schools and the purposes to which they are applied to proliferate. Two paramount tasks for school administrators at the present are to provide most, if not all, faculty members with the skills to use this new technology and to begin to engage teachers in critical discussions of computer applications in instruction.

Computer Applications 8
in Educational
Administration

Although most school administrators might like to think of themselves as educational leaders first and managers second, quite frequently, their credibility and success depend on good management of the masses of information to which they must have access. In today's highly politicized climate, school administrators often must produce information to show that the schools are effective and efficient organizations and they must be able to back up their decisions with complete and up-to-date data. Fortunately, this is an arena in which computers can help, provided the needed flow of information is carefully analyzed and systematically planned.

This is not a trivial proviso. Casual, poorly conceived computer use in information management can lead to disaster. As with instructional use of computers in schools, a decision to use computers in schools for information management requires a commitment to long-term planning, the adoption of a systems perspective, and the involvement of numbers of people whose work will be affected. This is where your leadership is needed, for a clear vision of the future must guide the planning process. The consistency and thoroughness with which you visualize your future administrative computing and communications system are critical, since the potential pitfalls are expensive and easy to overlook.

In earlier chapters, we discussed these issues of leadership in the context of planning computer implementation. Our primary purpose in this chapter is more concrete: to familiarize you with the many potential administrative applications of computers in schools.

We begin the chapter with an overview of information management in a school and the role computers can play in helping you handle this critical activity more efficiently and effectively.

INFORMATION MANAGEMENT: A SYSTEMS PERSPECTIVE

In a sense, every task performed in a school or school system may be seen as involving the more general activity of managing information. For example, in any classroom, department, school, or school district, it is necessary to keep track of people and things, to bring people into contact with resources, and to assess and report performance. To carry out these general tasks requires the establishment and maintenance of a variety of record-keeping systems, such as:

- Schedules
- Attendance reports
- Report cards
- Student records
- Personnel records
- Payroll records
- Inventory lists
- Financial records
- Purchasing records

These systems in turn require the collection, storage, and analysis of data; the development of procedures to control the uses and flow of this information; the design of an organizational hierarchy to carry out these procedures; and the assignment of personnel to that hierarchy.

As schools have become more complex, the challenge of accurately keeping track of people and things, efficiently using resources, and accurately assessing performance has become more difficult. Reliance on manual techniques for scheduling, communications, report preparation, inventory and budget control, evaluation, and other required tasks is likely to lead to serious difficulties, such as:

- Inaccuracy and inadequacy of records
- Lack of uniformity in records
- Difficulty in obtaining access to records
- Large amounts of time required to collect and process information
- Small amounts of time available for analysis of information and planning
- Near impossibility of integrating and cross-referencing information
- Inability to obtain or distribute desired and necessary information in a timely manner and appropriate format

One of the major challenges to school leaders today is to devise ways to gain control over the large volume of information available and to use it effectively.

Computers and the Flow of Information

Teachers, principals, department heads, and central office administrators all need information to make decisions. They need information about resources, about students and their learning needs, about budgets, and about staff. Some kinds of information are used primarily at only *one* level of administration. For example, purchasing, planning and research, transportation, and payroll are primarily central office concerns. The principal, in turn, is concerned with staffing, scheduling of classes, health records, and student activity funds. Many kinds of information, however, are used at *all* levels of school administration. Attendance, student achievement, student data, staff data, grades, and equipment and materials inventories all start at the classroom level as concerns of the individual teacher. Yet these types of information must flow to and be used by principals, department heads, and ultimately superintendents as well.

One of the advantages of using the computer administratively in schools is that each administrator can have electronic access to the same files of data and can retrieve them in the form which he or she needs at the moment. For example, using the same student information database, a teacher can generate a class list with addresses and phone numbers; a nurse can print a list of students who need immunizations along with their buildings and room numbers; a principal can integrate all tenth grader's parents' names into a mailing regarding planning for college and have each letter look personalized; a department head can print out book inventories by school compared to projected enrollments in classes; or an assistant superintendent can graph each school's achievement by class level and size.

Today, a number of different kinds of computer systems can make such shared use of centralized files possible. Chapters 9 and 10 provide details about various equipment and communications configurations to accomplish such an arrangement. Suffice it to say here that today's computer technology makes it possible to transmit data from school to central office and vice versa quite easily, and that the emphasis in the best of today's software is on allowing the user to manipulate data flexibly and on allowing the use of the same data by many different people and computer programs.

However, the key to successfully using computers to manage information in your school system is not hardware or software. Rather, it is the way in which you and your staff view your schools and the elements of information to be managed. Successful computerized information management requires a systems perspective, one that recognizes that a school system is indeed a system, that accurately identifies the elements of the system, and that anticipates the various potential connections between these elements. Without such a perspective, even the best hardware/software configuration in the world cannot work.

A Computerized Information Management System

With computers it becomes possible to develop an integrated information management system which facilitates the collection of data and the use of information across levels of school organization. Such a system can reduce the time needed for tasks, facilitate analysis and assessment, strengthen understanding of organizational functions, clarify priorities, and uncover areas needing change. The design of such a computerized information management system is based on a systems perspective, involving several interlocking definitions and relationships:

- Data is the raw material of information. Pieces of data are, in themselves, devoid of meaning.
- Information is the organization of data in particular ways that establish meaning. (Up to this point, we have used the word "information" more loosely to include "data.")
- A wide variety of types of information may be extracted from a common database.
- Similar information may be used in a variety of settings within an organization.
- Information in an organization flows from bottom to top (providing an empirical basis for decision making) and from top to bottom (structuring the activities of personnel).

Let us illustrate these relationships in a school system context.

Data is the raw material of information.   In order to make sense of school operations, hundred of thousands of pieces of data must be gathered. Some of these are indicated in the matrix in Fig. 8.1. Thus the location, characteristics, and condition of every piece of equipment in the entire school system are recorded in the form of discrete pieces of data as part of a district inventory procedure.

Information is the organization of data to establish meaning.   In order for these pieces of data to be useful, they must be organized in some way to yield information that is meaningful. Some of these ways are indicated in the matrix in Fig. 8.2. For example, the presence or absence of every student in every classroom, every period of every day is recorded as thousands of discrete bits of data which may then be organized to yield, among other information, the school attendance list for the day.

A variety of information may be extracted from a common data base.   Because data in and of itself is unorganized, it may be the basis of many different types of information, depending upon how it is subsequently organized. For example, individual student testing results may provide diagnostic information on an individual student, or may provide information on a particular group of students, as an indicator of program effectiveness, or may provide information on an entire grade, school, or district for comparative performance analysis.

Similar information may be used in a variety of settings.   In most school districts, certain types of information are utilized at many levels of operation: the classroom, department, school, district. As a result, time and effort may be saved by sharing

Subject of data

Nature of data	Students	Personnel	Equipment	Materials	Money	Space
Presence or absence	individual student name	individual personnel name	item name	item name		room number
Location	room	room or office	school building and/or room	room		school building
Characteristics	e.g. bilingual	e.g. tenured	description	description	category	e.g. size
Quantity	number	number	number	number	amount	number
Condition or Performance	individual student test result	performance checklist	checklist			checklist

Figure 8.1   Data

Subject of information

Nature of information	Students	Personnel	Equipment	Materials	Money	Space
Presence or Absence	school attendance list	individual teacher attendance record	school inventory	classroom inventory		plant management records
Location	individual student schedule	school master schedule	district inventory	building inventory		list of rooms by capacity
Characteristics	district demographic report	district list of tenured teachers	bid specification	teacher requisition	budget categories	
Quantity	district average daily attendance	district roster by school	district inventory	purchase order	bank account	district plants record
Condition or Performance	grade wide test scores	individual teacher performance evaluation	school inventory			

Figure 8.2 Information (Organized Data)

not only a common database, but also a common set of information (organized data). Some examples of information and the various levels of operation at which they might be used are shown in Fig. 8.3.

	Level of operation			
Type of information	*Classroom*	*Dept.*	*School*	*District*
Statements of goals and objectives	x	x	x	x
Scope and sequence descriptions	x	x	x	x
Descriptions of services	x	x	x	x
Annual schedule and calendar		x	x	x
Annual budget		x	x	x
Inventory lists	x	x	x	x
Purchase orders		x	x	x
Supply requisitions		x	x	x
Maintenance requests		x	x	x
Attendance reports	x	x	x	x
Personnel records			x	x
Program and service assessments	x	x	x	x
Student performance assessments	x	x	x	x
Staff performance assessments		x	x	x

Figure 8.3   Levels of operation at which information can be used

Thus a master list of instructional objectives may be used by a classroom teacher for lesson planning, by a department for creating a list of departmental objectives, by an elementary school for developing a K-6 scope and sequence in a particular subject, and by the district for establishing minimum competency requirements.

Information flows from top to bottom and bottom to top. Information is used to structure activities at various levels of operation and, conversely, it is derived from the outcomes of these very activities. For example, staff performance assessments are used to promote improvement in staff functioning, and they are derived in the first place from observation of such functioning.

DATABASE MANAGEMENT

Perhaps the most important aspect of computerized information management is the manipulation of vast quantities of data. Computers can perform unbelievably large numbers of complex data manipulations in equally as unbelievably short periods of time. They do so by means of software usually called database management systems. However, the software itself is incapable of performing the needed tasks unless the users have customized it to their purposes. And this is not a trivial task. It may be wise to involve a professional consultant in obtaining and customizing your database management system. Still, in the end, it is the user who must decide what data to store and what information to extract.

One important consideration in deciding what data to store is the amount of time necessary for initial data entry to start up the system, and another is the time required to maintain the data in an accurate and up-to-date form. Initial data entry is a huge task. Think of all the possible facts you may wish to store, just for starters:

Student name, residence, telephone, date and place of birth, sex, siblings, parent or guardian, immunizations, communicable diseases, T.B. tests, disabilities, I.D. no., schools attended, homeroom, counselor, courses, teachers, grades, credits, attendance, graduating class, aptitude test names, dates and scores, college board scores.

Textbook inventories, sports teams rosters and records, after-school clubs and advisors, scholarships, class schedules, course offerings.

Street name, map index, school assignment, walking distance, bus stop, safety area.

School building, valuation, square footage, construction, age, class, roof, number and size of rooms, grades, capacity, enrollment, type of fuel, storage capacity, burner specifications, boiler specifications, alarm systems, equipment specifications.

Employee name, address, telephone no., date and place of birth, sex, health record, education, degrees, certification, starting date, position, job code, school, department, grade, salary schedule, insurance, retirement fund.

Let's look more closely at what a school administrator might be able to do with such a vast array of data. Remember that good database software should allow you to use data from the database in letters and reports (via a compatible word processor) and in spreadsheets and tables that require calculated results (via a compatible spreadsheet program). Such compatible software is often called *integrated* since it allows you to integrate into one document data from your electronic files, paragraphs of analysis, charts or graphs produced from the data, and calculations performed initially on a spreadsheet.

Not all data base programs allow such integration, but even simple ones that might be used at the local school level or in a classroom allow users to search, sort and print out data in various formats. Let us look at several examples of reports that might be generated, using just these simpler functions of a database program.

Built-in sorting routines can rearrange data to meet the user's needs. For example, you may want to know the senior class rank or college board scores of students from a particular feeder school. The information from the computer might appear as in Fig. 8.4 showing only those high school students who originally attended Lincoln Elementary School.

ID#	STUDENT NAME	YEAR OF GRADUATION	ELEMENTARY SCHOOL	GRADE PT. INDEX	CLASS RANK	COLLEGE ENGLISH	BOARD SCORES MATH
1234	DOE, JANE	1988	LINCOLN	3.0	150/200	590	580
1371	SMITH, JOHN	1988	LINCOLN	2.5	100/200	510	490

Figure 8.4   Part of a list of students who attended Lincoln Elementary School

More sophisticated packages might calculate average scores or produce graphs contrasting students from several feeder schools.

For bus schedules and passes, you may need an alphabetic list of students by school and by bus stop. Data such as that shown in Fig. 8.5 can be used to generate such lists as well as to check for bus overloads.

ID#	STUDENT NAME	SCHOOL	YOG	HOME ROOM	ADDRESS	MAP INDEX	BUS STOP
1234	DOE, JANE	10	88	2010	100 MAIN ST.	G4	1200-03
1371	SMITH, JOHN	10	88	1030	32 CEDAR ST.	G2	1200-08

Figure 8.5   Part of a list of students sorted by school and bus stop

Employees can be grouped in order of job code, seniority, age, salary, or school. With integrated word processing and mailmerge software, the computer can then also be used to generate personalized letters to notify employees when to report for physical exams or TB tests. Fig. 8.6 represents a partial print-out of employees who were last tested for TB in February 1981 and are due for another test.

These are just a few examples of how administrators could use the sorting capabilities of database management software for analysis and for communication.

Other kinds of information that could be derived from such databases include grade point averages, class ranks, school enrollments, bus stop assignments, bus loadings, payroll (gross salaries, deductions, benefits, net pay and paychecks), seniority lists, preventive maintenance programs, energy usage, utility costs, building inspections, theft and vandalism records, and much much more. Moreover, with the proper software, the busy administrator can manipulate these data into charts or graphs and produce detailed fact-filled reports without manually tabulating, averaging, or assembling the figures.

SOC. SEC #	EMPLOYEE NAME	DATE OF BIRTH	JOB CODE	SALARY	DATE HIRED	SCHOOL	TB TEST
011-11-1111	BROWN, JAMES	09-13-46	12	27,750	09-03-75	05	FEB 81
022-22-2222	JONES, SALLY	06-23-39	15	36,250	08-15-62	11	FEB 81

Figure 8.6 Part of a list of teachers last tested for TB in Feb. '81

One of the biggest time-saving features of even simple data base management software, is the ability to put more zip into mass mailings. Mailing lists in school systems include students, parents, teachers, staff, alumni, PTA members, student newspaper subscribers, college admissions offices, booster club members, vendors, and association members. With database management software, the computer can easily sort these lists by zip code, state, city, alphabet, school, year of graduation, or any other specialized category (e.g., bus pass holders). Most computers can also then print the names and addresses on self-adhesive mailing labels. Sorting a bulk mailing by zip code to comply with postal regulations can be a very time-consuming activity if done manually. With a computer, it is a trivial task.

Among the other advantages of database managed mailing lists are:

1. A single database can be used for many purposes (mailing or otherwise) simply by altering the "sort".
2. It is easy to update and store the mailing list for future use, say, a graduating class used for later mailings.
3. Mailing labels can be generated that other departments in the system can also use (e.g., elementary school parents list passed on to junior high schools).

Database programs are considered standard software for all types of computers. As we have indicated, they range from sophisticated integrated systems to simple programs to store, search and sort through a limited amount of data. Some are very easy to use and to learn to use; others are poorly designed and confusing. It is extremely important that you "test drive" such software prior to purchase to be certain that its capacity (the magnitude of the task it can perform) and its features meet your present and anticipated needs.

The ideal situation is probably to have a large central database tied into offices and schools via terminals, modems on microcomputers, or a computer network. This configuration avoids duplication of data input, allows for quick updates, and makes information easily accessible to those who need it. However, if you can't afford the price of such a system or don't want to become involved in its complexities, it might still be worthwhile to have a small database management system for a given school (or even a given classroom) to keep updated class lists, health records, library overdues, or equipment inventories.

WORD PROCESSING

While designing and implementing a database management system is a time consuming and complex way to make a long term difference in administrative effectiveness, implementing the use of word processing in your system can reap immediate substantial benefits in the efficiency of information flow. Word processing is the fastest way for administrators, secretaries, and office staff to get hooked on computers. Besides everyday letters and memos, word processing can be used effectively for reproducing policy statements and written procedures, contracts, status reports, special studies, newsletters, bid specifications, bus schedules, lunch menus, minutes of meetings, and practically anything else that must be seen in hard copy.

Nearly all word processing software offers the user the ability to format, update, revise, correct, personalize, reproduce, search and replace, and store and retrieve any written document. Moreover, the identical letter may be sent to numbers of people such as school board and PTA members, each individually addressed and with the appearance of a typed original. And, by having the names and addresses stored on file in the computer, the operator can leave the office while the computer prints out the letters. Finally, with integrated software, these names and addresses can come directly from a database.

Word processing demonstrates its worth especially when a lengthy report requires several drafts, or a policy statement will be modified by various boards or committees. Second, third, and final drafts are ready in much less time than it would normally take to cut, paste, and retype them, since the operator can easily insert or delete any amount of text, and can move paragraphs around, seeing the results immediately on the screen. Drafts can be initially double or triple-spaced for easy hand editing, and then switched to whatever spacing is required for the final printed version.

Formatting.   School newsletters are a perfect application of the formatting capabilities of word processing. You can give your school publications a professional look by setting pages into columns (right and left justified) with room for headlines, pictures, and advertisements. Depending on the quality of the printer, you would have the options of different typestyles (fonts), body size and height (points), bold face, border lines and graphics. Using a word processor eliminates the expense and trouble of having to go outside for typesetting of many school publications.

Search and replace.   Bid specifications, bus schedules, telephone directories, and menus are ideal tasks for the search and replace features of word processing. Information which is subject to constant change and reissue can be typed into the word processor and then saved as a file on tape or disk. When it comes time to update the document, the user loads the file back into the word processor, has the word processor search the document for the specific places where changes are to be made, and enters the updated information. With word processing, it will never again be necessary to type the same list or document over and over again because of a few changes. It can be instantly reprinted each time changes are made.

Storage and retrieval.   Word processing also helps with filing and retrieval of information. After typing a form letter or annual report, the user can save it on disk or tape. At a later date, instead of searching through reams of paper or file drawers to find the document, the user simply calls it up from a directory on the computer screen. Work that repeats itself year after year is then ready in seconds to be updated using the search and replace functions described previously. Change the date and add a new sentence or two and, presto, this year's version can be printed out without retyping.

Word processing is available today for every type of computer. When choosing a word processing program from the myriad available, it is important to consider several factors: ease of use, editing features you'll need, formatting and printing options that you'll require, and the software's ability to work in an integrated way with other software such as database management systems, spreadsheets, or graphing utilities. In fact, it is advisable to purchase these four pieces of software for your computer at the same time to ensure such compatibility.

At the local school level, it may suffice to have a relatively easy-to-use word processing program with an inexpensive dot matrix printer, so that all staff can easily learn to use the word processor on an occasional basis. However, in the school office or at the central office, you will probably wish to consider a more complex and sophisticated system, perhaps integrated with other software, and certainly including a top-of-the-line printer which will produce letter quality output. For office use, it might be worth your while to invest in a more professional office computer, perhaps even a dedicated word processor. The vendors of such equipment usually include in the price training for secretarial, administrative, and clerical staff who will use it. With office word processing and/or computer systems, all users may be networked to a hard disk and to one or more high quality printers.

The results of providing word processing capabilities to a school will be astonishing—more and clearer communication, more secretarial time for new tasks, and the tendency to produce documents that are complete, clear, and entirely accurate. Word processing brings both greater efficiency and greater effectiveness to your system.

FINANCIAL ANALYSIS

Electronic spreadsheet programs can convert budget analysis from a nightmare into an exercise in administrative control. They can quickly give administrators a real sense of power over their budgets and the confidence to defend them. This is another example of a computer application which can be implemented fairly quickly and easily, with a big payoff right away. However, unlike word processing, learning to use spreadsheets effectively may require several days of training and practice with a knowledgeable instructor. Nevertheless, it will be well worth the costs and effort.

We have discussed electronic spreadsheets briefly in previous chapters. They are computerized, instantly revisable versions of large-sized accounting spreadsheets, with many rows and columns. The user defines by means of formulas the relationships among the entered numbers, and the computer does the calculating (totals, averages, percentages, etc.). The enormous power of an electronic spreadsheet comes from its ability to let the user change one or more values on which the other numbers depend and to recalculate the entire sheet on the basis of these changes. It allows the administrator to ask "What if . . . ?" about very complicated systems and get the answer immediately.

While useful to the individual principal for budgeting, electronic spreadsheets have become practically essential to central office administrators for use with salary schedules, salary costs and distributions, budget forecasts, long range planning, cash management and flow, balance sheets and budget reports, tax distributions, statements of revenue and expenditure, and comparative reports by building or department, to name but a few applications.

The following example leads you step-by-step through one use of an electronic spreadsheet program, so that you may see its features.

1. Define the objective. In this example, the objective is to develop a fuel budget for a school system.

2. Format column headings and row names. The user enters whatever column headings and row names seem appropriate. In Fig. 8.7, we've labeled the column headings with various heating fuel units and costs while the row names are the school buildings in the system.

```
                        FUEL BUDGET FY 1986
------------------------------------------------------------------------
                GAS           #2 FUEL OIL        #4 FUEL OIL        TOTAL
BUILDING    CCF      $        GAL      $         GAL      $          $
------------------------------------------------------------------------
SCHOOL A
SCHOOL B
SCHOOL C
SCHOOL D
SCHOOL E
------------------------------------------------------------------------
  TOTAL
```

Figure 8.7 Fuel budget spreadsheet column and row labels

3. Enter constants. In this example, we enter the annual fuel consumption, averaged over the last three years as in Fig. 8.8.

```
                       FUEL BUDGET FY 1986
-----------------------------------------------------------------------
              GAS         #2 FUEL OIL      #4 FUEL OIL         TOTAL
BUILDING   CCF     $      GAL      $        GAL      $           $
-----------------------------------------------------------------------
SCHOOL A   5700               0            165000
SCHOOL B   1350             750             46500
SCHOOL C   110                0             25650
SCHOOL D   100              750             23500
SCHOOL E   525                0             12500
-----------------------------------------------------------------------
   TOTAL
```

Figure 8.8   Fuel budget spreadsheet with fuel consumption "constants" entered

4. Enter variables. In this example, we have treated estimates of the unit prices for gas and oil for the coming year as variables. We will be allowed to change the prices later, if desired. For now, suppose:

Gas	$1.125/CCF
#2 Fuel Oil	$ .800/GAL
#4 Fuel Oil	$ .700/GAL

5. Enter formulas. These formulas provide the computer with instructions on how to calculate the unknown values in the spreadsheet from the "known" or given values. Such formulas must be written in terms of the spreadsheet labels and variable information.

Gas $ = Consumption x Unit Price
#2 Fuel $ = Consumption x Unit Price
#4 Fuel $ = Consumption x Unit Price
Total $ = Gas $ + #2 Fuel $ + #4 Fuel $
Total (Rows) = A + B + C + D + E

The computer computes the totals across and down. (See Fig. 8.9.)

FUEL BUDGET FY 1986

| | GAS | | #2 FUEL OIL | | #4 FUEL OIL | | TOTAL |
BUILDING	CCF	$	GAL	$	GAL	$	$
SCHOOL A	5700	6412.50	0	0.00	165000	115500.00	121912.50
SCHOOL B	1350	1518.75	750	600.00	46500	32550.00	34668.75
SCHOOL C	110	123.75	0	0.00	25650	17955.00	18078.75
SCHOOL D	100	112.50	750	600.00	23500	16450.00	17162.50
SCHOOL E	525	590.63	0	0.00	12500	8750.00	9340.63
TOTAL	7785	8753.13	1500	1200.00	273150	191205.00	201163.13

Figure 8.9   Fuel budget spreadsheet with all rows and columns filled

6. Analyze and revise variable(s). The total budget figure of $201,163 output by the computer seems reasonable, but "what if" oil prices were to go up ten cents per gallon? If we now input the percent increase, by changing the variable values, the spreadsheet program instantly recalculates the entire table, as shown in Fig. 8.10.

Gas	$1.125/CCF
#2 Fuel Oil	$ .900/GAL
#4 Fuel Oil	$ .800/GAL

FUEL BUDGET FY 1986

| | GAS | | #2 FUEL OIL | | #4 FUEL OIL | | TOTAL |
BUILDING	CCF	$	GAL	$	GAL	$	$
SCHOOL A	5700	6412.50	0	0.00	165000	132000.00	138412.50
SCHOOL B	1350	1518.75	750	675.00	46500	37200.00	39393.75
SCHOOL C	110	123.75	0	0.00	25650	20520.00	20643.75
SCHOOL D	100	112.50	750	675.00	23500	18800.00	19587.50
SCHOOL E	525	590.63	0	0.00	12500	10000.00	10590.63
TOTAL	7785	8758.13	1500	1350.00	273150	218520.00	228628.13

Figure 8.10   Fuel budget spreadsheet recalculated due to fuel oil price increases

7. Analyze and update constants. Sometimes even constants change as time

passes. In this example, "what if" it turned out to be a mild winter, so that fuel consumption was considerably lower than the average value entered as a constant. By late winter/early spring we would probably feel confident in entering new, lower values for the fuel consumption "constants" and thus projecting a budget surplus in this area of the budget. (See Fig. 8.11.)

```
                          FUEL BUDGET FY 1986
------------------------------------------------------------------------------

                  GAS           #2 FUEL OIL        #4 FUEL OIL         TOTAL
BUILDING    CCF      $         GAL      $          GAL      $            $
------------------------------------------------------------------------------

SCHOOL A   4500   5062.50        0     0.00      140000  112000.00    117062.50
SCHOOL B   1000   1125.00      600   540.00       30000   24000.00     25665.00
.SCHOOL C    80     90.00        0     0.00       20000   16000.00     16090.00
SCHOOL D    60     67.50      600   540.00       19000   15200.00     15807.50
SCHOOL E   400    450.00        0     0.00       10000    8000.00      8450.00
------------------------------------------------------------------------------

TOTAL      6040   6795.00     1200  1080.00      219000  175200.00    183175.00
```

Figure 8.11 Fuel budget spreadsheet recalculated due to lower than expected fuel consumption

The advantage of electronic spreadsheets is that they can be adapted to a tremendous variety of needs. They come in handy for budgeting, as well as for other tasks with financial aspects to them such as staffing, collective bargaining, school lunch pricing, and bid analyses. In fact, it is not uncommon today to see a computer at labor negotiations or budget hearings to quickly compute the financial implications of various proposals or modifications.

Electronic spreadsheet programs work on nearly every different type of computer. Different administrative levels would do well to have a spreadsheet program on their own computer and be able to use it at a moment's notice like a calculator.

GRAPHIC DISPLAYS

In certain situations, graphics may show more than words can say ("a picture is worth a thousand words"). Computer generated graphics displays can be used for a number of administrative purposes, especially to help school leaders get information across to various constituencies. For example, a pie chart, such as is shown in Fig. 8.12, representing a school system budget, school budget, or

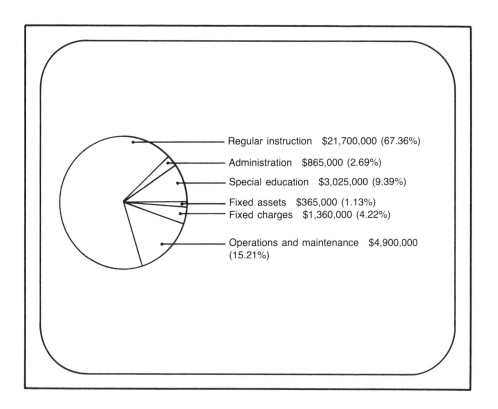

Figure 8.12   Pie chart of annual school budget

department budget, can help people see the budget breakdown without having to do heavy reading.

Graphics software packages are available for all types of computers. Some are more sophisticated than others, offering curve selections (bar graph, linear, stair-step), text entries (graph title, axis labels), custom lines and symbols, and multiple graphs. Some can even be integrated with a spreadsheet or database program, to display data from these programs graphically without your having to re-enter it. Some examples of the types of functions which graphics software can serve are as follows:

For research and planning, a pie chart can show the income levels of a school population, or what members of a class intend to do upon graduating.

A bar graph as in Fig. 8.13 may be used for emphasizing a particular point such as rising fuel costs.

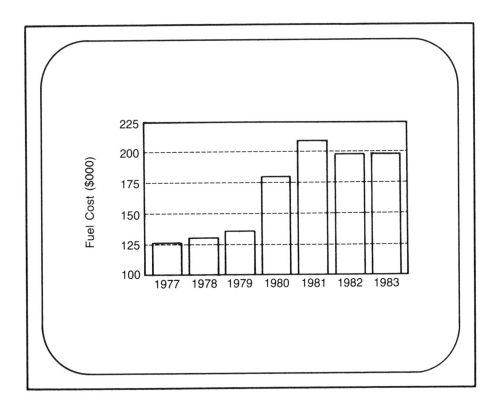

Figure 8.13   Bar graph showing annual fuel costs

A bar graph can also be used to compare a school's achievement test scores with national norms over a period of years. Looking at the scores graphically may uncover a trend that needs attention. Student/teacher ratios can also be shown in this fashion for staffing studies.

A line graph as in Fig. 8.14 may be useful for comparing actual expenditures against budgets for fuel, salaries, transportation, maintenance, and other budgetary line items.

Line graphs may also be useful in research and planning to show trends in enrollments by school system, school, grade, and course. Such graphs can then be included in reports relating to the hiring or laying off of staff, keeping open or closing schools, or retaining or cancelling courses.

The food services manager might question menus and prices after studying a line graph that shows declining participation in the school lunch program.

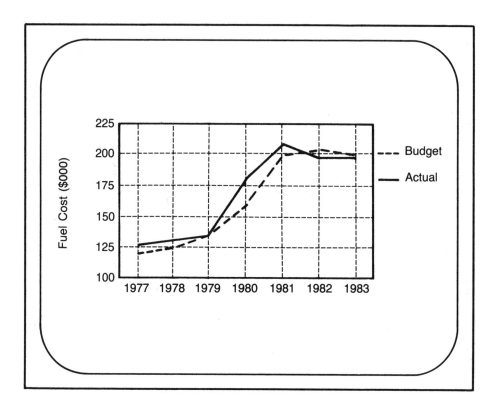

Figure 8.14   Line graph showing budgeted and actual expenditures

A classroom teacher can use a line graph to monitor test scores. The teacher can sit down with students and go over their progress right on the computer screen, or send home a progress report to the parents containing a print-out of the graph.

Computer graphics can also be used as an audio-visual tool in front of an audience by connecting the computer to a large monitor. This technique is much more versatile than using an overhead projector. The speaker can easily add new data or change variables on the screen and he or she has the additional options of color and animation. "What if" questions from the audience can often be answered graphically in seconds. New screens appear with the press of a key, instead of the presenter fumbling around trying to find a particular overhead. And the screen can be transformed at will into a print-out. For repeat performances (monthly, annually), the data can be stored and updated, which saves having to redo transparencies.

SCHOOL SPECIALTY PROGRAMS

In addition to these general purpose programs (database, word processor, spreadsheet, graphics), there are numerous special programs designed for schools. In this section we discuss several of these. However, before moving on, you might wish to consider the advantages of obtaining just the programs we have discussed above. First, there are only four, yet they are flexible enough to do nearly any office task. This means, too, that there are only four programs to buy and to learn to use. Further, if you purchase integrated packages, all of the programs can use the same data and their output can easily be merged into a unified whole, with charts, tables and graphics supporting text. These four types of programs all help you to relate data to one another in meaningful ways and to convey the resulting information efficiently and effectively. Moreover, their general nature permits their adaptation, so that among them, they can address just about any administrative task.

School specialty programs provide quite a different picture. There are large numbers of them, each tailored to a particular school administrative task. This means certain advantages and certain disadvantages in using them compared with general purpose programs. And indeed, for many tasks you will have the choice: adapt a general purpose program you already own to your needs or purchase a specialty program dedicated to that particular task. For example, as we have seen, mailing lists can be automated, using a word processer integrated with data base management software. Or you could buy dedicated mailing list software.

You must decide which way you want to go. You should recognize that it is more work to set up general purpose programs to do each task and it requires more expertise. But at the same time, such an application can be changed more easily to meet your changing needs. Moreover, since you already own the general purpose programs and have entered data into them, there is no new software cost incurred and probably no redundant data entry to be done. The chief advantage of general purpose programs is their flexibility and, conversely, your biggest concern in considering special purpose programs should be their potential lack of flexibility. Some are fine, of course, but many were designed with particular parameters in mind and cannot accommodate the different formats and structures which you might wish to use.

Implicit in this comment is another important contrast betweeen the two types of software: there is a great deal of specialty software that has been developed by school people in their districts and then marketed in limited ways by small, inexperienced software companies. In contrast, spreadsheets, word processors, database management systems, and graphics packages are generally published by experienced major publishers, with sophisticated national marketing, and extensive quality control behind the product. Thus it is very important in considering specialty software to read manuals carefully, and ascertain beyond doubt that their design and data capacities will be appropriate for your needs.

On the positive side, specialty programs are often much easier to use than your own adaptation of a spreadsheet or database application might be. Most are menu driven, so your choices are always on the screen and there is little for the operator to have to remember. An additional advantage is that for each of the applications listed in this section there are an increasing number of software packages from which to choose, so that your chances of finding one suited to your needs is greatly improved. Moreover, as the industry has matured, quality has gone up! Some companies even put out several specialty programs which are compatible and can therefore use the same data disks. This is a hopeful trend, for it reduces the time spent on data entry.

Course Registration and Class Scheduling

A smooth flow of information at scheduling and registration time creates a more efficient system, which takes less time from everyone and minimizes errors and mix-ups. Special purpose computerized scheduling programs can turn the nightmare of master scheduling by hand into an automated dream. Student and staff preferences are recorded, possibly on machine-readable cards, and swiftly generate neatly printed student and staff schedules, class rosters, lunch schedules, and faculty study hall assignments. The procedure is simple:

1. Course offerings are filed in the computer, including course number, title, periods per week, credits, prerequisites, days, times, department, location, and maximum class size.
2. Students fill out a registration form listing the courses they want to take. Information from these sheets is entered into the computer by a member of the school staff.
3. The computer assigns students to classes, prints student schedules, and lists closed-out courses after each run.
4. The process repeats itself until all students' schedules are completed.
5. Finally, the computer prints master student schedules and class rosters.

This process speeds up registration, assures conflict-free schedules, and stores and retrieves data for central record keeping. Sorts can also be used later for analysis of class sizes, teacher workloads, and course preferences. The program can even balance class sizes and eliminate the kind of teachers' schedules which require them to teach four classes without a break.

Although such scheduling software is available for most microcomputers, a medium to large size high school may be better off using a mainframe or minicomputer for such purposes. The reasons for this are; 1) a small computer may run out of data storage space; 2) with a larger system registration data could be integrated into central records already on the computer; and 3) with a more sophisticated computer, an optical scanner or card reader could be used to automatically enter the data, thereby further speeding up the process. Some of the newer, powerful business microcomputers may also be capable of providing these functions if linked to a hard disk for storage of data.

Attendance Reporting

Attendance is more than just marking students absent or late. Attendance reports, broken down by categories of students, are required for state reports and many grant applications, as well as by the offices of the principal, guidance counselor, and special education director, to name a few. Attendance reports are also cumulative, requiring perhaps, weekly, monthly, and quarterly versions of the same report, all of which are based on similar data. Attendance reports must be accurate; machines are better suited to preparing them than are people.

Fortunately, many programs exist to produce such reports. Your main concern is to find one which suits your district's procedures and produces reports in a format compatible with state and other requirements you must meet.

If your district has a centralized database and a program to handle it, you can store and retrieve attendance data in numerous formats for myriad purposes. A computerized attendance report from the main office can flag students who accumulate the maximum number of unexcused absences. The principal or department head can use classroom attendance summaries over a period of time to question teachers about student participation in class. Other reports can provide homeroom summaries, staff attendance, and long-term illnesses. Matching absences to days-of-the-week and holidays can help pinpoint abuses.

Doing such analytical attendance data retrieval manually is impractical because of time constraints. There is more important work for staff to do than sit and check off absences. Like scheduling, computerized attendance can be especially effective if it is tied into central administration student record-keeping, using terminals or microcomputers with modems.

Use of School Buildings

Most districts allow public use of school buildings. Classrooms, auditoriums, gymnasiums, and lecture halls are sometimes booked solid. Interested groups must often reserve facilities months in advance. Consider all the details that go into making up a schedule: area, organization, priority, dates, times, fees, staff, cancellations, equipment, attendance, preparation, and clean-up time.

Especially in a large high school, if the person in charge of reservations fills in time slots like a puzzle, he or she can expect to have to go back and make changes. A better way is to use one of many available computerized reservation programs like hotels and airlines use. As requests come in, the reservations software searches files to try to fit the activity into the schedule or offer the closest alternatives. If the request can be satisfied, the computer reserves the dates, times, and areas. This type of program can also print schedules for the people in charge, as well as permits, invoices, and usage reports. The result is much better control over the facilities. Such scheduling can be done through the central office or even at individual schools, using a microcomputer. While this sort of function can be performed using general purpose database software, a program specifically designed to facilitate reservations will prove easier to learn to use.

Student Activity Fund Accounting

Fundraising is as much a part of school as homework and sports. The existence of many after-school activities depends on money earned from concerts, car washes, bake sales, and concession stands. Money from fundraising usually comes in and goes out through the principal's office.

The Research Corporation of the Association of School Business Officials recommends that, "Every school district should have in effect rules, regulations, and procedures for accountability of student activity funds." A computer system for this purpose might work as follows:

1. Each club or activity establishes an account with the school bursar. These fund accounts are maintained in a permanent computer file.
2. The bursar also establishes the school's bank accounts in a computer file.
3. Club business is transacted using standardized deposit, withdrawal, and adjustment slips.
4. All transactions are entered into the computer directly from these slips, and a journal is produced on the printer.
5. The bursar is able to monitor the accounts on the computer's video display.
6. A trial balance and fund account statements are printed by the computer at the end of the month, as in Fig. 8.15.

Important considerations in adapting such a program are the number of accounts, monthly transactions, and dollar amounts the computer must handle. These will determine whether a stand-alone microcomputer can handle the job or whether you'll need more storage and memory capacity.

Library Circulation

A variety of library software is available for stand-alone microcomputers, all of which monitor circulation by title, author, call number, grade, subject, due date, and availability from other libraries. The computer tracks the location of every book and magazine and prints overdue notices. More elaborate software is also

```
            YOUR SCHOOL NAME PRINTED HERE STUDENT ACTIVITY FUND
                            TRIAL BALANCE
                            SEP 30 1986
```

	ACTIVITY FUND	PREVIOUS BALANCE DEBIT	PREVIOUS BALANCE CREDIT	NEW BALANCE DEBIT	NEW BALANCE CREDIT
001	PETTY CASH	262.89		223.39	
002	CHECKING ACCOUNT	3,537.83		2,300.00	
003	MUTUAL SAVINGS	644.13		644.13	
004	BAY BANK	3,421.99		3,635.74	
005	FIRST NATIONAL BANK	1,511.00		845.82	
006	VOLUNTEER TRUST	300.00		300.00	
007	GUARANTEE SAVINGS	1,252.15		1,248.10	
008	COOPERATIVE TRUST	406.74		406.74	
		---------		---------	
		11,336.73		9,603.92	
100	SCHOLARSHIP FUND		1,511.00		1,020.82
101	MARCHING BAND	79.00		54.00	
102	CHESS CLUB		55.10		55.10
103	GRADUATION		410.95		410.95
104	GREENHOUSE		201.45		139.95
105	AFRO AMERICAN CENTER		129.00		149.00
106	MATH CLUB		54.92		44.92
107	STUDENT EXCHANGE CLUB	81.38		31.38	
108	ATHLETICS		3,421.99		3,635.74
109	STUDENT COUNCIL		590.00		540.00
110	DRAMA CLUB		85.64		10.64
111	PHOTOGRAPHY		12.11	17.39	
112	CLASS OF 1987		875.00		875.00
113	CLASS OF 1988		493.25		393.25
114	CLASS OF 1989	116.10		20.15	
115	STAGE CREW		26.68		26.68
116	YEARBOOK		1,063.36		188.36
117	FIELD TRIPS		311.40		111.40
118	NEWSPAPER		201.00		213.00
119	OPEN CAMPUS		119.66		44.66
120	CHORUS		54.13		54.13
121	BROADCASTING		6.97	9.01	
122	SKI CLUB	19.51			40.49
123	C. BROWN SCHOLARSHIP		300.00		300.00
124	ALUMNI ASSOCIATION		91.10		91.10
125	OUTWARD BOUND		112.05	43.05	
126	ITALIAN CLUB		63.50		63.50
127	FRENCH CLUB	2.02		2.02	
128	GIRLS ATHLETICS		375.00		375.00
129	SHAKESPEAREAN PLAYERS		97.15		179.65
130	THEATRE		230.59		275.84
131	H. JAMES SCHOLARSHIP		406.74		406.74
132	PSAT		335.00		135.00
		---------		---------	
		298.01		177.00	
		---------	---------	---------	---------
		11,634.74	11,634.74	9,780.92	9,780.92
		---------	---------	---------	---------

Figure 8.15   Trial balance for school student activity fund

on the market which can connect school libraries with other libraries, such as college, town or state libraries, for a broader range of services. However, these applications involve a great deal of storage and quick access to large amounts of data, so they generally require a hard disk, and a more powerful computer.

Equipment Inventory

In the average school, equipment is dispersed everywhere. Locating any particular piece of equipment is often a difficult task. However, taking inventory manually every year is a big job. The results of manual inventories are frequently mixed bags of facts and figures of little real value.

A computerized equipment inventory system can provide the orderly and up-to-date property information that every administration needs for planning, operations control, evaluation, and reporting. Such software can simplify:

- Scheduling and monitoring the use of equipment.
- Recognizing and justifying equipment needs.
- Budget preparation.
- Selection and purchase of new equipment.
- Development of maintenance programs.
- Facility planning and space needs analysis.
- Insurance appraisals.
- Verification of losses in cases of fire, theft, or vandalism.
- Reporting to government bodies and funding agencies.
- Setting educational policies.
- Conducting educational research.

Inventory information stored for each item should include at least a description, serial number, manufacturer, model, curriculum area (if applicable), location, date of purchase, quantity, and cost (see Fig. 8.16). More would be needed if repair and maintenance information were desired. Print-outs should be available by curriculum area, description, manufacturer, and location. Then if designated staff enter additions, deletions, and revisions to the database as they occur throughout the year, annual inventory taking may be virtually eliminated. A random check would be all that is needed.

For an audio-visual department in a secondary school, a microcomputer-based inventory system would do fine. The information would be right at hand in the office. However, inventory control for an entire school system might require a minicomputer or a hard disk on a more powerful micro for the amount of data involved.

Achievement Test Scoring

After achievement testing takes place in schools, two methods are normally used to obtain results; the tests can be sent to the publisher for machine scoring or a person can hand score each test. The first method means increased cost and

```
SORT:CODE
AUDIOVISUAL                    EQUIPMENT INVENTORY           01/02/82          PAGE:1
------------------------------------------------------------------------------------
MSTR CODE   DESCRIPT.    SERIAL#    MFG./MODEL        LOC.   DATE   QTY   COST    TOTAL
------------------------------------------------------------------------------------
```

MSTR CODE	DESCRIPT.	SERIAL#	MFG./MODEL	LOC.	DATE	QTY	COST	TOTAL
1100-001	16MM PROJ	171948	BELL&HOWELL 552	2207	11/68	1 @	535 =	535
1100-002	16MM PROJ	170977	BELL&HOWELL 552	2207	11/68	1 @	535 =	535
1100-006	PROJ SCRN	NONE	KNOX TRIPOD	2207	03/81	3 @	56 =	168
1100-004	PROJ CART	1	WILSON WT26	2207	01/80	1 @	70 =	70
1100-005	PROJ CART	2	WILSON WT26	2207	01/80	1 @	70 =	70
1100-007	OVRHD PROJ	266420	3M 66AG	2208	09/64	1 @	115 =	115
1100-008	OVRHD PROJ	159118	3M 66AR	2208	10/70	1 @	225 =	225
1100-010	SLIDE PROJ	216017	KODAK HF2	2208	03/77	1 @	135 =	135
1100-009	SLIDE PROJ	445404	KODAK E2	2208	01/78	1 @	140 =	140
1100-038	35MM CMRA	763763	HONEYWELL K1000	2209	03/76	1 @	150 =	150
1100-039	35MM CMRA	7637081	HONEYWELL K1000	2209	03/76	1 @	150 =	150
1100-037	35MM CMRA	76600400	PENTAX K1000	2209	02/78	1 @	125 =	125
1100-031	8MM CAMERA	327639	MINOLTA 8D4	2209	09/73	1 @	60 =	60
1100-032	8MM CAMERA	328739	MINOLTA 8D4	2209	09/73	1 @	60 =	60
1100-033	8MM CAMERA	105080	SANKYO MF606	2209	10/75	1 @	190 =	190
1100-042	AMPLIFIER	274415	CALIFONE 25VBA	2209	04/59	1 @	100 =	100
1100-043	AMPLIFIER	RS17264	PIONEER SA600	2209	01/71	1 @	200 =	200
1100-012	CSSTTE REC	817805	REALISTIC CTR40	2209	11/78	1 @	50 =	50
1100-011	CSSTTE REC	817804	REALISTIC CTR40	2209	11/78	1 @	50 =	50
1100-041	FLMLOOP PJ	323986	TECHNICOLOR	2209	01/70	1 @	130 =	130
1100-040	FLMLOOP PJ	226116	TECHNICOLOR	2209	01/70	1 @	130 =	130
1100-034	FLMSTRP PJ	44338	INTERNATIONAL	2209	05/74	1 @	160 =	160
1100-036	FLMSTRP PJ	64686	SINGER RP50	2209	01/68	1 @	130 =	130
1100-035	FLMSTRP PJ	10267	VIEWLEX VR10	2209	04/74	1 @	200 =	200
1100-045	PA SYSTEM	57865	ARGOS 6040¦	2209	04/79	1 @	345 =	345
1100-044	PA SYSTEM	58297	ARGOS 6040	2209	04/79	1 @	345 =	345
1100-013	REC PLAYER	186400	CALIFONE 1875K	2209	01/72	1 @	150 =	150
1100-030	SPEAKER	220924	BELL&HOWELL	2209	11/67	2 @	100 =	200
1100-015	SPEAKER	45388	FISHER XP44B	2209	01/75	2 @	95 =	190
1100-016	SUP8 MOVIE	473021	SANKYO MF303	2209	01/75	1 @	200 =	200
1100-014	TAPE REC	5974	WOLLENSAK 2551	2209	09/74	1 @	267 =	267
1100-046	TV CART	1	REDITILT	2209	05/68	1 @	40 =	40
1100-019	TV 19 INCH	10981	GE CEM723BGA1	2209	02/72	1 @	250 =	250
1100-018	TV 19 INCH	11047	GE CEM723BGA1	2209	02/72	1 @	250 =	250
1100-017	TV 25 INCH	9026	RCA F596MV	2209	01/64	1 @	300 =	300
1100-021	TV CART	2	BRETFORD 754E	2209	10/77	1 @	50 =	50
1100-020	TV CART	1	BRETFORD 754E	2209	10/77	1 @	50 =	50
1100-022	VIDEO CMRA	52127	SONY AV3600	2209	11/71	1 @	600 =	600
1100-025	VIDEO MNTR	17052	SONY CVM115	2209	09/76	1 @	700 =	700
1100-024	VIDEO CSST	28935	SONY VO2600	2209	10/77	1 @ 1,500 =	1,500
1100-028	VIDEO EDIT	44344	SONY AV3650	2209	09/78	1 @	937 =	937
1100-026	VIDEO PORT	62170	SONY AV3400	2209	12/78	1 @	750 =	750
1100-023	VIDEO CMRA	33642	SONY AVC3450	2209	09/79	1 @	500 =	500
1100-027	VIDEO REC	62159	SONY AV3400	2209	10/79	1 @ 1,100 =	1,100
1100-029	VIEW FIND	17714	SONY AV3250	2209	09/78	1 @	200 =	200
1100-052	CSSTTE REC	17788	B&H 3081B	2210	09/78	1 @	50 =	50
1100-053	CSSTTE REC	17784	B&H 3081B	2210	09/78	1 @	50 =	50
1100-051	CSSTTE REC	17785	B&H 3081B	2210	09/78	1 @	50 =	50
1100-047	CSSTTE REC	25426	B&H 3079	2210	09/79	1 @	77 =	77
1100-055	CSSTTE REC	53988	WOLLENSAK 2520	2210	11/73	1 @	150 =	150
1100-054	CSSTTE REC	50429	WOLLENSAK 2520	2210	11/73	1 @	150 =	150
1100-056	R/R TAPE	70106182	WOLLENSAK	2210	01/68	1 @	225 =	225

Figure 8.16 Equipment inventory

time delays, while the second method is laborious and time consuming. Many present day computer programs can eliminate these shortcomings.

The teacher administers the test to a group of students in the customary way. Once this is done, student information and test responses are entered into the computer (card readers and optical scanners connected to the computer are available for automated scoring even on microcomputers). The computer program can provide teachers, administrators, and evaluators with quick, cost-effective scoring, norming, and diagnosing information. The output may include:

Individual Results
1. Total number of correct answers (raw score) by student.
2. Total number of questions answered by student.
3. Conversion of raw scores to standard scores—stanines, percentile bands, normal curve equivalents, grade equivalents and extended scale scores.
4. Diagnostic information based on student errors.

Group Results
1. Raw score, average and standard deviations.
2. Conversion of average raw scores to average standard scores—stanines, percentiles, normal curve equivalents, grade equivalents and extended scale scores.
3. Number of correct answers for each question and percent correct for the group.
4. Percent showing mastery within domains and item cluster.

Computer print-outs of test results may be used in various ways.

1. Individual results. Total score and subtest score norm data for individuals can be used in parent conferences, as a basis for judging growth from previous testing and as a preliminary screening device for more in-depth diagnostic testing.
2. Item analysis for individuals. The program may list the questions a student answered incorrectly. For the comprehension subtest, for example, it may give the correct answer and the student's answer. For vocabulary, it may give the word clue, correct answer, student answer and a possible interpretation of the error. This information can be used to diagnose error patterns and thus individual areas of weakness. Once identified, teachers can then plan specific instruction to overcome the weakness.
3. Group results. The program can give total score and subtest normative data for groups of students. Thus, it can indicate how the class as a whole is performing. This information can be used by the teacher to plan group activities and to describe how well the class achieves as a whole. It can be used by administrators and evaluators to monitor class progress and curriculum success.
4. Item analysis for groups. This part of the program may list each question,

the percentage of the class getting the item correct, and the percentage of the norming sample getting the question correct. It can be used as a basis for determining group strengths and weaknesses. If group weaknesses appear, group lessons can be planned to overcome the deficiencies. This output can also be used by administrators and evaluators to monitor the curriculum.

Everyone involved with testing can benefit from more detailed information, faster test results, cost savings, labor savings, and easy-to-read print-outs. National norm results are obtainable and can be built into the program as well. Most of the data analyses described above can be run on microcomputers and thus would be easily accessible to classroom teachers. For a large district that wants such results as part of a central data base, a more powerful computer would be required.

Grade Reporting

Most secondary schools have just a few days between semester finals and issuing report cards. The odds of beating the deadline and having more time to assess student performance are better with a computerized grade reporting system.

In addition, by printing summary reports for teachers, principals, guidance personnel, and others, the computer can help you transmit current grade information promptly to those who can use it most effectively.

The computer collates students' grades and figures credits earned, cumulative credits, grade point averages, and attendance. Grades can be stored on a disk or tape for permanent record-keeping. The result can be a professional quality report card that fits into a window envelope for easy mailing to students and parents. Although microcomputers can handle grade reporting, this use is probably best tied into the central administration hardware, both to avoid student tampering with files and to facilitate storage and use of large amounts of data.

Annual Purchasing

Annual school purchasing is the process for getting supplies and equipment into schools. Common bid items include instructional and art materials; custodial supplies; athletic goods; health and training room supplies; audio-visual equipment including computers, library books and software; industrial arts materials; and furniture.

Preparing bids involves writing specifications and determining quantities. Awarding orders means selecting vendors, calculating prices, and making up delivery schedules. Schools often encounter problems with deadlines, processing time, and errors in compilations.

A variety of microcomputer programs exist which can handle much of the paper work at each stage and can streamline the annual purchasing process.

One program, for example, may handle all of the following functions:

- Order quantities—enter purchase quantities by delivery location (warehouse, school, or department). Let the computer compute the totals for each item. Recall the orders when it comes time for the delivery schedules. (See Fig. 8.17.)
- Bid awards—enter the vendor, brand, and unit price. Let the computer compile total prices and print purchase orders and delivery schedules. Arithmetic errors are virtually eliminated.
- Budget—depending on how sophisticated a system is desired, the computer can compare quantities and prices over the years to use for inventory control and budgeting.

While the common microcomputer programs of this kind may not provide the space to handle detailed specifications, you can easily use a word processor to create descriptions and save them on a separate disk. You can then use these over and over again or modify them to appear in different formats for requisitions, bid sheets, and delivery schedules. In this way, tedious typing chores are eliminated.

With professional quality work expedited at the school end, there will be quicker responses from vendors and quite possibly better prices. The computer to use depends on the number and length of the specifications, the number of schools (requisitioners) involved, and the options your school purchasing agent wants in the program, such as inventory control.

Maintenance and Repair

A simple version of a maintenance and repair (M&R) report can be easily developed using word processing. As work orders come in, you can add them to an "outstanding" list (by school or craft). A code or comment beside each item gives its status, as in Fig. 8.18. When the job is finished, the M&R is deleted or moved to a file of completed work. The status report provides a quick check on the backlog of work.

More sophisticated customized maintenance and repair software might give queue lengths, labor and material costs, and a warning when work is running behind schedule. Microcomputers can handle such programs easily.

Food Services

The computer can be used in food services operations for recipes (preparation, ingredients, portions, nutrition, and per meal cost), food inventories (see Fig. 8.19), purchasing, meal counts, sales, and employee work schedules.

While such an application could be handled by a data base management

```
ABC SCHOOL SUPPLY CO.           DELIVERY SCHEDULE               PAGE 01
EAST HIGH SCHOOL                  ART SUPPLIES                   05/01/82
----------------------------------------------------------------------------
ITEM NO.    QTY   UNIT              DESCRIPTION             PRICE     TOTAL
----------------------------------------------------------------------------
                                  ADHESIVES
02-01-001   21    DOZEN      WHITE GLUE 8 OZ.: PLASTIC     $ 5.34   $112.14
                            SQUEEZE BOTTLE, NON-REMOVABLE
                            CAP.
                            BRAND/CAT#: ELMER'S
                                  CRAYONS
02-02-001   27    DOZEN      LARGE WAX CRAYON SET 16 STD.  $10.85   $292.95
                            COLORS: NON-TOXIC, LIFT LID
                            BOX.
                            BRAND/CAT#: CRAYOLA #336
02-02-002   25    DOZEN      STANDARD SIZE WAX CRAYON SET  $ 4.18   $104.50
                            16 STD. COLORS: NON-TOXIC,
                            LIFT LID BOX.
                            BRAND/CAT#: CRAYOLA #16
                                  PAINTS
02-03-001   17    CASE/6 QTS  TEMPERA LIQUID - RED:        $21.70   $368.90
                            NON-TOXIC, PLASTIC WIDE MOUTH
                            BOTTLE.
                            BRAND/CAT#: CRAYOLA
02-03-002   14    CASE/6 QTS  TEMPERA LIQUID - BLUE:       $21.70   $303.80
                            NON-TOXIC, PLASTIC WIDE MOUTH
                            BOTTLE.
                            BRAND/CAT#: CRAYOLA
02-03-004   17    CASE/6 QTS  TEMPERA LIQUID - WHITE:      $21.70   $368.90
                            NONTOXIC, PLASTIC WIDE MOUTH
                            BOTTLE.
                            BRAND/CAT#: CRAYOLA
                                  PAINT BRUSHES & TRAYS
02-04-001   10    DOZEN      FLAT WHITE BRISTLE BRUSH      $ 2.94   $ 29.40
                            1/2 INCH WIDE.
                            BRAND/CAT#: DELTA 261
02-04-005   26    DOZEN      WATER COLOR BOX & WHOLE PAN   $29.52   $767.52
                            W/NO. 7 BRUSH: NON-TOXIC,
                            SEMI-MOIST, PLASTIC BOX.
                            BRAND/CAT#: CRAYOLA 08W
                                          MERCHANDISE TOTAL:    $2,348.11
```

Figure 8.17   Delivery schedule for annual purchasing

```
----------------------------------------------------------------------------
BLDG      DATE      CONTROL NO.  MAINTENANCE/REPAIR   CRAFT  STATUS
----------------------------------------------------------------------------
SCHOOL A  5-3-83    42832        BROKEN WINDOW RM 10  G      CONTRACTOR CALLED 5-3-83
SCHOOL B  5-3-83    42833        EXIT SIGN BROKEN     C      PART ORDERED 5-3-83
```

Figure 8.18   Maintenance and repair report

program, the many calculations needed make it easier to purchase software especially designed to do the job.

ITEM CODE	ITEM DESCRIPTION	PACK DESCRIPTION	BEGINING INVENTORY	ISSUES	ADJUSTMENTS	ENDING INVENTORY	USAGES
0935	MILK HOMO	QT	1,248	25,462	-48	960	+25,702
0943	MILK SKIM	QTS	216	9,120	-96	192	+9,048
0960	BUTTERMILK	QT	14	20	+0	0	+34
0969	MILK 1/2 PT	.5PT	0	0	+108	0	+108
0986	CREAM SOUR	LB	20	20	+0	5	+35
0988	CREAM HEAVY	QT.	0	15	+0	0	+15
1020	YOGURT	QT	360	950	+0	200	+1,110

BEGINING PERIOD
3-NOV-79
FOOD INVENTORY ITEMS
DAILY DAIRY

ENDING PERIOD
7-DEC-79

Figure 8.19   Dairy inventory for food services department

Energy Monitoring

Energy audits surfaced in school systems when fuel costs began to cut significantly into education budgets. Detailed record-keeping is necessary to monitor and control energy consumption. A good energy monitoring program lets you know energy efficiency in terms of the building area and the number of occupants. Reports can be used to compare efficiency of buildings, pinpoint problems, forecast budgets, and set goals. Sophisticated software/hardware can even control energy use by turning off and on lights, air-conditioning, and heating in different areas of the building at different times of the day.

CONCLUSIONS

Administrative applications of computers are designed to expedite the flow of information and to enhance the quality of information that can be obtained quickly from data. Before such results can be obtained, however, you must give careful thought to the existing and the desired work flow. Consider tasks from a systems perspective: analyze each process by breaking down the present procedure into small steps and eliminating those steps that are meaningless or wasteful. Determine the amount of data to be put through this process, to get a handle on the magnitude of the application. Check, too, the format of the data when it is generated, so that you can be aware of any potential problems for data entry. Consult all who will use the resulting information and determine the format in which output is most useful to each one. Once you have done this, you have defined the input, the process, and the output. It is time to look for the appropriate software to do the task.

Finding the proper software will be much easier if you approach the marketplace armed with the above facts and analysis. If you know what you want, it is much easier to eliminate products which will not do the job. Do not forget to consider the general purpose tools, such as an electronic spreadsheet, wordprocessor or database management software, as possible answers to your search. Give your analysis of input, process, and output to the person in your system who knows these tools best (this may be your computer coordinator or even a parent, teacher, or student!) and get some advice on how much time it would take to set up the formats. Consider the expertise of the individual who will use the application in deciding whether a special purpose program, with its easy to use menus and prompts, may be a better choice.

Above all, do not rush into a decision. Be patient and deliberate, and recognize that implementation of your ideas will, inevitably, occur more slowly than you might wish.

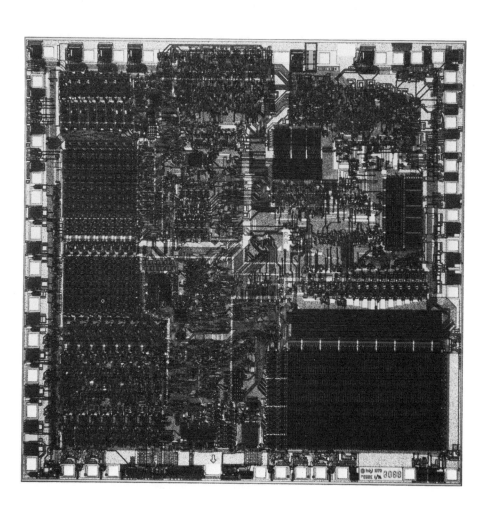

Bits and Bytes 9

This chapter might have been entitled "More Than You Ever Wanted to Know about Computers but Were Afraid to Ask." Its task is to help you, the school administrator, to understand how computers work. We have tried to steer a middle course between the twin perils of the overly general description that explains nothing and the overly technical description that explains too much. It is intended to be a useful introduction to computers, a basis from which you can readily acquire however much more knowledge your job demands. It is not the last word, but a beginning.

Do not worry about learning everything contained in this chapter. Your familiarity with computer systems will grow in appropriate ways over time, as your contact with computers increases. For now, just try to get a basic feel for the subject. You can always come back to this material for reference later on.

It is impossible to know it all—nobody does. So do not be embarrassed to admit your unfamiliarity with a given subject and openly to seek advice and information on any topic. There are many aspects of computers that most school administrators need never understand. Approach your learning about computers on a need to know basis.

Anyone who has spent even a small amount of time with a computer knows more about what it can do than a ream of words could explain. A first recommendation, then, is that every administrator arrange to spend an initial period of time with a microcomputer and a manual, exploring the workings and getting the feel of the machine. Even a brief hands-on exposure will provide a framework for what follows.

For purposes of simplification, most of the information here relates to microcomputers, although timesharing minicomputers and giant mainframes use much the same fundamental technology. The microcomputer is a self-contained system, and the primary computer functions are carried out with a minimum number of parts, which can easily be seen and identified. Today's small, stand-alone machines can do what room-filling systems were required for in the 1950s and 1960s. Where early computers were powered by banks of vacuum tubes, consumed significant quantities of electricity, occupied whole laboratories, and needed constant air conditioning and frequent maintenance, today's machines pack much greater computing power into microminiaturized circuits that occupy small space, use little power, stay cool, and need minimal maintenance. Instead of large vacuum tubes that heat up and require expensive cooling, computers have tiny transistors. Instead of painstakingly hand-wired circuits, they have circuits printed on small flat boards. Instead of millions of dollars per machine, they may cost thousands, or even hundreds. (Some cost less than one hundred dollars!) It is this increased computing power and reduced cost and size that have made computers a new force in education.

If computers seem bewildering, it is perhaps because they are such nonspecialized tools. To name but a few applications, we find computers running the fuel systems of our automobiles, writing our paychecks, producing our tax returns, and playing against us in chess. Computers are completely variable tools, ultimately capable of any task that can be broken down into a finite number of steps. We are accustomed to defining our tools by what they do. With computers, that's a questionable approach.

Yet the ideas behind computers are possible for the layman to grasp despite the complexity, diversity, and technological ingenuity with which these ideas are applied. Once the idea of a computer is understood, the vocabulary of the field is not hard to learn, and one can begin to think and communicate intelligently about computers. One warning: many of the terms used to describe computers and their operation have no precise definition. The jury of lexicographers is still out, and the words and meanings seem to keep changing almost as fast as the technology.

In this chapter we try to define technical terms when we first encounter them. Sometimes this is difficult to do, as in the case of "memory" below. If you encounter such an undefined term, try to ascertain its meaning from the context in which it is used or look it up in the glossary. Eventually the term will be explained in the text as well.

At its most fundamental level, a computer electronically manipulates symbolic information according to a list of instructions given it. Manipulating symbolic information is a little scary; it is very close to some of the processes we call thinking. Computers do in fact perform some of the functions we have formerly associated only with human mental processes—playing a pretty strong game of chess, for example. But the amazing thing about a computer playing chess is that some human has previously thought up the list of instructions that allows the computer to do so. Computers, for all their power, are entirely stupid, useless, and helpless without instructions from people.

Basically, a computer can perform just a very few operations. It can:

1. Obtain numbers from its memory.
2. Return results to memory as numbers.
3. Execute a list of instructions in memory.

4. Compare two numbers and execute different instructions depending on whether or not the numbers are equal.
5. Add two numbers.
6. Change zeros to ones and vice versa.

Not very remarkable, is it? So what's so great about computers? Three things: first, these simple operations can be combined to make much more powerful operations. Second, computers can perform these operations very rapidly. Adding two numbers is not particularly impressive; performing 100,000 such additions in a single second is very impressive. Third, the numbers that the computer manipulates can be interpreted as codes for letters, punctuation, and control characters (such as advancing the screen on a terminal or paper on a printer), with the result that the computer can manipulate text data as well as numbers.

COMPUTER SYSTEMS

The common electronic calculator is, in fact, an extremely simple computer system. You input numbers (data) and operations (instructions) via the keys; the computer calculates the result from step to step (processes each instruction as it is received); and outputs results on the display. This input-process-output cycle is typical of most computer operations. The procedure a person might follow to obtain a result from a calculator is analogous to a **program** in a computer. In that sense, the following is a "program" to compute the average of a list of numbers on a calculator:

1. Turn on the calculator.
2. Press CLEAR key.
3. Enter first number.
4. Press + (add) key.
5. Enter next number.
6. Repeat steps 4 and 5 until list of items to average is exhausted.
7. Press ÷ (divided by) key.
8. Enter number of items you are averaging.
9. Press = (equals) key.
10. Read result on display.

Let's see how this calculator procedure might appear on a simple computer system. A BASIC program has been loaded into the computer and is ready to run. You, the user, type the first command RUN, to which the computer responds. Thereafter you and the computer alternate responding to each other.

RUN
PROGRAM TO CALCULATE SUM AND AVERAGE OF A LIST OF NUMBERS. HOW MANY
NUMBERS TO AVERAGE?
3

```
ENTER 3 NUMBERS, EACH FOLLOWED BY A CARRIAGE RETURN
67.5
82.5
90
SUM IS 240.0
AVERAGE IS 80.0
AGAIN (Y/N)?
Y
HOW MANY NUMBERS TO AVERAGE?
```

In the example above, the computer system has been programmed to perform the simple, repetitive task of averaging several numbers. The program prompts the user for input, adds the numbers, divides the sum by the number of items being averaged, and prints the result. The outputs of the program are the prompts and the final result. As an added feature, the program is ready to continue averaging sets of numbers until the user wishes to stop.

A major difference between the computer and calculator examples is the degree of visibility of the process to you, the user. In using the calculator, you are involved with each operation and see each intermediate result as it is generated. Once you have accepted the minor marvel that the calculator does indeed perform its operations correctly, the whole thing becomes routine and trivial.

In the case of the computer example, all of the calculation is concealed from you: you enter the numbers, it gargles them and regurgitates an answer. The process by which the result is achieved is hidden. This is both good and bad. On the one hand, you, the user, are spared much that is boring, trivial, and repetitive; on the other, you are denied access (at least at this level) to the process by which your result is obtained. This often has the effect of making the computer seem more distant, forbidding, and magical than it really is. The user is potentially isolated from the process, and this isolation can be alienating.

This somewhat natural suspicion of unseen processes is not unfounded. Someone had to write that set of instructions to produce averages; except by careful testing of results, you have no way of knowing that the **programmer** did so correctly. It is easy to have a program announce a result with confidence; that confidence does not necessarily reflect accuracy. Many programs have errors in them, sometimes quite subtle ones. (Errors in programs are often referred to as **bugs** and the process of correcting a program is known as **debugging**.) You should cultivate a certain wariness of computer results, however imposing and reliable they may appear. The efforts of the people who program the computer make it a marvelous machine; those same people are as subject to human error as anyone.

However, it is possible for you, the user, to examine the program that allows the computer to compute averages. Then, if you have some knowledge of programming, you will understand how the results were obtained. If there were a bug in the program, you might find it by examining a **listing** of the program.

In BASIC, for example, to display the actual program listing on your computer's output device you type the command:

LIST

As a result the computer displays its program listing.

```
10 REM AVERAGE
20 REM PROGRAM TO DETERMINE SUM AND AVERAGE OF
25 REM A SET OF NUMBERS SUPPLIED BY THE USER.
30 REM AUTHOR: JANE T. GRAHAM & ALLEN L. WOLD
40 DIM A(100)
50 PRINT "PROGRAM TO CALCULATE SUM AND"
60 PRINT "AVERAGE OF A LIST OF NUMBERS."
65 LET T = 0
70 PRINT "HOW MANY NUMBERS TO AVERAGE?"
80 INPUT N
90 PRINT "ENTER "N " NUMBERS, EACH FOLLOWED"
95 PRINT "BY A CARRIAGE RETURN."
100 FOR I = 1 TO N
110 INPUT A(I)
120 LET T = T + A(I)
130 NEXT I
140 PRINT "SUM IS ";T
150 PRINT "AVERAGE IS ";T/N
160 PRINT
170 PRINT "AGAIN (Y/N)?"
180 INPUT A$
190 IF A$ = "Y" THEN GOTO 65
200 END
```

READY

Now, let us consider a more sophisticated example. Suppose your school has an administrative computer which has on its peripheral storage device a file of records—one for each student—including name, address, class, and some sort of identification number. Each school day, a list of absentees is entered into the computer which outputs the result to another file containing the student's ID number and the date absent. When an attendance report for each student is wanted at the end of some period of time, we run a program that does the following:

• Sorts the absentee file in student ID order (remember it was entered in date order).

- Prints the name and address of each student.
- Prints the dates each student was absent (if any).
- Prints the total number of days each student was absent.

The above is an example of data processing, something that a simple calculator cannot emulate.

As with stereo equipment, one can buy computer systems as integrated packages or as separate components. But unlike stereo equipment, which is all designed for the one purpose of playing music, the choice of computer hardware and software can result in very different computer systems designed for very different tasks. At a minimum, however, a computer system needs the following:

- A computer.
- A **peripheral device** for storing programs and data between sessions on the computer (e.g., a tape player/recorder or **disk drive**).
- Peripheral devices for putting instructions and data into the computer and receiving results back from the computer (e.g., **terminals**).

The rest of this chapter discusses each of these components.

THE CENTRAL COMPUTER

Pictured in Fig. 9.1 is a printed circuit board for a computer. Each rectangular block is a plastic or ceramic package containing a **chip,** which is basically a lot of electronics packed into a small area, capable of responding in certain predefined ways. Significantly, chips are cheap to build and buy.

The Central Processing Unit (CPU)

That largest rectangular block at the left of the board in Fig. 9.1 is the **Central Processing Unit (CPU).** The CPU is the "brains" of the operation. In older and larger machines, the CPU may be composed of several—or many—components. In microcomputers, all the elements of the CPU are combined in a single chip, called a **microprocessor.** It is this little device that can perform those basic operations we listed on pp. 194–195.

Building all of these functions of the CPU into one chip was the major technological breakthrough that has spawned the astounding price revolution in computers during the past few years. A **microcomputer** is a computer whose main CPU is a single microprocessor chip. What distinguishes microcomputers from older technology computers is not so much speed and power as price and size.

In order to process information, the CPU uses codes—somewhat like the Morse code of the telegraph—that are interpreted as letters, numbers, punctuation, and control characters. But instead of the long and short pulses of the telegraph,

Figure 9.1   Printed circuit board for a computer

the CPU uses electronic signals called **digital signals** to represent binary numbers, which are sequences of zeros and ones. A single zero or one is called a **bit** (short for **b**inary dig**it**.) and is the smallest unit of information in the computer. Groups of bits are then used as codes for instructions, for text letters and numbers, for punctuation marks, and for control characters. When you enter "The quick brown fox" into your computer, it is represented internally as a set of these tiny digital signals. In the old days of digital computing, each bit was stored in a vacuum tube that was either off or on, thus representing zero or one. Today, of course, the vacuum tubes have been replaced by microscopic transistors.

Communicating by code, whether it be Morse or computer, requires some clever manipulation of very limited variables. For example, how does the CPU know that one string of bits is a line of text, another a series of integers, another instructions, and so on? It knows the same way that people know to interpret "bear right at the intersection" as a direction to follow rather than as the location of a large animal: by context. If you tell the computer to "run" a certain program, it looks for instructions to execute. If you ask it to accept some numbers you are going to type in for summing and averaging, it expects numbers. You can confuse the computer by slipping it letters when it is expecting numbers.

Another requirement for communication by code is to indicate the division between strings of bits. In Morse code this is done by pausing briefly between letters. In computer codes this is done by assigning a specific number of bits to hold each character.

A group of eight bits, called a **byte,** turns out to be a useful size for coding one text character, be it a digit (0–9), a letter (A–Z, a–z), a punctuation mark (e.g., : ; , . - ! $ %.), or a control character (e.g., enter, return, linefeed). There are 256 combinations of eight zeros and ones from 00000000 (0) to 11111111 (255). An 8-bit CPU knows to process the bits in byte-size chunks, thus eliminating the need to pause between letters or other characters.

Currently, the full set of **ASCII** characters (**A**merican **S**tandard **C**ode for **I**nformation **I**nterchange, pronounced "as-key") uses 128 of the 256 possible byte-sized codes. "A," for example, is 01000001 in binary ASCII code (in decimal this is equivalent to 65). Generally speaking, then, a byte is eight bits and is capable of representing one letter, number, or special symbol. A short table of examples of ASCII computer codes and their decimal equivalents follows:

Character	ASCII Code	Decimal
A	01000001	65
a	01100001	97
8	00111000	56
?	00111111	63
linefeed	00001010	10
delete	01111111	127

However, not all computers process information in bytes, though the byte is still used when letters and digits are to be represented, at least within most microcomputers. Reference to "8-bit CPUs," "16-bit CPUs," and "32-bit CPUs," indicates how many bits the computer can process at one time. For text characters, this doesn't make much difference, but for numerical calculation, a 16-bit CPU can handle numbers (not digits) that are twice as large as those an 8-bit CPU can process.

The collection of bits processed at one time is called a computer **word.** Whether a computer obtains 8, 16, or 32 bits of data from memory at one time depends on the electronic architecture of the CPU chip. Although the 8-bit word is the one that has been implemented by most manufacturers of microcomputers, 16-bit and 32-bit micros are now available.

Why the different word sizes? A CPU that processes information in 16-bit chunks is roughly twice as fast at processing information as one that looks at 8-bit chunks, though for most practical applications there is little advantage to such differences in speed. Still, 16-bit computers have been gaining in popularity for business applications and school administrators should probably be considering them, especially for administrative applications, instead of the more common—and cheaper—8-bit systems. Where the speed and power of 16-bit machines makes a real difference is in **timesharing** and **resource sharing** systems, as we'll discuss later in this chapter and in the next chapter. Both of these kinds of systems are commonly utilized by school systems for their administrative computing.

Let us leave the ever-changing world of 8, 16, and 32-bit technology, and return to a consideration of the fundamental activities of the CPU. The CPU performs all of its logical and arithmetic functions internally, using special places called **registers** to hold numbers within the CPU. The registers have very limited capacity for storing information. To do its work the CPU transfers information stored in its memory (see discussion of memory in next section) to and from its internal registers. Memory is usually separated from the CPU; physically it is an array of chips.

At any given time, one portion of memory might contain a series of instructions to the CPU, another portion might contain data, the rest might be unused. For example, commanded to perform a set of instructions to add two numbers, the CPU will bring the first instruction into its internal instruction register. This instruction typically tells the CPU to load a number from memory location *A* into another internal register. Having done so, the CPU then fetches the next instruction, which causes the CPU to load a number from memory location *B* into a third register. The CPU then goes to the next instruction, which tells it to add the contents of the two registers. Finally, the last instruction causes the CPU to store the result in memory location *C*. Pretty tedious, isn't it? Don't worry, except for assembly language programmers, no one ever deals with the CPU at this level. Be thankful for high-level computer languages, such as BASIC, that shield us from all this tedium, and for applications programs that insulate us even more.

Memory

The easiest way to think of computer **memory** is as a long string of bits that are accessible in word-sized chunks (e.g., 8, 16, or 32 bits at a time). The CPU can get one word of information from anywhere in that long string (the 1st word, the 10th word, the 324th word, or the 52,401st word). The location of the word in that string is given a number (1, 10, 324, 52,401), which is called its **address.** One of the most important characteristics of computer memory is that the CPU can access the information in any address directly, without having to pass any other addresses. This is a very powerful, very important feature of memory (think how convenient it would be if you could go directly to any address in a large city without passing any other addresses).

Computer memory (also called **main memory,** or **main storage,** to distinguish it from its registers) comes in several flavors. All, however, have this direct access feature, which in the computer world is called **random access.** The most common type is in fact called **Random Access Memory (RAM).** This is somewhat misleading, since all computer internal memory is random access. Random Access Memory has the following characteristics:

- Data may move directly from any RAM address to the CPU (this is called **reading from memory**).
- Data may move directly from the CPU to any RAM address (this is called **writing to memory**).
- When you turn off the power to the computer all data held in RAM is lost (the information in RAM is thus called **volatile**).

In the photograph of the circuit board in Fig. 9.1, shown previously, RAM is the sixteen chips arranged in two columns at the far right of the board. Today's least expensive personal computers typically come with 64K bytes of RAM, although increasingly many are coming with or may be easily expanded to hold 128K, 256K, or even 512 bytes of RAM.

The other main type of memory is called **Read Only Memory (ROM).** It, too, is randomly accessible, and data may be read from it into the CPU, but it has the following additional characteristics:

- Data may not be written from CPU to ROM.
- Data in ROM is fixed, not volatile (when you turn off the power, the information is not lost).

In the photograph of the circuit board in Fig. 9.1, ROM is the two chips at the bottom right of the board.

RAM.   This is the computer's general purpose memory. (In older, large computers this general purpose memory was sometimes called **core memory,** after the process by which it was manufactured.) It is workspace for your programs and your data. Nothing stays there very long and, relatively speaking, it is a small amount of space. Every time you turn on your computer, you must reload RAM with the programs and data that you need. Furthermore, many small 8-bit computers are not capable of addressing (accessing) more than about 64,000 (64K) 8-bit bytes of RAM and ROM together. 64K bytes of text characters may seem like a lot, but it turns out to be very, very limited in its potential for storing a library of programs. (In computer usage K, short for kilo, really means 1024 or 2^{10}, rather than 1,000, which is represented by a lower-case k. Thus 64K RAM means RAM that can hold up to 65,536 bytes.)

Sixteen-bit computers are capable of addressing more memory—just how much depends on the specific CPU chip. They do this by using more bits to encode the address of each piece of data, meaning the location in memory where a computer word is stored. In an 8-bit computer, two bytes are used for each address, allowing 2^{16} or 65,536 different addresses (64K). Some 16-bit computers use an address of 20 bits and are thus able to address over one million computer words.

But even 8-bit computers can access more memory by means of a technique called **bank select** or **bank switching,** in which the computer can still access only 64K or 128K bytes at a time, but it can select which bank of memory it wants to use. It is like being able to open another volume of a multi-volume book, yet still being able to open only one volume at a time. The user is not aware of this switching back and forth between banks. The programs that allow it are more difficult to create than those that do not make use of this technique, but they can be larger and more complex.

ROM.   This kind of memory usually contains special operating system programs that will either be used very often—such as those controlling the keyboard, video display, and printer—or provide a limited set of simple commands that will allow the user to load more powerful programs as needed. Some microcomputer manufacturers provide the BASIC language in ROM to save the rather lengthy time it takes to load the language into memory from a peripheral storage device. Also, the game cartridges that you can load into some computers and video game machines contain their programs in ROM. This is so useful that a number of computer manufacturers are now providing in ROM applications programs that you use often and in which program speed is important, such as word processors and spelling checkers.

ROM comes in several variations. It can be in the form of single chips, which are installed inside the computer by the manufacturer; or boards that can be fitted by the user into slots provided inside the machine, as with the Apple II series and IBM-PC; or cartridges, such as are used by the many lower cost home computers. These cartridges can be plugged into a special slot without opening up the machine.

So with RAM for a workspace and ROM to store the special programs your computer needs to perform its functions, you're all set, right? Wrong. You still need to store programs you write or data you enter. ROM is difficult to use, expensive, and is like writing on stone, while RAM is volatile—you can't keep anything in it for long. What you need is something like paper, on which you can write down your ephemeral thoughts and temporary data, and which can be easily changed as your thoughts become clearer, and your data becomes permanent. That's what peripheral mass storage devices are all about.

PERIPHERAL DEVICES
FOR STORING DATA

Peripheral mass storage devices provide a means of storing programs or other information in such a way that the information can be either recorded by or played back to the computer. Information stored in this fashion is said to be

machine-readable. The advantage of having information stored in this form is that you don't have to reenter the information every time (e.g., via a typewriter-like keyboard). The gain in time and convenience, even with relatively slow peripheral storage devices, is immense.

Also, this is the only reasonable way to load commercially written programs into the computer. Without disks or cassette tapes, you would have to type the program in at the keyboard, and since many commerical programs are thousands of lines of **assembly language,** this is just not practical. The whole software industry depends on the existence of peripheral storage as a medium for making its products available to the customer.

Peripheral storage devices tend to fall into two broad categories: those that use magnetic tape as a medium and those that use magnetic disks as a medium.

Magnetic Tape Devices

As practically every stereo buff knows, the nice thing about magnetic tape is that one can both record on it and play back from it. The same is true with the tape systems used by computers. There are several varieties.

The cheapest and simplest is the audio cassette system in which a standard audio cassette player/recorder, such as the one pictured in Fig. 9.2, is attached

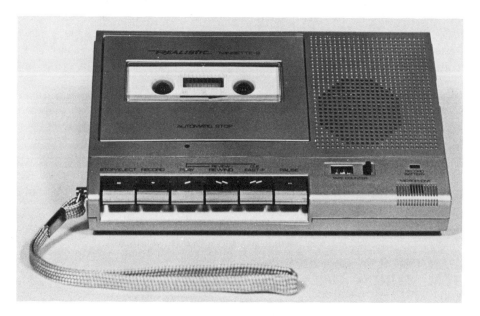

Figure 9.2   Audio cassette player/recorder

to the CPU via a special connection that converts the digital signals of the CPU into audio tones. These are then recorded on a tape cassette. When played back, the audio signal of the tape is converted to the digital signal of the CPU.

The only advantage of the audio cassette system is that it is cheap. Cassette recorders are available from $40 to $80 each, and the cassette tapes are approximately $2 each. The disadvantages of the system are that it is both relatively slow and somewhat unreliable. The more reliable cassette systems only operate at 30 characters per second, which means it can take several minutes to load a large program from the tape into memory. Unreliability is even worse than slowness, however. The frustration of finding that you cannot retrieve a long and complex program you thought you had saved on tape is very great, for it means that you will have to reenter the program manually. Thus there is a trade-off between price on the one hand and speed and reliability on the other. Not surprisingly perhaps, better performance tends to cost more.

There are also **tape drives** made specifically for storing computer output as a digital signal (rather than as an audio signal). These are much faster and much more reliable than audio cassette player/recorders. Until about 1983, such drives were also considerably more expensive (costing anywhere from several hundred to several thousand dollars, depending on the speed and sophistication of the drive). They are rapidly falling in price, however, and may soon become available as an alternative to either audio cassette or disk drives. The more sophisticated magnetic tape drives are widely used in large computer installations as an efficient means of storing very large volumes of information. These drives, such as the reel-to-reel drive shown in Fig. 9.3, tend to use half-inch-wide tape and take reels up to 16 inches in diameter.

Anyone who has used tape with stereo equipment knows that tape has an intrinsic design limitation: you cannot directly access any particular spot on the tape; you have to go forward or rewind until you find the place you want. This is fine if you want to play the whole tape (as you would if loading a small program from tape into RAM), but if you want only a couple of items here or there (as in most data-processing applications), skipping around to find them can be tedious. One of Murphy's Laws assures us that any data we want to access will be at the opposite end of the tape at the time we want it most.

Magnetic Disks

Magnetic disks are the answer to this access problem. Instead of using a long tape as a recording medium, information is recorded on the surface of a round, flat disk coated with the same surface material as magnetic tape. **Disk drives** rotate the disk very rapidly. Playback/record heads are fixed on an arm that can be positioned anywhere along a radius of the disk. The operating principle is very similar to a record player in an audio system. Like a record player, the

Figure 9.3   Reel-to-reel tape drive (1/2″ x 16″)

access to any spot on the surface is much faster than access to any given spot on a tape. Access times for disk systems are usually measured in thousandths of a second.

Magnetic disk drives for microcomputers come in two distinct forms: **floppy disk drives** and **hard disk drives.**

The floppy disk (or **diskette**) was originally developed by IBM to replace punched cards, but it has been widely used by the entire small computer industry as a fast, efficient, and highly cost-effective approach to peripheral storage for small computer systems. The hard disk is similar to the floppy in operation but is about ten times faster in access time and holds about ten times as much information in the same space. It is currently the most cost-effective approach to peripheral storage for larger systems.

The floppy disk is so called because it is made of a thin, flexible plastic that bends easily. Floppies come in two common sizes: 5 1/4-inch diameter and 8-inch diameter. They are permanently protected by a stiff envelope that has a window in it through which the heads of the drive contact the surface of the floppy disk. (See Fig. 9.4 showing a 5 1/4″ floppy disk with disk drive.)

Figure 9.4   5 1/4″ floppy disk drive

There is great variety in current disk technology. Depending on the manufacturer and system software chosen, a 5 1/4-inch floppy disk can hold anywhere from about 80,000 characters of information (80 kilobytes or 80K) to about 360,000 characters. The differences come from the density with which the information is recorded and the number of sides it is recorded on. **Double density** disks can hold almost twice as much data as single density disks, and some floppy disk drives work on both sides of a floppy disk at the same time, an option called **double-sided.** Eight-inch floppy disks can hold from about 250,000 characters to over a million (1 megabyte or 1M). Access times (the time it takes to access any given spot on the disk) and transfer rates (how fast information can be read or written once the starting point has been found) vary widely as well.

A form of floppy disk, called a **microdisk,** was developed in the early 1980s. As of this writing, the manufacturers have not determined a standard size for this disk, which may be 3″, 3 1/4″, or 3 1/2″ in diameter. Apple's Macintosh, for example, uses a 3 1/2″ microdisk, or "wafer", while Hitachi manufactures drives that use 3″ microdisks, and Dysan is manufacturing 3 1/4″ microdisks. Regardless of size, the microdisk is enclosed in a rigid plastic case, with sliding doors which cover the recording windows. Because the disk itself is stiffer than the larger floppy disks, it can hold more data for its size. Microdisk drives are not yet common, in large part because of this conflict of "standards", and which size will be the standard is anybody's guess.

Hard disks are made of rigid aluminum and are coated with a magnetic recording surface. They are generally much faster than floppy disk systems. That is, it takes less time for the CPU to get a chunk of information from a hard disk than from a floppy disk. For applications such as data processing that require a great deal of input from and output to data files, this is an important consideration.

Further, hard disks are much more reliable than floppy disks, which tend to take a terrible beating from users. Hard disks are contained in much more protected environments. The disk units are usually sealed so that there is much less chance of dirt or smoke fouling the recording surface or the heads. However, the drives are more sensitive to vibration and physical shock, and should not be casually carted around.

Hard disks are also larger in capacity than floppy disks. The smallest hard disks hold about 5 megabytes (5 million characters) of information, which is 5 times the capacity of the largest floppy disks and over 50 times the capacity of the smaller ones. Much larger hard disks (from 10 to several hundred megabytes) are available for more money. One of the reasons for this increase in capacity is that they can store characters more densely than floppy disks because the heads can read from or write to the hard disk surface without actually touching it. This means the heads must be very close to the surface, and therefore machinery of a very fine tolerance is required for reliable operation. A speck of dust can jam between a head and the surface and cause great damage, hence the need for protective environments.

Although hard disk drives cost more than floppy disk drives, the cost per unit of storage is much less than for floppy disk systems. However, the amount of storage available on a hard disk is more than a single user needs for most educational applications, so in schools the hard disk system is usually found in an administrative context or in a multiple user computer system. This latter could be either a timesharing system or an intelligent hard disk, shared by several single-user computers, as we'll discuss more fully later in this chapter and in the next chapter.

Until the 1980s, hard disk drives, such as the one shown in Fig. 9.5, were only affordable by those purchasing large computer systems, but a breakthrough known as **Winchester technology** has brought the price of these items down drastically. (See Fig. 9.6.) As with floppy disks, recording densities and access times vary tremendously but are at least ten times the densities and speeds of floppy disks. Hard disks are available that can hold from 5 million characters (5M) to well over 100 million characters (100M).

Even newer technologies involve the storing of data on laser disks such as the compact disks (CDs) used to play back movies on your television and music on your stereo system. One of the problems with such disks, however, is that they are more like ROM than RAM; that is, once the data is stored, it cannot be

Figure 9.5   Hard disk drive

easily erased, as the recording process burns physical holes in the recording medium. This problem, however, is now being worked on by engineers.

At this point, we have discussed the central computer and peripheral storage. So far all we've got is some electronic devices talking to each other. The item missing from this cozy arrangement is you, the user. You need a way to communicate with the CPU and memory, both sending information (instructions or data) to the CPU and receiving results back. The section on peripheral storage devices was about communications between the computer and its library files. This next section is about communication between the computer and you.

Figure 9.6 Winchester hard disk drive

PERIPHERAL DEVICES
FOR THE USER

Some peripheral devices provide communication between the computer and the user. Examples of such human interfaces to computers include input devices such as keyboards, light pens, game paddles, bar code readers, optical character readers, digitizers, and mark sense readers. Figs. 9.7, 9.8, 9.9, and 9.10 show some of these. Other examples include output devices such as cathode-ray tube monitors, printers, plotters, voice synthesizers, tone generators, and AC line controllers. Increasingly, some of these devices are combined into **I/O (input/output) devices.** For example, a keyboard and a video screen are often combined into a **video terminal,** such as the one pictured in Fig. 9.11, or a printer and a keyboard are combined into a **hardcopy terminal,** as in Fig. 9.12. The actual computer itself is often so small that it is easily tucked away in a box largely dedicated to a peripheral device, such as a video terminal. Several manufacturers even incorporate into one unit a computer, video terminal, a pair of floppy disk drives, and connections for a printer and other peripheral devices, as shown in Fig. 9.13.

Terminals

Despite recent advances in voice input technology and the growing popularity of pointer-like input devices such as the *Mouse*, the vast majority of terminals use typewriter-like keyboards as their primary input component. Each time the user strikes a key, the terminal sends off to the computer a set of electronic pulses that are eventually changed into a 1-byte digital signal that reaches the CPU. If the CPU is accepting information from the user at this point, it will put the character received somewhere in its memory and (by way of confirmation) send a copy back that is reproduced on the output device.

Terminal keyboards vary in style and quality. Some have actual keys like a typewriter, some have buttons like those on a calculator (snidely called "chicklets"), and others use a flat touch-sensitive panel. Some keyboards will have an additional numeric keypad for faster entry of numbers, and/or a set of special function keys. Some of these function keys always do the same thing, such as "print," while others can be defined by particular pieces of applications software. With some keyboards, all keys can be redefined by means of a special program. Most keyboards are easy to use; however some are very awkward.

Terminals vary in their output component. Video terminals have a **Cathode Ray Tube (CRT),** which is very much like a TV tube but with some significant differences. Hardcopy terminals, on the other hand, have a printer instead of a CRT and look very much like a large typewriter. Video terminals are usually capable of receiving information from the computer at a much faster rate than

Figure 9.7   3-D spatial digitizer

Figure 9.8   Mouse

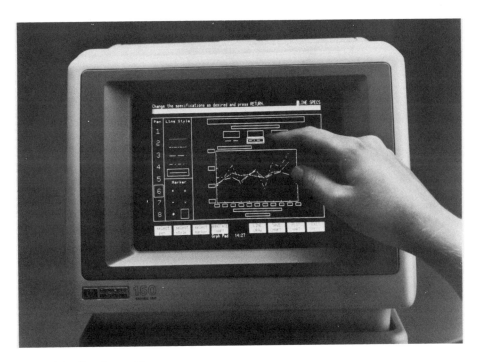

Figure 9.9   Touch-sensitive screen

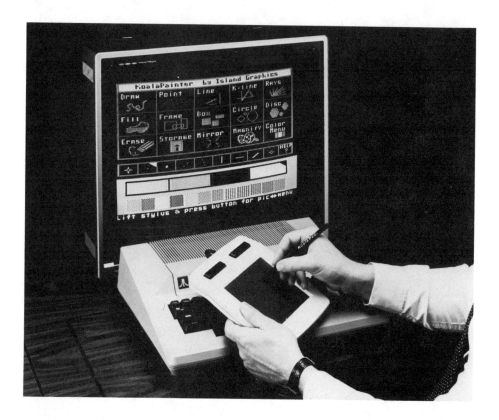

Figure 9.10   Digitizer tablet

a hardcopy device, are much quieter, and don't chew up reams of paper un-necessarily. Also, a video terminal can be a much more flexible medium for graphics, as you can move the **cursor** anywhere on the screen with relative ease, draw and erase lines or graphic symbols readily, and can have color. On the other hand, hardcopy devices provide you with an ongoing record of your entire terminal session (although this may often be more than you really want). And while most printers are only black and white, some can produce colors by means of special ribbons, and more recently by means of colored inkjets. Most users do want results printed out at some point, so with a video terminal a printer may also be necessary.

Video terminals have screens of varying size, usually from 5″ to 14″ measured diagonally. Most good quality terminals provide a screen that is capable of displaying

Figure 9.11   Video terminal

24 lines of 80 characters each, which is virtually the industry standard. (Many computers, of course, actually display fewer lines or fewer characters per line.) Some more expensive models can display up to 132 characters in a line, though there are some that, alas, provide much-reduced formats. Some video terminals are capable of graphics (which simply means you can draw pictures as well as display text); some only handle text.

Figure 9.12 Hardcopy terminal

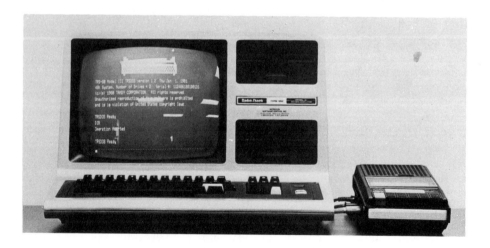

Figure 9.13 Computer, including video terminal, two floppy disk drives and connections for peripherals, shown here connected to audio cassette player/recorder

A CRT without a keyboard is called a **monitor.** (See Fig. 9.14.) While some computers can use a regular TV set, a TV has limitations on the degree of **resolution** it can display. TVs, for example, cannot clearly show an entire line of 80 characters. A good video terminal or monitor can cost as much as (or more than) a good color television set. Some CRTs display white characters on a black ground, others have a green or amber display, and others are full color. The only real advantage of a TV, if your computer will allow it, is that you can use an existing set rather than buying another expensive piece of equipment. However, for some uses, such as word processing and high resolution color graphics, a monitor is ultimately the only reasonable choice.

Most terminals these days are **intelligent,** which means that they have a microprocessor inside them to handle the terminal's functions and communications with the host computer. The so-called **dumb terminal** leaves all the chores to the host computer. A TV is a good example of a dumb terminal, though it is really serving the purpose of a monitor. Most *home* computers rely on TVs for their displays.

Figure 9.14   CRT monitor

Printers

A **printer** is an output device; that is, the computer can send information to it but not receive information from it. It allows you, the user, to receive output from the computer on a piece of paper so that you can read it, analyze it, mark it up, file it, or dispose of it. The main difference between a printer and a hardcopy or printing terminal is that a printer lacks a keyboard. There are, however, several printing devices on the market that can be purchased with or without a keyboard. These options are usually indicated by the acronyms **KSR (Keyboard Send/Receive)** or **RO (Receive Only).** The KSR printer is, of course, a hardcopy terminal.

As with everything else in this chapter, printers such as those pictured come in seemingly infinite variety. They vary in:

- The process used to produce a character on paper (dot matrix, daisy wheel, ink jet, laser, thermal, electrostatic).
- The forms of paper handled (rolls, continuous pin-feed, single sheets).
- The width of paper handled (from 4 1/2″ to 15 3/4″).
- The speed of printing (from 10 characters per second to over 200 characters per second).
- Price (from a few hundred to several thousand dollars).

But the purpose of all printers is the same: to transfer computer information to the printed page. The two most common and least expensive types of printer are the dot matrix and daisy wheel. Figs. 9.15a and 9.15b and 9.16a and 9.16b show examples of the print elements and print appearance of these.

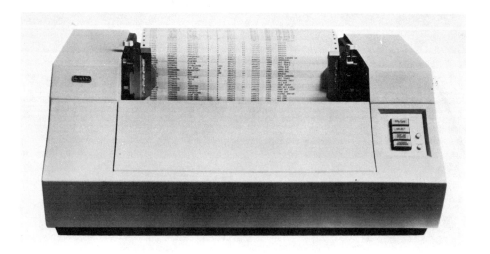

Figure 9.15a   Dot matrix printer

Epson FX-80 Print Sample

One reason Epson sells more p
in the world is the crisp, cl
PICA sample. However, ELITE is
smaller print, you can use CONDENSED.

But just having different siz
Epson. Epson printers have h
is the ability to mix *italic*,
<u>underlines</u> within the text th
emphasis, try doublestrike, e
lines.

TRY TITLES IN
Subheads can be emphasized do
The body of the text can I
portional mode using the popular

You can even mix text and gra
line as these examples of int
traffic signs show:

Engineers, scientists, and ma
appreciate the **superscript** an
for equations and formulas: K^3
$[Y^2 + 2X^{11}]$.

The FX even contains' eight fu
International characters:
à ° ç § è ù é ¨ Ä Ö Ü ä ö ü ß
ø å Ø É Ò ì ſt ¡ Ñ ¿ ñ ¥

User defined characters (incl
control codes) may be printed
© ♫ ☐ α β √

Figure 9.15b Dot matrix printout

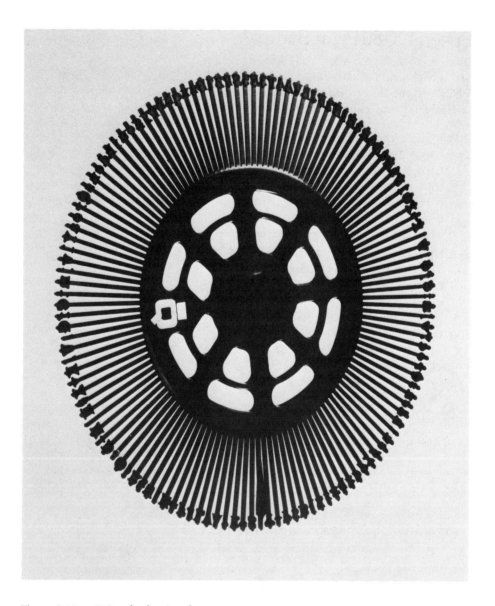

Figure 9.16a   Daisywheel print element

QUME PRINTWHEEL LISTING

SEQUENCE	TYPESTYLE	PITCH	PART NUMBER	CHARACTER SET (IN ASCENDING ASCII ORDER)
WP	BOOKFACE ACADEMIC	10	82061	@ABCDEFGHIJKLMNOPQRSTUVWXYZ[®]©_ °abcdefghijklmnopqrstuvwxyz§¶†"_ |!"#$%&'()*+,-./0123456789:;<=>?
WP	COURIER	10	82050	@ABCDEFGHIJKLMNOPQRSTUVWXYZ[®]©_ °abcdefghijklmnopqrstuvwxyz§¶†"_ |!"#$%&'()*+,-./0123456789:;<=>?
WP	ORATOR 90%	10	82057	@ABCDEFGHIJKLMNOPQRSTUVWXYZ[®]©_ °ABCDEFGHIJKLMNOPQRSTUVWXYZ§¶†"_ |!"#$%&'()*+,-./0123456789:;<=>?
WP	PICA	10	82051	@ABCDEFGHIJKLMNOPQRSTUVWXYZ[®]©_ °abcdefghijklmnopqrstuvwxyz§¶†"_ |!"#$%&'()*+,-./0123456789:;<=>?
WP	PRESTIGE PICA	10	82058	@ABCDEFGHIJKLMNOPQRSTUVWXYZ[®]©_ °abcdefghijklmnopqrstuvwxyz§¶†"_ |!"#$%&'()*+,-./0123456789:;<=>?
WP	COURIER	12	82086	@ABCDEFGHIJKLMNOPQRSTUVWXYZ[®]©_ °abcdefghijklmnopqrstuvwxyz§¶†"_ |!"#$%&'()*+,-./0123456789:;<=>?
WP	COURIER ITALIC	12	82060	@ABCDEFGHIJKLMNOPQRSTUVWXYZ[®]©_ °abcdefghijklmnopqrstuvwxyz§¶†"_ |!"#$%&'()*+,-./0123456789:;<=>?
WP	DUAL GOTHIC	12	82059	@ABCDEFGHIJKLMNOPQRSTUVWXYZ[®]©_ °abcdefghijklmnopqrstuvwxyz§¶†"_ |!"#$%&'()*+,-./0123456789:;<=>?
WP	ELITE	12	82070	@ABCDEFGHIJKLMNOPQRSTUVWXYZ[®]©_ °abcdefghijklmnopqrstuvwxyz§¶†"_ |!"#$%&'()*+,-./0123456789:;<=>?
WP	LETTER GOTHIC	12	82089	@ABCDEFGHIJKLMNOPQRSTUVWXYZ[®]©_ °abcdefghijklmnopqrstuvwxyz§¶†"_ |!"#$%&'()*+,-./0123456789:;<=>?
WP	LIGHT ITALIC	12	82182	@ABCDEFGHIJKLMNOPQRSTUVWXYZ[®]©_ °abcdefghijklmnopqrstuvwxyz§¶†"_ |!"#$%&'()*+,-./0123456789:;<=>?
WP	PRESTIGE ELITE	12	82052	@ABCDEFGHIJKLMNOPQRSTUVWXYZ[®]©_ °abcdefghijklmnopqrstuvwxyz§¶†"_ |!"#$%&'()*+,-./0123456789:;<=>?
WP	SCRIPT	12	82181	@ABCDEFGHIJKLMNOPQRSTUVWXYZ[®]©_ °abcdefghijklmnopqrstuvwxyz§¶†"_ |!"#$%&'()*+,-./0123456789:;<=>?

S-118

Figure 9.16b   Daisywheel print sample

221

Another very useful output device, for producing graphs, charts, and pictures, is the plotter. Fig. 9.17 shows an example, along with a sample of the kind of output a plotter can produce. More expensive versions can produce a full range of colors as well.

Figure 9.17   Graphics plotter

INTERFACES AND I/O PORTS

You may have been wondering exactly how the CPU communicates with the various peripheral devices we've discussed. After all, the CPU only understands patterns of electronic pulses or digital signals. How do such signals become typed letters on a video screen or a printer? The missing pieces are **interfaces** that change the signal of the CPU to some other kind of signal that the peripheral device in question can recognize, and vice versa. The interface for a video screen is different from that needed for a printer and different again from the interface needed for a tape drive. In addition to simply converting the signals back and forth, interfaces perform other functions like resolving different device speeds.

(It is no good sending a signal to a device faster than it can process it—compare the lightning speeds of the CPU with a 10 character per-second printer.) The interfaces themselves are connected to the CPU via chips and connections called **input/output ports** (an I/O port is pictured projecting out from the top right of the circuit board in Fig. 9.1). A port is just a way in and out of the CPU.

Although different devices require different sorts of interfaces, the industry has managed to standardize two such interfaces: the RS232-C Serial interface and the Centronics Parallel interface. A **serial interface** transmits or accepts information one bit at a time. In contrast, a **parallel interface** accepts or transmits information a computer word at a time, by having (at least) eight wires to carry the eight bits simultaneously. All communications over the telephone lines are serial; eight lines would be required to support a parallel interface.

Finally, what ties together all these elements (central processing unit, memory, input/output ports, interfaces, and so forth) is a set of parallel wires and connections called a **bus.** One of the breakthrough concepts in recent years has been to standardize bus structures so that different printed circuit boards from different manufacturers can plug in and work immediately. There are several competing standard bus structures on the microcomputer market, the most widely adopted of which is the S-100 bus. Some computer manufacturers have their own proprietary bus structure, such as for the Apple or IBM-PC.

A standardized plug-in bus structure is called a **mother board** (or sometimes a **cardcage** or **backplane**). A mother board, such as is inside an Apple, is a large circuit board that also has special connectors into which other circuit boards can be plugged. A cardcage, on the other hand, is just a frame to hold a number of circuit boards, with cables from the connectors to other parts of the computer. In either case, you can plug in printed circuit cards with various chips designed for specific purposes. There are cards for virtually any purpose you can think of: interfaces, special graphics boards, voice recognition boards, language boards. Many of these come with their own central processing unit and/or ROM with some special programs on them. A cardcage with circuit cards plugged in is shown in Fig. 9.18.

COMMUNICATIONS EQUIPMENT

Computer users can do a lot with wire: string it from building to building or even run it halfway across town to connect remote pieces of equipment together. Using wire in this fashion, you can connect terminals all over a building or campus to a central computer, or you can link several computers together in a network. But running your own wire at some point becomes impractical, and it begins to make sense to use that great network of wire that is already in place: the telephone system, including its communications satellites.

Figure 9.18   Cardcage with circuit boards

However, the telephone system is set up to convert voice noises into electronic signals and then reassemble the voice noises at the other end. Thus communication between computer devices through the telephone requires a special interface that will take the digital signals of the computer and convert them to appropriate electronic signals before sending them on their way. And at the other end, the computer needs a box that will take the electronic signals produced by the telephone and convert them back into digital signals recognizable by the computer device again. Such a device is called a **modem** (**mo**dulator/**dem**odulator).

There are two variations of modems: **direct-connect modems** and **acoustic couplers.** Acoustic couplers send and receive their signals directly through the mouthpiece and earpiece of the telephone, while direct-connect modems send and receive through wire connections between the computer and the telephone jack; otherwise, they are identical in function.

Recall that interfaces between telephone lines and computer devices are serial in nature; that is, the bits of information or the tones representing them go through the phone line one at a time. Not only do the bits travel serially, but each group of eight bits (or each byte) is preceded by a start bit and followed by a stop bit. Thus it takes ten bits of information to transmit one character via modem.

The speed at which bits are transmitted and received becomes a real consideration for reasons of cost and efficiency. This rate is usually measured in bits per second and is called the **Baud rate.** The commonly used Baud rates are 110, 300, 600, 1200, 2400, 4800, 9600, 19200. Currently, 1200 Baud (bits per second) or 120 characters per second (remember: transmission requires 10 bits per character) is the maximum rate attainable over ordinary public telephone voice lines with commonly available modems. Higher Baud rates require **dedicated data lines** and/or special and expensive modems.

There is lots more to hardware peripheral devices, but they all work on the same principles described above. They are either devices that allow you, the user, to make input to the computer or to obtain output from the computer, or they are peripheral storage devices that allow you to save programs and/or data between sessions.

SOFTWARE

But all this great hardware is worthless without software to run it. The classic error school systems make when first buying computers is to put all of their money into hardware and have none left for software. It is analogous to buying a record player without having any records to play on it. In the horror stories that abound in the short history of computing, one that seems to crop up over and over again is of the school system that bought a $50,000 computer, which then lay idle for two years for lack of software to run it. (Software is a collective name for programs, those lists of instructions that tell the CPU what to do—whether to play chess or print the payroll.)

The process of acquiring a computer system should really start at the software end. The school administrators who bought that dormant computer should have first decided what use the school system wanted to make of the computer, next identified and priced the software necessary to perform those tasks, and only then chosen the hardware. Your purposes in acquiring a computer can be very general and educationally oriented, but you will need software to fulfill those purposes.

There are two basic types of software: **applications software** and **systems software.** You have already been introduced to applications software: it comprises programs like the one to average numbers and the one to print the payroll checks. The effect of applications software is to insulate the user from the obscure and trivial operations down inside the CPU. A programmer has already figured out how to make the computer average numbers: the user doesn't need to deal with that side of the problem any more. Applications software, then, is what makes the computer useful in doing the tasks we want it to do.

Systems software falls into two rather broad and somewhat overlapping categories. The first is essentially applications software for programmers. It enables them to think about programming in more human terms, instead of in machine terms, thus making it much easier for them to write the programs to perform desired applications. Users only interested in specific applications and not intending to develop any applications programs of their own are prone to think that they need not care about this kind of systems software. Perhaps, but many applications packages will eventually require modification and then the users will care. Further, if the systems software is poor and hard to use, then fewer good applications packages will be available for that system.

The second type of systems software includes the programs that enable the computer to function at all, and in certain important ways. It is systems software that makes it possible for one computer to be shared by several users at the same time, that provides for efficient management of files on the disk drives, and that allows the use of various computer languages.

Systems software usually consists of an **operating system program,** several **utility programs,** and one or more **high-level language translators.** The distinction between these is somewhat blurred. Sometimes, for example, the operating system is made part of the language translator. Whether a particular function is included in the main operating system program, in a separate utility program, or in a language interpreter is the decision of the designers. How it is done is not terribly important, so long as the main functions are covered.

The operating system, generally speaking, allows the user to run programs and to control the movement of data to and from the computer memory and peripheral devices. A **disk operating system (DOS)** for example, should allow you to name disk files, to obtain a list or **directory** of those names, and to copy files from the disk to another peripheral device. It should keep track of where all your files are on the disk—so you don't have to know or care.

Utility programs may include some sort of program to copy the entire contents of one disk onto another, a program to preformat new disks, some sort of text-editor to facilitate the typing in and changing of programs, and an **assembler,** which is a primitive language translator that makes giving instructions to the CPU a little easier. An **assembly language** is just one step up from the binary codes that the CPU uses. Instead of giving the CPU a binary code meaning "add," you can give the assembler a mnemonic instruction (perhaps ADD) and let the assembler translate that into binary code. Generally speaking, there is a direct one-to-one correspondence between an assembly instruction and a binary CPU-level instruction.

Assembly languages are sometimes referred to as **low-level languages** because of their close relationship to the actual operation of the CPU. **High-level languages,** such as FORTRAN, BASIC, COBOL, APL, Forth, C, Pascal, and Logo are, in contrast, quite removed from the operation of the CPU. A single instruction in a high-level language may generate several CPU level instructions. With a high-level language, you don't have to worry about the minute details of the computer's operation at its most fundamental level. The trade-off is in efficiency. No one has yet written a high-level language that performs as well as assembly language: we pay for ease of use. But as the technology allows the speeds of computers to increase and their prices to drop, it is a small cost to bear—and the benefits of high-level languages are many. For one thing, it takes less time to write a program in a high-level language. Also, a program once written is easier to understand in its high-level form, thus making updating and correcting easier. Even amateurs can write reasonably useful programs in BASIC and Pascal.

However appealing high-level languages may be to humans, they must be translated somehow into computer code for the CPU, since that is the only thing it understands. There are two types of translators: **compilers** and **interpreters** (an assembler is a special case of a compiler). Most high-level languages are compiled rather than interpreted. A language is usually one or the other, although BASIC is available in both compiled and interpreted versions.

A compiler works as follows: the user writes a program in a high-level language (such as FORTRAN, which is a compiled language) and stores that program in a file. The user then runs a FORTRAN compiler program, which translates the original program into machine code and stores that code in another file. Then the user tells the computer to load the machine code file into its memory and execute the instructions in it.

An interpreter works somewhat differently: the user loads a BASIC interpreter (for example) into memory, then gives the interpreter a BASIC program to run. The interpreter looks at the program one line at a time, translates, and executes that line, and then goes on to the next. Interpreters are easy to use and great for the "quick-and-dirty" program. But if a program is intended to be run often, it is better to write it in a compiled language, since an interpreter must repeat the translation process every time the program is run.

At the United Nations there are two kinds of human language translators: those who give a complete and uninterrupted translation when the speaker is done, and those who translate a speech line by line as it is being given. Compilers and interpreters are analogous to these two sorts of human translators. Clearly, each has a different function, though the end result is the same.

Most high-level languages were devised with a particular class of problems in mind. FORTRAN (**For**mula **Tran**slator) was designed to solve scientific and engineering problems easily and efficiently. COBOL (**CO**mmon **B**usiness-**O**riented **L**anguage) was designed for commercial data processing and reporting applications. BASIC (**B**eginners **A**ll-purpose **S**equential **I**nstruction **C**ode) was designed to be simple for laypeople to learn and use in its rudimentary forms, and yet to be very powerful in its full capability. Logo was designed to give children access to the full power of a computer, as well as to be a powerful and elegant language for adults. Pascal was designed as a language to teach computer programming, and combines the power of FORTRAN and COBOL with the more elegant logical structures of ALGOL (**ALGO**rithmic **L**anguage). The language C was designed to facilitate the writing of systems software, such as operating systems and compilers. Forth was originally created to control astronomical observatories, and is widely used for that today, but is also used to create graphics and to write games. LISP is one of a class of languages used in the study of artificial intelligence, as are SNOBOL and Smalltalk. Each of these languages has its own "feel," just as human languages are different from each other.

In addition to being better or worse for certain classes of problems, high-level languages have a way of defining your computer environment, including the way you perceive your computer system and the way you use it. The situation is a little like the difference between hearing a play on the radio, seeing it on television, and attending it in person. The difference can be quite profound. Logo, for example, was specifically designed to create an environment in which children could experiment with and learn sophisticated mathematical concepts in a manner analogous to the way we learn our first spoken language. That a computer language can create an environment for exploring and experiencing "mathland" is a profound and extraordinary fact.

Yet another class of high-level languages is the **author languages.** These languages determine your programming needs from your responses to a series of questions. The author language program then produces a perfectly ordinary program just as though you had written it yourself. The effect is to allow you to write programs in a computer language without knowing much about the language.

Today there are literally hundreds of languages (and **dialects** of languages, which are different versions of the same mother tongue). Which ones you choose for your computer system will depend on what purpose you would have it serve.

TIMESHARING AND NETWORKING

These are two major methods of allowing multiple users to share expensive computer resources: **timesharing** and **networking.** Timesharing is an older technology, generally associated with mainframe or minicomputer systems. Networking has grown in popularity in recent years due to the desirability of sharing resources among microcomputers.

Timesharing

Timesharing is the use of one computer by several concurrent users. Typically, each user has a terminal that is connected to the shared computer. The connections can be made either through direct wires to ports on the computer or through modems and the telephone system.

Timesharing is based on the recognition that it is unusual for a single user sitting at a terminal to keep a central processing unit entirely occupied. By sharing the use of a CPU among several users, the cost and power of one computer and its peripherals may be shared by many.

However, you should note that the CPU can only do one thing at a time: it does not, as some think, actually process several user requests simultaneously. Rather the CPU will process one user's request for some small fraction of a second (called a **timeslice**), and then it will take up some other user's request. Timesharing operating systems are generally complex. The operating system must keep track of all the different users and where each user was last suspended, while actually only servicing one user at a time. The timesharing system must also resolve contending requests for its services—not unlike a teacher in a crowded classroom with many students simultaneously clamoring for attention. Further, the computer activity of each user of a timesharing system must be insulated from every other user, so that one user's programs and data are not altered or lost by the interference of another user.

Timesharing usually requires fairly large and powerful hardware resources: a fast CPU, a great deal of memory, a large volume of hard disk space, a magnetic tape drive for back-up of information on the disks, sophisticated communications equipment, and a fast line printer. Thus school systems generally use timesharing for central administrative purposes, not for classroom instruction. However, timesharing *can* work in a much less powerful environment, although usually the constraints of such an environment make timesharing more trouble than it is worth. For example, while timesharing may be implemented on a system using only floppy disks for peripheral storage, this almost always results in a wrangle between the users over which disks will be on which drives. Nonetheless, in an appropriate environment, timesharing can result in a very cost-effective system on a per-user basis, even for instructional purposes.

Networking

Networking is the communication between or the sharing of resources by two or more different computers. There are three broad categories of networks:

1. Resource-sharing networks.
2. Communications networks.
3. Distributed processing networks.

While timesharing is the sharing of one central computer among several users, **resource sharing** is the sharing of one or more peripheral devices among several computers. As single-user computer systems have increased in usefulness and decreased in price, the idea of sharing the more expensive peripherals has gained currency. For example, a school might wish to provide one printer for every four classroom instructional computer units. This printer could be shared by providing a rotary switch that controlled the actual connection between the printer and a single computer.

With the appropriate systems software to handle conflicting requests for the shared equipment, almost anything is possible. Any device that is not worth buying for every computer unit may potentially be shared by several units. Devices that have been effectively shared include high-speed printers, letter-quality printers, plotters, hard disk drives, and high-speed tape drives.

In **communications networks** the individual computers can send files or messages back and forth between the nodes (the computers) of the network. Communications networks can be particularly useful in instruction. Communication, after all, is a great deal of what education is about. Such networks can make possible a class of geographically separated students, can provide connections to large information systems (such as CompuServe or The Source), or simply provide a means of sharing ideas, programs, problems, and news, as for example, on a Computer Bulletin Board.

In **distributed processing networks** some data processing is done at smaller remote computers and then transmitted to a large central computer **(uploaded)** for more complex processing with results then sent back to the remote computers **(downloaded)** for review and more processing. In such a network, all communication is between the central computer and the units connected to it. Communication between the individual units, if any, is handled entirely by the central computer. Distributed processing is like timesharing, except that the terminals are replaced by computers capable of doing some of their own processing. However, unlike timesharing, distributed processing is unlikely to have many instructional applications. Its value is for the many data-processing intensive tasks faced daily by school administrators.

Networking is only in its infancy at this time. It is an area in which we may expect great technological change and numerous creative applications over the next few years.

CONCLUSIONS

We've covered a lot of ground in this chapter, and some of it rather quickly, but by now you should know enough about computers to be able to understand most of the technical issues with which you, as an administrator, may need to deal. In the next chapter, you'll get to apply that knowledge to the important task of specifying the computer system most appropriate for your district and its goals.

Choosing Your Computer System 10

Probably the most important, and most expensive single decision you will ever make as an administrator is to determine what computer system your district will purchase. Whether the decision is ultimately yours or you are making recommendations to the ultimate decision-maker, the significance of the decision is equally weighty. Even if you are only a computer coordinator for an elementary school, deciding on the purchase of two or three relatively inexpensive personal computers, the decision is extremely important in the context of your situation.

However, you should not let the significance of this decision intimidate you. We have known too many school administrators who have allowed the scope and apparent technicality of this decision paralyze them to the point where they either abdicated responsibility for making it or "closed their eyes and took a stab in the dark." This book was written, in part, to combat this counterproductive reaction of administrators to the daunting prospect of purchasing computers for their schools. Once you've finished reading and digesting what we've shared with you from our experiences and research, you should be prepared to make this decision with confidence, albeit probably not with certainty.

The first six chapters of this book laid the managerial foundation for your decision by walking through a systematic planning and implementation process. This included long-range planning procedures, political and financial strategies, procedures for annual planning and implementation, approaches to staff development, and detailed suggestions for coping with the myriad tasks of day-to-day operation of a computer facility in the schools. This foundation should have provided you with most of what you need to know to be able to confront the purchase decision.

However, we suspect that many readers, after reading Chapters 1–6, may still have lacked sufficient knowledge about computers and their potential applications to make these decisions with confidence. Thus, Chapters 7 and 8 were written to provide an overview of potential uses for computers in instruction and administration. The decisions you and your staff make about which of these applications you want to carry out will significantly determine what kind of computer system you should purchase. Yet, you should keep in mind that priorities change so that the more flexible a system you choose, the more likely it is that you'll be able to use it to accommodate new instructional and administrative objectives.

Finally, Chapter 9 was written to provide you with as much technical information as you'll ever need to make the important purchase decisions. For some of you, it may have been partially or entirely a review, but we suspect that for most readers it has provided that last new bit of information they need to feel sufficiently knowledgeable to make the purchase decisions with confidence.

In this chapter, we present a general approach to the complex questions of choosing a computer system and offer school administrators some basic guidelines for the slippery questions of hardware, software, and system specification. Too many school systems buy a certain computer system because of pressure from parents or teachers, or because they have been sold on it by an enthusiastic sales representative, or because a local high-tech industry will provide it at substantial savings, or for some other less than rational reason. It is our hope that after reading this chapter, you will provide the kind of informed leadership to your staff that will result in a rational approach to computer system selection. There is still no guarantee that you will make the most appropriate choice, but your chances will be considerably improved with forethought and planning.

A RATIONAL APPROACH TO SYSTEM SELECTION

The key to rational decision-making about computer system selection, and purchase, like every other aspect of computer implementation, is that it must be consistent with the educational goals of the district and the long-range district computer implementation plan. The aim is to specify a computer system that will allow you to attain your goals for computer use at a price that seems worth it. The idea is for you and your staff to determine what your computer system must do and how much that will cost. This gives the people who will eventually allocate funds for the computer (perhaps, you!) a reasonable grasp of the decision they must make and creates a climate of reasonable expectations for the computer's performance. This approach should be taken whether you are the administrator of a small funded program contemplating the acquisition of a single personal computer for your area or the superintendent of schools, seeking to select a far more powerful computer system to serve myriad functions in your district. This approach should increase both your chances of adequate funding and the likelihood that your staff and others will regard this purchase as a success.

The central question is, "What uses do we intend to make of computers now, and what further uses might we make of them in the future?" Those involved in the specification of a computer system should ask this question of every constituent group who might be affected by computer purchases. The answers will vary widely and will be constantly changing, but the question needs early and ongoing attention. The formulation of a catalog of desired computer applications is perhaps the single most important process you can undertake in evaluating and acquiring a computer system. It is essential, of course, that this "wish list" have some connection with the reality of both the technology and your budget. That this may be so, you and your staff may wish to use the worksheets in Appendix A. These are intended to assist you in matching desired applications with necessary components at a range of prices. But before using the worksheet, as a leader in your school system, you need to know a little more about computer system configurations, involving both software and hardware, and how to evaluate them. You do not need to become an expert but you need to know enough to understand the "experts" when they make their recommendations. This chapter is a primer, designed to provide you with such a level of understanding.

LEARNING ABOUT COMPUTER SYSTEMS

To begin with, you and your staff need to gain a concrete, hands-on grasp of what a computer can and cannot do. Then you will be able to specify a cogent list of appropriate goals, based on your own knowledge and experience—especially experience. There is only so much that you can learn from books on this subject. Hands-on experience is critical. You need a "messing about" stage. That being the case, make gaining such experience your first goal. Purchase or lease several different inexpensive computers so you and those involved in the computer system selection process can learn more about the state of the art and the art of the possible. Let the short range goal be to expose staff to computers, to gain some knowledge and experience, and to see where you might go from there.

One argument for obtaining several trial computers might be to compare your situation to trying to learn to drive a car without ever getting behind the wheel. These first computers need not be of the same kind as those you think you would like later, and need not have all the bells and whistles. It is far better to spend several hundred dollars to learn what you need and then dispose of those computers, if you must, than to spend $40,000 on a system only to discover you can't use it, or that computing is not appropriate to your situation, and then be unable to recover your loss.

Do not try to implement a major installation of computer hardware and software unless you know what you are doing. Move within the range of your competence and experience. Remember, the bigger the installation and commitment of funds, the larger the potential for disaster. And Murphy's Laws are very active in the computer field. If the system you are contemplating is more complex than several stand-alone computers, it is best to hire a consultant—after you have done as much technical, political, and budgetary research as you can. Professional confirmation of your conclusions will be reassuring to you, and to those who allocate the funds.

Having easy access to a computer is the best way to learn about computers, but it is not the only way. The classic approaches to learning about new fields apply to computer systems as well: Read the literature and talk to those who have already acquired knowledge and experience. In addition to this book, there are a number of good, nontechnical publications to help you get started (see the Resources section: Periodicals).

If another school in your area has already gone through the process of computer selection and implementation, that is by far the best place to start. Information can also be obtained from your state department of education, educational collaboratives, regional educational centers, and large area user groups. Other knowledgeable people include local computer store personnel, educational equipment dealers, and sales representatives from the hardware manufacturers. The most useful stores or dealers are the independents, the ones not committed to any particular brand. But talk to them all; a good knowledge of local resources is essential to your acquisition decision. Find out what systems they are selling and why; tell them that you are a beginner in the field; solicit their advice and help. But be considerate of their time—the retail computer business is highly competitive and profit margins are very narrow, so the salespeople are usually running behind schedule and are a little harassed. If you want to see the other end of the spectrum, go to a manufacturer of larger computers, such as IBM, Wang, Hewlett-Packard, or Digital Equipment Corporation. They will give you all the personal attention of one of their sales reps for as long as you want it. Their profit margins are better.

Often, computer stores will have the equipment they sell set up for demonstration. Test drive it as much as you can. Borrow or buy the manuals—the computer system's **documentation**—and read them, particularly the manuals for beginners. There are basically two kinds of manuals: those intended to be instructional (like a text) are aimed at beginners, while those intended to be used for reference (like a dictionary) are aimed at the more experienced user. Judge for yourself if the manuals are useful, readable, and complete. (This will be easier for you, as a beginner, to do with the first kind than with the second.) But be warned, good documentation is hard to come by. Unintelligible manuals do not mean a bad product, but do mean you will have a harder time learning about the product. On the other hand, beautifully written manuals do not necessarily signify a superior product, but it is an indication of that, and will make your evaluation far easier.

EVALUATING COMPUTER SYSTEMS

Evaluating a computer system is a three-pronged effort: The hardware, the operating environment, and the applications to which the system will be put must all be considered in parallel. This is complicated by the fact that sometimes it is difficult to distinguish the three elements. Some computers come with their operating system built in, while others require the addition of a commercial operating system. Some computers come bundled with (sold together with) various applications packages, while others come with nothing at all in the way of software. Sometimes the operating system is a separate entity within the computer, and at other times it seems to be a part of the primary programming language (usually BASIC). Sometimes the computers in a network seem almost totally independent, at other times their interdependence is all too obvious. Also, hardware can come in pieces, or it can come all enclosed in a single cabinet.

It is hard to make rules for evaluating a computer system. In some cases, a system, a software package, or a hardware component will be a good buy, even if it violates one or more of the rules. Those are the exceptions, but you should be on the look-out for them. If you find a product that seems especially suited to your particular needs, you may wish to base your decisions for the rest of the system on finding what will make use of that specific item.

We have formulated a number of guidelines to help you evaluate hardware, software, and operating environment. Some of these guidelines are more general, others (especially those dealing with applications software) more specific.

1. Look for Local Sales and Service

It is tempting, when looking at the ads in magazines and seeing the discounts some dealers offer, to try to buy your equipment mail order. If you know what you are doing, you can save from 20 percent to 50 percent that way. And indeed, for some minor software packages, or some less important pieces of hardware, this can be a good option. But only after you know what you are doing, and only if you know that the vendor will stand behind the product. Those savings are totally illusory if those who will be using the computers need help in setting up the equipment, help in running the software, or any kind of service at any time. It is of utmost importance that your district establish a good relationship with a local dealer, who can get you started, ease you over the rough spots, and handle repairs and maintenance quickly. Computers are generally reliable, but when they do break down, they do so in obscure, hard to define, and sometimes intermittent ways. Software, no matter how well documented, will generate questions from its users. To handle these situations, you need local support. Local dealers are not eager to service products they haven't sold. For hardware, investigate a maintenance contract, which should normally cost about 1 percent of the value of the hardware per month. It is best if your dealer is able to handle the maintenance, rather than having to send it off somewhere. Your dealer should also be able to provide training in the operation of your system, and should respond to telephoned questions. Select your dealer for his good service, rather than for his good prices.

2. Obtain and Read the Documentation before Purchasing Products

The documentation for much hardware and software can be purchased separately from the products. The prices may look formidable, but it is better to have spent the $20.00 or so for the documentation only to learn that the product is not right, than to spend perhaps several hundred or several thousand dollars for the product and then discover it will not suit your needs. The documentation should describe in detail all the features and limitations of the product, and this knowledge will make an actual demonstration or test more meaningful and comprehensible. And remember that good documentation can be an indicator of a good-quality product.

3. Talk to Users and Owners of the System You are Considering

Bear in mind that it will be a little like talking to the proud owner of a new car. Most new owners will be quite pleased with their choice, whatever the true merits of the case. Only a very few will admit to making a mistake. Long-time owners can be far more objective, and their reports of experiences with their systems will be very useful in your evaluation of a particular system or product, especially if you have researched that product independently and read the documentation. Even if the owners praise a particular program or computer, what they like about it may be something you will not. The people you talk with may even be willing to give you a chance for more hands-on experience with their systems.

4. Check for Expandability and Compatibility

It is common for most new users to expand their computer use far more than anticipated in the first year or two. It can be frustrating if your system does not allow you to upgrade (say by adding hard disks or a second terminal), or if your software is not compatible with other related products (such as a spelling checker that works with only one word processor). Such products were never meant to be expanded. These should be avoided unless you purchase them only with the intention of learning the ropes before buying a larger system, or of meeting a very specific and limited need. The great majority of educational software packages need not be compatible with each other, but major applications software, such as spreadsheets, word processors, and database systems have to be compatible with each other to a certain extent. Also, commercial software frequently requires a specific version of the computer's operating system, and won't run on earlier versions; for example, a package that requires Apple DOS 3.2 will probably run on DOS 3.3, but not vice versa. Certain limitations on expandability and compatibility cannot be avoided, but if the product shows an obvious dead end, check out alternatives.

5. Beware Untested Products

Almost all hot new products go through a shakedown phase involving their hard use by consumers. During this time, problems and bugs are discovered and hopefully rectified. Unless you want to be a part of this testing process, stay with products that have been on the market long enough for them to have been thoroughly debugged. Also, be wary of obscure systems, which may sound more powerful or less expensive in the advertisements. Some of these, over time, may prove worthy of your funds, others will prove faulty or will even disappear. Hardware and software are constantly being upgraded and updated. It is best, unless you absolutely need some particular feature, to stay with those products that have a good record of performance and reliability.

6. Look for Good and Well-Documented Systems Software

Most of the popular personal computer systems come with their own particular systems software built in, more or less. Others use one of the more general operating systems, such as CP/M or MS-DOS. Besides the operating system, systems software can include language interpreters or compilers, assemblers, disk formatting and copying programs, disk operating software, and a variety of utilities such as text editors (not to be confused with word processors) and debuggers. Whether the systems software is a part of the system, or an addition to it, you should check out its strengths and weaknesses. What might otherwise be a highly desirable system could prove less than worthless if the only operating system for it doesn't do what you need it to do, or does so only very slowly, or clumsily. Obtain a competent review, from a consultant or computer magazine, of any operating system you are considering. You should get a similar review of the BASIC interpreter (or indeed any prospective language translator that will run on your system) before purchasing. This is especially important if one of your major purposes in acquiring a computer is for instruction in programming. Not all BASIC dialects are created equal. There are some very poor interpreters on the market. If the one that comes with the system is not up to par, you may have to buy a different one. Your BASIC should handle decimal numbers as well as integers, plus text character strings as well as numbers. BASIC was developed as a language that handled text more naturally and powerfully than its predecessors. Beware of stripped-down interpreters that lack these essential pieces.

7. Choose a System with More Than One Language Available.

BASIC is very good, but you may later find that some of your needs are better met by FORTRAN, Pascal, Forth, Logo, C, or COBOL. The point is that you cannot anticipate every need, but you can have a better chance of meeting most needs if you choose a computer for which a wide variety of languages have been written. A computer that will run only its own dialect of BASIC will not serve you well.

8. Look for Systems with a Lot of Available Applications Software.

That others have written many programs for a computer is an indication of the popularity of the computer and (less certainly) ease of programming, including support from the manufacturer, which in turn suggests quality in the operating system, language translators, keyboard, screen editing, and other components. Further, availability of packaged software may be essential in itself: most school people do not have the time to write the programs they want to use. It is nice to know that many of them have already been written by professionals.

Hardware—A Special Note

In addition to the above guidelines, you should also look for quality workmanship in your hardware. Some systems that might be eminently suitable for home use won't stand up to the rigors of a classroom or office environment. You should pay special attention to the durability of the keyboard (as well as odd key arrangements), a steady screen image, the quietness of components (especially disk drives—printers are noisy by nature), and just plain sound construction. If the cabinet is cheap or fragile, you can hardly trust what is inside.

If students are going to use equipment, it has to be rugged. Further, cheap construction or sloppy work anywhere should be regarded as a sign of poor quality work throughout. You cannot afford it.

EVALUATING SOFTWARE

In a very real sense, a computer is the software it runs. The machine that is doing word processing feels different from the way it feels when it is running a programming language or an educational game. The software tends to define the computer.

It has often been suggested that prospective purchasers of a computer system first determine what software they want to run, and then find the hardware that will run it. Depending on the relative importance of a specific package in the scheme of your district's needs, a choice of software package may indeed dictate your choice of computer. If you are in need of one or more major software packages (a sophisticated record-keeping system for basic competencies, for example), this can be the soundest approach. Even though you might prefer computer X to computer Y, if a software package essential for your needs will not run on X, forget it. For example, if the computer language APL is high on your list of software priorities for mathematics students in your system, then your hardware options are reduced considerably, since, as of this writing, APL has been fully implemented on only a few systems and usually requires a special keyboard not commonly available.

The options aren't always that well-defined, however, and you may find yourself with a computer system and then have to find the software that fits. Applications software (including courseware) tends to be central to the question of what the computer is going to do, which is at the heart of our system selection process. Here are some further guidelines, specific to software selection and evaluation. They are applicable to courseware as well as to any more complex and important piece of software, but bear in mind that the more expensive the software, the more important that it follow the guidelines.

1. Establish and Verify Software Support

No matter how well-documented, every significant piece of software generates questions from its users. Even software that has been carefully designed and written can have defects (bugs) in it. This is especially true of custom software. Someone familiar with the software on a technical level must be available to answer those questions and fix those bugs (if they exist). Ideally, that person will be in your local calling area, will know you, your equipment, and your specific needs, and may have sold you the hardware, the software, and a maintenance contract. If this ideal is not available, you should be able to get telephone support from the group or company that produces the software, again, especially if your software is custom-designed or is a large and complex package. Research and test this long-distance option (even if local support is available). Some software companies are very helpful; some are not. In addition to software maintenance, you may need your local dealer for training. Even with good documentation and relatively experienced users, a short but intensive training session from a person already familiar with the software can save untold time and trouble.

2. Buy Software That Does What You Need It to Do

Substantial differences in quality and performance are hidden under deceptively similar packaging. It is your task to break through the packaging to the operational substance of the software. Many vendors will try to reshape your needs to fit their package, rather than providing a package with the flexibility to meet your needs. For example, you may find a grade-book management package that expects grades to be reported in numbers from 50 to 100. If your own system is based on letter grades or on some other method, this package may prove a poor choice. Another problem might be software that is far too powerful for your needs. For example, you don't need a database management program generator if all you want to do is keep a simple address list. But approach the matter flexibly; a package may appear a poor fit because it is a better approach than the one you had thought out, and you may find uses for the program you once thought too powerful.

3. Thoroughly Test the Software.

The larger and more complex (and expensive) the software is, the more important it is to actually try it out and see how it will work for you. While even a $50 instructional game should be previewed, a $500.00 accounting package requires rather extensive testing. If possible, this should be done at an installation that already has the package up and running full steam. Many of the real drawbacks of a piece of software will not reveal themselves until it is fully laden with data and in constant use. Also, a full-dress demonstration of a package will suggest questions to you that you had not yet thought to ask. Make sure your test is "hands on."

4. Look for Good Error Checking

If you enter a letter in response to a request for a number, does the program crash (that is, fail—perhaps losing all the work you've just entered), or does it merely indicate that your entry was unacceptable and ask you to try again? Well-designed software will trap all such errors internally, give you a plain-English statement of the problem, and send you back to correctly enter the response that caused the problem. With poorly designed software an unexpected response will often cause the program to fail or to provide incorrect results.

5. Look for Consistency and Good Design in Prompts and Program Commands

Some software will lead you through a series of menus with no clear-cut way to get back to the main menu. Others will use commands that look similar but perform different operations at different times. No matter how powerful or potentially useful the software, if you can't find your way around in it without a prolonged learning session, or if the commands don't do what you expect them to do every time, it is not the software for you.

6. Demand Fast and Flexible Data Retrieval

There is little that is more irritating than having information stored on a computer system that you cannot retrieve easily. Fast responses to queries are indications of sophisticated file design and handling. For example, if a district were to institute a basic competencies tracking system, qualified people ought to be able to display the record of a given student on request. Such a request ought to be fulfilled by the computer in a matter of a few seconds. If it takes more than that, the system is probably not worth your further consideration.

7. Buy Software That Makes the Computer Do the Work

If you are constantly being asked by the program to change disks or tapes, or to enter the same information more than once, it could be a sign of inadequate hardware, inferior software, or both. In any case, continual shuffling of disks or tapes is more trouble than it is worth and should be avoided. Multiple entry of data is anathema.

A FURTHER CAUTION

The price revolution in computing has put much hardware and software within easy economic reach, but it has also led to a widespread belief that all computing is cheap. That is not so. Some computing is very cheap, but much of it is still very expensive—especially if you make mistakes. Large corporations pay hundreds of thousands of dollars for computer systems, while owners of small personal computers pay a few hundred. Do the corporations pay more because they want to? Is there any difference between the thousand-dollar system and the hundred-thousand dollar system? Of course there is, although the differences may not always be worth the differences in cost. It is the task of prospective purchasers of computer services to discover if their intended applications for a computer system are, in fact, within their means.

You should also be aware that two computers that look much the same might be very different inside. To further confuse the issue, two computers with entirely different external appearances may operate in much the same way, or offer much the same capabilities. Thus you are forced to judge the book by its cover and then to disregard the cover for a second evaluation.

Here are two last thoughts to consider when evaluating a computer system as a whole, after you have eliminated those computers and programs that will not serve you.

1. Don't Rush Anything

Haste is a sure way to guarantee an unpleasant result. If everything takes three times as long as you expected, you are right on schedule. That's just the way it is in the world of computers.

2. Remember That All Rules Have Exceptions

Use the guidelines discussed above, but do not be bound by them into doing something less than intelligent.

You are now ready to consider the type of computer system most appropriate for the needs of your schools. There are four basic hardware configurations from which you may choose: non-disk, single-user disk, timesharing, and resource sharing. The characteristics, appropriate applications, advantages, and disadvantages of each are described in the following sections.

NON-DISK SYSTEMS

Non-disk systems are essentially single-user systems, though an increasing number of portable computers and even hand-held computers such as the one shown in Fig. 10.1 come equipped with a modem, enabling them to emulate a timesharing terminal or otherwise communicate with other computers. Many of these small computers can be connected to disk drives and thus they become disk-based systems. By themselves, however, they use other forms of mass storage, which may include magnetic cards, bubble memory chips, or sometimes special digital tape cartridges. They range in price from under $100 to nearly $8,000.

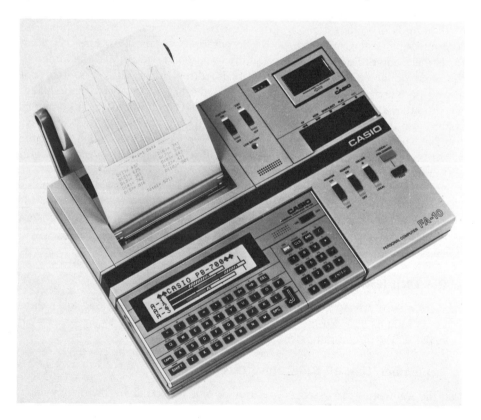

Figure 10.1   Hand-held computer connected to a printer and a tape expansion

Truly hand-held computers can be as small as 5 5/16 by 2 3/4 by 3/8 inches, such as the Sharp PC-1250, which uses 128K bubble memory cartridges for peripheral storage. Some so-called portables, on the other hand, can weigh over 30 pounds, and are more the size of a large briefcase. Many of these larger "portables" come with built-in disk drives and should therefore be considered in the next section.

The most common means for off-line storage for non-disk computer systems is the audio cassette tape and its drive. These systems, such as the Timex/Sinclair 1000, the Radio Shack Color Computer, the Texas Instruments TI-99/4A, the Atari 400, or the Commodore VIC-20, can be very inexpensive, cheap enough that a computer can be provided for each student in a class. (Although many of these systems are no longer manufactured, discontinued computers can be excellent buys, as long as there's no need for new software. These computers can be bought at drastically reduced prices and may be ideal for programming or computer literacy classes.) The cassette drive (and a TV or monitor) must usually be purchased in addition to the computer itself, but a complete system can be put together for under $500, and sometimes for a lot less. If you already have TVs and cassette players, the cost per system can be reduced considerably.

A cassette-based system is also the simplest to learn and the easiest to use, since sophisticated data processing and file management are next to impossible to implement on them. Thus there is no need to learn how to deal with those features and functions. The two sides of this coin are obvious.

Cassette-based microcomputer systems were at the heart of the initial rapid growth of the home-computing and school-computing markets in the late seventies. Here is where Apple, Radio Shack (TRS-80), Commodore (PET), Atari, and other microcomputer manufacturers did most of their early business. Most of these companies still offer cassette-based systems, similar to the one pictured in Fig. 10.2 although the majority of their systems are now intended to be used with disk drives.

Cassette-based systems range widely in quality, features, and price, and it is often hard to make accurate comparisons from one vendor to another. One company will include a video monitor in its package, others will not. One company has a full-stroke key typewriter keyboard, another will offer a flat-panel membrane instead. One will offer easy expansion via plug-in boards, another will not be expandable—but much cheaper. Comparisons are tough.

Cassette-based systems are the bottom of the line for each vendor. This does not mean they are necessarily of poorer quality, but it does mean that they will be the most basic version of a computer that you can buy. In compensation, such elementary systems are excellent for introducing students to computers, for introductory computer literacy, and for elementary programming. Though disk systems now predominate, there are still games, educational programs, calculation programs, graphics packages, and even a few computer languages available on cassette tape. The BASIC language interpreters in such systems can be fairly powerful and are very good for teaching beginning BASIC.

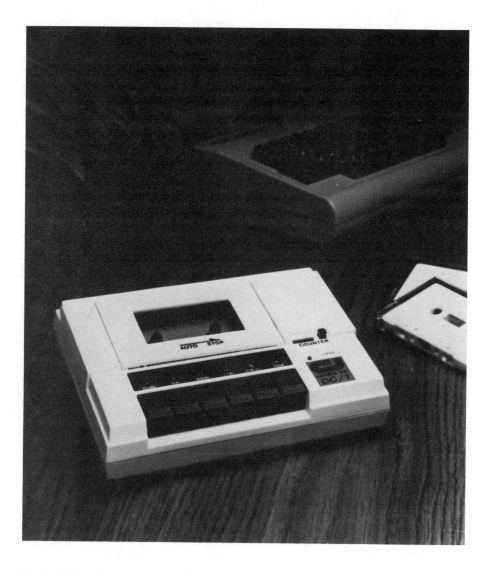

Figure 10.2   Microcomputer with cassette option

There are even some quite powerful (relatively speaking) applications programs, such as word processors and spreadsheet programs written for cassette-based systems, though these all suffer from the inadequacies of sequential access, as opposed to the random access available with disk drives. Hence these programs are of limited usefulness in a classroom or office situation.

Most of the smaller systems, however, come with very little RAM for workspace, and some cannot be easily expanded. Most screen displays are less than the 24 lines by 80 characters which is almost standard with larger computers. Not all have color, although most have graphics of some kind. Many do not have lower case letters, sometimes replacing these with graphics characters. Some have no provision for upgrading to a disk-based system.

Moreover, precisely those features that make cassette and other non-disk systems so easy to learn and use are also the features that limit their overall utility. Although in theory, such computers can do anything more powerful machines can do, the cassette drive's usefulness is really limited to storing and retrieving only small programs or text files. It is too slow and unreliable for applications requiring frequent storage and retrieval of data, such as in any data processing activity.

In summary, the most important disadvantages of a cassette-based system are:

- It takes a relatively long time to load a program from a cassette into the computer or vice versa. An ordinary 16K program can take as much as ten minutes to load at 300 Baud (bits per second).
- Some of the cassette systems are unreliable. It is irritating to save a program that you have spent hours developing and then find at a later time that the computer won't accept the playback.
- Cassette systems are nearly useless for any application that requires the storage and retrieval of any significant amount of data. The data is stored sequentially so that if you want a particular item, you must read through all the preceding items, instead of going to it directly, as you can with a disk drive. If you recognize from the start that applications that process data files are beyond the scope of a cassette-based system, you will have a much easier and more rewarding time with your system. Don't try to make a pick-up truck do the work of an eighteen-wheeler. Allow for the limitations of your tools.

The great advantage of the cassette-based systems is that they are cheap, so a school can afford to provide sufficient units to work with a whole class. It is very frustrating to have too few units. For most classroom uses, one system for every four students is considered the maximum productive computer-to-student ratio.

SINGLE-USER, DISK-BASED SYSTEMS

The great strength of computers lies in their ability to perform certain repetitive tasks faster and, on the whole, more accurately than people can. Thus speed of operation is important, and a computer that wastes five minutes of your time just loading your instructions from a cassette is not doing its job very well. Cassette-based computers have their place, but virtually everyone who owns a cassette-based machine yearns for a disk system. If you start with cassettes, be sure to incorporate a better peripheral storage system into your plans for the future.

A disk operating system expands the usefulness of a computer considerably, primarily by managing disk files. It is this capability which distinguishes disk operating systems, or DOSs, from the simpler cassette operating systems. A DOS enables the user to read data from or write data to permanent storage quickly and conveniently. Text, programs, and other information may be grouped in "files" on the disk with your own identifying names for easy retrieval.

Loading and saving programs on a disk-based system is quick and painless; the reliability of file storage and retrieval is generally much higher than in cassette systems; and floppy disks allow you to make effective use of the computer for applications requiring repeated access to a specific file. This is what data processing is all about.

Disks also generally have larger capacity than cassette tapes—they can store far more data. This becomes especially important in word processing. While most tapes may hold just short documents, most disks can be used to store long reports, articles, and even whole books (such as this one).

Perhaps one of the most useful aspects of a disk-based system is that programs can be written that are larger than the computer's RAM workspace. This is done by dividing a program into segments, which are read from the disk as they are needed, temporarily overlaying other portions of the program that are not in use at the moment. Sophisticated word processing, accounting, and spreadsheet programs all make use of this capability, as do an increasing number of educational programs. With a cassette-based system, this is nearly impossible.

There are some disadvantages to floppy disk-based systems, however. The first is that they are more expensive. If your school intends to have a great many computer units, it may not be very cost effective to buy a floppy disk system for each of them. You may instead want to consider timesharing or networking (resource sharing) as we'll discuss below.

Secondly, disk-based systems are more complex. The more powerful disk input/output routines in disk BASIC and other languages usually prove to be difficult for new users to master. The increased complexity may be bewildering to some users. It is harder to drive an eighteen-wheeler than it is a pick-up.

The increase in complexity also creates increased demands on memory. A floppy disk drive is a highly sophisticated piece of electromechanical equipment and requires an equally sophisticated operating system. In order to take advantage of the drive's ability to store and retrieve data quickly and easily, the DOS must be larger and more complex than a cassette operating system. This means, in turn, that the computer must have a certain minimum amount of memory dedicated to DOS, usually more than comes with a basic cassette system, and

Figure 10.3   Microcomputer with built-in floppy disk drives

Figure 10.4   Microcomputer with stand-alone disk drives.

enough to allow you room for your applications programs and still have workspace left for your inputs.

Nonetheless, single-user, disk-based systems definitely have their place. The following educational uses of the computer begin to make sense with such systems. Our comments refer mostly to floppy disk systems, but they are equally true of those systems with a hard disk drive.

1. Word processing. The ability to edit and rewrite papers on computers with relative ease is nothing short of marvelous. The key to it is the ability to keep the manuscript on a disk, since disks are able to employ random rather than sequential searches for files; store and retrieve far more quickly than tape; and with some word processors, permit files far larger than the computer's RAM workspace. Word processing is useful for teachers, for students, and for administrators.

2. Classroom administration. It now becomes possible to do sophisticated record keeping on the computer. Again, it is the random access to files and to records within a file that is important. The disk operating system stores your data; you don't have to worry about where it goes. And files can be far larger than on a cassette tape. There are programs that will track basic competencies, attendance, or any number of record-keeping functions.

3. School administration. The business office can choose from a wide range of accounting programs, library programs, payroll, and inventory programs. With a disk, class scheduling and other administrative functions become a lot easier.

4. More complex computer-based instruction programs. Any learning situation where it would be helpful to have the computer "remember" where students were when they left off last time can be handled easily by a floppy disk-based system. Further, it is possible to tie all kinds of curricular applications into record-keeping routines.

5. Statistical analysis of raw data. With one of the good statistical packages available you can collect data, store it on floppy disk, and then run analyses on it. This is great for teachers who like to put classes to work doing surveys, as well as for administrators who need to make pupil population and other statistical projections.

6. Spreadsheet analysis. Financial planning of all sorts, such as budgeting, forecasting, or projecting cash flow needs, is far easier using an electronic spreadsheet. Such a program can also become an important educational tool. Spreadsheet models can be created in almost any format; for example, as an IRS 1040 form, a purchase order, a comparison of several methods of depreciation, or a sophisticated accounting ledger. Spreadsheet programs have done more to sell computers than any other form of software, and their capabilities and features are increasing with each new release.

7. Any application that requires the processing of data, provided the volumes of data are not too large. For example, a disk-based computer in a science lab could track laboratory equipment inventory as well as record data from actual experiments.

Each of the above applications, and others, requires a certain amount of computer power, by which we mean the capacity, speed, and reliability of random access peripheral storage. You must be sure that your peripheral storage is sufficient to meet the demands made on it by the software you will be using. That is not always easy, but it is almost certain that you will need more capacity than you think. It may be a good idea to look into hard disks drives, even though you may not need them at the moment.

TIMESHARING SYSTEMS

As mentioned previously, if your school needs a great number of computer units with disk capabilities, it may be less expensive to create a timesharing system than to buy numerous stand-alone floppy disk-based computers. With a timesharing system, the most expensive computer resources, such as the CPU, main memory, disk drives, and printers are shared by several users, each of whom has his or her own computer terminal, usually a video display and keyboard. However, the effectiveness of a timesharing computer depends on how many requests for processing it receives in a given time frame and how fast it can take care of those requests. It is extremely doubtful that an 8-bit floppy disk-based microcomputer could act as a satisfactory core for a timesharing system. This is where a 16-bit computer (or larger) becomes desirable, especially in conjunction with a hard disk drive.

The advantage of such a system is the per-user cost saving possible through such sharing. The major disadvantages are that the system as a whole requires a greater outlay of money at the start and that expansion must be carefully considered at the beginning. If you have the initial resources, however, it is an option well worth exploring.

Such computer systems (like the one pictured in use in a school in Fig. 10.5 are capable of supporting from 4 to 64 simultaneous users, depending upon the power and configuration of the machine. The evaluation, configuration, and acquisition of such a system requires careful study, expert consultation, and a lot of money. Prices start at $16,000 and go up from there. Usually the acquisition of such a machine implies the employment of at least one full-time computer systems manager.

Figure 10.5   High school computer room with a mainframe computer and terminals

It is not that such systems perform any great tasks that a stand-alone 8-bit disk-based computer cannot. Rather, such systems are simly capable of doing their tasks faster, handling a greater volume of data, and providing access to a larger number of users for less money. A large timesharing system might be capable of handling the academic and administrative computing for an entire school district; a single-user system is more appropriate for administrative use in a single school or instructional use in a single class.

If you buy a traditional timesharing computer from one of the major manufacturers (such as Digital Equipment Corporation, International Business Machines, Prime Computer, Hewlett Packard, Honeywell, Wang or National Cash Register), be aware that the software for such computers tends to be qualitatively different from that available on the 8-bit microcomputers now so popular. It is generally more sophisticated, often of an older generation of software development, and quite possibly more cumbersome to use. The same critical judgments we discussed in evaluating software above should be applied to these software packages as to any others. A high price tag is no guarantee of high quality or appropriateness for your needs. In particular, there tends to be very little courseware available for these systems, so don't expect to do much of your instructional computing, other than student programming, on these systems. However, administrative applications can be far more powerful on such systems and may justify purchase for such purposes alone.

The potential advantage of such large systems is cost per unit. A $30,000 system (including terminals) that will support 16 concurrent users costs under $2,000 per user, which is cheaper than some floppy disk-based systems for single users. With the additional advantages of far greater range of power and sophistication, this is potentially a very attractive proposition. In addition, some of the vendors of large computers are open to negotiating substantial discounts for eductional buyers.

One special advantage of a timesharing system is the availability to computer science students of the more complex operating systems that run them. Familiarity with Unix or VMS or MP/M can be very useful to any student who chooses computer science as a profession. Also, since there are more languages available for larger computers, the range of exposure to these is greater. Some commercial software is available only for larger computers, which is another possible plus.

However, the larger the system, the more potential there is for disaster. The planning and budgeting process for acquisition of a $50,000 system is obviously a much weightier matter than the process of acquiring a $2,000 microcomputer system. The selection and acquisition of such computers is a matter that is ultimately better done with the help of a professional consultant.

RESOURCE-SHARING NETWORKS

We have discussed timesharing as a means of providing more computing power for your dollar by sharing the more expensive elements of a computer system among several concurrent users. However, the basic problem with timesharing is that it requires a large initial investment and might not take advantage of any stand-alone computers that the school may already have. Resource-sharing is a technique that can potentially avoid this dilemma.

With resource-sharing systems, often called local area networks, or LANs, individual computers run under their own operating system but are connected to a network controller. This is actually another computer that runs the network operating system and which in turn has access to hard disk drives, printers, plotters, and other devices that not every user needs all the time.

The high-speed, high-capacity hard-disk drive is the core of the system. It has its own special purpose computer to manage its operation and to communicate with the network controller. Whenever a user needs access to the hard disk, the controller puts the request into a **queue,** and deals with it according to some internal algorithm. It is like timesharing, but with only access to the hard disk being shared, not CPU time. Printing, plotting, and other tasks can be initiated from any computer, either by putting jobs in a queue, or by personally requesting the use of the desired peripheral.

This resource-sharing approach has only been around for a few years and its capacities and limits are not yet well understood. Corvus, a manufacturer of intelligent disk systems, uses its *Omninet* LAN system or its older *Multiplexor* system to provide for attaching up to 64 computers to its disk systems. Corvus also allows different types of computers to be attached. With *Omninet*, you can have an Apple, an IBM-PC, a Corvus, and a DEC LSI-11 computer all accessing the same disk and printer concurrently. (The *Multiplexor* besides Apples and IBM-PCs, can also connect TRS-80s, and S-100 bus CP/M machines.) Each computer is given access to a separate physical area of the disk, and each has a special interface to make the connection to the intelligent disk system. Other companies produce different systems with different compatibilities and differing numbers of users.

There are several configurations for connecting computers in a network, such as *star* (with all stations connected directly to the controller), *ring* (as its name implies, with the controller just a section of the ring), and *bus* (with each computer connected to the next in a line with the controller at one end). Which configuration is best will depend on your specific needs. Again, you will probably need the services of a professional consultant to advise you.

Besides the operating system software itself, perhaps the key element in intelligent disk systems is the rate at which data is transferred between a computer and the disk system. The higher that rate, the better the disk system will be able to handle many concurrent requests for I/O.

One drawback to local area networks is that they require special cables for connecting the computers to each other, to the controller, and to the peripheral devices. In a timesharing system, terminals may be connected by either an RS-232C cable and interface (a standard form of connection) or by phone lines with modems. The network, however, needs more sophisticated cabling to handle the higher speeds and volumes of data transferred. Depending on the network, these cables have limits in length, as phone lines do not. In some cases, users can be only a few hundred yards apart; in others they can be up to 50 miles apart. Such cables and the interfaces that support them are rather expensive.

Standards for networking are still being established, complicated by the wide range of configurations and possible applications and by almost weekly advances in both hardware technology and software development. Thus it is difficult to predict which system, method, or technique will become well-established in the future.

To specify and purchase a networking system for your needs, you will need to find a vendor who is well trained, knowledgeable, and dedicated to the field. This may not be easy, but because of the complexity of networking, incomplete knowledge will not suffice.

Installing a network is not as easy as plugging in a RAM card or a printer interface. You'll need good technical assistance. Networks are far from being off-the-shelf products.

In spite of this, networking installations are becoming more and more popular, and in many situations can provide for more than either single-user systems or timesharing systems in the way of exciting applications.

COSTING OUT YOUR WISH LIST

Now that you know what configurations of computers are needed for what sort of applications under various circumstances, you and your staff are ready to develop a wish list that represents perceived needs. Then, using vendor catalogs and the blank worksheets in Appendix A, you can cost out your various desired applications.

Suppose, for example, that you and your staff have decided on the following purposes or applications for a computer in a school.

- The English teachers would like to make word processing available to students for writing papers.
- The social studies teachers would like some simulations of various key situations in American politics (e.g., the Hayes/Tilden election). They would also like a statistics package that would be able to analyze survey data.
- The math teachers would like a series of tutorial and practice programs on math topics and the programming language APL.
- The art teacher wants a sophisticated graphics package and color plotter.
- The assistant principal wants the beginnings of a school-wide computer literacy campaign with as many students as possible exposed to computers in a hands-on and unthreatening way. She would like students to begin learning to program a computer, but has no particular preference as to which language should be used.

Now you would duplicate and then fill out the blank worksheets supplied in Appendix A, using one or more pages for each application. It will take a lot of research and legwork to fill out the worksheets in full detail. When you are done, you will have a good idea of what products are available for your desired applications and what each one would cost if a computer system were solely dedicated to that application.

The next step is to look across the list of applications for pieces of the system that can be shared. Ideally, you will find a configuration of hardware that supports decent software packages for each application. Practically, however, this will often involve compromise: the machine that supports most of your packages may not support all of your top priorities.

Then you need to factor in some general considerations for the system:

- How many people will use the system concurrently?
- Are you going to locate all the equipment in one place, distribute it to different locations, have it portable, or some combination of the above?
- Are you going to want to use your system for administrative applications as well as the specified instructional applications?

Now you are ready to cost out your entire system as:

- Several single-user systems.
- A timeshared system.
- A resource-shared system.

Typically, you will find that your original wish list far exceeds potential funding for this project, no matter how you configure the system. Now you must go back to the charts and look for the applications that are most expensive to implement. There is an old adage that states that 90 percent of your computing incurs 10 percent of the cost. If your desired applications are within the 90 percent range, you may be able to put together a very useful system for comparatively little money. It is almost axiomatic, however, that the most interesting applications fall into the 10 percent that will incur 90 percent of the cost. So it goes.

In your search for inexpensive ways to maximize the effectiveness of a computer, look for those applications that require the least computer time per user. For example, in some of the better simulations, one computer provides information to each of several groups using the simulation. The groups then go off and work independently of the computer, organizing their information and formulating their next set of decisions in the simulation. Typically, groups will finish at different times and thus their need to consult the computer will be staggered. On the other end of the scale, use of computers for word processing will tie up computer units for hours, especially if student users are just learning to type.

You may find that you have so exceeded your resources that you have to go back to square one and begin anew. Your time has not been wasted—you have gained a lot of knowledge and information that will be very useful in the future.

Charting out the applications you intend to use your system for is a very useful approach, but it does not tell you anything about quality. There is a substantial quality difference between a BASIC interpreter that will handle character strings and one that will not, or between a word processor that limits document size to the amount of RAM available (but is very fast) and one that constantly updates the document on disk, allowing very long documents (but operates much more slowly). You must determine for yourself the relative worthiness of the package.

Whether you hire a computer consultant or not, you and your staff will have to establish priorities for your desired applications, according to your sense of educational needs, budgetary constraints, technical considerations, and the political realities of your school. In order to do this, you may want to share the costed-out application list with members of the various constituent groups in your school to ask them for their priorities. Doing this maximizes participation of eventual computer users, although it also makes the decision-making process a bit more cumbersome.

Eventually, of course, you and your staff will have to make a proposal to those who allocate the money. If you have done your job, the proposal will ask for computer equipment for one or more carefully defined purposes. You will have spelled out the benefits and detailed the costs. You will have created a set of reasonable expectations in the event that the proposal is funded. Now it's up to the keepers of the treasury.

CREATING BID SPECIFICATIONS

The final step in deciding on what equipment to purchase is to write a set of bid specifications for the system you have determined you want. In most states, this is required for purchases in excess of $4,000. Most manufacturers' sales representative will help you to write up these "specs" free of charge, although obviously their doing so will tend to bias the spec toward their bid. So, you may wish to use an independent consultant to create this document.

Although the content and format of bid specifications may vary to accommodate state laws or local requirements, certain categories of information are likely to appear in most bid specifications, as follows:

Introduction (or Overview). A summary statement of what is to be purchased along with intended uses. A brief description of the school district may also be included.

Bid requirement procedures. Information on format and when bid is to be filed and opened. Included also are requests for demonstrations, consultant help, financing method. Evidence of good standing on the part of the bidder may also be part of the requirement.

Equipment specifications. A listing of all the performance requirements which the equipment is expected to meet. Specific reference to model numbers and manufacturer may also be added. The tighter the specifications, the more you are assured of being able to get the desired product. The comment statement "or equivalent" should be added in the event a desirable alternative is available. Finally, the quantity should be listed.

Requirements may also refer to the hardware's capacity to operate peripherical equipment from a different manufacturer, as well as to provide for future capabilities. It is highly desirable to have all bids specify a one year warrantee on parts and labor.

Each vendor will then respond to your bid specification with a bid statement that will, usually, provide a cost summary sheet that clearly indicates the cost per item plus the total cost and the amount of discount if any. This applies to all items contained in the bid (hardware, software, installation, training and service). The bidder also should insert a statement to indicate that the option to buy at the total price or unit price rests with the bidding institution.

Bidders are also usually required to.

- Document all exceptions.
- State a delivery date for installation.
- Identify third party responsibilities.
- Include connectors, modulators, and other electronic interfaces with equipment.
- Deliver a specified number of manuals with the award.

Finally, the designated person(s) from your district will carefully review, analyze, and compare the various bids to make recommendations for bid awards. The recommendation to award a bid is not always made to the one selling at the lowest price. Consultant services, maintenance provisions, and delivery dates all influence the final decision. In most school districts, the superintendent makes the final recommendation to the district school board as to which bidder should be awarded the bid.

CONCLUSIONS

Some last warnings:

1. Don't try to do too much with too little computing power. Do not, for example, expect an 8-bit CPU to support a major timesharing system of 16 terminals. Limit your initial expectations to tasks that are well within the capacity of the system you have budgeted. Avoid disappointment.
2. Don't try to buy too much computing power for too little money. There are manufacturers who have become price competitive by lowering the quality of their components rather than by technological breakthrough. Be especially careful to purchase top quality electromechanical devices (e.g., printers and disk drives), since these are more prone to failure than electronic components and are harder to fix.
3. Listen very carefully but don't believe everything you hear. Demand tests and demonstrations whenever possible. Be suspicious of claims.

So if you read the literature, evaluate your needs, follow all these guidelines, and avoid all the indicated traps, will you make the right choices of hardware and software? The answer is, "Not necessarily." It may be that there are no good choices for your particular need and budget. Or if there are good choices, they may not be locally available. Much depends on you and your own savvy. Be tough and thorough, but be flexible and open to new ideas at the same time. Learn as much as you can, but be aware that your information will never be complete and that there will always be much more for you to learn. Take heart in knowing that everyone, including the professionals, is in the same boat. There is simply no way of knowing all there is to know about computers.

Transforming the Schools 11

We began this book by observing that the nation's schools were under fire from every corner. Let us conclude with a discussion of how computers may help to usher in a new era of effectiveness for American schools. By this, we do not simply mean that with computers schools will do better at what they attempted to do previously (although that is certainly occurring already). More importantly, we wish school leaders and citizens to consider the ways in which computers may allow us to transform the very nature of mass education to forms and purposes more suitable for children who will live the majority of their lives in the 21st century.

Not everyone will welcome this vision of the future of education. There are many who cling to traditional views of what they believe the schools have "always" done and should continue to do. "It was good enough for me; it should be good enough for my kids!" is a refrain heard all too often at school board meetings and school budget hearings. The trouble is: "It ain't so". Even if we grant that it *was* "good enough for us"; (which we doubt, if one carefully considers who "us" is—women, minorities, poor people, foreign-language speakers, and the handicapped, for example), the fact is that the times have changed. The tragedy is that our nation's schools have failed to keep pace with those changes.

Computers and related technologies such as laser disks, satellite communications and fiber optics are revolutionizing every aspect of our lives. The stores in which we shop, the offices and factories where we work, the cars we drive, the banks that handle our money, the games we play, even the television sets and telephones in our homes and the appliances in our kitchens are being radically altered by new electronic technologies.

Yet, according to some futurists, the computer revolution our society is currently experiencing is but a tremor, presaging a worldwide upheaval that could transform our entire civilization. Such futurists envision a cataclysmic change in lifestyle, family structure, work habits, and education emerging out of technological break-throughs and spurred on by rapidly diminishing sources of fossil fuels. In one such vision of the future, described in detail in Alvin Toffler's book *The Third Wave*, people would stay closer to their homes and families. They would no longer commute to work, but instead "communicate" their work on computers over telephone lines. They would no longer travel long distances to shop and visit, but do so over computerized videophones. They would no longer go to school for their education, but instead learn through interactive computer systems, linked to other people and to information sources. And these are but a few of the changes envisioned by some futurists.

However, many of us haven't yet caught up with the current computer revolution, mere tremor though it may be, and we are certainly not prepared to consider future social upheavals of the magnitude predicted by Toffler and others. Nevertheless, as educational leaders, it is incumbent upon us to consider seriously the challenges and opportunities computers present for transforming the nature of schools as we move into the final decade of this century.

Will Computers Transform the Schools?

Computers are changing the face of business, both on the assembly line and in the office. They are altering the way many Americans, especially children, are spending their leisure time. They have revolutionized the ways information is generated, stored, and transmitted in our society. But will they transform the schools?

Among today's advocates for educational computing are a number of optimists who would answer an unequivocal yes. They point to the tremendous expansion in the number of schools using computers in the last few years, and suggest that computers are slowly but surely bringing about many of the changes in schools long sought by educational reformers and concerned citizens. In their view, school people are beginning to take advantage of the power of the computer to make significant improvements in the conduct and effectiveness of the school. These optimists cite some of the marvelous features of even today's relatively unsophisticated microcomputers: video, color, high-resolution graphics, animation, sound, speech synthesis, speed, accuracy, and the capacity to manipulate vast amounts of data. Computers are already beginning to free teachers, staff, and administrators from the drudgery of repetitive managerial tasks, so they can give their attention to the more personalized aspects of education. Further, a growing number of teachers are using the computer as a tool with which children can think and learn in new and exciting ways. Still other teachers are using computers to augment and make more effective their regular curriculum and methods.

This optimistic view sees the current flurry of interest and activity in educational computing as leading eventually to the development of a new generation of computer systems specifically designed for us in schools. Equipped with these new systems, educators would then be able to develop even more effective ways of using computers to accomplish long-standing educational goals and objectives such as improving basic literacy and computational skills, teaching students concepts, promoting student inquiry, individualizing instruction, mainstreaming special needs children, matching teaching and learning styles, and compensating for deficiencies in students' environments. Computers would be used to address the learning needs of students who are physically handicapped, bilingual, learning disabled, mentally retarded, unmotivated, emotionally disturbed, gifted and talented, homebound, chronically absent, delinquent, school phobic, or geographically isolated. This is indeed a bright and hopeful view of what could be done with computers in schools.

But is it realistic? Others in the educational community are far more skeptical about what will happen when computers go to school. They regard the optimistic vision described above as being naive about computers and about schools. They cite grave deficiencies in the current generation of computers—machines that don't work properly and are hard to get serviced; computer programs that won't run on different machines even of the same make; programs that stop working when a user makes even minor input errors such as striking the wrong key on the computer keyboard; a dearth of quality educational software; the limited number of people who can use a small personal computer at the same time, and the high cost if large numbers of such computers must be purchased; the quickly reached limits of the inexpensive personal computers to handle large amounts of data; and the often unclear, overly technical instruction manuals for computers and their programs. According to the skeptics, if teachers encounter such problems in their early experiences with computers, they will quickly sour on them and remain disenchanted for a long time to come, no matter how much computers are later improved.

As if this were not enough, the skeptics observe that schools and teachers are no more ready for computers than the machines are ready for them. Given the other demands of teaching, most teachers have neither the skill, the time, nor the inclination to develop or modify existing computer materials. When teachers do create their own programs, most of these seem to involve trivial uses of the computer and student materials that are little more than electronic ditto sheets or, at best, video textbooks. The skeptics continue: Just as educational television programs used in schools were unable to capture children's attention despite their addiction to TV, educational computer programs used in shools will be unable to capture their attention despite their love for computer games. Still worse, some argue that even though the computer is becoming as ubiquitous as the television in our society, many teachers and some students seem to regard computers as threatening and alienating. To them the news that "the computers are coming" sounds more like an ominous warning than the announcement of a bright new day.

Most educational computing advocates are unimpressed by the arguments of the skeptics. Some retort simply that if schools are not responsive to the educational potential of computers, the schools will shrivel up and die out as institutions of education in our society. They will be replaced by learning networks of home computers and public information sources.

Most knowledgeable educators, including many computer advocates, find this retort to be both irresponsible and naive. Schools perform too many invaluable functions in our society to be abandoned in favor of home computers and utopian learning networks. They are crucial instruments in the process of developing good citizens and an appropriately trained workforce; they socialize children to become adults and to carry on the cultural traditions of our society; they are custodians to our children while we work; they provide compensatory attention to those who may lack a proper diet, hygiene, medical care, basic literacy skills, or the ability to speak English; they are the primary route to economic success in our society. As long as there are societies, there will need to be schools. While many families now and in the future may supplement their children's learning with home computers, it seems unlikely that they would wish to deprive their children of the important formative influences experienced in schools.

Computers Will Affect the Schools

Despite sharp disagreements among educators concerning the revolutionary potential of computer use in schools, there would seem to be few who would dispute the assertion that computers will affect schools in some fashion and to some degree. Just as the widespread use of the automobile, the telephone, the airplane, and the television changed the face of society and therefore of schooling as well, so too is the increasing computer presence in our society likely to alter, at least indirectly, the nature of schools. These earlier technological innovations created the conditions for the emergence of a country of relatively prosperous suburbanized metropolitan areas and regionalized rural areas, all with architecturally similar schools, an emerging national curriculum, and a kid culture, shaped by the media. Television, in particular, seems to have contributed to creating a student body that many teachers find to be extremely homogeneous, worldly but jaded, relatively passive and uncreative, barely literate, all too often violence-prone, and largely unimpressed by the experiences we non-electronic teachers can offer them.

In light of these past indirect effects of technology on schools, some of us have mixed feelings about the possible fallout the schools may experience as a result of a computerized society.

When we are feeling optimistic, we see:

1. Schools drawn into the large-scale information networks that are almost certain to emerge soon, allowing students and teachers ready access to a quantity and quality of information heretofore too expensive to obtain.
2. Family bonds becoming stronger, as computers allow more people to work at home, leading to less alienated children and greater parent interest in their children's school experiences.

3. The re-emergence of smaller, more local schools, although now, through computers, without the resource disadvantages from which small schools once suffered.
4. An end to problems with the basic skills of reading, writing, and arithmetic, as these become unnecessary in the forms we know them today and as people master new computer-based basic skills by using them in their lives.
5. Computers becoming an antidote to many of the ill effects of television, as their use promotes active, creative, individualized behavior in children.

On the other hand, when we are feeling pessimistic, we see:

1. A further decline in necessary computational skills as computers handle more and more of our daily uses of numbers.
2. More resistance to learning and more truancy from schools which cannot provide the immediate excitement of computer games.
3. More violent behavior in schools as students spend more time and money killing space invaders and eating energy pellets in quarter arcades.
4. An erosion of the print-based culture on which schools are based as more time is spent with computers and less with books and magazines.
5. New and greater pressures on schools to provide equal opportunity in a society in which computers are likely to widen the gap between the rich and the poor, the powerful and the powerless.

As educators, we need to prepare ourselves for computer fallout in the schools. One way to do so is to use computers in schools to promote our educational goals in the best way we know. This book has been written with that task in mind. We hope that by reading it and engaging in some of the activities we have suggested you have begun to get a sense of the possibilities and the limits of computer use in schools. You should now be ready to decide what, if any, uses you will make of computers in your school.

TRANSFORMING THE PROCESSES OF TEACHING AND LEARNING

While it is true that computers can greatly improve the administrative functioning of schools, this is probably not the arena in which profound changes will occur in mass education. Managerial effectiveness will increase to be sure, but it is in the classroom and through the processes of teaching and learning that schools may change in ways to meet the challenges of today's complex society.

This may not be self-evident. To date, educators have primarily used computers to augment their current repertoire of methods and materials in pursuit of traditional educational objectives.

But, a new day is dawning for educational computing; traditional computer-based instruction is slowly giving way to a new generation of educational software and a new image of how the computer can be used educationally. The new software does not emulate traditional curricular methods and materials: textbooks, workbooks, chalkboards, filmstrips, overhead projectors. Rather, it exploits the vast memory, logical structures, and impressive graphics capabilities of computers to produce an interactive, flexible, and powerful medium for teaching and learning. The corresponding new image of the computer in education is as a tool for learning, rather than as the latest audio-visual device. And for the various disciplines, this new image includes the computer as a tool for *doing* the central activities of those disciplines: doing mathematics, doing social science, writing English, performing scientific investigations.

However, in the last thirty years, new technologies and techniques have promised similarly dramatic changes in the way students are taught and learn. Radio, typewriters, film, mimeograph stencils, spirit masters, television, overhead transparencies, film strips, slide-tape presentations, film loops, Polaroid cameras, photocopies, electronic calculators, thermofax machines, videotape, and others all have raised high hopes for educational improvement. And, all have failed to make much of a difference in children's learning or even in the ways we teach. So, teachers have a right to be skeptical about claims that computers will usher in a new age in education.

Nevertheless, the potential exists for computers to transform how we teach and how students learn. It is up to school leaders to unlock that potential.

The Computer as Problem-Solving Tool

Computers were originally designed to be used to solve scientific and business problems. As a result, they are powerful problem-solving devices with which students can probe problems, store and retrieve data, test out solutions, simulate problem situations, and calculate results. These problem-solving capacities of the computer enable students to work with much more interesting and complicated problems than they were able to before. They can ask "What if?" questions and attack problems in any number of ways. Most important, with computers, students have a new-found freedom to explore, to test strategies, and to play, all of which are at the heart of problem solving.

In the past, the difficulties of teaching problem solving have prompted educators to invent various recipes for it, some resembling old snake oil cures. The "scientific method," the best known of these recipes, has had surprising vitality despite the insistence of creative scientists that it is pure fiction and that, as a method, it hinders the problem solver more than it helps. These recipes each offer the one "true" path to all problem solving. But there is no one way to solve problems; there are many paths, many techniques, and many tools for exploring problems, identifying patterns, and finding solutions. People who learn problem solving well are like actors who play many different roles. They have wide and varied repertoires of tools with which to define and solve problems. The computer culture has appropriated, incorporated, and enhanced many of the most powerful of these tools. These exist primarily in sophisticated forms as business software that can be used by high school students.

Numerical-anaylsis tools developed for business and scientific applications, such as spreadsheets can be adapted for use by students in mathematics, science, social studies, business education, and industrial education. With them, students can keep track of and separate variables and store and display data. One of the most powerful features of spreadsheets is the ease with which students can alter variables to test out alternative hypotheses. Numerical analysis programs can also help students solve problems by making it easy for them to sort out variables and formulas, keep track of intermediate solutions, and even record their mistakes. Appropriately used, these professional programs can make problem solving more structured and less frustrating for many students.

Such software can perform many of the "messy" computational tasks that so often frustrate students in their problem-solving efforts. This suggests a change in role for students doing problem solving. No longer need they be concerned with making trivial arithmetic errors that cause them to "get the problem wrong." Instead, they can focus on figuring out how to solve the problem. Of course, this runs counter to the traditional pattern of providing students with a model solution and then asking them to solve a set of virtually identical problems. Instead of this rote-practice approach to problem solving, such software promotes thinking through problems each time they are encountered.

Students can use such software to check their own work as they wind their way through complex problems. As a result of using these programs, students can approach formula-based problem solving as a structured, planned activity, rather than as a guessing game based on trial and error. Students can take problems one step at a time and see what they have done in each step. Seeing their work neatly displayed in a standard format also can make it easier for students to see their mistakes.

Moreover, the next generation of educational problem-solving tools is just around the corner. With these, students will be able to input problems as English sentences, separate the elements of the sentences, collect those elements, and later join them together as the solution to the problem. The programs will directly assist students to explore problem situations, keep track of what they have learned, and find patterns in what remains to be done. The students will make the decisions and do the thinking; the programs will be the working tools. These programs will be, in essence, powerful but limited computer languages that students would use to program their own problem solving. Using such programs, students will be able to solve surprisingly complex and realistic problems, extrapolate results, and do trial runs on new data. Such power will be in the hands of students sooner than most of us expect.

The use of the computer as a problem-solving tool has the potential to transform how problem solving is taught and learned in school. Tool programs such as those discussed in chapter seven are already causing some teachers and students to reconsider the meaning of finding solutions, to question the need for a single correct answer to a problem, and to focus instead on problem-solving methods and the notion of finding a range of possible solutions.

This new view is being reflected in educational software development, as well as in classroom practices. Courseware packages such as the *Search Series* promote group cooperation and record keeping as social studies problem-solving activities. Simulation languages, like MicroDYNAMO, permit students to model problem situations in science and social studies and to test their solutions against real-world data. And in some classrooms teachers are beginning to alter their lesson objectives, assignments, and grading practices. They are encouraging and rewarding student creativity. They are asking students to try alternative approaches to problems, even when they have arrived at appropriate solutions. They are recognizing that some problems cannot be completed within a class period or even a week. And they are giving students credit more for setting up problems than for getting answers.

These departures from standard teaching practice are not yet widespread. They may never be. There may be too much inertia in school and classroom traditions to be overcome. But, if ever there was an opportunity to transform classroom problem-solving activities so that they become more like real-world problem solving, the computer appears to be providing it. The onus is on educational leaders to take up this challenge.

The Graphics Revolution

Prior to the development of video displays, computer terminals could only print output on paper. This led educators to write programs that used the computer more or less like an automated workbook or reading machine. Video computer monitors have changed all that. Now high-resolution color displays enable students to create, see, and manipulate images and to use them to discover patterns, trends, and alternative perspectives.

Students can use the graphics capabilities of computers in a wide variety of ways in classes, ranging from traditional graphing activities to creative art to informal geometric explorations to sophisticated three-dimensional designing. Teachers can encourage students to put visual images of phenomena on the computer for study and manipulation. For example, students can graph demographic information or equations to help them visualize these sometimes abstract entities.

A variety of graphing programs are commercially available, from simple ones that can be used for graphing particular equations to complex and elegant general programs, originally designed for industrial applications. Most of the best plotting programs are still those developed for business, but there are beginning to be some excellent, sophisticated, general graphing programs specifically designed for education. Educators who have not yet seen these graphing programs are in for a pleasant surprise. Finding the best program for current use is less important than getting started and encouraging students to graph problem solutions to see if their answers are reasonable.

Students can also visualize problem elements by using one of the increasing number of two-dimensional drawing programs. For example, students can draw, or even animate on the screen, the common geometry problem which asks students to calculate the angles at which a ladder of a given length leans against a house at various heights. Using more sophisticated three-dimensional drawing programs, now available for even low-cost microcomputers, students can draw three-dimensional figures, manipulate them, and investigate problems involving such shapes.

Drawing programs can also be used with elementary school children. Teachers, or even students, can create shapes, such as circles or squares, which can then be used in learning to count, sort, classify, and to recognize patterns in numerical relationships, such as fibonacci numbers and perfect squares.

Such supplementary use of the computer's graphics capabilities in the curriculum only scratches the surface of possible applications. Entire units or even courses can be built around the graphics computer. Logo's graphics features can be used to teach programming to elementary school children, geometric and algebraic concepts to junior high and high school students, and vectors to high school or college students. With minimal instruction from the teacher, students at all grade levels can adopt Logo as a personal and powerful tool with which they can translate abstract and complex mathematical problems into accessible, concrete, and simple forms.

The graphics capabilities of computers offer teachers and students a learning tool of nearly infinite flexibility and variety. Even an activity as straightforward as learning graphics programming in BASIC can provide students with dozens of practical applications of concepts ordinarily covered in high school mathematics, science, and social studies courses. Educators have only just begun to tap the vast educational potential that could emerge from the marriage of computer and video screen.

A New Medium for Teaching and Learning

Computers can provide an exciting new medium for teaching and learning because of their flexibility and potentially interactive nature. Most computers are capable of carrying a varitable tool kit of programs that can transform the computer now into a word processor, now into a sophisticated calculator, now an accounting worksheet, now a set of drafting tools, now a slide projector, now a primitive animation device, and more. Most of these capabilities are generic. They can be applied to any field—engineering, creative writing, economics; to any task—typing a letter, estimating costs, projecting election results; to any situation—home, school, business, government; and to any student—gifted and talented, unmotivated, handicapped.

Computers have the potential to be used interactively. Students can test out their own solutions and hypotheses on the computer, receiving immediate and appropriate feedback. They can explore microworlds to discover patterns, system dynamics, logical relationships, or natural laws. They can program computers to solve problems or to perform tedious tasks, such as calculations, and difficult ones, such as drawing diagrams. They can use computers to query data bases, store and retrieve information, manipulate and analyze data, and display results in myriad forms.

Or, they can do none of this. Teachers can disregard the interactive capabilities of computers. They can use them to provide students with drill and practice of basic skills or with tutorials that lead students through a series of brief questions and answers to arrive at some statement of a concept. They can see computers as electronic page turners and grade books, and "high tech" demonstration screens or arcade-like behavior modification devices. It's up to educators to decide how they will use computers. Interaction is only potential in computers; if it is to become actual in classrooms, educators must release it.

TRANSFORMING THE CONTENT OF THE CURRICULUM

During the past thirty years, there have been numerous on-going efforts to transform the K–12 curriculum. In the 1960s, there was an alphabet soup of massive federally funded programs such as: SMSG (School Mathematics Study Group—the so called "new math"), PSSC (Physical Sciences Study Committee), HPP (Harvard Project Physics), CHEM Study (Chemical Education Material Study), CBA (Chemical Bond Approach), BSCS (Biological Sciences Curriculum Study), ESCP (Earth Sciences Curriculum Project), ECCP (Engineering Concepts Curriculum Project), MACOS (Man: A Course of Study), ESS (Elementary Science Study), COPES (Conceptually Oriented Progam in Elementary Science), IPS (Introductory Physical Science), SCIS (Science Curriculum Improvement Study) and many more. Most of these curriculum projects were based on the assumption that when students were taught the underlying structures of a discipline, they would better understand and be better able to perform the basic skills of that discipline.

On the whole, these curricular reforms were failures, not necessarily because their premise was wrong, but because their politics were naive. Most parents were bewildered by the new kind of homework their children brought home. Many elementary school teachers, just barely comfortable with the old curricula, were so afraid of these new approaches they consciously and unconsciously subverted them. Even high school teachers who were familiar with the new approaches from their college courses weren't always confident in their ability to teach them.

But the curriculum developers were undaunted. They established in-service training workshops, summer institutes, and even evening courses on the new curricula for anxious parents. These efforts were to little avail. They were too few and too late. The backlash was formidable and came from many quarters: minority parents complained that their children weren't being taught the real-world skills they needed; business leaders lamented the decline in workers with adequate basic skills; some proponents of the "Back to Basics" movement viewed the new curricula as a conspiracy on the part of university intellectuals to deprive children of a basic American education; and even the various teachers' organizations had little praise for these new approaches.

The developers and proponents of these curriculum reform projects made several crucial errors that doomed their efforts from the start. First, theirs was a "top-down" reform, originating with university professors and a hand-picked elite of secondary and elementary school teachers operating under federal funding, mostly from the National Science Foundation. There was never much grass-roots involvement, either during the planning stage or during implementation. Second, these new curricula were simply too much of a departure from what parents, students, and any teachers were used to. They didn't begin where people were and move them along from there; they began with ideas, concepts, and methods that were alien and that only got stranger as they were developed. Third, these reforms demanded too much of teachers. They required them to learn new content and new methods, to become accustomed to new texts, new problem activities, and new types of test questions. Teachers were pressured to attend workshops and summer institutes, just so they could keep up with the changing curriculum. Fourth, the excesses of some of the new curricular approaches opened the entire effort up for ridicule in the public press. Fifth, the new curricula ran afoul of a growing political conservatism in this country, which focused its wrath on the new curricula and the "effete intellectuals" from universities who were "destroying" basic education. And sixth, the proponents of these projects failed to keep up with the other changes in society that impacted all of education, including mathematics.

The new curricula, particularly in science and mathematics, were born in the late 1950s as a reaction to Sputnik. In the meantime, an increasingly militant civil rights movement in the 1960s, a brief flurry of political and educational progressivism in the early 1970s, the emergence of neo-conservatism in the late 1970s, and the deepening world economic crises of the 1980s all made themselves felt in the schools. The new curricula were inconsistent with virtually every political development and educational philosophy that was influential in the past twenty-five years.

The political failure of these new curricula are not unique among educational reform efforts. In his book, *Transformation of the School*, educational historian Robert Cremin traces the collapse of the progressive education movement to virtually identical factors. Others have suggested the same explanations for the decline of the free school movement of the 1960s, the open-school movement of the 1970s, and all the other various new curriculum efforts of the past twenty-five years. Might not the educational computing revolution experience a similar failure?

Indeed, it might. It is incumbent upon those who wish to see computers transform the processes and content of education to be aware of these past failures and to learn from them. There are signs that this is happening to an extent in the small but growing ranks of educational computing advocates. The best sign is that educational computing is, in many ways, a grass-roots movement. It has grown out of, and has been nurtured by, personal computer enthusiasts: parents, teachers, and students. It has received almost no support from the federal government or the elite funding foundations. And few of the real successes of educational computing have come out of the universities.

Perhaps as important to its successs is the almost inherently up-to-date nature of educational computing. Because computers promise to be a dominant feature of western civilization for some time to come, educational computing is unlikely to fail to keep up with important sociopolitical developments.

However, educational computing does contain some seeds of failure. It can be very demanding of teachers, requiring retraining, changes in pedagogical practices, and an entirely new body of knowledge to master. The most exciting uses of computers in education are a radical departure from current educational practices and could be threatening to educators and parents alike. These same uses, as well as some of the least exciting applications, such as drill, are perfect targets for media attention and ridicule.

Nevertheless, the signs of a successful curriculum reform movement are prevalent. Across the nation, innovative educators are slowly infusing computer activities into their lessons and courses. These pioneering efforts have been largely self-supported. No national curriculum projects or funding measures are helping them. These educators read avidly, experiment with their computers in their classes, and attend workshops sponsored by the growing number of educational computing consortia or organizations. Occasionally, they may take a college course, but when they do, it is more likely to be offered by the education department than by the computer science department, and it is more likely to be taught by an adjunct instructor who is also an elementary or high school teacher than by a college faculty member.

The transformation of curriculum content is likely to be a slow process, as indeed it should be. Students, parents, and teachers need to get used to new and different ways of understanding the disciplines. The new content should emerge naturally from the old. With computers, traditional topics can be recast in more realistic and complex forms. Problems from the real world can be introduced and interdisciplinary activities considered. Such approaches are likely to find favor with both the progressively minded and advocates of the basics. Students will learn and use the skills they will need while solving problems of genuine relevance to their current interests and emotional maturity. As the computer becomes a more accepted and familiar feature in a given school or classroom, the transformation of content may become more rapid and more radical. With computers, students may consider issues heretofore the province of scholars. Sophisticated concepts in computer science and programming may become quite accessible to even elementary school children. Some of the goals of the "new" curricula may yet be realized.

Realistic Activities

A typical seventh-grade mathematics textbook problem asks students to find the time it would take a car traveling at 40 miles per hour to go from New York to Boston, a distance of 212 miles. Such a problem is then usually followed by another that asks the same question for other cities and then another and another, always asking the same basic question. Because of limited space available on problem-solving pages and because of a textbook's inability to check answers, textbook authors must rely on such repetition, and cannot build either realism or complexity into their problems. (When was the last time someone drove a car at 40 mph from New York to Boston?)

But, using a computer, it would not be difficult for a teacher with some programming experience to create a program that generates a variety of more realistic and complex problems. Such a program might begin with the same sort of question, but would include a map of a region familiar to the student, state the problem in terms of that region, and display a car traveling along the roads on the map so that students could get a visual sense of the problem. A clock on the screen and the moving car could then simulate the situation, providing students with a visual means to check their solution. The computer wouldn't need to tell them if their solution were right or wrong. They would be able to see it on the screen.

This idea could form the basis of a more elaborate commercial program that might add a "window" to provide the student with a scratchpad for doing calculations on the screen, as well. (See Fig. 11.1.)

Such a program might also have provisions to branch to a tutorial or to ask the same question for two different towns, if the student got the answer wrong, and to pose the same problem but for different routes between the same cities if the student got the problem right. The program could also add each successfully calculated route to the map as a mark of the student's progress and keep a record of distances, times, and speed limits correctly calculated for each route in a table. For some routes the computer could change the speed limit; for others it could add obstacles and towns, which slow a car up. Students would thus be solving similar but increasingly sophisticated problems, while at the same time buiding up a realistic road map and a table of useful information. (See Fig. 11.2.)

Becoming even more sophisticated, such a program could ask students to become travel agents, plotting a family's vacation, stopping points, the fastest possible route, and gas savings. This is the sort of problem involved in planning

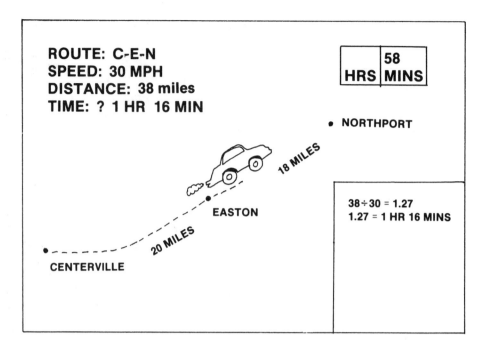

Figure 11.1

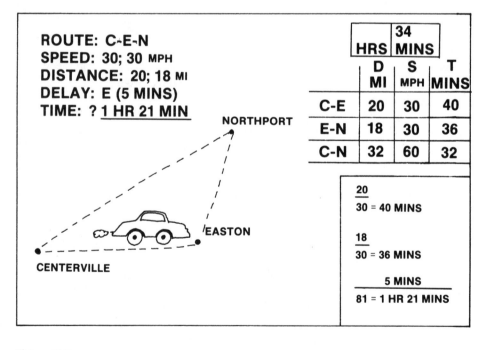

Figure 11.2

school bus routes, mail delivery routes, or a traveling salesperson's route. To solve such problems, students would have access to similar maps and tables of information as in earlier problems but for a new region. The program could also provide a simple authoring language that would allow students to transform all the roads into straight lines and all the stops into points. This would move students to a new level of abstraction in understanding and visualizing a problem.

Such a powerful and flexible program would give teachers the ability to create different problems for different students and to save a student's work for later use. Although this program does not exist, it easily could—the product of a talented teacher-programmer or a forward-looking curriculum developer and publisher. But educators need to let publishers know that this is the direction curriculum materials should be taking.

Real World Activities

Unfortunately, thus far computer use in schools has been provided primarily for the college-bound, usually wealthier segments of the school population. Yet, experience in using computers is clearly appropriate for students who will be going straight to work after high school. Many of them will work directly with computers in the office, on the assembly line, or in stores. If one of the missions of American public education is to prepare young people for the world of work, then today's public schools must provide a reasonable degree of computer education to all of their students.

This admonition is particularly directed toward university-based educators who, in their funded curriculum projects, have tended to focus their attention on college-bound students and on their understanding of the underlying structures of the various disciplines. While it is certainly worthwhile for some students to learn and appreciate the more abstract aspects of a discipline, the vast majority of students will have little use for such knowledge after graduation. In contrast, all students will need to use the English language and mathematics in a variety of settings, many of them involving computers as well. Yet, few curricular materials provide applications or examples from life.

Because computers are real-world tools and do not belong to any one field or academic discipline, they are an ideal medium through which students may learn to use a variety of skills they will encounter in their lives. For example, the classic business mathematics unit on income taxes can be transformed from a mechanical task into a creative activity that may raise issues and questions about tax laws and tax fraud, both matters of relevance to most citizens.

There are already business computer programs that fill out the 1040 form, and hardcopy versions of the forms themselves are free, in quantity, at IRS offices, banks, and post offices, so that students can work with pencil and paper, as well as with the computer. Students could be given various parameters for income tax problems by using a computer's random number generator. These parameters would include income, number of family members, expenses, business losses, stock market gains, and so forth. The students would then use the computer to fill out their tax forms and find out what their income tax would be. The teacher could pursue many creative variations of this problem; for example, tell students to find ways for someone with a large income to pay little or no taxes, or ask students to determine the difference between the taxes paid by a married couple with two incomes filling out a joint return and those paid by two single persons with the same combined income. This relatively traditional business education topic could then be extended beyond what is ordinarily treated in high school courses to problems dealing with the stock market, the start-up of new companies, business accounting, or car sales. Software publishers have been coming out with new and improved simulations, like Scarborough Systems's *Run For The Money*, that do just this.

Presumably, the great concern for basic competencies for high school graduation is a function of the need for citizens to successfully manage such activities. Yet, so much instruction ignores the practical context in which the skills to be mastered will be practiced. Computer simulations like *Run For The Money* provide effective and motivating means of learning practical skills for a wide range of students.

But real world activities need not be limited to simulations. Students can use problem-solving tools like spreadsheets to do real-world problem solving for their family, their school, their organizations, and themselves in such diverse areas as: energy conservation, budget management, investment strategies, purchasing, strategic decision making, efficiency studies, and many others.

One of the important reasons for learning skills is to be able to use them in the real world. Computers make it much easier for students to do so now, while they are being taught the skills, and thus make it more likely that they will actually learn the needed skills and use them later.

Interdisciplinary Activities

But how will there be room in the curriculum to include these additional activities and approaches? As it is, there are ever more increasing demands on schools to provide coverage of new subjects: drug education, driver education, health education, environmental studies, women's studies, various ethnic studies, and so on. This is coupled with competing and often opposing pressures to spend more time on the basics and less on such "frills" as lab sciences, social studies, art, and music.

Now, computers can provide at least one approach to settling some of these competing demands through meaningful interdisciplinary activities. Not that computers are required for interdisciplinary studies, but they certainly make such activities more interesting, more realistic, and more useful to students.

Two programs from Scarborough Systems, *Songwriter* and *Patternmaker*, allow students to use the computer in an intuitive way that combines mathematics with music and art. *Songwriter* displays music like a player piano and lets the user invent or change the music in significant ways (see Fig. 11.3). In the program, the student sets the length of a note either by using the number keys alone or in combination with an operation key (addition, subtraction, multiplication, or division). The student changes the length of a measure in the same way. Musical notes are fractions; thus, while students learn music with *Songwriter* they also learn fractions. Not only do they see how mathematical operations with fractions are performed, they see them in a graphic and dramatic way.

With *Patternmaker*, students design and explore tesselation (tiling) patterns and symmetry. Students can view these patterns artistically and mathematically. The program enables students to take patterns of boxes and perform on them any of the symmetry operations: translation, rotation, or reflection. These operations are carried out on the screen graphically where students can observe the resulting changes in patterns. They can specify a series of operations that combine artistic design with some fundamental algebra. In this way, students can use *Patternmaker* to solve design problems mathematically, or mathematical problems graphically.

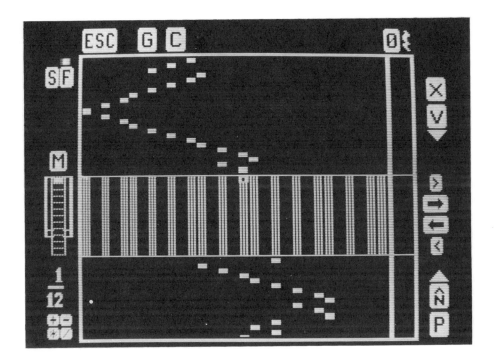

Figure 11.3 Screen from *Songwriter*

Real Activities

Traditional instruction rarely provides opportunities for students to make their own discoveries. Most curricula are taught convergently. The text and teacher present the concepts. The students are expected to follow the logic of the argument and to answer questions derived from that content. Only rarely are elements of discovery incorporated into curricular materials, and even then such inclusion is often contrived.

With computers, students are much more able to make genuine discoveries and to seek the solution of problems that they themselves identify. Even very young children can pose problems for their own explorations. For example, many students are fascinated by numerical patterns such as fibonacci numbers. Computers make it "child's play" to search out patterns among the prime numbers or the perfect squares or the multiples of 9 or the factors of consecutive numbers.

Even a novice programmer can develop a simple program that searches prime numbers for relationships. The first element of the program would extract prime numbers from the natural numbers using the Sieve of Eratosthenes, in which each whole number is tested to see whether it is divisible by the whole numbers before it.

In the next step of the program, the prime numbers could be grouped by 100s, those from 1 to 100, 101 to 200, and so forth, and the primes in each group counted. These results could then be displayed on a graph to see whether they show any patterns or tendency. This is precisely the method used by mathematicians through the centuries in searching for elusive relationships among primes. But with computers, even elementary school children stand a better chance of finding a relationship than the best mathematicians of earlier days. Students can generate an almost infinite number of primes, group them in as many different ways as they can think of, perform any mathematical operation on them or on the intervals between them, display them in a wide variety of ways graphically, and all of this effortlessly and errorlessly. What power to be in the hands of students! With computers, the once mysterious realm of number theory can become a reasonable subject for exploration throughout the K-12 curriculum.

Similarly, sophisticated graphics packages make it possible for students to explore geometric patterns and relationships instead of waiting for these to be presented to them as a series of theorems whose significance is usually unclear. Whether students "discover" relationships that are already known or really make new discoveries is irrelevant. The importance of such explorations is the genuine sense of discovery students get when they pose their own problems, devise their own methods of solution, and recognize some pattern or relationship that they never noticed before. This can help students to see subjects like mathematics or social studies as living, changing disciplines of which they can be a part.

Computer Science

For some time now many universities have offered a computer science major. The trickle-down effect is beginning to be felt in secondary schools, reinforced by the interests of students who have home computers and parents who want their children to be prepared for a computerized world. High school mathematics departments are slowly responding to these pressures, primarily by integrating the computer into existing courses. However, mathematics departments will soon need to offer entire courses in computer science. Some computer enthusiasts are even suggesting computer science departments at the high school level.

Courses in computer science would include far more than programming, just as programming should be part of many courses besides computer science. Much of what is loosely classified as "computer literacy" would be included as objectives in most computer science courses: consideration of social, economic, political, and ethical issues related to computing; an awareness of important historical developments in computer technology; the ability to use computers for a range of purposes, including programming; understanding how computers work, from the level of electronic switches to high-level programming languages.

Of course, the treatment of topics will vary in sophistication depending on the age, experience, abilities, and goals of the students, but every student in school today needs a modicum of exposure and skill in these areas. The world in which they are living and will be working is dominated by computers and is certain to be more so. People will need computer know-how simply to exercise their basic rights and responsibilities as citizens: voting intelligently, obeying and being protected by laws, working, being informed and informing others, engaging in financial transactions, participating in military service, and so on. Every aspect of our society and culture will be affected by computers. Today's students need to know and understand as much as they can about this major influence in their lives, and educators in every discipline will be expected to take a role in the creation of lessons, units, and courses that address this need.

COMPUTERS AND THE FUTURE OF EDUCATION

The 1980s promise to be a watershed for the schools. Pressures from society and from within the educational community, coupled with the revolutionary potential of the computer, are already changing how some teachers are teaching topics in the curriculum. And this may be only the beginning of far more pervasive changes. All indications are that such a transformation is underway.

Public figures from government, industry, and academia have, for the past few years, been calling attention to the need for many more high technology workers, from engineers and inventors to technicians and computer programmers.

At times, these public pronouncements have reached a fever pitch, akin to the scare that followed the Soviet Union's launch of Sputnik and precipitated the herculean crash programs to upgrade science and mathematics education in the 1960s. Indeed, members of the science, mathematics, and education communities appear to be hoping for and encouraging a similar reaction to the technology gap of the 1980s. This time the scare is less military than economic, less symbolic than real. Politicians like former California Governor Jerry Brown and the so-called "Atari Democrats" in Congress are claiming that many of our economic woes are a result of our failure to replace traditional industrial activities with high technology, to replace steel and automobiles with semiconductors and computers. They warn that unless the United States takes quick and drastic action to develop and adequately capitalize new high technology industries, we will experience a serious technology gap in which other industrial countries such as Japan and Germany will dominate the world economy. In the pessimistic version of this scenario, the economy of the United States is reduced to a shambles with chronic high unemployment and a state of almost perpetual recession.

While such dire warnings are undoubtedly dramatized for political purposes, the pressures to close the technology gap are real, as are the concommitant needs of people for skills and knowledge befitting citizens of the 1980s. Unfortunately, the majority of the K–12 curriculum in all subjects reflects values and needs more appropriate to the 1950s, or even the 1940s. This is especially true in science, social studies, and mathematics, where many of the innovations of the ill-fated curriculum reforms of the 1960s have been abandoned or so diluted as to be unrecognizable and largely ineffective.

Equally unfortunate is the shortage of qualified teachers, particularly in science and mathematics, to prepare people for life and work in a high technology society. The conventional wisdom regarding this shortage is that industry is so desperate for people with science and mathematics training that they are luring them away from teaching with high salaries and excellent benefits. This line of thinking leads inevitably to proposals for financial incentives for science and mathematics teachers and crash programs to train them.

While neither of these approaches to the problem is particularly objectionable, they suffer some drawbacks and more importantly, they do not address the more significant problem: the outmoded content of today's science, mathematics and social studies curricula. No increase in numbers of science and mathematics teachers, particularly if many of them are overnight converts from the "breadlines" of English teachers, can produce technologically literate high school graduates if the curriculum doesn't reflect this as a goal. Yet, technological literacy is not currently a central feature of the K–12 curriculum, either in words or deeds.

Indeed, many would argue that there is no room in the K–12 curriculum for yet another set of goals and objectives. It is hard enough to attain basic literacy ojectives in reading, writing, and arithmetic without worrying about high technology objectives in database utilization, word processing, and computer programming.

Others counter that the so-called basics have changed; that computer-accessed databases and interactive video are permanently altering what it means to read; that with word processors, educators may at last really be able to teach people to write; and that electronic calculators and computers make basic arithmetic skills unnecessary. According to such educational futurists, basic skills are indeed important, but they must be the skills students will need for life and work in the 1980s and beyond, not those of a pre-technological era.

While it is uncertain that such a view of basic skills and needed educational objectives will prevail, it is clear that computers stand ready to be the vehicle for implementing such a vision. In virtually every curriculum area, computers offer opportunities to learn new content, in different sequences, and with a higher degree of sophistication at every age level. They provide educators with an unprecedented opportunity to reconsider why they teach what they teach and whether they should be teaching other skills and ideas altogether.

One of the most interesting and provocative side effects that has already emerged from using computers with elementary school children is the challege this use poses to traditional concepts of cognitive development. Child-appropriate programming languages like Logo, powerful simulation languages like Micro-DYNAMO, the various graphics capabilities of computers, and their capacity to handle very large and complicated calculations quickly, all provide children with tools and the means to think and learn differently from the way children learned even five years ago. This makes possible, and perhaps necessary, a radical alteration in the way topics have been sequenced in the curriculum.

Topics can now be taught much more often on a need-to-know basis, rather than according to some logical hierarchy or cognitive developmental framework. Computers can make accessible, even to young children, advanced concepts from higher mathematics, linguistics, and the social sciences. Teachers may have to shift their expectations about what children of a certain age can and cannot learn. They may also have to change their modes of communication and methods of instruction to better fit the new learning styles of children reared on television, computers, and video games.

A Future Scene

Anne had been fascinated by the weather for years. During summer evenings in Washington State, she loved to watch the clouds that appeared over Mt. Ranier, as moist air was forced over the summit where, as it cooled, it sank, then warmed up and formed a cloud which finally disappeared into the sky. Her family called this the Mt. Ranier Cloud Show.

Anne, now in the sixth grade, had just gotten home from school. She had thought of Mt. Ranier today in geography class because they had been discussing weather. Her teacher had stated at some point during the class that a good rule of thumb to remember was "go north, go cold; go south, go warm." Anne had just finished reading about Napoleon's disasterous invasion of Russia, when most of his troops froze to death. She realized that Napoleon had gone east and had gotten very cold indeed. Her teacher's rule of thumb bothered Anne, and she wanted to find out more about how temperatures are distributed globally.

Anne turned on her family's computer terminal and selected the LIBRARY option. A prompt appeared on the screen, telling her that she had successfully hooked into the National Data Bank and asking for her account number. She responded, and a menu with many options appeared on the screen. She selected CATALOG and then WORLD TEMPERATURES. After a pause, the screen filled up with possible sources. She selected the DATA option and requested a list of average temperatures for all the major cities of the world. A message appeared on the screen telling her to turn on her printer, and shortly she had a complete list of all the major cities, arranged alphabetically, with their average temperatures.

She was puzzled by the list because the temperatures were all about the same. Ann thought about this for a moment and realized that she had requested the wrong data. She had just finished some work in her math group at school on statistics in which the teacher had explained averages. She now realized that the statistic she wanted was the average coldest temperatue per year for each city, or the "average extreme cold." The data she had did not give her this.

She sat and thought for a couple of moments and was startled when her older brother David came into the room and asked her what she was up to. She told him, and explained the problem she was having. David told her about a special map he had seen at his school, called the Dymaxion Air Ocean Map, designed by Buckminster Fuller. He said it was a weird shape, but it contained a great deal of information, like temperatures.

Anne asked for another CATALOG, and this time requested information about the Dymaxion Air Ocean Map. In a couple of seconds she had a list of sources in front of her. Unfortunately, most of them sounded pretty technical so she asked to see a copy of the map.

David was right; it was weirdly shaped and certainly didn't look like any map she had ever seen before. Anne typed in a command that caused a colored copy of the map to appear on her printer, but she couldn't make much sense of what the colors represented. When the computer displayed the explanation of the colors on the screen, Anne knew she had found what she was looking for. The map was color-coded to show the average extreme low temperature for each place on the globe. The map showed clearly that, in many cases, the temperature gets colder as you go east, not as you go north. As one moved from Paris to Moscow, the colors became progressively bluer. Anne thought for a moment about what would have happened if Napoleon had used this map.

The more she looked at the map, the more fascinated she became. All the land masses seemed to be the proper size, with Greenland appearing as the relatively small island that it is. Also, there were no longer three oceans but only one. Anne noticed also that the shortest distance from Chicago to Europe and points East was over the pole.

As Anne sat staring at the screen, David took the color printout of the map and cut it out. He then folded it and joined the edges, making a solid object, called an icosahedron. David held it up for Anne and said, "I've got the whole world in my hands." Anne laughed, appeciative of the joke.

The map continued to amaze Anne, and she wanted to learn more about it.

"David, how does it work? Why doesn't it distort the shapes of the continents like other maps do?"

David had just finished a unit on transformations in his math course, so he had a partial answer to her question.

"I know why other maps are distorted; it has to do with the method of projection that is used."

"What do you mean by projection?" Anne asked.

David sat down at the terminal and requested information on Mercator projections. He asked for a demo and then said to Anne, "Watch. This will show you how one type of projection works."

A white sphere appeared on the screen. Below it appeared a question

DO YOU WANT LINES OF LATITUDE (LA) AND/OR LONGITUDE (LO)?

LA and LO

The computer drew the great circles on the sphere as requested by David. It then asked a second question.

DO YOU WANT POLITICAL BOUNDARIES DRAWN ON THE LAND MASSES?

Yes

Again the computer responded to the request, filling in the territorial lines of the countries of the world.

The sphere now rotated slowly around the poles and stopped after one revolution. Beneath the sphere appeared a brief description of the Mercator projection process, which then began to happen on the screen. The sphere was enclosed in a translucent cylinder that was tangent to the sphere at the equator. A ray originating at the center of the globe appeared with its end on the equator. The top of the ray traced out the equator and then moved on to trace out all the other lines of latitude and longitude on the cylinder. Points on the sphere were being transformed to points on the cylinder.

As this was happening, Anne could see why Mercator maps were so distorted: lines of latitude are equally spaced on the sphere, but their projections on the cylinder become further and further apart as they get closer to the poles.

The computer now traced each country onto the cylinder and colored it appropriately. It did not include anything above 70 degrees North or below 70 degrees South, because there would be too much distortion.

Once the tracing process had finished, a cut appeared on the cylinder and the cylinder slowly unfolded into a rectangle. There it was: a Mercator map of the world. Anne asked for a copy and now had two maps in front of her, the dymaxion map and the Mercator map.

It was getting late, so Anne and David signed off from the Data Bank. As she left the room, Anne made a mental note to ask her teacher about icosahedrons, because she wanted to know how Buckminster Fuller had made the Dymaxion map.

Although the preceding vignette is fictional, all the technology referred to in it now exists. Large databases are getting easier and easier to access. Solid modeling systems are being perfected for microcomputers. Multicolored printers capable of printing the maps Anne used are now available at relatively low cost. In the near future these features are likely to be found in schools, libraries and many homes.

Developments such as these promise to bring about dramatic changes in how traditional school subjects are learned and taught. One major change, evident in this vignette, is that more and more learning is likely to take place at home, at least for families with the means to buy the latest in computer technology. The impact of such a shift, on schools and on society, is difficult to predict at this time. Will schools become less important as more learning takes place at home? Or will they take on even more critical roles as equalizers by providing computer access to lower socioeconomic groups who may not be able to afford elaborate home computer systems? Will teachers become mere computer technicians, or will they need to be even more creative, developing curricula capable of exploiting computer capabilities? Will students develop more creative learning styles as in the exploration carried out by Anne in this vignette? Or will parents view computers as a way of providing their children with a competitive edge over their classmates, and so insist that they be used to reinforce skills and knowledge learned in school?

Largely because of computers and related technologies, we stand at a crossroads in our educational system. The potential is there for computers to bring on the next Gutenberg Revolution in society and in education. Computers can open up vast new areas of knowledge and understanding to all the citizens of the world. But the potential is also there for computers to spur on an Orwellian nightmare in which they help "Big Brother" and the "thought police" to limit our knowledge and understanding, and so our control over our own lives. Which road we take is in our hands, as citizens and educators of a free society.

Appendix A
Costing Out
Your Wish List

Form I

Fill out a separate Form I for each application (e.g., spreadsheet analysis, word processing, simulation) to be considered.

Application: What application do you want to do? Specify the application as precisely as possible, e.g., say "computer-aided drafting," not just "graphics."

_____

_____

Use Requirements: What type of software is needed, e.g., "word processing for grades 3–6," or, "secretarial word processing system for reports, mailing lists, business letters, etc."? What special features should the software have?

_____

_____

_____

_____

Software Packages: What software packages exist that will do this?

Product Name	*Vendor*	*Price*

Form II

For each software package listed in Form I, fill out a copy of Form II.

General Requirements

Computer Compatibility: If known, specify each computer on which the package will run, or with which the package must be compatible.

1. _____
2. _____
3. _____

Operating System: Especially if the OS is not standard with a specific computer, e.g., CP/M, MP/M, UNIX, etc., or if a specific version of an OS is needed, e.g., DOS 3.3, etc.

_____

Memory Requirements: Where known, specify minimum memory to run the package, e.g., 48K, 128K.

_____

Mass Storage: Specify type, e.g., cassette or disk, and where applicable number of drives, minimum capacity, e.g., 2 drives 360K each, or hard disk with 40M and tape backup, etc.

_____

Special Requirements

Monitor/Terminal: e.g., is a color monitor required as opposed to monochrome; is 80 columns required rather than 40?

_____

Printer/Plotter: e.g., if a printer, is dot matrix acceptable or is a daisy wheel to be preferred; is high speed required or is low speed acceptable? If a plotter, single color or multi-color, etc.

_____

Modem/Communications: If required, what capabilities are necessary, e.g., do you wish to only connect two computers, will you need a modem, is networking necessary, is 300 or 1200 Baud preferable? Use a separate worksheet to specify in detail.

_____

Special Input: e.g., light pen, joystick, digitizer. If additional supporting software is necessary for these, use a separate worksheet to specify in detail.

Special Output: e.g., voice synthesizer, analog controller, etc. If additional supporting software is necessary for these, use a separate worksheet to specify in detail.

Form III

Using the information contained in Forms I and II, choose and cost out the basic hardware, peripherals, and software that will allow you to carry out the activities you most want to do, considering price, reliability, etc. Try to make choices that will be flexible, that will allow you to meet the needs of as many different applications as possible.

System Component 1. _____
Vendor or Manufacturer _____
Local Sales & Service _____
Remote Service _____
Remarks _____ Price _____

System Component 2. _____
Vendor or Manufacturer _____
Local Sales & Service _____
Remote Service _____
Remarks _____ Price _____

System Component 3. _____
Vendor or Manufacturer _____
Local Sales & Service _____
Remote Service _____
Remarks _____ Price _____

System Component 4. _____
Vendor or Manufacturer _____
Local Sales & Service _____
Remote Service _____
Remarks _____ Price _____

Total Price: _____

Appendix B
Educational Software Evaluation Form

The purpose of this form is to guide you in previewing software and to record your responses for the information of others who may be interested in the same package.

Following are a number of questions previewers might wish to ask about a software package. They are divided into three sections because, in general, three different people have the expertise to answer them. A *teacher* might be expected to answer the questions about ease of use, a *curriculum specialist* or department head would answer those about the software's relationship to the established curriculum, and a *person trained in software evaluation* would answer the more technical questions. Conceivably one person might answer all of the questions (e.g., a department head who teaches and who also knows quite a lot about computer software). After filling in identifying information, fill in the rest of page one last, as a summary.

Page One

Subject Area _____
Grade level(s) _____

Program title _____
Disk, cassette or package title (if different) _____
Microcomputer brand _____ _____ K memory needed
Language _____ Peripherals needed _____
Source of program _____
_____

Cost _____
Catalog description

Prerequisite skill: _____
_____

Functional description of program: _____
_____
_____

Strengths: _____
_____
_____

Weaknesses: _____
_____
_____

Reviewed by: _____
_____
_____

NAME	GRADES/SUBJECTS TAUGHT	KNOWLEDGE OF COMPUTERS
_____	_____	_____
_____	_____	_____
_____	_____	_____

Final Recommendations: _____
_____

SOFTWARE EVALUATION QUESTIONS – TEACHER

Page Two

> Questions about the program's *ease of use:*

---

1. To what degree is what it teaches of educational value?

2. How do *students* respond to it?

3. Can students read the *directions* and understand what to do?

4. Are there *materials* accompanying it? _____ Are they complete and helpful to the teacher? _____ Please explain.

5. How *easy to use* is the software? _____ Does it help the teacher? _____ How?

6. Can it be used with a *range of learners*, adapting to the needs of several levels?

7. Could it be used with groups as well as individuals? _____ How?

In summary, is it usable in the classroom? _____ Why or why not?

SOFTWARE EVALUATION QUESTIONS – CURRICULUM SPECIALIST

Page Three

> Questions about the program's *relationship to the established* curriculum:

1. Is what it teaches of *educational value?*

2. Is it *accurate?* _____ Does it *correlate with the curriculum? Where* does it fit?

   If it is outside the present curriculum's scope, should it be added anyway? _

   Why?

3. Is its *pedagogical style* (view of learning, educational philosophy) desirable and consistent with our goals?
   How does it *respond* to wrong answers?

4. Does it *present* or reinforce a skill or concept in a better way than we can without the computer?

5. What *level of skills* (knowledge, application, analysis, etc. à la Bloom) does it tap?

6. Is it free of racial and sexual *stereotypes?* _____ Is it free of violence?

In summary, does it enhance the curriculum? _____ Why or why not?

How would you suggest it be used?

SOFTWARE EVALUATION QUESTIONS – COMPUTER SPECIALIST

Page Four

Questions about the program's technical quality:

---

1. What is the degree of *user control?*

2. Is *error trapping* complete?

3. Are *format*, visual impact, paging, help, use of abbreviations acceptable?

4. Are *graphics* intrinsic?

5. Is *branching* employed?

In summary, is it well done technically?

Does it use the computer's capabilities? _____ Explain.

Glossary

The words in this glossary are defined consistently with their use in the body of the book. Definitions of some terms may be different from definitions of those same terms in a more technical work. Terms used within a glossary definition that are themselves listed in the glossary are *italicized*.

Acoustic coupler   See under *modem*.

Address   In computing usage, the location of a computer *word* within the computer's *memory* or the location of a record on a disk storage medium.

ALU   The Arithmetic Logic Unit, the part of the *CPU* where all arithmetic and logic operations are actually performed.

Applications software   See *software*.

Artificial intelligence   A branch of computer science that has the aim of developing machines capable of carrying out functions normally associated with human intelligence, such as learning, reasoning, self-correction, and adaptation.

Artificial intelligence language   A computer language, such as LISP, used in artificial intelligence research.

ASCII   Acronym for **A**merican **S**tandard **C**ode for **I**nformation **I**nterchange, pronounced "as-key." This is a binary code using seven *bits* to represent 128 letters, numbers, punctuation and other special marks, and control characters. A *byte* of eight bits could encode 256 such characters, but the eighth bit is not used in ASCII code, so only 128 characters are encoded.

Assembler   A special program that translates *source programs* written in *assembly language* into machine code.

Assembly languages   Sometimes referred to as *low-level languages*, since there is a one-to-one correspondence between assembly code and machine code. These languages are different for each type of *CPU*, and allow a programmer to write a program using word-like instruction codes instead of binary number machine code.

Audio cassette player/recorder   A form of *peripheral storage device*. Computer *digital signals* are converted to sounds (tones), which are recorded on the tape. The tones are converted back into digital signals when the program on tape is *loaded* into the computer. Compare with *tape drive*.

Author languages   High-level languages that allow the user to program without having much knowledge of a computer language. Some author languages determine programming needs through the user's responses to a series of questions and then provide an appropriately formatted program.

Backplane   See *card cage*.

Bank select   A technique for enabling a computer to access more RAM than the CPU can address at one time by providing additional "banks" of memory that the computer can access instead of its regular memory.

Bank switching   The process of switching from one bank of memory to another while using *bank select* addressing techniques. The user is not aware of this process.

Baud rate   A measure of the speed at which information is transmitted through serial *interfaces*, roughly the same as bits per second (e.g., 300 Baud = 300 bits per second).

Bit   Acronym for **bi**nary dig**it**, a bit (represented as being a zero or a one) is the smallest possible unit of information in a computer.

Boot   Short for "bootstrap" which is the process of loading the *operating system* of a computer into main memory and commencing its operation.

Bug   An error in a computer program. The process of eliminating such program errors is known as *debugging*.

Bus   A set of wires and connections that provides links between various components within a *CPU*, such as *registers*, *ALU*, and *input/output ports*, etc., or between the CPU and other devices, such as *RAM*, various *interfaces*, *circuit cards*, etc.

Byte   A computer word of eight *bits*. Typically, one byte is required to store one character of text. A byte is made up of eight bits in various combinations of 0s and 1s that represent text, numbers, control characters, and intructions in computer code.

Card cage   A metal frame in a computer with slots and connectors into which various *circuit cards* can be plugged. Contrast with *mother board*.

Cathode ray tube (CRT)   Also called a video display unit, a CRT is that part of a *monitor* or *video terminal* where images are formed. A TV picture tube is also a CRT, though a computer CRT generally has much finer resolution than an ordinary television.

Central processing unit   See *CPU*.

Chip   A small (e.g., ¼″ × ¼″), flat piece of silicon on which electronic circuits are etched.

Circuit card   A small board on which chips and their electronic components are mounted, and with connectors to the computer's *bus*. Circuit cards can hold extra *memory*, special controllers such as for a *disk drive*, *interfaces*, etc.

Communcations network   The connection of several individual computers so that files of messages can be sent back and forth between them. Communications networks can provide multiple connections to large information systems or connections to share ideas and programs between individual users.

Compiler   A computer language translator program that translates another program written in a high-level language into machine code. It translates the *source program* all at once and stores it for later use. COBOL, FORTRAN, and Pascal are languages that use a compiler. Compare with *interpreter*.

Computer   An electronic device that manipulates symbolic information according to a list of precise (and limited) instructions called a *program*.

Computer-based instruction   Sometimes called *computer-aided* or *assisted instruction (CAI)*. These terms have undergone several changes in usage. Originally they were applied only to computerized tutorials. Now some people use them to refer to any instructional application of computers. We use them to mean those computer applications applied to traditional teaching methods such as drill, tutorial, demonstration, simulation, and instructional games.

Computer-based testing (CBT)   Testing programs that use computers in any number of ways.

Computer literacy   A term with many meanings to different people. We use it to mean the general range of skills and understanding needed to function effectively in a society increasingly dependent on computer and information technology. (See Chapter 2 for a detailed discussion of computer literacy.)

Computer-managed instruction (CMI)   Primarily classroom management systems that use computers to help teachers to organize and manage teaching and record keeping for classes.

Computer system   What most people mean when they say "computer." A computer system consists of a computer and all the *hardware* and *software* used in connection with its operation. A computer system requires at least a *CPU* (central processing unit), *memory*, some form of *peripheral storage device*, an *input device* (such as a keyboard) and an *output device* (such as a *monitor*).

Courseware   Educational *software*, usually accompanied by a range of ancillary materials.

CPU   The "brains" of a computer. The CPU (*central processing unit*) controls what the computer does. It contains the circuits, including the *ALU* (arithmetic logic unit), *registers*, and others that interpret and execute instructions.

Cursor   A position indicator on a video display screen that can be moved in various directions, such as left or right one space, character, or word, and up or down one line or to the top or bottom of the screen.

Database   A large collection of related data, often in several files generally accessible by computer, in which case it is commonly said to be *on-line*.

Data processing   Performing a programmed sequence of operations on a body of data to achieve a given result; also known as information processing. More commonly, a term used to refer to the manipulation of large amounts of data by a computer.

Debug   To find and correct errors in a computer program.

Dedicated   Refers to any component of a computer system (such as a data line or terminal) set aside for a specific purpose or user only.

Dialects   Different versions of the same computer language, such as the different versions of BASIC that run on different computers.

Digital signals   The actual form of information within a computer, electronic signals which may be high or low, representing zeros or ones in machine code.

Direct-connect modem   See under *modem*.

Directory   A list of files stored on a *peripheral storage device*, such as on a disk. Directories are usually obtainable from the *operating system*.

Disk drive or **magnetic disk drive**   See *hard disk drive* and *floppy disk drive*.

Diskette   See under *floppy disk drive*.

Disk operating system (DOS)   An operating system that, in addition to its other functions, controls the operation of a disk drive, the reading of information from and writing of information to the disks, and the management of the file structure of the disks. See also *operating system*.

Distributed processing networks   Connections between a central computer and remote computers in which data is transmitted to a central computer (*uploaded*) for complex processing and then sent back to remote computers (*downloaded*) for review and more processing. Like *timesharing*, distributed processing networks share the cost and time of expensive central computers.

Documentation   The collection of manuals and instructions that explain the proper use and possible applications of a given piece of *hardware* or *software*. Also, the explanatory comments sometimes included in the written *listing* of a program.

Double density   See under *floppy disk drive*.

Double-sided   See under *floppy disk drive*.

Download   See under *distributed processing networks*.

Dumb terminal   An input/output device without an internal *CPU*. Dumb terminals require host computers for operation, as compared with *intelligent* terminals, which have internal *CPUs* to handle the terminals' functions and communications.

Floppy disk   See under *floppy disk drive*.

Floppy disk drive   A *peripheral device* for storing programs or other information on disks made of thin flexible plastic with a magnetic recording surface (called a *floppy disk* or *diskette*). Floppy disk drives may record on only one side of a disk, or they may be *double-sided*, recording on both sides at the same time, thus being able to store twice as much data. Some drives are rated as *double-density*, which means they can store (almost) twice as much data as single density drives. Compare with *audio cassette player/ recorder, tape drive, hard disk drive, Winchester technology*.

Hardcopy terminal A terminal that uses a *printer* as its output device. See *KSR (Keyboard Send/Receive) unit*.

Hard disk See under *hard disk drive*.

Hard disk drive A *peripheral device* for storing programs or other information on disks made of rigid aluminum, coated with a magnetic recording surface (called *hard disks*). This can refer to either the large disk drives used in larger computer systems or to the newer *Winchester technology* disk drives used with microcomputers. Also compare with *floppy disk drive, tape drive, audio cassette player/recorder*.

Hardware More properly called computer hardware, it is the collection of physical devices which make up a computer system, including *chips, disk drives, circuit cards, terminals*, etc.

High-level languages Languages such as FORTRAN, Forth, BASIC, COBOL, C, Logo, APL, PL/I, Pascal, and many others that use English-like commands to keep the user from having to use machine code or *assembly language* to communicate with the *CPU*. Typically, one high-level language statement will be equivalent to several machine-level instructions.

High-level language translators See *compiler* and *interpreter*.

Input Information entered into the computer.

Input device A *peripheral device*, such as a keyboard, light pen, or digitizer, that allows the user to enter information into the computer.

Input/output (I/O) device A *peripheral device*, such as a *video terminal* or *KSR unit*, that has both input and output components.

Input/output ports (I/O ports) Electronic connections that link the *CPU* to various *peripheral devices*.

Intelligent Any component (such as a disk drive or terminal) that contains its own *CPU*, enabling it to execute instructions without the host *CPU*. Dumb components, on the other hand, require the *CPU* of the host computer to process all instructions.

Interface An electronic and physical connection between various electrical and electromechanical devices, the most important of which are between the computer and various *peripheral devices*. A *serial interface* transmits or accepts information one *bit* at a time, whereas a *parallel interface* transmits or accepts information one computer *word* at a time.

Interpreter A computer language translator that translates and executes another program written in a *high-level language* one line at a time. BASIC and APL are languages that use an interpeter. Compare with *compiler*.

KSR (keyboard send/receive) unit A printer that also includes a keyboard thus making it an *input/output device*, also known as a *hardcopy terminal*.

Listing   A printout of the lines of instructions making up a program.

Load   To enter a program into the memory of the computer from some *peripheral storage device* (or sometimes from a keyboard).

Log-in or **log-on**   A sign-on procedure for users of a *timesharing* system.

Low-level language   See *assembly language.*

Machine-readable   Information stored in such a way that it can be read by a computer. Programs and data stored on disk are machine readable, as is information printed in bar codes, in OCR (Optical Character Recognition) characters, or in MCR (Magnetic Character Recognition) printing.

Memory (also called **main memory** or **main storage**).   The integrated circuits of a computer in which information is stored that is directly accessible to the *CPU*, as opposed to peripheral storage, which is accessible only via interfaces. See *RAM (random access memory)* and *ROM (read only memory).*

Menu   A list of options from which a user can choose while running a program.

Microcomputer   A computer whose *CPU* is a *microprocessor.*

Microprocessor   An integrated circuit that executes instructions. Also a *CPU* on a single *chip.* Computers whose main *CPU* is a microprocessor are called *microcomputers.*

Modem   Short for **mo**dulator/**dem**odulator, this device provides communication between computers over phone lines by converting a computer's digital signals to audio tones and then back to digital signals for the computer at the other end. One type of modem called an *acoustic coupler* sends and receives its signals directly through the mouthpiece and earpiece of the phone, while *direct-connect modems* send and receive through wire connections to the phone.

Monitor   A *cathode ray tube* when used as a dumb output device, also known as a VDU (video display unit). The term "monitor" is also used to name a particular kind of *utility program* that is used to observe the running of another program as an aid to *debugging.*

Mother board   A printed circuit board, usually the main board containing the *CPU* and its support chips, which also contains slots onto which can be plugged various other circuit boards. Contrast with *card cage.*

Networking   The communication between, or the sharing of resources by, two or more computers. See *resource-sharing networks, communications networks,* and *distributed processing networks.*

On-line   A technical term referring to the location and connection of devices so that they are immediately accessible to the *CPU* of a computer. However, in common usage it has come to refer to information that can be accessed directly from a computer as compared with information from a book, radio, television, or other medium.

On-line database   See under *database.*

Operating system   *Systems software* that manages the computer and its *peripheral devices*, allowing the user to run programs and to control the movement of data to and from computer *memory* and peripheral devices. See also *disk operating system*.

Output The information sent from the *CPU* to any *peripheral device*.

Output device A *peripheral device*, such as a printer, monitor, or voice synthesizer, that allows the user to receive information from the computer.

Parallel interface See under *interface*.

Peripheral device Any device not actually a part of the computer itself, including all *input/output devices*, *peripheral storage devices*, etc. Some peripheral devices, such as a *CRT* or *disk drive*, may be built into the same housing as the computer.

Peripheral storage device Any device other than the computer's main memory and internal *ROMs* to which information can be written and from which information can be read. See *audio cassette player/recorder, floppy disk drive, hard disk drive, tape drive*. Other forms of peripheral storage include bubble memory, laser disks, and punched card readers.

Printer An output device that prints characters on paper. A printer without a keyboard is a pure output device, sometimes designated RO (Read Only). See also *KSR (Keyboard Send/Receive unit)*.

Program The list of instructions that tells a computer how to perform a given task or tasks; see also *software*. Programs are written by *programmers*, and when a program is loaded into a computer, we say that the computer is *programmed*.

Queue A waiting line within a computer system for use of some component, e.g., several files waiting to be printed constitute a *print queue*. Queues most often occur in a timesharing or resource-sharing system where there is contention among several users for a device.

RAM (**random access memory**) The computer's general purpose memory, sometimes called read/write memory. RAM may be written to or read from by the *CPU*. Information on RAM is usually *volatile*; that is, it disappears when power to the computer is turned off.

Reading from memory The process of moving data from memory to the *CPU*.

Registers Locations inside the *CPU* that store temporary results or intermediate calculations and are used repeatedly by the *CPU*.

Resource sharing networks The connection of several computers with one or more *peripheral devices*, such as high-speed *printers* or *hard disk drives*, which devices are shared by the computers in the *network*, rather than having one of each device for each user.

RO (**receive only**) See under *printer*.

ROM (**read only memory**) Intergrated circuits in which programs are permanently stored during the manufacturing process. Programs stored in ROM cannot be changed, and remain even when the power is turned off. ROMs are typically used to store special system programs that will be used often; to provide a set of simple commands enabling more powerful programs to be loaded; and, in the form of ROM cartridges, to store the games used in home video game machines.

Run To perform or execute a given program; when a computer is executing a program, we say the program is being run. Also, the BASIC command (RUN) to run a program.

Serial interface See under *interface*.

Software Computer programs. There are two basic types of software. *Systems software* enables the computer to carry out its basic operations. Examples include *operating systems, language interpreters,* or *utility programs. Applications software* consists of programs that instruct the computer to perform various real-world tasks such as accounting, word processing, games, or testing students.

Systems software See *software*.

Tape drive A *peripheral device* for storing programs or other information in digital form (rather than audio form) on magnetic tape. It is more reliable than an *audio cassette player/recorder*.

Terminal An *input/output device* that allows a user to communicate with a computer. See *dumb terminal, printer, video terminal*.

Timesharing The concurrent use of one computer by several users. In general, timesharing is the connection of several users at different terminals to a shared computer. The connections are either through direct wires (*dedicated* lines) or through *modems* and telephone wires.

Timeslice A fraction of a second during which the *CPU* of a *timesharing* system is handling a user's request.

Upload See under *distributed processing networks*.

Utility programs *Systems software* that enables the computer to carry out certain basic functions such as copying the contents of one disk onto another, tracing the run of an applications program (see under *monitor*), determining the length of the files stored on disk, etc.

Video terminal A terminal that uses a video display unit (*monitor, CRT*) as its ouput device. See *cathode ray tube*.

Volatile Information that disappears from memory when the computer power is turned off. RAM is volatile.

Winchester technology A form of *hard disk drive* designed to be used by microcomputers. In most Winchester drives, the single hard disk is not removable. Winchester disks can store much more information than *floppy disk drives*, and are faster.

Word In computing usage, the number of *bits* processed and addressed at one time by the *CPU*. An 8-bit word is called a *byte. Modem* communications frequently use a 10-bit word—a byte and two extra bits. A 16-bit computer is one that uses either a 16-bit word or two bytes.

Writing to memory The process of moving data from the *CPU* to RAM.

Resources

These resources were originally compiled as part of a more extensive database of educational computing resources for the *Computers in Education* series at Intentional Educations. They have been updated by Ellen Chaffin and Helen Goldstein of Addison-Wesley to reflect changes in the field that have occurred since then. The following criteria were used to select resources from the vast and growing quantity of microcomputer materials available.

- Entries of greatest value to educational administrators
- Entries referenced most often by educators
- Entries of established reputation
- Entries guiding administrators to sources of answers to their most frequently asked questions.

Special thanks for assistance go to: Inabeth Miller of the Gutman Library at the Harvard Graduate School of Education for her consultant expertise; Karl Zinn for the use of Dataspan-produced information; Newton Key for organizing the Intentional Educations/Classroom Computer News database; and Nancy Upper for her major revision of the database. A portion of the ERIC listing under Bibliographies and Indexes were produced by an ERIC search through Dialog Information Services by Carlla Hendrix, Lesley College Library.

All addresses and phone numbers of these resources were correct as of publication, but may have changed since that time.

RESOURCES CONTENTS

PUBLICATIONS

Written materials on computing provide the most accessible source of computer-related information for educational leaders. This section includes seven categories of publications, covering the most useful literature on educational computing.

Periodicals

Magazines and Journals

The following magazines are directed specifically toward educational computing, include regular columns on computers in education, or publish frequent articles of interest to computer-using educators. Warning: magazine publishing is a fickle business; more magazines fail than succeed. It is likely that within a year of publication of this book, one or more of the magazines below will have ceased publication.

AEDS Journal and AEDS Monitor
Association for Educational Data Systems
1201 16th Street, NW
Washington, DC 20036
(202) 822-7845

The *AEDS Journal* is a professional/academic quarterly that publishes reports on original research, project descriptions and evaluations, as well as theories relating to educational computer use. Many articles focus on problems in instructional design and administrative applications and are prefaced by an abstract and a list of keywords. The *AEDS Monitor* reports bimonthly on research and applications of computers in education. Research and reviews from other groups, such as ERIC and MECC (see ORGANIZATIONS), are regularly included. *Journal*: $8/copy; $32/4 issues. *Monitor*: $5/copy; $28/6 issues.

Byte
70 Main Street
Peterborough, NH 03458
(603) 924-9281

Byte offers technical information for the microcomputer enthusiast. The monthly magazine contains detailed discussions of new microcomputer hardware and software and includes exceptionally well-researched special-focus issues. Educators interested in developing their own programs and evaluating and comparing products for possible purchase may find this a valuable source of information. $3.50/issue; $21/12 issues.

Classroom Computer Learning

Peter Li, Inc.
19 Davis Drive
Belmont, CA 94002
(415) 592-7810

Classroom Computer Learning links computer-based instruction with traditional classroom teaching. Published eight times a year, it features teacher-developed classroom ideas, original programs, software reviews, and a two-sided pullout poster for classroom use. Manufacturers' product news and a calendar of educational computing events are included in each issue. $3.00/issue; $22.50/8 issues.

Collegiate Microcomputer

Rose-Hulman Institute of Technology
Terre Haute, IN 47803
(812) 877-1511

Collegiate Microcomputer is a quarterly journal devoted to microcomputers in the college and university curricula. It features reviews of hardware and software, results of research and experiments, and presentations of student projects. The journal serves as a forum for exchange of ideas related to microcomputers in the higher education environment. $28/4 issues.

COMPUTE!

COMPUTE! Publications, Inc.
PO Box 5406
Greensboro, NC 27403
(919) 275-9809

COMPUTE! The Leading Magazine of Home, Educational, and Recreational Computing, is an applications-oriented publication for Apple, Atari, Commodore, IBM, and TI personal computer users. It focuses on computer use at home and in school and features reader feedback columns, applications programs, games, product information, and articles for both children and adults. $2.95/issue; $24/12 issues.

COMPUTE!'s Gazette

COMPUTE! Publications, Inc.
PO Box 5406
Greensboro, NC 27403
(919) 275-9809

COMPUTE!'s Gazette, for Commodore Personal Computer Users, is a monthly magazine devoted to owners and users of the Commodore 64, Commodore 128, Plus 4 and 16, and VIC-20 computers. Each month it features articles, step-by-step tutorials, reader feedback columns, original games, and applications programs for home, educational, and recreational computing. The programs from each issue of the magazine may also be purchased separately on *COMPUTE!'s Gazette Disk*, a ready-to-load floppy disk. $2.95/issue; $24/12 issues.

Computer Update

The Boston Computer Society
One Center Plaza
Boston, MA 02108
(617) 367-8080

This bi-monthly features commentary and reports on news in personal computing. Regular columns include "The Learning Curve" and "Straight Talk." Subscription is included with membership in The Boston Computer Society. Membership fee: $28.

Computers in the Schools

The Haworth Press, Inc.
28 East 22nd Street
New York, NY 10010
(212) 228-2800

Computers in the Schools is an interdisciplinary journal devoted to the theory, practice, concerns, and issues surrounding the use of microcomputers in the school curriculum. It features articles on research, computer languages, software, hardware, educational psychology, and instructional and administrative applications. Individuals: $26/4 quarterly issues. Institutions: $32/4 quarterly issues.

The Computing Teacher

International Council for Computers in Education (ICCE)
University of Oregon
1787 Agate Street
Eugene, OR 97403
(503) 686-4414

The Computing Teacher publishes general and technical articles on the instructional uses of computers and on teaching about computers. Offered as part of the membership in the International Council for Computers in Education, it emphasizes precollege education and teacher training. Teachers in the field write most of the articles. It also includes programming suggestions; computing problems; software and book reviews; news items on conferences, projects and resource centers; and technological developments in computers. $3.50/issue; $21.50/9 issues-USA.

CRLA: Computers, Reading and Language Arts

Modern Learning Publishers, Inc.
PO Box 13247
Oakland, CA 94661
(415) 530-9587

Computers, Reading and Language Arts provides nontechnical information on the use of computers in the teaching of reading and written language skills at elementary and secondary levels. Each issue contains reviews of language arts software, prepared by educators who relate their reactions based on classroom experiences with commercial courseware. Each issue also includes articles on innovative language arts curricula, overviews of research in the field, and descriptions of how computers may enhance teaching skills in the language arts. Individuals: $16/subscription. Institutions: $22/subscription.

Educat's Curriculum Product Review
125 Elm Street
PO Box 4006
New Canaan, CT 06840
(800) 227-2410, in Connecticut (203) 972-0761

Published nine times a year under a controlled circulation, *Educat's Curriculum Product Review* features short descriptions of audiovisual materials, textbooks, supplementary materials, and free or inexpensive educational materials, all less than a year old. All products are listed by subject matter; topics include computer learning, curricula, learning technology, social studies, science, testing and guidance, mathematics, special education, language arts, early childhood, and computer courseware.

Electronic Education
Electronic Communications, Inc.
Suite 220
1311 Executive Center Drive
Tallahassee, FL 32301
(904) 878-4178

Electronic Education addresses the needs of today's teachers and administrators from middle school through college levels with up-to-the-minute news on products, trends, and classroom applications for computer and other technologies shaping tomorrow's classrooms. It profiles individuals who have had a profound effect on, or are just beginning to influence, these technologies and it chronicles the opinions of those involved in the day-to-day applications of these technologies. All of this is presented in an easy-to-read format with illuminating graphics and art, providing readers with unique insights into the field of electronic education. $3/issue; $18/8 issues.

Electronic Learning
Scholastic, Inc.
730 Broadway
New York, NY 10003
(212) 505-3000

Electronic Learning provides nontechnical introductions to educational computing applications. News columns—including a Washington report and international items—report on innovations and official receptivity to computers in education. A group of educators evaluates commercial software and discusses the merits and faults of classroom software applications. Regular features include a primer for teachers with minimal computer literacy, teachers' suggestions for simple computer-based classroom activities, and guides to proposal writing and funding sources for the purchase of educational technology. $3.50/issue; $19/8 issues.

Journal of Computers in Mathematics and Science Teaching
ACMST
PO Box 4455
Austin, TX 78765
(512) 244-1771

This is the official journal of the Association for Computers in Mathematics and Science Teaching. The journal is published quarterly by ACMST, a professional, non-profit organization whose purpose is to promote the improvement of college, elementary, and secondary mathematics and science instruction through the use of computers. Each issue includes feature articles, reader contributions of problems and solutions, classroom applications of results of new studies, tutorials, lists of reviews of the newest books, and Association news.

Infoworld
Popular Computing, Inc.
1060 Marsh Road, Suite C-200
Menlo Park, CA 94025
(415) 328-4602
East Coast Bureau:
375 Cochituate Road
Framingham, MA 01701
(617) 879-0700

A newsweekly for microcomputer users that reports on all aspects of computer technology. Each issue includes a department on educational computing and educationally oriented software. $1.75/issue; $31/52 issues.

Mathematics Teacher
National Council of Teachers of Mathematics
1906 Association Drive
Reston, VA 22091

This journal emphasizes practical ways of helping teachers in secondary schools, two-year colleges, and teacher-education institutions to teach mathematics effectively. Contains articles on issues concerning the use of computers in mathematics education; features classroom activities, tips for teachers, reviews of microcomputer software, and descriptive information about new instructional programs.

Media and Methods
1511 Walnut Street
Philadelphia, PA 19102
(215) 563-3501

Media and Methods features regular columns on media reviews and electronic teaching; also includes departments of general interest to educators, including software reviews and previews. Computer-oriented articles are in every issue, along with articles relating to other aspects of media education. Special features include the annual Showcase section of news on hardware and software, and the annual Buyer's Guide, listing computer sources of all kinds. $27/5 issues.

Microzine
Scholastic Inc.
730 Broadway
New York, NY 10003
(212) 505-3556

Microzine is a bimonthly magazine-on-a-disk for the Apple II Plus and Apple IIe computers. Each disk is 2-sided, with full-length programs designed for grades 4 through 8. Programs include utilities, databases, interactive stories, and special features. A 32-48-page handbook and teaching guide are included with each disk, plus a back-up disk. $169/5 issues.

Personal Computing
Hayden Publishing Company, Inc.
10 Mulholland Drive
Hasbrouck Heights, NJ 07604
(201) 393-6000

Personal Computing has editorial content designed to serve people whose curiosity about the benefits of personal computer use is developing into serious interest and active involvement. Articles and features meet readers' needs without demanding years of experience or advanced knowledge of the technology. $2.50/issue; $12/12 issues.

Popular Computing
70 Main Street
Peterborough, NH 03458
(603) 924-9281

While primarily focused on the needs of the business market, this magazine offers concise articles on microcomputer hardware and software, new technologies, and their applications to increasing productivity. Information can be useful for product price and feature comparison.

The School Microcomputing Bulletin
Learning Publications, Inc.
5351 Gulf Drive
Holmes Beach, FL 33510
(813) 778-6818

The *SMB* is written and read by educators who test and evaluate computer products, programs, and practices in school settings. The *SMB* specializes in short, readable but professional articles which will help teachers and administrators bring about more effective school administration and improve classroom instruction. $28/10 issues; $50/20 issues (2 years); Additional $20 outside North America; Additional copies same address $12/year; back issues available.

Teaching and Computers
Scholastic Inc.
730 Broadway
New York, NY 10003
(212) 505-3000

Teaching and Computers provides information and practical suggestions for integrating computers into the classroom. It includes nontechnical information about how computers work, teacher-developed lesson ideas, and information on new books and resources. The publication is geared to elementary school teachers. $3.50/issue; $19/8 issues.

T.H.E. Journal
PO Box 992
Acton, MA 01720
(617) 263-3607

Technological Horizons in Education (T.H.E.) Journal features general theoretical discussions and reports on applications of educational technology. *T.H.E. Journal* is published six times a year and is available free on a limited basis to qualified educators. Reviews of software, projects, and publications are linked to an inquiry service card so that additional information can be obtained from the publisher or manufacturer. Material included is geared towards promoting educational technology. However, much state-of-the-art information can be gleaned from the magazine.

3-2-1 Contact
Children's Television Workshop
One Lincoln Plaza
New York, NY 10023
(212) 595-3456

3-2-1 Contact is published by the Children's Television Workshop, the creators of *Sesame Street*, and *The Electric Company*. *3-2-1 Contact* is a magazine of science and technology aimed at 8-14 year olds. The magazine features stories about nature, animals, computers and the new technology, and scientists working in unusual places doing unusual things. In addition, the magazine features puzzles, games and activities, computer programming, and computer software news and reviews. For subscription information, write: *3-2-1 Contact Magazine*, $E = MC^2$, PO Box 2932, Boulder CO 80321. $11.95/10 issues.

Videodisc and Optical Disk
Meckler Publishing
11 Ferry Lane West
Westport, CT 06880
(203) 226-6967

This bimonthly journal assists readers in keeping abreast of videodisc, optical disc, videotex, and other computer and communications technologies. Each issue focuses on a particular topic of video application; for example, the role and use of instructional theory on the development of the videodisc as an educational, instructional, and training tool. *Videodisc and Optical Disk* features a regular column by the Director of Market Support and Educational Services of Pioneer Video. A biweekly companion newsletter, *Videodisc and Optical Disk Update* is also published by Meckler. $75/6 issues. Per vol. year, the journal is $75 (6 issues). Per vol. year, the newsletter is $157/22 issues.

Newsletters

CMC News
Computers and the Media Center
515 Oak Street North
Cannon Falls, MN 55009

CMC News is published three times an academic year. It features articles on the uses of microcomputers in library/media centers, reviews library software, and provides listings of libraries using microcomputers. $5 prepaid, $6 billed.

C.U.E. Newsletter
PO Box 18547
San Jose, CA 95158
(408) 244-2559

The California-based group, Computer Using Educators, publishes this useful "newsletter" six times per year. Practically a full magazine, it contains material of interest to computer educators, including announcements, letters, opinions, programs, teaching ideas and curricula, and software or hardware reviews contributed by members. Also included is information on upcoming conferences. C.U.E. membership is $8 and includes the newsletter.

EPIEgram: Equipment
EPIE Institute
PO Box 839
Water Mill, NY 11976
(516) 283-4922

Published monthly during the school year by the Educational Products Information Exchange, this user-oriented newsletter reports on all types of equipment used in education—frequently including news and inside background information on microcomputers. A "Feedback" form included in each issue generates answers to questions and solutions to problems sent in by readers. $40/9 issues.

EPIEgram: Materials
EPIE Institute
PO Box 839
Water Mill, NY 11976
(516) 283-4922

Published 8 times during the school year by the Educational Products Information Exchange, this user-oriented newsletter reports on a wide range of instructional materials and copyright issues and frequently includes news and inside background information on microcomputer courseware. A "Feedback" form included in each issue generates answers to questions and solutions to problems sent in by readers. $40/8 issues.

ERIC/IR Update
Syracuse University
ERIC Clearinghouse on Information Resources
School of Education
Syracuse, NY 13210
(315) 423-3640

The semi-annual bulletin reviews microcomputer-related items from the ERIC microfiche collection as well as books that are available from commercial publishers. To receive the newsletter free of charge, write to the ERIC Clearinghouse.

FOLLK-Lore
FOLLK
Friends of LISP/Logo & Kids
PO Box 22094
San Francisco, CA 94122
(415) 753-6555

Published by Friends of LISP/Logo & Kids, this journal is a forum for information on Artificial Intelligence. Ideas for using Logo in the classroom, problems and puzzles for children, and discussions of new computers and programs appear in each issue. Subscriptions free with membership. Memberships $15/students and senior citizens; $25/families and individuals; $100/institutions.

Hands On!

Technical Education Research Centers (TERC)
1696 Massachusetts Avenue
Cambridge, MA 02138
(617) 547-0430

This newsletter provides information and commentary on educational computing. Each issue contains programs, book and software reviews, news on conferences, idea exchange forum, and "Classroom Computing" and "Special Needs" columns. A $10 contribution is requested.

Library Systems Newsletter

American Library Association
50 East Huron Street
Chicago, IL 60611
(312) 944-6780

This newsletter is published monthly by Library Technology Reports. It reports on various subjects of interest to librarians, such as the differences between in-house files and database services, videodisk updates, and cataloging and other automated library systems. A one-year subscription is $35.

MECC Network Newsletter

Minnesota Educational Computing Corporation
2520 Broadway Drive
St. Paul, MN 55113
(612) 638-0600

This periodical, published four times a year, focuses on MECC software, services, and general computing news.

Microcomputer Digest

201 Route 516
Old Bridge, NJ 08857
(201) 679-1877

Microcomputer Digest summarizes articles from a wide variety of microcomputing magazines, journals, and press releases, especially chosen for their educational focus. Topics covered include: funding sources, new developments, product reviews, and practical applications of microcomputers in education. The editors say that a school administrator would have to subscribe to dozens of magazines to obtain the same information contained in one issue of *Microcomputer Digest*. Annual subscription: $29.95/$50.00 two years (11 issues Sept.–July).

Microcomputers in Education
2539 Post Road
Darien, CT 06820
(203) 655-3798

Microcomputers in Education is a newsletter, which focuses on the commercial educational software marketplace. Besides describing new educational programs, the newsletter also summarizes software reviews from other magazines and notes where the reviews first appeared. *Microcomputers in Education* regularly carries announcements of new products, publications, workshops, and projects. This newsletter is available for $38 per year.

MICROgram
EPIE Institute
PO Box 839
Water Mill, NY 11976
(516) 283-4922

This is EPIE's consumers' newsletter, containing purchasing advice and commentary on major issues facing users of computing products, plus update information on the EPIE-CU program.

NCTM News Bulletin
National Council of Teachers of Mathematics
1906 Association Drive
Reston, VA 22091
(703) 620-9840

Included in this newsletter are reports on new publications, national issues such as the shortage of mathematics and science teachers, and committee and conference news. A pullout section, "NCTM Student Math Notes," is included in each issue. The newsletter is published five times a year and is sent to NCTM members only.

SALT Newsletter
50 Culpeper Street
Warrenton, VA 22186
(703) 347-0005

A publication of the Society for Applied Learning Technology, it is geared toward higher education. *SALT* reports current research and innovations in instructional technology.

SIG Bulletin
International Council for Computers in Education (ICCE)
Special Interest Group for Educational Administrators
1787 Agate Street
Eugene, OR 97403
(503) 686-4429

ICCE's Special Interest Group for Administrators (SIGADMIN) provides a forum for superintendents, principals, and other school management personnel to discuss the administrative implications of the use of microcomputers in public schools (K–12). The *SIG Bulletin* features nontechnical articles on instructional uses of computers and issues in computer education as well as articles on applications in the school and district office (word processing, data base management, communications, networks, spreadsheets, and business graphics). Published quarterly. $10 for U.S. ICCE members, $12 for non-U.S. ICCE members, $15 for U.S. non-member, $17 for non-U.S. non-member.

Small Computers in Libraries
Meckler Publishing
11 Ferry Lane West
Westport, CT 06880
(203) 226-6967

Small Computers in Libraries discusses the internal and public access library applications of microcomputers. As a clearinghouse, it includes glossaries, tutorial articles, and reports on uses of computer library management systems. Subscriptions are $24 per year for this monthly publication.

Special Issues of Magazines

Following is a selection of special issues of magazines devoted entirely to a single topic of interest to microcomputing educators. Some of the magazines listed publish annual directories of resource information in addition to special issues, as a benefit of subscription. Addresses for the magazines listed (unless otherwise noted) may be found in the previous Magazines and Journals portion (pp. 307–314) of the Resources section.

BYTE
March 1984, Vol. 9, No. 3

SIMULATION.   Eight major theme articles in this issue explore the use of software models to solve real-world problems. What computer simulation is and how it is done on microcomputers is explained in detail; there are articles on simulating reality with computer graphics; specific examples are discussed; and a compendium of conferences, organizations, books, and software for microcomputer simulationists is included.

BYTE
October 1984, Vol. 9, No. 11

IBM Special Issue: Guide to the IBM Personal Computers

BYTE
December 1984, Vol. 9, No. 13

BYTE Guide to the Apple PCs.

CLASSROOM COMPUTER LEARNING
August 1984, Vol. 5, No. 1

Directory of Eductional Computing Resources

ELECTRONIC LEARNING
January 1984, Vol. 3, No. 4

NATIONAL DIRECTORY OF SOFTWARE PREVIEW CENTERS, Part I.   The first of a two-part series that lists places where educators may preview software prior to purchase. This issue (Part I) includes at least one government or privately run preview center for each state west of the Mississippi.

ELECTRONIC LEARNING
February 1984, Vol. 3, No. 5

1. NATIONAL DIRECTORY OF SOFTWARE PREVIEW CENTERS: Part II
   This issue completes the Directory of Software Preview Centers with a listing of at least one government or privately-run preview center for each state east of the Mississippi and the District of Columbia.
2. TECHNOLOGY AND SPECIAL EDUCATION
   Four feature articles discuss how the microcomputer is helping handicapped children to learn basic skills and to communicate with the world; state education agency initiatives in special education; and special education books.

ELECTRONIC LEARNING
March 1984, Vol. 3, No. 6

FUNDING.   Entitled "Money for Micros 1984/85: EL'S Guide to Funding," this issue includes a seven-page guide listing the foundations and government agencies where one might look for funds, and suggests some strategies for getting them.

ELECTRONIC LEARNING
April 1984, Vol. 3, No. 7

1. VIDEODISCS
   EL terms this issue "The first published complete guide to educational interactive videodiscs." Includes articles on how to make commercial videodiscs interactive and a Buyer's Guide to videodisc players and interactive devices.
2. THIRD ANNUAL GUIDE TO SUMMER COURSES
   The issue also includes *EL*'s annual guide to summer courses, a directory of courses and workshops for learning or sharpening educational computing skills.

ELECTRONIC LEARNING
September 1984–June 1985, Vol. 4

Computers in the Curriculum: Reading, Science, Writing, Math, Science, Foreign Language, Math, and Social Studies (respectively).

Bibliographies, Indexes and Sources of Book Reviews

So many books and journal articles on computers in eduation have been written or revised in the past few years that only the most recent bibliographies, indexes, and sources of book reviews have been included here. The reader is advised to consult current bibliographies published in the various educational computing, microcomputing, and education periodicals as well.

Bibliographies

Annual Bibliography of Computer-Oriented Books
The Computing Newsletter, Publisher
PO Box 7345
Colorado Springs, CO 80933
(303) 593-3239

This bibliography includes a total of more than 1,000 books from 170 publishers. Books are separated into subject categories, type (e.g., reference, textbook, handbook), and style of presentation (e.g., programmed instruction, case study, narrative). Though not specifically geared toward educational computing, it is one of the most comprehensive listings of computer books available. It is important to note, however, that the bibliography's aim is to be comprehensive and up-to-date, rather than selective, and books of lesser quality are also included.

Computer Assisted Instruction for Handicapped Children and Youth
Council for Exceptional Children
1920 Association Drive
Reston, VA 22091
(703) 620-3660

Reprints of abstracts from computer searches of the Exceptional Child Education Resources (ECER) and ERIC databases. The searches were done by the Council for Exceptional Children. Price: $10; CEC members, $8.50. Order from: Council for Exceptional Children. Stock #506

Computers and Gifted Students
Council for Exceptional Children
1920 Association Drive
Reston, VA 22091
(703) 620-3660

Reprints of abstracts from computer searches of the Exceptional Child Education Resources (ECER) and ERIC databases. The searches were done by the Council for Exceptional Children. Price: $10; CEC members, $8.50. Order from: Council for Exceptional Children. Stock #528

Computer Managed Instruction for Handicapped Students
Council for Exceptional Children
1920 Association Drive
Reston, VA 22091
(703) 620-3660

Reprints of abstracts from computer searches of the Exceptional Child Education Resources (ECER) and ERIC databases. The searches were done by the Council for Exceptional Children. Price: $10; CEC members, $8.50. Order from: Council for Exceptional Children. Stock #532

ERIC Clearinghouse on Information Resources
Pamela McLaughlin, User Services Coordinator
Syracuse University
School of Education
Syracuse, NY 13210
(315) 423-3640

The ERIC Clearinghouse has user service materials such as mini-bibliographies and ERIC digests available on the topic of microcomputers. It has a publications list of information analysis products about current issues and developments in the microcomputer field and publishes a newsletter, *ERIC/IR Update* (see Newsletters) twice each year. These items are available with a self-addressed stamped envelope.

The Reader's Guide to Microcomputer Books
Michael Nicita and Ronald Petrusha
Golden-Lee Book Distributors, Inc.
1000 Dean Street
Brooklyn, NY 11238
(212) 857-6333

This is a critical guide to microcomputer books, reviewing and rating over 1000 titles for content and quality of presentation. Books are categorized within six subject areas: microcomputer introductions, microprocessors, operating systems and hardware design, programming, software and applications, and specific systems. The second edition was published in Sept. 1984 and is available in both paperback at $14.95 and hardcover at $29.95.

Use of Computers in Regular and Special Education Teacher Education
Council for Exceptional Children
1920 Association Drive
Reston, VA 22091
(703) 620-3660

Reprints of abstracts from computer searches of the Exceptional Child Education Resources (ECER) and ERIC databases. The searches were done by the Council for Exceptional Children. Price: $10; CEC members, $8.50. Order from: Council for Exceptional Children. Stock #509

Indexes

ACM Guide to Computing Literature
Association for Computing Machinery
Order Department
PO Box 64145
Baltimore, MD 21264
1-800-526-0359 x75 (1-800-932-0878 x75 in NJ)

This annual guide lists current scientific books, papers, and reports in over 200 computer science categories. Six separate indexes list titles, authors, keywords, topics, sources, and reviewers. Items from ACM's *Computing Reviews* (see Sources of Book Reviews), papers from ACM conferences, and literature published by other societies, government agencies, and sources are indexed. Copies of the guide are $100, or $50 for ACM members.

Computer and Control Abstracts
The Institute of Electrical Engineers/IEEE
445 Hoes Lane
Piscataway, NJ 08854
(201) 981-0060

This monthly publication contains abstracts of journal articles, bibliographies, books and conference proceedings, all indexed by subject. Abstracts cover topics such as CAI, educational-administrative data processing, and other educational computing areas. Subscription price is $705 per year.

Current Index to Journals in Education (CIJE)
ORYX Press
2214 North Central at Encanto
Phoenix, AZ 85004

Produced by the Educational Resources Information Center (ERIC), *Current Index to Journals in Education (CIJE)* is an excellent source for locating journal articles. Using subject terms from the *Thesaurus of ERIC Descriptors*, such as "microcomputers," "computer literacy," "computer assisted instruction," many relevant citations can be found. Each entry is annotated.

Microcomputer Index
Database Services Inc.
885 North San Antonio Road
Suite H
Los Altos, CA 94022
(415) 948-8304

This is the most important computer index for those interested in instructional computing. Available both in printed form and online, through Lockheed's Dialog system, it is one of the few indexing services that deals solely with information on microcomputers. Approximately 75 periodicals are indexed, including many of the popular microcomputing magazines not indexed anywhere else. Articles, books, hardware and software reviews, columns, and letters are all referenced.

Resources in Education (RIE)
Educational Resources Information Center (ERIC)
National Institute of Education (NIE)
U.S. Department of Education
Washington, DC 20208

This is a unique abstracting service which indexes educational materials that are not accessible through any of the other indexes or abstracting services. Most of the literature is unpublished and available on microfiche from the ERIC Document Reproduction Service. Types of documents include research reports, directories, resource guides, bibliographies, conference proceedings, and curricula. RIE has a wealth of information on microcomputers that can be located using subject headings such as "microcomputers" and variations on the word "computer(s)."

Sources of Book Reviews

In addition to the sources of book reviews listed below, see also the *Microcomputer Index* (under Indexes) under the name of the specific book. Books are also reviewed in many of the educational computing journals, the general microcomputing magazines, the educational technology journals, the general education periodicals, and the library journals in their book review sections.

Computer Book Review
Comber Press
735 Ekekela Place
Honolulu, HI 96817
(808) 595-7337

Computer Book Review critically reviews and rates the latest microcomputer books. All subjects, most publishers. This bi-monthly publication covers approximately 150 books per issue. An electronic edition of *Computer Book Review* is issued weekly on NEWSNET.

Computing Reviews
ACM Subscription Department
PO Box 9209
Church Street Station
New York, NY 10249
(212) 869-7440

This monthly publication of the Association for Computing Machinery provides reviews of current literature on computing science and applications. Critical evaluations of new books, papers, articles, reports, and other materials are included from over 300 serial publications. Complete bibliographic information is included for each review. A one-year subscription is $60, or $19 for ACM members.

Book Review Digest
Wilson Publications
950 University Avenue
Bronx, New York 10452
(212) 588-8400

Book Review Index
Gale Research
Book Tower
Detroit, MI 48226
(313) 961-2242

Directories

These comprehensive guides provide invaluable information on the thousands of materials available to educators using microcomputers. Only the most inclusive directories are listed here, to assure adequate coverage of the rapidly growing number of resources in the field.

Instructor's Computer Directory for Schools
545 Fifth Avenue
New York, NY 10017
(212) 503-2888

A buyer's guide to the selection of microcomputers and peripherals, courseware, computer-assisted and computer managed instruction systems, books and resources, magazines and journals, and free materials.

Datapro Directory of Online Services
Datapro Research Corporation
1805 Underwood Boulevard
Delran, NJ 08075

A comprehensive, two volume independent information service dedicated to detailed coverage of all varieties of online services. Designed as a tool for management and technical staffs at all levels, the directory presents concisely all the facts and evaluations you will need to know about the burgeoning online services market. Actually two services in one, Volume 1 covers the Information Retrieval Services industry. It includes a user's guide; company/database index; subject index; indepth company reports; company and database profiles; user ratings; and feature reports. Volume 2 covers the Remote Computing (Timesharing) industry. It includes a user's guide; general index; applications index; company reports; company profiles; user ratings; feature reports; and a glossary. Subscribers also receive a monthly newsletter and the use of an inquiry service.

Directory of Published Proceedings
Series SSH: Social Sciences/Humanities
InterDok Corporation
PO Box 326
Harrison, NY 10528

This is a quarterly publication that reports conference proceedings and papers. Using the index of key words from the conference titles and the sponsors' names, relevant conferences can be located using such terms as "microcomputers," "computer-based instruction," and "educational computing." The directory is found in most university libraries and includes information for ordering manuscripts.

Directory of Resources for Technology in Education
Far West Laboratory for Educational Research and Development
1855 Folsom Street
San Francisco, CA 94103
(415) 565-3166

This is a comprehensive publication of technology information listing a contact person; address; telephone number; description and purpose; list of publications, if applicable; membership criteria and fees; and current events for the following: national and regional associations, resource groups, public access centers, state-by-state instructional TV personnel, summer institutes, degree programs, conferences, periodicals, databases, electronic bulletin boards, software evaluation agencies, hardware companies, and funding foundations.

Microcomputer Directory: Applications in Educational Settings
Monroe C. Gutman Library
Harvard University
Graduate School of Education
Cambridge, MA 02138
(617) 495-4225

Published in 1982, this unique directory describes schools and alternative settings that use microcomputers for either instructional or administrative purposes. Over 1200 sites in the United States are included, with entries from elementary and secondary schools, computer camps, museums, prisons, alternative learning sites, and colleges and universities. Listings are by state and include a brief description of each program. There is also a subject index that provides an additional access point to the programs in the directory. A new directory of 6,000 entries has been prepared to be published electronically on CompuServe, Consumer Information Service. It is searchable.

Microcomputers in Education: A Resource Handbook
Technical Education Research Centers, Inc. (TERC)
1696 Massachusetts Avenue
Cambridge, MA 02138
(617) 547-0430

This resource handbook, developed originally for participants in TERC's National Workshop series, provides a reference tool to help teachers and administrators who wish to orient themselves in the complex field of microcomputers. The directory is divided into four chapters: Hardware Resources, Software Resources, Educational Organizations, Bibliographies and Terminology. $10 plus $2 for postage/handling.

ON-LINE INFORMATION PROVIDERS

The "big three" search services used by academic institutions, businesses and public libraries are BRS (Bibliographic Retrieval Services), Dialog, and SDC (Systems Development Corporation). CompuServe and The Source are mostly for business and home use, but people in academic settings are showing increasing interest in them. Nexis serves the corporate marketplace, but is beginning to turn its attention to educators. The following databases belong to one or more of these six major vendors of on-line search services, as indicated. An asterisk following the title of a database signifies that an authority list or thesaurus exists for use in subject searching.

CompuServe
CompuServe Information Service
5000 Arlington Center Boulevard
Columbus, OH 43220
(614) 457-0802

CompuServe is a utility offering a wide range of programs in information retrieval and communications. Representative of the types of information are financial, electronic encyclopedia, shopping, banking, and research databases. Of particular interest to those in education are Grolier's Academic American Encyclopedia (full-text, searchable by title only, but soon to be enhanced) and the files of ERIC and the MECC software catalog.

Educational Resources Information Center* (Dialog, BRS, SDC)
ERIC Processing and Reference Facility
4833 Rugby Avenue, Suite 301
Bethesda, MD 20814
(301) 656-9723

The mission of ERIC is to bring the literature of education under bibliographic control for access by and dissemination to all levels of the educational community. The ERIC database encompasses both the Report (or "Fugitive") literature and the Journal Article literature and extends across the entire field of education, in its broadest sense. Through 1984, there are more than one-half million items in ERIC; a list of the topics covered may be obtained from the ERIC Processing and Reference Facility at the above address. Although the database is nearly all English-language materials, there is a significant body of literature dedicated to education in other countries, especially developing nations.

Educational Testing Service Test Collection* (BRS)
Educational Testing Service
Test Collection
Princeton, NJ 08541
(609) 734-5737

ETS has more than 7000 descriptions of tests, evaluation tools, and assessment/screening devices. Educational tests (achievement, aptitude. subject mastery, etc.) account for the preponderance of the materials; however, personality, aptitude, self-concept, and aptitude tests and measures are found in the file. A particular effort is made to put research instruments in the database.

Exceptional Child Education Resources* (Dialog, BRS)
Council for Exceptional Children
1920 Association Drive
Reston, VA 22091
(703) 620-3660

ECER online corresponds directly to the quarterly print product with the same title. It is intended for use by those researchers, educators, and psychologists who are concerned with all areas of exceptionality, including the handicapped and the gifted. Journal articles, curriculum materials, books, program descriptions, convention and conference papers, and dissertation citations are contained in the database, plus ERIC documents. This file of over 55,000 items is updated monthly.

Knowledge Index (Dialog)
Dialog Information Services, Inc.
3460 Hillview Avenue
Palo Alto, CA 94304
(800) 227-1927 or (800) 982-5838 (in California)

Over twenty-five databases are available for searching through Knowledge Index. They cover the broad areas of medicine/psychology, corporate news/ business and legal information, computers/electronics/engineering, magazines/news/books, and education and government publications. The system is designed for searching by the layperson. Knowledge Index also offers you DIALMAIL, an electronic mail service. A manual and free time are given to enable new users to begin searching Knowledge Index in two hours. Some of the specific databases included are ERIC, Computer Database, Microcomputer Index, National Newspaper Index, Standard and Poor's News, and Biological Abstracts. Further information and order forms are available from the address above.

Mental Measurement Yearbook* (BRS)
Buros Institute of Mental Measurements
University of Nebraska, Lincoln
135 Bancroft Hall
Lincoln, NE 68588
(402) 472-1739

More than 1800 tests are included in this database, drawn from the most recent editions of the *MMY*. The complete record, with the exception of references, but including professional reviews, is available for online or offline printing. Approximately 40 new records are added monthly. Among available fields to search are test name, author(s), publisher, population, scores, manual information, and reliability/ validity data.

Microcomputer Index (Dialog)
Database Services Inc.
885 North San Antonio Road
Suite H
Los Altos, CA 94022
(415) 948-8304

Microcomputer Index appeared online one year after the appearance of its print counterpart. It provides access to some 75 popular microcomputer magazines of which 30 to 35 are indexed cover to cover. File content numbers some 30,000 items with monthly updates of approximately 1000 records. Representative of the topics covered are the broad areas of business, law, and education. Of particular use is the capability of searching for reviews: hardware, software or book. Further, reviews are categorized as favorable, mixed, or unfavorable.

National College Database (BRS, Viewtex, Dow Jones News Retrieval)
Peterson's Guides, Inc.
PO Box 2123
166 Bunn Drive
Princeton, NJ 08540
(609) 924-5338

This file is the online counterpart to the two annual volumes which comprise *Peterson's Annual Guide to Undergraduate Study*. Full-text or field searching may be done by college name, state name, undergraduate profiles, freshman data, enrollment patterns, majors, etc. Category code searching permits access to information which includes admissions requirements and patterns, level of competitiveness, percentage of part-time students, and demographic information. Approximately 3,000 profiles of United States and Canadian two- and four-year colleges and universities are contained in the database.

National Database of Interactive Technology Applications in Educational Settings* (CompuServe)
Harvard Graduate School of Education, Monroe C. Gutman Library
Appian Way
Cambridge, MA 02138
(617) 495-9021

This is a nationally accessible online database of educational technology information developed in 1984–85. The file draws from a survey of school districts and institutions of higher education nationwide. Gutman Library will test, revise, add to, and update entries regularly, and will produce disk copies for those institutions unable to access the file through telecommunications.

NEXIS
Mead Data Central
9333 Springboro Pike
PO Box 933
Dayton, OH 45401
1-800-227-4908 (toll free) or 513-865-6800

NEXIS searching permits access to the full text of more than 130 leading newspapers, magazines, newsletters, and wire services. One can elect to search the entire database or to search specific files such as the *Encyclopedia Britannica 3* or *The New York Times*, singly or in combination with other individual or group files (e.g., all newspapers plus

Fortune and *Business Week*). Coverage ranges back to 1975, with daily publications being updated each day, weeklies within a week after publication, and monthlies several weeks after issue. The NEXIS service also offers access to EXCHANGE, a library of SEC filings and analyst reports written by top brokerage and investment banking firms on thousands of companies and industries; The Federal Register; The Code of Federal Regulations; the Forensics Services Directory; the TODAY service of news summaries from *The New York Times*; The Associated Press Political Service; the National Automated Accounting Research System, a database of annual reports and proxy information; and LEXPAT, a database of the full text of patents since 1975.

Resources in Computer Education* (BRS)
Northwest Regional Education Laboratory
300 S.W. Sixth Avenue
Portland, OR 97204
(503) 248-6800

RICE is funded by NIE and operated by the Northwest Lab. It contains information on educational computer applications in the following categories and approximate numbers: producers of application packages for computers in education, 300; the software packages themselves, 3000; computer literacy materials, 160–170; projects, 80. Each record includes contact information, hardware type, system requirements, grade level, and evaluations if available.

Social Sciences Citation Index* (Dialog and BRS)
Institute for Scientific Information
3501 Market Street
Philadelphia, PA 19104
(800) 523-1850 x 1371

Currently, *SSCI* contains some 1,064,000 records drawn from over 5,200 journals. The majority of retrievable literature is journal articles; however, book reviews, discussions, editorials, biographical items, letters, meetings, and literature reviews are included. ISI's computer-based operation permits database searching within two weeks of item receipt. *SSCI* on-line is Social SCISEARCH.

The Source
1616 Anderson Road
McLean, VA 22102
(800) 336-3366

The Source is a menu-driven multifaceted system of more than 700 programs. Areas fall broadly into the catagories of news and information (UPI, Associated Press, stock market quotes, etc.) business services, entertainment, publishing, travel (including airline schedules), career information, and word processing. The Source is applicable to classroom use for promotion of computer literacy. The system permits storage, transfer, and retrieval of information as well as communication. Rates differ for prime and nonprime time use.

SpecialNet
NASDSE
1201 16th Street
Suite 404E
Washington, DC 20036
(202) 822-7933

The National Association of State Directors of Special Education, in cooperation with Education Turnkey Systems, operates the first national electronic mail/bulletin board on microcomputer applications in education through the Special Education Communication Network (SpecialNet). SpecialNet includes electronic mail, access to databases, electronic bulletin boards, data collection and information management systems. SpecialNet is presently used by more than one thousand local school districts and state education agencies.

RESOURCE AND DEVELOPMENT CENTERS

The following centers are either nationally known for their innovative educational developments, extensive resources, and research excellence or have made a name for themselves regionally as outstanding institutions in the field of computers in education, with growing resources available to a large number of people.

Bank Street College of Education
610 West 112th Street
New York, NY 10025
(212) 663-7200

Bank Street College is an important teaching and research institution made up of the following divisions: Graduate School, which prepares students for careers in schools, museums, hospitals, social agencies, and educational settings using microcomputers; School for Children, an on-site laboratory and school for 450 children; School and Community Services Division, which conducts outreach training in communities throughout the United States; Research Division, which focuses on the development of children and adults in school and family settings, and which is conducting research on the effects of microcomputer technology; Center for Children and Technology, a part of the Research Division exploring the contribution of new technology to learning, development, and education; Media Group, which develops books, software, and television productions that support the College's goal of improving the quality of life for children and families.

Center for Learning Technologies
Gregory M. Benson, Jr., Director
Cultural Education Center, 9A47
NYS Department of Education
Empire State Plaza, Albany, NY 12230
(518) 474-5823

The CLT promotes and supports the installation of instructional technology systems in the educational and cultural institutions of New York State. Initiatives relating to computer literacy, equity and access, research and development, and demonstration, distribution, and duplication of hardware and software have been designed for elementary, secondary, and continuing education, cultural education (including museum and library), vocational rehabilitation, and higher education. The center also manages instructional television production and teleconferences and administers public radio and television broadcasting. In addition, it operates computer training programs and distributes instructional videotapes and technology guidebooks.

Center for Social Organization of Schools
Henry Jay Becker, Project Director
The Johns Hopkins University
3505 N. Charles Street
Baltimore, MD 21218
(301) 338-7570

This center is involved in sociological research, with projects related to classroom instruction. In 1983, the Center completed a major survey of microcomputer-owning public and private elementary and secondary schools, focusing on how these schools use microcomputers. Over 1100 teachers participated in the survey, representing about 70 percent of a nationally representative sample. A report series, *School Uses of Microcomputers: Reports from A National Survey*, is available by subscription for $3. Reports from the survey are issued periodically.

Computer Education Resource Coalition (CERC)
c/o Lesley College
29 Everett Street
Cambridge, MA 02238
(617) 868-9600

This coalition of several organizations is a resource for teachers in the Boston area using educational technology. Their meetings focus on current research on integrating technology into education. CERC is sponsored by Lesley College, The Boston Computer Society, MIT, Bolt Beranek and Newman, Harvard University, Educational Collaborative (EdCo), the State Department of Education, and several local school systems.

ECCO (The Educational Computer Consortium of Ohio)
Teacher Center 271
1123 Somcenter Road
Cleveland, OH 44124
(216) 461-0800

ECCO is a group of individuals and school district members interested in instructional computing. Membership in ECCO includes use of its educational software library, which contains public domain software that members can copy and commercial software to preview. Members also have access to the organization's library of computer books, journals and audiovisual materials, a subscription to the newsletter, *The Output*, and consulting services for school districts. ECCO runs a series of workshops for novice and experienced computer users, an annual Educational Computer Fair, a statewide spring meeting, college student fairs, and hands-on Logo and Computer Literacy workshops, in which participants take home a computer for one month.

Educational Products Information Exchange (EPIE) Institute
PO Box 839
Water Mill, NY 11976
(516) 856-6945

The Educational Products Information Exchange (EPIE) Institute is the country's only educational consumer advocacy group that gathers and disseminates descriptive and analytical information on instructional materials, equipment, and systems. From October to June they publish two monthly newsletters, the *EPIEGRAM: Materials* and the *EPIEGRAM: Equipment*, as well as publishing quarterly *EPIE Materials Reports* and *MicroProfiles*, which furnishes evaluations of computer software. These publications identify inferior, unsafe, or questionable products. They also publish *MICROgram*, which reports on educational hardware and software.

Educational Technology Center
Harvard Graduate School of Education
Gutman Libary
337 Appian Way
Cambridge, MA 02138
(617) 495-9373

The Center, operated by a consortium of research, school, and production organizations, was founded at Harvard in the fall of 1983. It is one in the system of seventeen research and development laboratories and centers funded by the National Institute of Education. The center's mission is to examine the present and potential roles of technology in education. It concentrates its efforts on the roles computers can play in the learning and teaching of mathematics and science and the ways students learn about computers themselves.

Educational Technology Center
University of California, Irvine
Irvine, CA 92717
(714) 856-6945

Under the leadership of Dr. Alfred Bork, the Educational Technology Center maintains research and development projects on computer-based materials for all levels of the curriculum. The Development of Learning Skills in Early Adolescence project produced computer-based modules specifically for junior high school students, while the project on scientific literacy in public libraries is designed to improve public understanding of science.

A new project concerns weak students in beginning science classes. The Center has also developed college-level science and math units. Information on these projects is provided in their literature and books.

Educational Testing Service
Educational Technology Laboratory and Software Resource Center
Martin B. Schneiderman, Director of Computer Education Programs
Princeton, NJ 08541
(609) 921-9000

The ETS Educational Technology Laboratory and Software Resource Center houses more than 3000 commercial and public domain software packages. A series of seminars are offered to elementary through higher-level educators, focusing on instructional and administrative applications of computers.

Houston Independent School District
(HISD)-Department of Technology
Dr. Patricia Sturdivant, Associate Superintendent
5300 San Felipe
Houston, TX 77056
(713) 960-8888

The HISD is considered a leader in education in an urban environment. It was one of the first school districts to address the growing opportunities of technology; its goal is to acquire a computer for every student in the system. The Department of Technology is the only one of its kind in the country. Six divisions in the department address seven major areas: needs assessment and planning, technology training for teachers, technical applications, centralized procurement, maintenance, systems design, and special projects support. Future plans include software lending libraries, magnet schools offering specialized training, and more business connections that will provide experts and/or financial assistance.

Lesley College
Computers in Education Department
Dr. Nancy Roberts, Director
29 Everett Street
Cambridge, MA 02138
(617) 868-9600

Lesley College was the first graduate program and development center for computers in education. The Department offers Master's of Education and Certificate of Graduate Study degrees; conducts ongoing training programs at six outreach locations around the United States; sponsors an annual, nationally attended Computer Conference on campus; and hosts an annual week of workshops for computer educators from Sweden, an indication of the Department's growing international reknown.

Microcomputer Education Applications Network (MEAN)
256 North Washington Street
Falls Church, VA 22046
(703) 536-2310

MEAN, a division of Education Turnkey Systems, is involved in the following activities: workshops for administrators on the applications of microcomputers in administration and instruction, including reference handouts, demonstrations, purchasing guidelines, and hands-on opportunities; slide show presentations and accompanying equipment demonstrations on emerging technologies which are expected to impact education at all levels during the next few years; microcomputer software to assist the special education administrator in managing record keeping for handicapped pupils. The Modularized Student Management System (MSMS) maintains a pupil database and prints reports. MEAN also helps local districts and state agencies develop specific educational computing programs.

Microcomputer Resource Center
Teachers College
Columbia University
New York, NY 10027
(212) 678-3000

The Microcomputer Resource Center at Columbia University conducts seminars and workshops on curriculum materials, plus field-based training for the use of computers in the classroom. It is also a clearinghouse for hardware and software information.

Minnesota Educational Computing Corporation (MECC)
3490 Lexington Avenue North
St. Paul, MN 55112
(612) 481-3500

MECC, the nation's preeminent statewide instructional computing network, provides services for students, teachers, and administrators in schools and colleges. MECC offers in-service training and curriculum guides, as well as developing and distributing educational software. MECC is an excellent source of software and written materials for use with Apple II, Atari, IBM, Radio Shack, and Commodore 64 microcomputers. MECC has also directed a project to develop computer learning packages for use in science, mathematics, and social studies courses. The MECC newsletter and courseware catalog are free to members.

The National Center for Research in Vocational Education
Development Division
Harry N. Drier, Associate Director
Ohio State University, 1960 Kenny Road
Columbus, OH 43210
(614) 486-3655

The Development Division studies problems of local, state, and federal agencies relating to technical, occupational, vocational, and career education. Three computer-related projects have been recently completed at the center. *Microcomputer Analysis*, sponsored by the U.S. Department of Education, analyzes possibilities for the application of microcomputers in vocational education. *Adaptation of the Career Planning System to Microcomputers*, also sponsored by the U.S. Department of Education, modifies the *Career Planning System*, a print-based curriculum package, for use with the microcomputer. Computerized Guidance supplies training and consultation services to purchasers of *Choices*, a career information and guidance system that can be accessed by microcomputer.

NEA Educational Computer Service
4720 Montgomery Lane
Bethesda, MD 20814
(301) 951-9244

This service provides teachers with a comprehensive source of information about computers. In addition to assessing and endorsing software, the *Educational Computer Service* provides consultation and offer seminars and courses. Product information is published in *The Yellow Book of Computer Products for Education*. All products are offered for sale through a distributor.

SMERC Library Microcomputer Center
San Mateo County Office of Education
Ann Lathrop, Library Coordinator
333 Main Street
Redwood City, CA 94063
(415) 363-5472

The product of a joint project by Computer-Using Educators (CUE) and the San Mateo County Office of Education, the Microcomputer Center maintains SOFTSWAP and exhibits a variety of computers and commercial software for examination by educators. In addition, the Center maintains a software library and clearinghouse for California TEC Centers. The Center serves primarily the teachers and administrators of San Mateo County, although educators from outside the county are welcome to use the Center's resources by appointment.

Technical Education Research Centers (TERC)
Computer Resource Center
1696 Massachusetts Avenue
Cambridge, MA 02138
(617) 547-3890

The Computer Resource Center (CRC) of TERC houses information on microcomputer hardware and software and a library of technical and educational publications. The center also has various microcomputers and educational software available for inspection and sample use. TERC conducts workshops by contract on using microcomputers in education.

Teachers are invited to visit the center but must call ahead to arrange their visit. TERC is a non-profit research and development group with ongoing projects in special education and using microcomputers in school teaching.

SOFTWARE

Software Directories

The Blue Book Family of Computer Directories
WIDL Video Publications
8135 North Monticello
Skokie, IL 60076
(312) 673-4050

The Blue Book is published separately for the Apple, Commodore, Atari, and IBM computers, including product listings for software, hardware, and accessories. Apple and IBM directories cost $24.95; Atari and Commodore directories are $17.95, plus shipping, and can be ordered from the publisher or found at computer stores and bookstores. *The Blue Book* is also distributed as a reference book to schools, colleges, and public libraries.

Educational Software Directory
A Subject Guide to Microcomputer Software
Libraries Unlimited
PO Box 263
Littleton, CO 80160
(303) 770-1220

This directory provides subject access to over 900 educational microcomputer software packages (grades K–12). It contains information on programs for many different micro-computer systems. Each entry includes the name of the software package, publisher, grade level, format, language, price, and a lengthy annotation. There is also a publisher and distributor index. The price of the directory is $27.50.

Instructor's Computer Directory for Schools
attn: Order Department
PO Box 6177
Duluth, MN 55806
(800) 346-0085

Software listings in this semi-annual publication are organized by content area, machine, and alphabetically by company. Information about selecting computers, peripherals, books, and other resources is also provided.

Micros for Managers: A Software Guide for School Administrators, Revised Edition
Little, Mackey, Tuscher, Eds.
New Jersey School Boards Association
PO Box 909
Trenton, NJ 08605
(609) 695-7600

This guidebook provides essential information for over 300 software packages in the area of school administration. Also listed are names of experts on each program, locations of product reviews, and current users in schools around the country. The price of the book is $25, plus $3 for shipping and handling.

Micro-Software Guide and Directory
Online, Inc.
11 Tannery Lane
Weston, CT 06883
(203) 227-8466

This guide describes over 700 software packages that can be located in the index by producer, application, distributor, and package name. Also included are an annotated bibliography, industry resource section, glossary, and articles on buying and using software. Cost for the directory is $40; $30 for annual supplements. First annual supplement contains 300 new and/or updates to packages in the main directory. An outgrowth of the directory is an online database, FileSOFT, available publicly on BRS. FileSOFT contains over 4100 microcomputer software descriptions and is updated monthly.

Microcomputer Marketplace
R. R. Bowker Company
205 E. 42nd Street
New York, NY 10017
(212) 916-1600

This directory includes company background data for software publishers and distributors and listings of suppliers and manufacturers. Also included are listings of microcomputer associations, magazines, newsletters, producers, developers, consultants, and a calendar of events and meetings. The price for the directory is $75, plus shipping and handling.

The Personal Computer—An Industry Sourcebook
Chromatic Communications
Enterprises
PO Box 3249
Walnut Creek, CA 94598
(415) 945-1602

This over 800-page directory is a reference manual designed specifically for dealers and members of the microcomputer industry. Companies are listed in 15 categories such as

Hardware (six subcategories), Software (four subcategories), publishers, and distributors. The listings include name, address, phone, key contacts, sales volume, year started, year incorporated, number of employees, means of distribution, and a brief product line description. The publication is a biannual looseleaf service with quarterly updates. Currently it includes over 4,500 microcomputer companies, 12,000 industry executives, and 15,000 product lines. Price: $295 per year.

SOFSEARCH

2973 E.Coronado
Anaheim, CA 92806
(714) 632-6671

SOFSEARCH is a software locator service, utilizing a constantly updated database of information on computer software products. Information in the database is obtained from thousands of software vendors. A subscription to *SOFSEARCH* includes five regular search reports containing information on software products meeting subscriber specifications. Reports are updated quarterly and additional searches are available at reduced rates. Annual subscription fee is $175; nonsubscribers pay $60 per single search report.

The Software Catalogs

Elsevier Science Publishing Company
52 Vanderbilt Avenue
New York, NY 10017
(212) 370-5520

These directories derive information on software products from .MENU™—the International Software Database™, published by Elsevier. Over 15,000 entries are included, covering a wide range of interests including education, games, professional applications, systems software, utilities and others. Thorough cross-referencing and key-word indices are helpful in locating appropriate software. *The Software Catalog: Microcomputers* is published twice each year, winter and summer. An update is published approximately six months after each edition appears. Catalog price: $95.00; updates $15 each. *The Software Catalog: Minicomputers* is published once a year, with one update a year. Catalog price: $125.00; updates $25.

Software in Print: A Resource Guide to Microcomputer Software

Technique Learning Corporation
40 Cedar Street
Dobbs Ferry, NY 10522
(914) 693-8100

Software in Print is a series of software directories designed to be issued for particular microcomputers, applications areas, and operating systems. USMI-registered software publishers contributing data classify each of their products in one of four major market segments: business/professional, education, home/entertainment, technical applications. Each *Software in Print* directory contains four indexes: author, title, subject, publisher.

The publisher index lists all software packages produced by the publisher and provides the publisher's address, telephone number, and specific program requirements. The system is available on-line through Newsnet.

T.E.S.S. The Educational Software Selector
EPIE Institute
PO Box 839
Water Mill, NY 11976
(516) 283-4922

TESS is the most comprehensive and detailed source of information about the availability of microcomputer software, telling who makes what to run on whose hardware to do which educational jobs. *TESS* also tells readers, in summary form, how reliable reviewers have rated the quality of individual products. Features include: almost 7,000 software product descriptions from over 550 suppliers; coverage of products for all the microcomputers found commonly in schools; indexing of instructional software by subject for over 100 subjects, as well as administrative and guidance software; over 2000 citations of software reviews; in-depth coverage of software suppliers.

The USMI: Market Directory
A Profile of Software Publishers
Technique Learning Corporation
40 Cedar Street
Dobbs Ferry, NY 10522
(914) 693-8100

The USMI: Market Directory is a loose-leaf service profiling all USMI-registered software publishers in the micrcomputer industry. The directory is divided into two sections: (1) Basic Reference, Indexes: includes alphabetic, numeric, geographic, key word, operating system, and computer system indexes; (2) Publishers Profiles: an alphabetically sequenced index composed of information-packed profiles of each software publisher. An updating service is provided to all subscribers to the directory on a bi-monthly basis.

Sources of Software Reviews

Courseware in the Classroom: Selecting, Organizing and Using Educational Software
Ann Lathrop and Bobby Goodson
Addison-Wesley Publishing Company
Menlo Park, CA 94025
(415) 854-0300

This book includes criteria for evaluating courseware, how to organize and maintain a courseware library, plus a resource section with recommended courseware, sources of reviews, and publishers. The price of the book is $9.95.

Courseware Reviews
c/o San Mateo County Office of Education
333 Main Street
Redwood City, CA 94063
(415) 363-5472

There are fifty programs evaluated in each annual issue for all curriculum areas. These reviews have been compiled by educators all over California. Besides describing each program, the reviews include noted strengths, weaknesses, and student responses. Wherever applicable, they also list other publications which have published critical reviews of the programs. The cost for this publication is $10 per annual issue. Checks should be made out to: County School Service Fund.

The Digest of Software Reviews: Education
School and Home Courseware, Inc.
301 West Mesa Suite F
Fresno, CA 93704
(209) 431-8300

This professional publication is published monthly nine times a year during the school year. The first issue in August contains 60 titles and each of the other issues contains 30 titles for a total of 300 titles reviewed. *The Digest* searches 150 journals for software reviews and lists all sources of these reviews. The four indexes are by subject, by title, by micro-computer, and by publisher. Back issues of the first three volumes are available comprising 570 titles. A one-year subscription costs $147.50.

Foreign Language Teaching Program for Microcomputers: ERIC Clearinghouse on Language and Linguistics
Center for Applied Linguistics
3520 Prospect Street NW
Washington, DC 20007

The reviews in this volume, comprising programs published through 1983, were written by teachers or supervisors of foreign languages from twenty-nine high schools in six states. Twenty-five programs covering French, German, Italian, Russian, Spanish,and general areas are reviewed. Evaluations include quality of content, relevance to the subject area, suitability to the computer medium, appropriateness to the target audiences, technical reliability, ease of operation, graphic design, technical documentation, content documentation, and ease of entry by the instructor. Comments from the reviewer are given at the end of each review. A final product listing contains publisher information, system requirements, and price for all programs reviewed, including additional programs that are not reviewed in the volume.

Library Software Review

Meckler Publishing
11 Ferry Lane West
Westport, CT 06880
(203) 226-6967

A review of the computer programs for library and educational applications, *Library Software Review* also contains articles on software concepts and evolution. The review is published quarterly in 1984; six times a year in 1985.

Media Review

1611 North Kent Street
Suite 508
Arlington, VA 22209
(703) 528-1082

This monthly publication comprises all media including microcomputer software evaluations covering a range of subject areas in each issue. Reviews are a composite of several evaluations, with at least one the result of field-testing in the classroom. Program reviews are cumulatively indexed by title, publisher, and subject. One edition of *Media Review* is available for K–College at $99/issue.

Micro-Courseware/Hardware/Pro/Files and Evaluations

EPIE Institute
PO Box 839
Water Mill, NY 11976
(516) 283-4922

Pro/Files are two-to-four page software evaluations covering all major curriculum areas and grade levels. The purchase of this evaluation product includes a file box with course reviews divided into various subject areas. Typical review information includes analyst's summary, capsule evaluation, user comments, sample forms, student comments, other reviews of the program, how the teacher and students use the program, instructional/educational value, and documentation evaluation. Subscription price includes bi-annual updates to the files and the *MICROgram* newsletter, published nine times a year. Initial year $360. Subsequent renewals: $200.

Software REPORT CARDS

Infoworld
530 Lytton Avenue
Palo Alto, CA 94301
(415) 328-4602

Software reviews from the weekly publication, *Infoworld*, are collected in this publication and sent free of charge to *Infoworld* subscribers. Software is reviewed in the following categories: word processing, math/finance, file management, integrated systems, education, programming/operating systems, and utilities. Each review summarizes the product's content and gives a thorough description of its features, performance, system requirements, ease of use, error handling, documentation, and manufacturer support. *Infoworld Report Cards* are published quarterly.

Statewide Microcomputer Courseware Evaluation Network
Region IV Education Service Center
PO Box 863
Houston, TX 77001
(713) 462-7708

This project has received 500 courseware packages relating to the basic skills objectives for reading/language arts, mathematics, science, business education, and vocational education. These evaluations for Apple, Radio Shack, and Commodore microcomputers are available online through BRS (Bibliographic Retrieval Services). This project is in the process of reviewing computer literacy courseware and courseware compatible with IBM computers.

ORGANIZATIONS

American Association of School Administrators
1801 North Moore Street
Arlington, VA 22209
(703) 528-0700

AASA Provides leadership through the development of highly qualified leaders and by supporting excellence in educational administration. They publish several books throughout the year. AASA has published a new critical issues report entitled *High Tech*, which deals with modern technology in the schools.

American Association of School Librarians
50 East Huron Street
Chicago, IL 60611
(312) 944-6780

The AASL, with a membership of 7000, is composed of school library specialists at both the building and district levels, who have an interest in computerized library management and integrated instructional programs. In 1985, AASL presented its first annual Micro in Media Award for an individual and a school introducing the most innovative programs using microcomputers in the schools and in the school currciculum.

The American Computer Science League
PO Box 2417A
Providence, RI 02906
(401) 331-ACSL

The ACSL, composed of almost 800 participating schools in the US and Canada, administers monthly computer science contests and awards prizes at the end of the year for junior and senior high school students.

American Educational Research Association
1230 Seventeenth Street, N.W.
Washington, DC 20036
(202) 223-9485

AERA is an organization of university researchers and has special interest groups for members interested in computer-assisted instruction. Publications include: *Educational Researcher*, *Educational Evaluation and Policy*, *American Educational Research Journal*, *Review of Educational Research*, and *Contemporary Education Review*.

American Library Association
50 East Huron Street
Chicago, Illinois 60611
(312) 944-6780

The ALA is the oldest and largest library association in the world. Its nearly 40,000 members represent all types of libraries: state, public, school, academic, and speciality serving persons in government, commerce, armed services, hospitals, prisons, and other institutions. The ALA is an advocate for people to achieve and maintain high-quality libraries and information services. The educational uses of computing are a frequent topic at annual conferences, as well as at regional workshops, institutes, and conferences.

Association for Computing Machinery (ACM)
11 West 42nd Street
New York, NY 10036
(212) 869-7440

The ACM deals with all aspects of computing. The two sections of ACM that deal specifically with instructional computing are the Special Interest Group on Computer Uses in Education (SIGCUE), and the Elementary and Secondary Schools Sub-Committee. Publications that may prove useful are *Computing Reviews*, *The ACM Guide for Computer Science and Computer Applications Literature*, and the *ACM SIGCUE Bulletin*, the latter being especially worthwhile for educators.

Association for Computers in Mathematics and Science Teaching
PO Box 4455
Austin, TX 78765
(512) 244-1771

This professional organization serves college and secondary mathematics and science teachers interested in educational uses of computers. The Association's purpose is to advance the use of computers in mathematics and science education, primarily through its publication, *Journal of Computers in Mathematics and Science Teaching.*

Association for the Development of Computer-Based Instructional Systems
ADCIS Headquarters
Miller Hall 409
Western Washington University
Bellingham, WA 98225
(206) 676-2860

This association advances the use of computer-based instruction and management by facilitating communication between product developers and users. It also reduces redundant activities among developers of CAI materials. Its members include elementary and secondary school systems, colleges, universities, businesses, and government agencies. ADCIS maintains several special-interest groups active in educational technology. Publications include: *The Journal of Computer-Based Instruction*, *ADCIS Newsletter*, annual conference proceedings.

Association for Educational Communications and Technology (AECT)
1126 Sixteenth Street, N.W.
Washington, DC 20036
(202) 466-4780

AECT is a professional membership association for anyone interested in the use of media and technology for education and training. Publications include: *Educational Communication and Technology Journal*, *Journal of Instructional Development*, *Tech Trends*, *Guide to Microcomputers*, *Learning with Microcomputers*, and Project BEST videotapes.

Association for Educational Data Systems (AEDS)
1201 Sixteenth Street, N.W.
Washington, DC 20036
(202) 822-7845

AEDS is a professional organization serving educators and data processing professionals at all levels of education interested in instructional computing, computer science, and administrative computing. Activities include workshops, seminars, and an annual convention.

Twenty-five chapters in the U.S. and Canada are affiliated. Publications include: *AEDS Newsletter*, *AEDS Monitor*, *AEDS Journal*, and *AEDS Layman's Guide to the Use of Computers in Education*.

Association of Supervision and Curriculum Developers
225 North Washington Street
Alexandria, VA 22314
(703) 549-9110

ASCD is an educational association composed of superintendents, principals, directors, supervisors, professors, and teachers who have joined together for the improvement of curriculum instruction and supervision. ASCD's program provides its members with effective information and training through publications, tapes, institutes, and an annual conference. ASCD has published several educational computing journal articles on the implications for instruction and training, the fusion of computers and video, and computer technology and curriculum. They have also just formed a technical committee of educators who will meet via CONFER once a month and keep in touch with educational computing needs as well as resources.

International Communications Industries Association
3150 Spring Street
Fairfax, VA 22031
(703) 273-7200

ICIA is a trade association that advocates the use of educational technology. ICIA offers information on funding for classroom computer use through its markets research program and through updates in its newsletter. Its annual equipment directory of audiovisual, video, and computer products gives details on microcomputer hardware and other technology.

National Association of Elementary School Principals
1615 Durce Street
Alexandria, VA 22314-3406
(703) 620-6100

The NAESP, founded in 1921, is a professional organization serving more than 22,000 elementary and middle school principals and other educators throughout the United States and overseas. They occasionally publish articles on educational computing in their magazine.

National Association of Independent Schools
18 Tremont Street
Boston, MA 02108
(617) 723-6900

NAIS is a non-profit organization of more than 900 independent elementary and secondary schools in the US as well as 100 schools abroad. NAIS compiles statistics on its member schools, publishes educational surveys, studies, periodicals and books; and provides administrative and academic services. The organization will make available copies of *Twenty Questions about Computers in Education*, questions schools should ask themselves pertaining to the philosophical basis of using computers in education. They also published the *1984 Study of Instructional and Administrative Use of Computers in Independent Schools*.

National Association of Secondary School Principals
1904 Association Drive
Reston, VA. 22091
(703) 860-0200

NASSP is an association serving all school administrators at the middle and senior high levels. NASSP provides a broad range of programs and publications, including legal counsel and information, research studies, conventions and conferences. Other special resources include *School Tech News*, educational software reviews published 6 times a year.

National Council for the Social Studies (NCSS)
3501 Newark Street, NW
Washington, DC 20016
(202) 966-7840

NCSS is interested in the use of simulations and other computing programs for teaching social studies. In 1984, NCSS published a position statement entitled, "Social Studies Microcomputer Courseware Evaluation Guidelines." Selected issues of its journal, *Social Education*, also review social studies courseware.

National Council of Teachers of English (NCTE)
1111 Kenyon Road
Urbana, IL 61801
(217) 328-3870

NCTE has formed a committee on Instructional Technology which has prepared guidelines for the evaluation of software in language arts. The NCTE Conference on College Composition and Communication has also formed a committee on Computers and Composition. In conjunction with the ERIC Clearinghouse on Reading and Communication Skills, NCTE has published its first monograph on classroom applications of computers titled *Computers in the English Classroom: A Primer for Teachers*. National and regional meetings highlight educational computer applications. Publications include: *College Composition and Communication, College English, English Education, English Journal, Language Arts, Research in the Teaching of English*, and *Teaching English in the Two-Year College*.

National Council of Teachers of Mathematics (NCTM)
1906 Association Drive
Reston, VA 22091
(703) 620-9840

NCTM encourages classroom computing at all grade levels and has published a policy statement on educational microcomputer applications. Two of its publications, *Arithmetic Teacher* and *Mathematics Teacher*, include software reviews and articles on math education computer use. The NCTM's *Guidelines for Evaluating Computerized Instructional Materials* is a valuable guide to software evaluation. Publications include: *Arithmetic Teacher*, *Mathematics Teacher*, *Journal for Research in Mathematics Education*, *NCTM News Bulletin*, and the best-selling 1984 yearbook *Computers in Mathematics Education*. Other council publications on computers are available.

National Education Association (NEA)
1201 16th Street, NW
Washington, DC 20036
(202) 822-7200

The NEA is a national organization serving teachers. They publish a newsletter, *NEA Today*, that frequently includes articles on educational computing. In addition, the NEA has started the NEA Educational Computer Service, providing a comprehensive guide to courseware. The NEA Educational Computer Service may be reached at (301) 451-9244.

National Science Teachers Association (NSTA)
1742 Connecticut Avenue, NW
Washington, DC 20009
(202) 328-5800

NSTA includes in its journals articles that discuss use of small computers in science teaching. Projects initiated by NSTA include developing interdisciplinary software for energy and education. Six software units on energy are available from NSTA. Presentations at each annual NSTA conference deal with computer-based science instruction. Publications include: *Science and Children*, *The Science Teacher*, *Energy and Education Newsletter*, *Science Scope*, and the *Journal of College Science Teaching*.

Society for Applied Learning Technology
50 Culpeper Street
Warrenton, VA 22186
(703) 347-0055

SALT serves professionals concerned with instructional technology. It is geared toward higher education and research, but is also a useful source of information on technological innovations. Proceedings from SALT-sponsored conferences as well as books on microcomputers in education and educational technology are available from SALT. Publications include: *Journal of Educational Technology Systems* and *SALT Newsletter*.

Young People's Logo Association (YPLA)

1208 Hillsdale Drive
Richardson, TX 75081
(214) 783-7548

YPLA publishes *Turtle News* and *TLComputing*, which contain information about Logo, BASIC, PILOT and member-contributing applications. YPLA has a software exchange library of public domain programs and sponsors programming activities. A series of local chapters of the group and turtle learning centers are being set up nationwide. YPLA has its own electronic Logo bulletin board in Richardson, Texas and sponsors the Logo Forum on CompuServe. Membership is $25 per year. Add $15 for international air mail.

Index

The Addison-Wesley Series on Computers in Education

The future of computers in education is in your hands, and this outstanding new series of books from Addison-Wesley will show you why.

Each book in the Series on Computers in Education is intended to provide teachers, school administrators, and parents with the information and ideas that will help them meet the challenge of computers. These books will help you:

- Appreciate the potential and the limits of computers in education.
- Develop an understanding of computers.
- Overcome fears about computers.
- Introduce and integrate computers into a school.
- Use computers creatively and effectively.
- Evaluate the myriad computer-related products now being offered.
- Consider seriously the ethical, political, and philosophical issues surrounding computer use in education.

Your interest and involvement in the educational applications of computers will determine whether the computer will be the textbook, the TV, or the chalkboard of education for the next generation.

The Authors

Daniel S. Cheever, Jr. (Ed.D. Harvard Graduate School of Education) is president of Wheelock College. He served ten years as the superintendent of the school systems of Lincoln and Weston, Massachusetts. Prior to that, he was a classroom teacher. He is the author of numerous articles and has co-authored two books.

Peter Coburn (M.A. University of Vermont) is the president of Commercial Logic, Inc., a software consulting firm with offices in Burlington and Norwich, Vermont. He is also a lecturer in the computer science department at the University of Vermont. He is a co-author of *Practical Guide to Computers in Education.*

Frank DiGiammarino (Ph.D. Syracuse University) is Director of Planning for the Lexington, Massachusetts public schools. He spearheaded the computer education program in Lexington. He has been with the Lexington school system for twenty-nine years, beginning as a social studies teacher.

Peter Kelman (Ed.D. Harvard Graduate School of Education) is Vice President, Product Development for CBS Software. He was formerly editor and associate publisher of *Classroom Computer News* and prior to that was assistant professor of education at Dartmouth College. He frequently lectures, writes articles, and conducts workshops on a variety of educational topics. He is series editor and has co-authored three other books in the Addison-Wesley Series on Computers in Education: *Practical Guide to Computers in Education, Computers in Teaching Mathematics,* and *Computers, Education, and Special Needs.*

Beth T. Lowd (Ed.M. Boston University) is a specialist for computers in instruction for the Lexington, Massachusetts public schools and has served in that capacity for six years. Prior to that, she taught English and reading in Massachusetts and Pennsylvania public schools.

Adeline Naiman (B.A. Radcliffe College) is Director of Software at HRM Software, a division of Human Relations Media, and a trustee of Lesley College, both in Cambridge, Massachusetts. She writes monthly columns for two journals: *Computer Update* and *Personal Computing.* She formerly served as managing director of The Technical Education Research Center (TERC) and on the service staff of Educational Development Center.

Gus A. Sayer (Ph.D. University of Maryland) is assistant superintendent for curriculum in the Weston, Massachusetts public schools, with responsibility for planning the introduction of computers into the school system. He formerly taught in the Franklin, Massachusetts public schools, at Boston Latin School, and at Haverford College.

Kenneth Temkin (M.E.A. George Washington University) is Administrative Assistant for the Newton, Massachusetts public schools. His specialty is systems analysis and design. He is a founder of School Management Arts, Inc., Boston.

Isa Kaftal Zimmerman (Ed.D. Harvard) is assistant superintendent of the Lexington, Massachusetts public schools. She was formerly principal of the Hamilton-Wenham (Massachusetts) Regional High School.